CLASSICAL PRESENCES

General Editors

Lorna Hardwick James I. Porter

CLASSICAL PRESENCES

Attempts to receive the texts, images, and material culture of ancient Greece and Rome inevitably run the risk of appropriating the past in order to authenticate the present. Exploring the ways in which the classical past has been mapped over the centuries allows us to trace the avowal and disavowal of values and identities, old and new. Classical Presences brings the latest scholarship to bear on the contexts, theory, and practice of such use, and abuse, of the classical past.

Ancient Greek Women in Film

Edited by

KONSTANTINOS P. NIKOLOUTSOS

UNIVERSITY PRESS

Great Clarendon Street, Oxford, OX2 6DP,
United Kingdom

Oxford University Press is a department of the University of Oxford. It furthers the University's objective of excellence in research, scholarship, and education by publishing worldwide. Oxford is a registered trade mark of Oxford University Press in the UK and in certain other countries

First Edition published in 2013

Impression: 1

Published in the United States of America by Oxford University Press
198 Madison Avenue, New York, NY 10016, United States of America

British Library Cataloguing in Publication Data
Data available

Library of Congress Control Number: 2013945563

ISBN 978–0–19–967892–1

As printed and bound in Britain by
CPI Group (UK) Ltd, Croydon, CR0 4YY

Acknowledgements

This volume had its genesis in a panel of the same title organized at *Feminism & Classics V: 'Bringing it All Back Home'*, which took place at the University of Michigan in May 2008. The panel laid the foundations for an ongoing collaboration among an international group of classicists, the result of which is the present collection. I would like to thank the OUP anonymous referees for their insightful comments and suggestions, as well as the series editor, Lorna Hardwick, for embracing the project enthusiastically since its inception. A special debt of gratitude is due to Mary-Kay Gamel for soliciting three of the essays included here when she acted as co-editor. She made important recommendations, on both a theoretical and practical level, for which I am most thankful. She contributed immensely to the success of the project and was with us all the way in spirit after her withdrawal. Special thanks are also owed to the OUP commissioning editor, Taryn Das Neves, and the production editor, Kizzy Taylor-Richelieu, for their help and guidance with all matters related to the publication of this volume. The College of Arts and Sciences at Saint Joseph's University generously provided funds for the creation of the index, for which I am most grateful. Finally, I would like to thank all my contributors for their commitment, patience, and support during the entire process.

Ruby Blondell's essay was previously published in *Classical Receptions Journal* 1 (2009): 1–26 and is reprinted by kind permission of Oxford University Press. Some paragraphs from my own chapter are included in an article in *Classical World* 106.2: (2013): 261–83 and are reproduced by permission of the Classical Association of the Atlantic States. Many of the images are DVD stills taken under fair use policy for academic use.

Konstantinos P. Nikoloutsos
Philadelphia
15 October 2012

Contents

List of Figures

List of Contributors

Annette M. Baertschi is Assistant Professor in the Department of Greek, Latin, and Classical Studies at Bryn Mawr College. Her research interests include Roman literature, especially imperial poetry, Greek and Latin epic, ancient drama and performance, Latin meter as well as the reception of the classical world. She has published articles and reviews on Lucan, Seneca, and witches and sorceresses in ancient literature, and has co-edited a large collection of essays entitled *Die modernen Väter der Antike. Die Entwicklung der Altertumswissenschaften an Akademie und Universität im Berlin des 19. Jahrhunderts* (Berlin 2009). Currently, she is finishing her book *Necyiae: Visions of the Underworld in Neronian and Flavian Epic*.

Anastasia Bakogianni received her Ph.D. in Classics from the University of London. She is currently a Lecturer in Classical Studies at the Open University. She also holds a post as a Research Fellow at UCL. Her first monograph, *Electra Ancient and Modern: Aspects of the Reception of the Tragic Heroine*, was published by the Institute of Classical Studies in 2011. She has also edited a forthcoming two-volume collection of essays entitled *Dialogues with the Past* on aspects of the reception of Greco-Roman culture. Her interests lie in Greek tragedy and culture and its reception, particularly in opera, cinema, art, and poetry. She has published articles on all these aspects of the reception of Greek drama.

Ruby Blondell is a Professor of Classics at the University of Washington in Seattle. She has published widely on Greek literature, philosophy, and the reception of myth in popular culture. Her books include *Helen of Troy: Beauty, Myth, Devastation* (Oxford University Press, 2013); *The Play of Character in Plato's Dialogues* (Cambridge 2002); *Women on the Edge: Four Plays by Euripides* (co-authored) (Routledge 1999); *Helping Friends and Harming Enemies: A Study in Sophocles and Greek Ethics* (Cambridge 1989).

Kirsten Day is Associate Professor of Classics at Augustana College in Rock Island, IL, USA. Her research interests include women in classical antiquity and classical representations in popular culture, on which topics she teaches classes and has published several articles. She also edited a special issue of *Arethusa* (41.1: 2008) entitled *Celluloid Classics:*

New Perspectives on Classical Antiquity in Modern Cinema and served as chair for the 'Classical Representations in Popular Culture' area at the Southwest Texas Popular/American Culture Association conferences from 2002–2013.

Edith Hall is Professor of Classics at King's College London and Consultant Director of the Archive of Performances of Greek and Roman Drama at Oxford University. Her numerous publications include *The Theatrical Cast of Athens* (OUP, 2006), *The Return of Ulysses* (2008), *Greek Tragedy: Suffering under the Sun* (OUP, 2010), and *Adventures with Iphigenia in Tauris: A Cultural History of Euripides' Black Sea Tragedy* (OUP, 2012).

Lloyd Llewellyn-Jones is Senior Lecturer in Ancient History in the School of History, Classics and Archaeology at the University of Edinburgh. He specializes in Achaemenid Persia, Greek socio-cultural history, ancient dress, and the reception of antiquity in popular culture. He is the author of *Aphrodite's Tortoise: The Veiled Woman of Ancient Greece* (The Classical Press of Wales, 2004), *Ctesias' History of Persia: Tales of the Orient* (Routledge, 2010), *King and Court in Ancient Persia* (Edinburgh University Press, 2013) and the forthcoming *Designs on the Past—How Hollywood Created the Ancient World.* He has published extensively on the use of antiquity in cinema and popular culture and served as a historical advisor to Oliver Stone during the making of his movie *Alexander*.

Hallie Rebecca Marshall currently holds a Social Sciences and Humanities Research Council of Canada Postdoctoral Research Fellowship at the Archive of Performances of Greek and Roman Drama at Oxford University. Her postdoctoral research is on classical reception in the late eighteenth century. She has published articles on the work of Tony Harrison, Jocelyn Herbert, Ted Hughes, Sarah Kane, and Aristophanes.

Konstantinos P. Nikoloutsos is Assistant Professor of Latin and Ancient Studies at Saint Joseph's University in Philadelphia. He has published a number of articles in the fields of Roman elegy, ancient history on film, and the classical tradition in Latin America and the Caribbean. Besides this volume, he has also edited a special issue of *Romance Quarterly* (59.1: 2012) entitled *Reception of Greek and Roman Drama in Latin America.* He is the recipient of the 2008 Paul Rehak Prize from the Lambda Classical Caucus and the 2012–2013 Loeb Classical Library Foundation Fellowship from Harvard University.

Kirk Ormand is Professor of Classics at Oberlin College. He is the editor of *A Companion to Sophocles* (Blackwell, 2012), and author of *Controlling Desires: Sexuality in Ancient Greece and Rome* (Praeger, 2008), *Exchange and the Maiden: Marriage in Sophoclean Tragedy* (University of Texas, 1999), and articles on Hesiod, Euripides, Sophocles, Lucan, Ovid, and Clint Eastwood. His next book, *The Hesiodic Catalogue of Women and Archaic Greece*, is forthcoming from Cambridge University Press.

Joanna Paul is a Lecturer in Classical Studies at the Open University. Her research in the field of classical reception studies covers a number of different areas, with a particular focus on reception in contemporary popular culture. She has published on a variety of cinematic receptions of antiquity, from Fellini to *Alexander*, and her monograph on *Film and the Classical Epic Tradition* is also part of the Classical Presences series (OUP, 2013). Her current projects include further work on the modern reception of Pompeii, and research into childhood engagements with antiquity, in both pedagogical material and children's literature.

Arthur J. Pomeroy is Professor of Classics at Victoria University of Wellington, New Zealand. He is the author of *The Appropriate Comment: Death Notices in the Ancient Historians* (1991), *Arius Didymus: Epitome of Stoic Ethics* (1999), *Theatres of Action: Papers for Chris Dearden* (co-edited with John Davidson, 2003), *Roman Social History: A Sourcebook* (with Tim Parkin, 2007), '*Then it was destroyed by the Volcano': Classics on the Large and Small Screen* (2008), and various articles on a wide range of Latin authors and on the reception of the ancient world in modern film and television.

Susan O. Shapiro received her Ph.D. in Classics from the University of Texas at Austin. She is Associate Professor of History and Classics at Utah State University. Her articles on Herodotus, Greek intellectual history, and Catullus have appeared in *The Classical Journal, Classical Antiquity, Transactions of the American Philological Association*, and *Syllecta Classica*. She is also the author of *O Tempora! O Mores! Cicero's Catilinarian Orations: A Student Edition with Historical Essays* (University of Oklahoma Press, 2005).

Bella Vivante is Professor of Classics at the University of Arizona. Her numerous publications include 'The Primal Mind: Using Native American Models to Study Women in Ancient Greece' in *Feminism and Classics* (1992), *Women in Ancient Civilizations* (1999), translator, with commentary, of Euripides' *Helen*, in *Women on the Edge: Four Plays by Euripides* (1999), *Events That Changed Ancient Greece* (2002), *Daughters of Gaia: Women in the Ancient Mediterranean World* (2007/2008), *Helen: Ancient and Modern Icon of Femininity and Poetic Creation* (forthcoming).

Introduction[1]

Konstantinos P. Nikoloutsos

This collection examines cinematic representations of women from the realms of ancient Greek myth and history. The chapters discuss how female figures from these two domains are resurrected on the big screen at different historical junctures and are embedded in a narrative that serves different purposes (artistic, commercial, political) depending on the director of the film, its screenwriter(s), the studio, the country of its origin, and the time of its production. Nearly all the chapters included in this volume engage in a comparative analysis of ancient accounts and their cinematic adaptations, but expand the scope of their search beyond the question of whether or not filmic recreations of antiquity are faithful reproductions of the details of the source text(s). Employing a diverse array of hermeneutic approaches (gender theory, feminist criticism, gaze theory, psychoanalysis, sociological theories of religion, film history, viewer-response theory, and personal voice criticism), the essays assembled here aim to cast light on cinema's investments in the classical past and decode the mechanisms whereby the female figures under examination are extracted from their original context and are brought to life to serve as vehicles for the articulation of modern ideas, concerns, and cultural trends. The goal of the collection as a whole is to explore not only how antiquity on the screen represents and in this process often distorts, compresses, contests, and revises antiquity on the page but also, most importantly, why cinema reconstructs the classical past in a frequently eclectic fashion.

[1] I am grateful to the OUP anonymous referees, as well as to the following readers for their insightful comments, suggestions, and criticisms that helped me sharpen the focus of my argument: Anthony Corbeill, Lorna Hardwick, Maria Marsilio, Pantelis Michelakis, and Martin Winkler. All mistakes remain with me alone.

Written by established and emerging authorities in classical reception studies from across the globe, the thirteen essays that make up this volume examine a wide range of films (in terms of genres, budget, distribution, and audience appeal) produced in different countries[2] during a period of ninety years (1917–2007). The volume discusses both big studio features and independent productions. The films fall into the following categories: silent, black-and-white, epic, peplum, action, adventure, drama, comedy, made-for-television, art house, and poetry films. These are either films set in Greek antiquity or reworkings of ancient themes situated in a modern setting. The commercial success and critical acclaim of individual films are of interest here insofar as they can illuminate the social, economic, and cultural context of a film's production and reception.

The book is divided into five sections. The first three are devoted to Helen, Medea, and Penelope respectively. These female figures have captivated the imagination of many directors from both sides of the Atlantic and are therefore granted a special place in the collection. The fourth part examines representations of women from the realm of Greek myth that have received a lesser degree of attention in the medium, but nonetheless carry a high cultural, artistic, and political charge. The list of these mythical figures includes Clytemnestra, Iphigenia, Iole, Deianeira, Omphale, Io, and the Nereids. The last section of the collection focuses on three historical figures: Gorgo, Olympias, and Cleopatra.

ANCIENT GREEK WOMEN IN FILM AND CLASSICAL RECEPTION STUDIES

The study of ancient Greek women on the screen has not received adequate attention in current scholarship on the reception of classical antiquity in cinema and on television.[3] This book aims to fill this critical vacuum and make an original contribution to this field by enriching our

[2] Most of the films are American, Greek, and Italian productions or co-productions. The volume also examines films from Denmark, France, Germany, and Great Britain.

[3] This is the first collection devoted entirely to a topic that has been treated sporadically in recent scholarship on classics in film. Previous studies include McDonald (2001: 90–1, 95–6, 98–100); Cyrino (2007b); Allen (2007); Cavallini (2008); Roisman (2008); Blondell (2009); Potter (2009); Shahabudin (2009: 206–14); Winkler (2009: 210–50); Carney (2010); Nikoloutsos (2010); Bakogianni (2011: 153–94); Blanshard and Shahabudin (2011: 73–5; 118–21; 210–13). This is by no means an exhaustive list of works on the topic. See also the essays in this volume for further bibliography. I regret I have been unable to consider Michelakis (2013) as well as the various essays in Renger and Solomon (2012) and Cyrino (2013). These publications were not available by the time the final typescript of this volume was sent to press.

knowledge of the ways in which the ancient world is recreated, used, and (almost always) abused in modern popular culture. The arrangement of the essays in thematic units allows the readers of the collection to trace the reception history of Greek women in the medium across time, region, and genre, and obtain a clear picture of the commonalities, variations, and cultural patterns involved in their filmic transplantation. One of the collection's main objectives in examining representations of the same female characters in films produced in different countries and historical periods is to illustrate not only their enduring appeal and polysemous role in the narratives in which they are inserted but also the mutability and continuous adaptability of their screen image. As the essays illustrate, this image is not static, or consistent with the features that these women are attributed in ancient literary and visual sources. It changes, in most cases radically, according to the sociocultural norms and stereotypes of the time in which the film is produced; the economic and technological conditions of its production; the political climate in which it is made; the vision of the producer, director, and screenwriter; the star image and nationality of the actress who plays the part, as well as her physical characteristics that are often taken advantage of in order to connote issues of power and transgression; the aesthetic expectations and moral sensibilities of the audience; and the stylistic and other conventions of the genre through which ancient female figures are revived on the big screen.

These parameters determine both the way ancient Greek women look and the way they act on screen. For example, as Bella Vivante discusses in her essay, in conforming to stereotypes of female beauty in post-World War II American society, the Helen of Robert Wise's 1956 epic film *Helen of Troy* is cast as a platinum blonde, fair-skinned bombshell, projecting onto Homer's heroine the glamour and sex appeal of a pin-up girl. By contrast, in Michael Cacoyannis' 1971 adaptation of Euripides' *Trojan Women* Helen has olive skin and jet-black hair as an embodiment of Mediterranean femininity, passion, and sensuality. Cacoyannis' film builds Helen's screen image upon a fundamental principle in the history of classical reception, that of repetition with difference. In keeping with the textual tradition, it acknowledges Helen's power to victimize men with her looks; at the same time, the film exploits her iconic attraction on a metacinematic level by casting a Greek actress, Irene Papas, in the role of classical antiquity's most notorious femme fatale, thereby making a statement about ethnic continuity between ancient and modern Greece. Drawn from the pages of Athenian tragedy, Helen is fashioned in accordance with, and operates as a vehicle for the propagation of, notions of popular history, memory, and the nation. *The Trojan Women* is one of several case studies examined in this collection which illustrate that filmic recreations of the classical past are not neutral or disinterested. They have affective dimensions, and are deeply implicated in contemporary cultural and political discourses.

Arthur Pomeroy's essay shows how similar popular perceptions about hair colour, body type, and national identity inform the portrayal of female characters who surround Hercules in Italian peplum films. For example, the role of Antea, the sexually voracious, vampy queen of the Amazons, in Pietro Francisci's *Le Fatiche di Ercole* (1958) is played by Gianna Maria Canale, whose dark black hair and curvaceous figure fit the stereotypical look of the southern Italian woman, termed *maggiorata fisica* (buxom beauty),[4] which was popularized by physically imposing actresses, such as Sofia Loren and Gina Lollobrigida. By contrast, Iole, the princess from Iolcus who is rescued by the mythical hero and falls in love with him, is cast as a slender, delicate girl played by Sylva Koscina. Her light hair and fair complexion suggest to the viewer either an American-style 'girl next door', most typically portrayed in cinema by stars like Doris Day and even sometimes by Marilyn Monroe, or an upper class Italian lady, since in Italy these features were traditionally associated with the affluent north or the Frankish aristocracy of the south. Antea is dark-haired and looks demonic; Iole has light auburn hair and looks angelic.

The examples discussed by Pomeroy show that identifying the multiple influences (industrial, technological, aesthetic, sociocultural) that shape celluloid antiquity requires methods and approaches other than the purely philological. Tracing these influences will help us develop a critical idiom for analysing cinematic versions of the classical past and investigate, more effectively, the complex ways in which they are produced to function as commentaries on the present. The image of the women who populate peplum films about Hercules and his adventures is not informed only by Italian history and geography. It is also symptomatic of American cultural hegemony and media imperialism in the age of globalization, which started in the 1920s and reached its peak in the 1950s and 1960s (and continues to this day). Extracted from the world of ancient Greek myth, the women of Hercules are reanimated on the big screen and are allocated a hybrid look that bears testimony to the blurring of artistic boundaries between Europe and the United States in the post-war era and to the transcontinental dissemination and fusion of cultural elements and aesthetic trends caused by the massive migration of people at the time.

My own essay also investigates how antiquity and modernity intersect with each other on the big screen. Filmed at the height of the Cold War,

[4] For this trend in Italian cinema, see Celli and Cottino-Jones (2007: 81–82).

Rudolph Maté's *The 300 Spartans* (1962) implicates Gorgo in the US ideology of 'Containment' and homemaker lifestyle of the 1950s and early 1960s, projecting an image of her as a loving mother and wife who is devoted to her family and tends to her domestic duties. Almost half a century later, when Gorgo is resurrected on screen through Zack Snyder's smash hit *300* (2007), she is fashioned to suit the rhetoric of gender equality and is depicted as a dynamic queen who is actively involved in public life, despite the very fact that there was no such office for royal women in fifth century BC Sparta. My analysis shows that at different historical moments the same female figure from ancient Greek history is deployed in the medium to advance completely different modern positions.[5] This method of character reconstruction, termed *neo-mythologism* by Italian director Vittorio Cottafavi,[6] finds a parallel in ancient tragedy, in which female characters were appropriated from the realm of epic and were adjusted to serve the agendas of the playwrights and reflect the values and attitudes of Athenian society. Some of the surviving tragedies preserve different and sometimes even contradictory versions of the same myth. Electra, for example, continues to live at the palace at Mycenae and enjoy her royal status after the murder of her father, Agamemnon, in Sophocles' tragedy. Euripides, by contrast, portrays her as a peasant who is dressed in rags and lives in a poor household in his own play. Tragedy, the popular culture of fifth century BC Athens, undermines the idea of a canonical story with fixed details. The films examined in this volume form part of the same artistic tradition of reimagining and reinventing the ancient world for popular consumption.

In classical literature, this discursive method of refiguration applies to historical persons as well. In the aftermath of her defeat at the battle of Actium in 31 BC, Cleopatra VII Philopator is divested of her political powers and titles as a Ptolemaic ruler and enters the poetry of the early Augustan period in the form of a mistress from the dissolute East charged with an extraordinary amount of erotic allure and perversity. From protective queen of a powerful kingdom, as her public image is promoted on coins, inscriptions, and other visual material from pre-Roman Egypt, she is transformed into a barbarian whore in the work of Propertius, Horace, and Virgil, as Maria Wyke has most notably shown.[7]

5 See also Martindale (2006: 4) and Kallendorf (2007: 3).
6 See Winkler (2005); (2009: 16).
7 Wyke (2002: 195–243).

In the last essay of the collection, Lloyd Llewellyn-Jones traces a similar process of identity erasure in Hollywood recreations of the life of Cleopatra. With the exception of Joseph Mankiewicz's 1963 film, where her Greekness is acknowledged, albeit briefly and in jest, US filmmakers in general subdue her Macedonian ancestry and portray her, in terms of both narrative and costumes, as a Pharaonic monarch, thereby exploiting, for aesthetic and commercial reasons, the exotic and glamorous aspects of her Egyptian connection. The Hellenistic world that Cleopatra inhabited is anachronistically replaced on screen by buildings, symbols, and dresses from the time of the Egyptian New Kingdom.

Llewellyn-Jones' chapter calls attention to the conditioned and mediated character of cinematic antiquity. Although in promotion material they cultivate the expectation of a historically accurate portrait, Hollywood films perpetuate an identification of Cleopatra with Pharaonic Egypt, which has been firmly established in the western imagination since the mid-nineteenth century. Sold to audiences as accessible versions of ancient history, the Cleopatra biopics reproduce modern myths, clichés, and misconceptions about her, thereby proving to be a form of entertainment that pretends to offer high art, but in reality surrenders to the temptation of popular acceptance and profit. This treatment of Cleopatra reflects the attitudes of Hollywood producers and directors during the studio era toward what constitutes ancient history: a combination of folklore and factual information loaded with visual opulence, operatic music, and narrative ellipses, disjunctions, and eclecticism. This is not the history of Hellenistic Egypt, but rather a collage of fragments or 'sheets'[8] of history from different epochs.

Many of the films examined in this volume have been inspired by, and respond to, specific contemporary political events. The female characters in them are shaped to serve the propagation of the director's view about these events. Anastasia Bakogianni examines how modern Greek history informs Michael Cacoyannis' third adaptation of a Euripidean tragedy titled *Iphigenia* (1977). She argues that the film, produced in the aftermath of the collapse of the Greek dictatorship and the retaliatory Turkish invasion of Cyprus in 1974, places renewed emphasis on the intersection between the public and the private spheres in Euripides' play by depicting the longing of men for war and power as a catalyst for the severing of the strong mother–daughter bond that characterizes the relationship between Clytemnestra and Iphigenia. The annihilation of the family and the forcible separation of the mother from her child in the

[8] I borrow the term from Landy (1996a: 153).

mythic past are, according to Bakogianni's reading of the film, a powerful allegory for the suffering of the Greek-Cypriot nation in the present and the images of thousands of mothers, shown in the media at the time, who were mourning the loss of their dead and missing children in the wake of the 'Attila' operation.

As Bakogianni's essay demonstrates, cinema extends tragedy's project of blurring the boundaries between myth and national history, thus pointing out the manifold ways in which the classical past can be used to shed light on and problematize the present. Hallie Rebecca Marshall builds an argument along similar lines in her essay on Tony Harrison's *Prometheus*, a film/poem in which the British writer draws on Aeschylus' play, as well as the reception of Prometheus in later European literary tradition, to discuss both the legacy of the coal mine closures that precipitated the bitter strike of 1984 by the National Union of Mineworkers in the UK and the concurrent collapse of the socialist dream in Eastern Europe. Investigating how and for what purpose Harrison reshapes the female figures of *Prometheus Bound*, Marshall argues that the chorus of the anonymous Nereids is used to express communal suffering. Io, on the other hand, becomes a symbol for the destruction of a single household due to severe economic hardship. Past and present are interblended on the big screen to provide a critique about social identity and political change.

This recontextualization of ancient Greek myth and its employment as a powerful tool whereby to expose and condemn political decisions and social practices at moments of national crisis illustrate the central position that classical antiquity occupies in modern artistic imagination. This, however, is hardly a new finding, for almost every publication in classical reception studies has sought to link the past to the present under the rubric of 'cultural continuity' and by identifying parallel constructed versions of myth and history in ancient and modern media. Charles Martindale has, alarmingly, pointed out this 'wider [scholarly] trend to collapse reception into cultural studies'.[9] This collection responds to this concern and shows that, as much as it is legitimate, it is also reductive to treat filmic reenactments of the ancient Greek world as a form of art that is filtered only through the lens of contemporary sociopolitical reality. A number of the films examined here do not draw, directly or exclusively, on ancient sources. Rather, they are responses to, and often symptoms of, modern appropriations of the ancient Greek world in film or fiction. These receptions form an important intertext that cannot be ignored in critical analysis.

For example, Zack Snyder's *300* is based on Frank Miller's 1998 comic book of the same title, which was in turn inspired by the 1962 historical

[9] Martindale (2006: 9).

epic *The 300 Spartans*. In other words, the 2007 blockbuster is the most recent in a 'chain of receptions'[10] of the battle of Thermopylae in contemporary popular culture. Snyder's Gorgo, as I show in my essay, cannot be examined in isolation from this artistic framework and be compared only to her Herodotean counterpart, since she is also constructed to evoke her cinematic and graphic precursors. Similarly, as Annette Baertschi demonstrates, Lars von Trier's 1988 telefilm *Medea* is not directly informed by Euripides' homonymous tragedy, but is based on its modern reception transmitted through a mediating text, the script of an unrealized film by renowned Danish director Carl Theodor Dreyer. Dreyer, who drew loosely on the Greek play, had planned *Medea* to be his first film in colour and had allegedly travelled to Paris to offer the title role to Maria Callas, but he suddenly died of pneumonia in 1968, a year before the famous soprano played the part in Pasolini's film. Von Trier resurrects Medea on Danish television by reproducing both the thematics and the aesthetics of his master's script.

Baertschi's essay shows that an investigation of the reception of Greek antiquity in the medium needs to take into full consideration the history of a film's production—in particular the various routes through which ancient texts, images, and ideas have travelled, physically and metaphorically, across time, place, and media, and have come to influence modern directors and scriptwriters. Tracing these routes can shed light upon the artistic trends and stylistic innovations that shape antiquity on screen and can explain the shifts, variations, and inconsistencies in the reception history of its iconic figures within specific national contexts. As Lorna Hardwick has cogently put it, acknowledging the diasporic nature of classical texts:

> ... recognizes the shaping forces of the subsequent filters that have conditioned understanding of the texts without assuming that only one set of filters matters. It leaves room for investigating why any particular ante-text re-emerges under particular cultural conditions and for considering the extent to which the dynamics of its relationship with its ancient context are replicated or revised.[11]

Susan Shapiro, in turn, makes an eloquent case for the need to consider context when we examine cinematic reconstructions of the classical world. Her essay discusses Pier Paolo Pasolini's *Medea* (1969) and illustrates that the film is a synthesis of dominant theoretical approaches

[10] I borrow the term from Jauss (1982: 20). For the use of the term in classical reception studies, see, Kallendorf (2007: 2); Martindale (2007: 300); Paul (2010a: 15) and (2010b: 148).

[11] Hardwick (2007: 47). See also Hardwick (2003: 4, 32).

to myth and religion, advanced by some of the most influential philosophers of the last two centuries, such as Karl Marx, Sir James Frazer, Carl Jung, Mircea Eliade, and Antonio Gramsci. Informed by these theories, Pasolini casts Medea as both innocent victim and vengeful sorceress. On the one hand, she represents the beneficent powers of nature and fertility and, on the other, the destructive forces of retribution and irrationality. The belief in and veneration of these elements are characteristics of the religious systems of archaic civilizations, as well as of those of the African nations, which were considered to be primitive civilizations in economically developed countries at the time of the film's production.[12] As Shapiro maintains, Medea and the Colchians symbolize the people of pre-industrialized societies who were forced to submit to the colonial powers of the modern world, as portrayed by Jason and the Argonauts. Pasolini appropriates the myth of Medea from classical literature and (in keeping with ancient mythopoeic practices) he transforms it into a new foundation story. Produced at the end of a decade that witnessed the collapse of European colonialism in sub-Saharan Africa, the film 'decolonizes' Medea's story and antiquity in general. It liberates them from the normative epic style in which Hollywood studios—a multimillion-dollar empire—sought to portray the classical world in the 1950s and early 1960s, and opens them up to innovative, counter-hegemonic interpretations.

The essays outlined above illustrate two interrelated aspects of the reception of ancient Greek women in the medium. First, their screen image is the product of a process of hybridization between ancient depictions and modern cultural trends and ideologies. Second, their refiguration takes place at a particular historical moment, and the pastiches that make up their cinematic portrait are contingent upon that moment. The plasticity and adaptability that directors perceive as the very characteristic of the women of Greek myth and history undermine the expectation of a faithful rendition of the source text that some classicists may have[13] and illustrate a 'fusion of horizons'[14] that opens up new pathways for research into the diverse ways in which cinema draws on and transforms the classical world. For, in addition to films that recreate

[12] On the interpretation of Greek tragedy with primitive rituals in postcolonial contexts, see also Nikoloutsos (2010: 95–103).

[13] As Winkler (2009: 247) astutely remarks regarding the attitude of classical scholars to judge films set in the classical world on the basis of their historical or literary accuracy: 'Scholars who despair over the extent to which modern media distort the supposed truth of ancient myth or dismiss such versions as hopelessly inaccurate and therefore *infra dig* might do better to remember the ancients.' See also Paul (2010b: 146–47); Nikoloutsos (2013: 282–3).

[14] I borrow the term from Gadamer (1991): 306–7, 374–75.

episodes from Greek mythology and history, or update them to modern times, there are also motion pictures seemingly unrelated to classical antiquity in which, nonetheless, classical themes can be traced and echoes of the classical past can be heard. This is precisely the point that Edith Hall makes in the second half of her essay, where she examines both direct and 'masked' descendants of Penelope in films as diverse as Jean-Luc Godard's *Le Mépris* (English title: *Contempt*, 1963), Jon Hiller's *Penelope* (1966), Barry Levinson's *The Natural* (1984), Jon Amierl's *Sommersby* (1993), Mike Leigh's *Naked* (1993), Theodoros Angelopoulos' *Το βλέμμα του Οδυσσέα* (English title: *Ulysses' Gaze*, 1995), Joel and Ethan Coen's *O Brother Where Art Thou?* (2000), Anthony Minghella's *Cold Mountain* (2003), and Wim Wenders' *Don't Come Knocking* (2005), among other titles.

Films like the above merit consideration here not only because they illustrate the catalytic influence of Penelope's figure upon contemporary artistic imagination and her employment as a model for the construction of the ideal wife in European and American film narrative. They also invite a reassessment of the role of the Homeric heroine in the world of the *Odyssey* by shedding light on certain aspects of her character that have been underexplored in classical scholarship. This does not mean that we will be able to retrieve the Penelope of the epic poem, as 'Homer' visualized her and ancient audiences understood her; the context of her original conception and reception is forever lost and irrecoverable. An exploration of her cinematic offspring, however, will enable us to identify and rethink the 'accretions',[15] perceptions, and misconceptions that have been embedded in and have shaped her image through centuries of continuous appropriation and reinterpretation. This, of course, is an epistemological benefit that the reader of the collection will gain from the analyses in the rest of the chapters.

ANCIENT GREEK WOMEN IN FILM AND GENDER STUDIES

The essays outlined above demonstrate that ancient Greek women are revived in various shapes in cinema and that the examination of their reception in the medium is a complex venture that leads to conclusions

[15] On 'accretions' and classical reception studies, see Hardwick (2003: 107); Martindale (2006: 12).

important for more than one interdisciplinary field. The second such area in which the collection inscribes itself is gender studies. From Monique Wittig and Hélène Cixous to Luce Irigaray and Jacques Lacan, twentieth-century French criticism has regularly used ancient Greek myth as a particularly useful tool with which to theorize sexual desire and analyse gender categories. Such appropriations of antiquity continue to provide impetus, such as in the recent collection edited by Vanda Zajko and Miriam Leonard under the title *Laughing with Medusa*. The anthology focuses, *inter alia*, on the importance of Greek myth and its female inhabitants for the development of post-1970 feminist thought, and investigates how the stories of these mythic figures have been revised and retold in order to destabilize the hierarchies that uphold the symbolic systems and institutions of western societies.

This collection pursues the same line of inquiry in a different discursive terrain, by exploring the instrumentalization of the women of ancient Greek myth and history in a medium defined, predominantly, as male. The producers, directors, and screenwriters of the films under examination here are all male. As a result, the films reflect the patriarchal value system of their time and, as the essays demonstrate, employ women as conduits for the propagation of dominant ideologies of femininity and as paradigms of the intersection of gender and politics in contemporary European and American culture. In this respect, the films that the collection places under critical scrutiny are important not only from an artistic but also from a socio-historical point of view. Although they have nothing new to contribute to our knowledge of gender and sexuality in the ancient world, they constitute a valuable source of information about the variations and changes in perceptions of, and attitudes to, these issues in recent decades.

Joanna Paul examines Mario Camerini's *Ulisse* (1954) and shows that the film is far from providing an accurate picture of the role of women in Homeric society. Camerini hired the same Italian actress, Silvana Mangano, to play the roles of both Penelope and Circe; Mangano also lends her voice to the Sirens. Paul explains this artistic innovation by situating the film within its sociopolitical context. Produced in the aftermath of World War II and during the war in Indochina, which led to the war in Vietnam in 1955, the film casts Odysseus as a figure for the soldier who roams away from his country. Mangano, in turn, symbolizes both the loyal wife who patiently awaits the return of her husband home and the foreign ('other') woman who might lure that man away from his mission and thus endanger the nuclear family and by extension the nation. The Madonna/whore dichotomy that informs the representation of the central female characters in *Ulisse*, an Italian-US co-production, is in line with the rhetoric of the restoration of traditional gender roles in post-war America and Europe, which entailed the confinement of women in the domestic sphere and the return of men to the role of the breadwinner. Cinema and television, its competitor in the 1950s, did not provide just a popular form of mass entertainment; they also served as vehicles for the idealization and endorsement of the patriarchal life style. Penelope and Circe, as Paul's essay illustrates, are revived on the big screen in order to reproduce in an ancient Greek garment, and thus validate in the eyes of their spectators, stereotypes of femininity on both sides of the Atlantic—the roles, that is, that women had to perform in order to gain social acceptance or rejection. *Ulisse* also invites us to rethink the parameters, determinants, and subject matters of filmic recreations of Greek antiquity in the years following the collapse of the Third Reich and the division of the world into spheres of influence during the Cold War era. For, as Wyke has shown about films set in ancient Rome,[16] so too films based on Greek myth or history reflect, and at the same time seek to deflect, the traumas of war and fascism, as well as the paranoia of the West about the spread of Communism beyond its borders. In her role as Circe, Mangano destabilizes, but as Penelope she ultimately reinforces ideas about power, male identity, hierarchy, and homeland security.

Although the films examined here do not provide an accurate picture of the role of women in Greek society, their storylines replicate the male bias of the ancient sources. As Ruby Blondell argues in her essay, the supreme beauty that Helen possesses makes her an extremely dangerous woman. Most Greek authors respond to the threat that she poses by limiting her power and denying her agency. Wolfgang Petersen's *Troy* (2004) extends the Greek project of disempowering Helen. Instead of celebrating the lethal powers of female beauty, the film reduces Helen to an everygirl and, as is the case of the *Iliad*, relegates her to the margins of the narrative in order to keep her from outshining the real star, Achilles/Brad Pitt. A similar representational strategy is followed in Don Chaffey's *Jason and the Argonauts* (1963). As Kirk Ormand shows, Medea's inclusion in the film is unavoidable; she is a central figure in the Golden Fleece quest in classical literature and thus cannot be ignored. Although she possesses extraordinary powers as a sorceress—powers on which Jason

[16] Wyke (1997).

depends to accomplish his mission—her role in the film is diminished significantly, and she is cast as a passive object of desire without clear self-motivation. The narrative of Chaffey's film is purely androcentric, revolving around the adventures of Jason and the Argonauts.[17] Medea appears in a few scenes only to add a romantic touch to the story. Her identity is voided of the dynamism and transgressiveness that characterize her in ancient literary sources. This suppression of female agency allows Jason to emerge, in the eyes of his male viewers, as a true hero who can achieve his goal and obtain the Golden Fleece without the help of a superwoman, no matter how many obstacles are put in front of him. Medea is evoked but then 'contained' in order for male ambition and potency to triumph.

The marginalization of women in filmic recreations of Greek antiquity that focus on the deeds of men is also the subject of Edith Hall's essay. Hall examines the portrayal of Penelope in various cinematic and televisual excursions into the world of the *Odyssey*, as well as in films that reinscribe Penelope's archetypal character in modern settings. She shows that, whereas we might have expected Homer's heroine to emancipate herself from the patriarchal constraints of her archaic plotline and be refigured in the wake of feminist activism, her reception in the medium during the period 1963—2007 demonstrates a regression of her image in terms of gender equality and women's empowerment. Penelope's screen substitute in Hollywood productions is deprived of the complexity and moral agency that her Homeric counterpart possessed and reaffirms modern male fantasies of the female psyche as masochistic, depressive, or even hysterical. The films examined in Hall's essay celebrate an iconic woman from Greek myth, as well as modern perceptions of Penelope as an ideal wife/mother and a symbol of conjugal devotion in narrative trajectories that deny her individuality.

An exception to this Hollywood rule is the depiction of Olympias in two historical epics, Robert Rossen's *Alexander the Great* (1956) and Oliver Stone's *Alexander* (2004). As Kirsten Day's essay illustrates, both directors portray Alexander's mother as a strong, ambitious woman who pursues power by manipulating information, taking advantage of her sexuality, and capitalizing on her relationship with her son. While both films attempt to offer insight into the power and gender dynamics at Alexander's time, they nonetheless provide a picture of the position of elite women in fourth century BC Macedonia that is filtered through modern beliefs and understandings. Thus, Rossen's film suffers from

[17] Most of the plot involves the journey of the Argonauts before they arrive at Colchis. As opposed to Medea, Hera receives prominent attention in the plot.

an imposition of a post-World War II intolerance of female individuality and dynamism, and erases Olympias from the narrative once Alexander decides to step into Asia to wage war against the Persian Empire. Stone's biopic, on the other hand, psychoanalyses Olympias' relationship with Alexander and attaches to it Oedipal overtones. Films like these, as Day points out, are most productively viewed as dialogues between the past and the present. Not only do they illustrate why Greek antiquity continues to engage modern film-makers and audiences. They also offer us an opportunity to learn about the present by examining 'the veneer of modern social and artistic agendas superimposed on historical realities'.

The purpose of this introductory chapter has been to delineate the theoretical and methodological approaches used in the volume as a whole and provide an overview of the rest of the chapters in order to demonstrate the contribution of the collection to two major interdisciplinary fields: classical reception studies and gender studies. The book does not aim by any means to offer an exhaustive treatment of the subject. Cinematic depictions of Antigone, Electra, and Phaedra, for example, are not considered here, though we do hope that the analyses that follow will generate critical interest in them as well.[18] The goal of the collection is to restore to visibility the polysemous role of the women of Greek myth and history in the films under examination and to explore, through some notable case studies, the interplay and coalescence of tradition and innovation—or 'the dialectic of continuity and rupture', to borrow terminology from literary theorist and critic Fredric Jameson[19]—that characterizes their appropriation in the cinema. The collection, thus, will appeal both to classical scholars who are interested in knowing the ways in which the ancient world has been used, and abused, in contemporary mass culture and to film historians who seek to trace the impact of classical antiquity on the medium. The book is also meant to reach a wider audience of academics and students in various disciplines in the humanities and social sciences, such as women's studies, history (European or American), Italian studies, Modern Greek studies, and cultural studies.

The essays identify and address new issues—theoretical as well as practical—and thus add a significant dimension to research on the reception of the classical world in the cinema. Although there are several similarities in the cinematic portrayals of the various female figures under consideration, each film and heroine represent a distinct case. One of the main goals of the book is to concentrate on individual films

[18] For Electra in the cinema, see Bakogianni (2011: 153–94).

[19] Jameson (2002: 23). On 'temporal continuity and disjunction' in classical reception, see Brockliss et al. (2012: 5).

or characters in order to avoid generalizations and develop a theoretical framework based on specific examples that could apply to a wider range of films set in the classical world. Binding the different case studies together is the common goal to investigate the diverse ways in which the classical past is reanimated on the screen in order to suit the ideological, technological, aesthetic, and commercial needs of its cinematic narration. As the essays that follow demonstrate, once they are transplanted into film, the women of ancient Greek myth and history are no longer ancient or Greek, but become the property of an international community of directors, screenwriters, producers, viewers, and academics, all of whom seek to impose different meanings and interpretations upon them.

Part I

HELEN

1

Gazing at Helen: Helen as Polysemous Icon in Robert Wise's *Helen of Troy* and Michael Cacoyannis' *The Trojan Women*

Bella Vivante

> Avoid looking at her, lest she seize you with desire.
> For she captures the eyes of men.[1]
>
> Eur. *Trojan Women* 891–2,
> Hecuba speaking to Menelaus about Helen

Hecuba's words from Euripides' play locate Helen's power of seduction through the eyes of the men who look upon her. This gaze is dangerous, like looking upon Medusa, but instead of turning men to stone, gazing at Helen melts men, causing them to become impotent, understood polysemously.[2] The popularity of the fifth-century vase paintings that show Menelaus with sword raised rushing to kill Helen on one side while on the other, in pre-Freudian symbolism, he drops his sword upon sight of her, visually testifies to this power attributed to Helen when men look at her.[3] Interestingly, while Greek pottery depicts Helen as clothed in these scenes, Euripides refers to Menelaus' melting at sight of her bare breasts.[4] This concept of the male gaze contrasts sharply with the typical configuration of the gaze in film criticism. Since the publication of Laura Mulvey's foundational 1975 article, 'the gaze' has been posited as that of the male spectator by and for whom most images, especially those of the

[1] All translations from the Ancient Greek are my own. I wish to thank Martin Winkler and especially the volume editor Konstantinos P. Nikoloutsos for their valuable comments on this chapter.

[2] More on Helen and Medusa below. Blondell (this volume) asserts that Helen 'exercises supreme erotic power through her blinding impact on men's eyes', but she does not pursue this line of inquiry further.

[3] Kahil (1988: 542–4, image numbers 260–77, pp. 337–41).

[4] *Andr.* 629; cf. the scholiast on this passage = Ibycus 296 PMG.

female, are fashioned. Images of women in cinema and other media are shaped to gratify heterosexual male (sexual) desire. Examples of female figures constructed according to male projections and to fulfill male desires are rife from ancient Greece to modern western literature and art. Helen, as she is conceptualized in both ancient and modern media, epitomizes the '*to-be-looked-at-ness* [of]... woman displayed as the sexual object... of erotic spectacle'.[5] Hecuba's warning suggests a different approach to the male gaze, one that constructs it as vulnerable, weak and powerless when sighted on the immense power of the female. With the attribution of this power over the male gaze to her, the figure of Helen may be seen as focalizing three different constructs of the gaze. First, throughout the western cultural tradition she has served as the iconic female to be gazed upon to stir men's desire. Second, she evokes the danger men risk from gazing upon a sensual, sexually potent female. Third, through Helen we shall also witness the power of the female gaze.

My goal in this paper is to examine how the depictions of ancient Greek Helen in two films produced in the third quarter of the twentieth century cinematically display these three concepts of the gaze: Robert Wise's 1956 *Helen of Troy*,[6] starring Rossana Podestà, and Michael Cacoyannis' 1971 *The Trojan Women*, an adaptation of Euripides' eponymous tragedy, with Irene Papas as Helen.[7] Both directors underscore the first meaning of the gaze, as the cameras repeatedly display for the spectators' view virtual still shots of the iconically beautiful Helen. Cacoyannis, more than Wise, explores the danger of gazing upon Helen, although Wise alludes to this danger, and Cacoyannis vividly dramatizes the power of Helen's own gaze. Despite being based on the same ancient Greek figure, these two films portray Helen's physical appearance and conduct very differently. Both use skin and hair colour, hairstyle, and costume to convey their messages about Helen's status and her thematic and social significations. Furthermore, both films accentuate these concepts of gazing upon Helen by dramatizing key aspects of ancient Greek Helen: foremost, in most ancient sources, as the icon of beauty and eroticism; as a goddess associated with the cycle of vegetation and adolescent girls' transitions; as a

[5] Mulvey (1975: 11). See also Berger (1972). On feminist and gendered film criticism on the gaze, often as coinciding with western hegemonic imperial gaze, see Kaplan (1997: 67–93), (2000), Bean and Negra (2002), MacKinnon (2002).

[6] Since the film was produced in 1955 and officially released in 1956, both dates occur in references.

[7] Scholarly interest in cinematic Helens has skyrocketed in the last decade, especially on Helen in Wolfgang Petersen's *Troy*: Cyrino (2007b), Roisman (2008), Blondell (this volume, first published in 2009).

member of Sparta's royal lineage; and morally as a woman capable of transgressing gender and social boundaries with relative impunity. The diverse ways in which Wise and Cacoyannis incorporate these ancient characteristics into their cinematic Helens, and particularly the two actresses who are respectively cast to perform Helen, deliver distinctive messages about women and sexuality. Helen is fashioned by one director in general accord with the gender stereotypes of his time and by the other as a figure through which to interrogate accepted ideas about femininity and female sexuality. The respective cinematic conceptualizations of Helen and the films within which they are set offer comments, whether deliberate or not, on current political issues, including women's placement in larger political movements.[8] Despite their many differences, these two films form an interesting comparative pair. Distinguished, first, from the other major English-language film portrayals of Helen by their closer proximity in date—between one in 1927, Alexander Korda's *The Private Life of Helen of Troy*, and two in the early 2000s: John Kent Harrison's 2003 cable tv production, *Helen of Troy*, and Wolfgang Petersen's 2004 *Troy*—these two films stand out for portraying Helen as a complex, multi-layered figure of power, however differently each film projects her power.[9]

ROBERT WISE'S *HELEN OF TROY*

Impelled by the success of the biblical dramas *Quo Vadis?* (dir. Mervyn LeRoy, 1951) and *The Robe* (dir. Henry Koster, 1953), Warner Brothers released *Helen of Troy* in a mid-decade wave of films on ancient Greek themes, and concurrently with Cecil B. DeMille's biblical blockbuster *The Ten Commandments* (1956).[10] Filmed in Cinemascope, the new

[8] Scholars have noted cinema's crucial role as a new medium for political commentary. See, e.g., Negra (2002: 375), Ross (2002: 4), and Russell (2007: 31, 45).

[9] I list the major productions only; for brief overviews of films featuring Helen, see Pomeroy (2008: 61–2), Roisman (2008: 127–8).

[10] See Solomon (2001a), Russell (2007), Pomeroy (2008), and Paul (2013) for a discussion of historical epic films from the beginning of cinema. Following almost a decade of no films drawing on classical antiquity, the late 1940s saw a resurgence of films featuring ancient Greek themes, including Eugene O'Neill's *Mourning Becomes Electra* (dir. Dudley Nichols, 1947). The films produced during the 1950s, the 'golden age of historical epic' (Russell, 2007: 5) when 40 per cent of films were set in the past (Russell, 2007: 24), include *Orphée* (dir. Jean Cocteau, 1950), *Alexander the Great* (dir. Robert Rossen, 1956) starring Richard Burton, *Ulisse* (dir. Mario Camerini, 1954) starring Kirk Douglas, *Hercules* (Pietro Francisci, 1958) starring Steve Reeves, and the brilliant Brazilian film *Orfeu Negro* (dir. Marcel Camus, 1959) starring Bruno Mello.

technology for historical epics first used in 1953, the film was Wise's only foray into the epic genre.[11] Because it is a US-Italian co-production made in Rome's Cinecittà studios, like *Ulisse* (dir. Mario Camerini, 1954), scholars consider *Helen of Troy* a precursor to the Italian peplum films produced by the hundreds in the period 1958–65.[12] In the peplum films, the muscle-bound male hero is on display for much of the film, bare-chested and in skimpy tunic—available for the (conscious or not) homoerotic gaze of the male spectators—complemented by comparable displays of the female lead, who can conversely appeal to all audience segments.[13] According to the codes devised by Italian director Duccio Tessari about peplum films, preferable plotlines favour an erotic triangle of two men pursuing one woman; colour should be used to convey a character's moral qualities—white or yellow for 'good' characters, red or black for the 'bad'.[14] While these are conventional, that is, patriarchal, social and cinematic features, *Helen of Troy*'s dramatization of a good female heroine rather than the masculinist heroics of its male lead radically differentiates its plot and dramatic focus from the later peplum films. Scholars interpret the preponderance of visual imagery over dialogue in the peplum films as glorifying brawn over intellect and as an attempt to appeal to less educated, lower socio-economic classes.[15] In sharp contrast to peplum films, *Helen of Troy* plays to a putatively educated audience open to learning and who would respond favourably to the intellectual subtleties of the film.[16]

Helen of Troy illustrates two significant cinematic trends of the 1950s: a focus on historicity and a concern with contemporary social attitudes, especially in regard to women's roles and images.[17] In its pre-release

[11] Russell (2007: 10–11) notes the unique connection established between historical event and cinematic spectacle by filming historical epics in the new Cinemascope technologies.

[12] Günsberg (2005: 101); Pomeroy (2008: 61). In general on pepla, see Günsberg (2005: 97–132), Nisbet (2006: 47–55), Pomeroy (2008: 29–59), Nikoloutsos (2013), and Paul and Pomeroy (both this volume).

[13] Dyer (1997: 145–83), MacKinnon (2002), Günsberg (2005: 102, 130–1), Turner (2009).

[14] On the erotic triangle, see e.g., Shahabudin (2009) and Pomeroy (this volume). See Günsberg (2005: 103) for the colour associations.

[15] Günsberg (2005: 101–4), Pomeroy (2008: 33), Nikoloutsos (2013: 264–72).

[16] '*Helen of Troy* particularly shines as a thoughtful, literate screenplay' (Nisbet 2006: 33). Nisbet adds that screenwriter Hugh Gray's handling of some ancient features provides 'treats for classicists' (34).

[17] Regarding social signification, Ross (2002: Introduction) observes that since their inception in the 1890s movies have always exerted a major influence on social values and customs, both conforming to dominant social trends as well as advancing alternative ideas. Most feminist and gendered film criticism addresses how cinematic portrayals of female

promotion Warner Brothers touted the film's historical importance in perpetuating the myth and history of the Trojan legend into a new generation.[18] According with the cinematic spirit of the time, the film's opening minute-plus establishes the story's historical background. While the voiceover presents a historically credible foundation, the film's historicity is contested. As in most films set in ancient Greece, the architecture, costumes, and hairstyle are an inauthentic amalgam of Hollywood set and costume designers' vision of classical antiquity that suggests ancient Greece by any, more often Roman, ancient-like image.[19] Troy, as in Petersen's 2004 film, is modelled on the ancient Minoan city of Knossos on Crete, replete with Minoan-style downward tapering columns, myriad 'horns of consecration', and Minoan and Mycenaean-like wall paintings; however, the statuary within the Trojan palace suggests sixth–fifth century Greek sculpture.[20] While many of the men's costumes and armour are not authentic, Helen's outfits in her opening scenes are reminiscent of ancient Spartan women's dress: short and long sleeveless tunics fastened on one or both shoulders (more below), scarf (rather than veil) covering head and shoulders, and a simple cloak covering head and body when she goes out.[21] Finally, her royal robe at Sparta echoes that of apparently royal women on some Mycenaean wall paintings.[22]

More subtly, knowledge of ancient Athenian drama and literary portrayals of Helen permeate the film in imaginative ways, as the opening scenes richly illustrate. Evoking the tale of the judgement of Paris, statues of the three goddesses, Hera, Aphrodite, and Athena stand prominently in the Trojan palace room. Paris is chided for worshipping Aphrodite too much and ignoring Athena, thereby echoing, though with different goddesses, Euripides' *Hippolytus* and its protagonist's devotion to Artemis while neglecting Aphrodite.[23] Evoking the judgement's outcome, the

figures advance or interrogate women's social and cultural roles. Sieglohr (2000: Introduction), Negra (2002: 377), and Gundle (2007: xvii–xxiii) discuss how female stars come to represent national identities.

[18] Pomeroy (2008: 61); Winkler (2009: 12) notes that from its beginning cinema has reincarnated Homeric epic. Russell (2007: 16, 42–5) discusses the role of 1950s epic film-makers as public historians and the marketing publicity of historical epics as making serious social, educative, and spiritual comments.

[19] See Nisbet (2006: 34) on both set and costume designers' tendency to Romanize ancient Greek images in order to make them more 'familiar' and acceptable to American audiences. See further Nikoloutsos (2013: 272–8) and this volume.

[20] García (2008: 21–3).

[21] Pomeroy (2002: 31–2, 43, fig. 4).

[22] Cavallini (2005: 73, fig. 42).

[23] Nisbet (2006: 33–4).

shipwrecked Paris utters upon seeing Helen approach him through the surf, as she is arising out of the sea: 'Aphrodite'; the scene recalls both Hesiod's tale of Aphrodite being born from the foam of the sea (*Theog.* 191–7), and, probably more familiar to most modern spectators, Botticelli's painting of Venus floating up on the sea on a clamshell. Paris' unique arrival at Sparta in rags, shipwrecked on the coast (which of course justifies the extended cinematic focus on his almost nude body) invites multiple allusions, ancient and modern. It echoes, most immediately, Kirk Douglas' 1954 Ulysses washed up on the beach, lying face down (Paris lies face up) by a mast tangled in ropes, while Rossana Podestà as Nausicaa greets him.[24] At the same time, the scene alludes to Euripides' *Helen*, where Menelaus enters in rags fashioned from his shipwrecked sailcloth.[25] Regardless of how many ancient allusions modern audiences are able to recognize (on which see more below), their presence reveals the writers' (classicist Hugh Gray and John Twist) familiarity with the ancient material and Wise's ability to dramatically incorporate these allusions into a modern film.[26] As Gideon Nisbet remarks, Gray's script 'demonstrates its respect for the textual sources by engaging with them knowledgeably and creatively'.[27]

This idea of edification links the educational historical representations with the film's social messages. Based on an ancient Greek theme, rather than the more common Roman or biblical, especially Christian subjects, *Helen of Troy*, like other post-World War II American and European films, stressed the re-establishment of traditional gender roles.[28] In Wise's film, a blonde Rossana Podestà dramatizes Helen's story from her first meeting with Paris to the end of the Trojan War as a proud yet vulnerable American beauty, emblematic of female American screen stars. Consequently, despite portraying the most renowned adulteress in the western cultural tradition, Podestà's Helen projects the wholesome, good girl image typical of American films at the time. While she displays

[24] Nisbet (2006: 34). In *Rosanna* Podestà also emerges out of the sea in a skimpy two-piece costume and has a steamy scene with her leading man, Crox Alvarado, on the beach, behind a fishing net with the sea lapping behind them. On the movie's IMDb site, a reviewer notes: 'Rossana Podestà epitomizes some kind of Goddess, of Eve before the fall. A Madonna's face but a sensual body and a false innocence: it was not surprising Robert Wise would cast her as Helen of Troy' [spelling, spacing, and punctuation of the original corrected] <http://www.imdb.com/title/tt0046233/> accessed 1 October 2012.

[25] Pomeroy (2008: 62) identifies Euripides' *Helen* as the basis for the 1964 Italian film, *Leone de Tebe* (*The Lion of Thebes*), called in France, *Hélène, reine de Troie*, directed by Giorgio Ferroni (Filmes).

[26] Gray was also the screenwriter for *Ulysses*.

[27] Nisbet (2006: 32).

[28] See Fraser (1988) and Sieglohr (2000).

the regal bearing of a queen of Sparta, Helen's sweet demeanour virtually obliterates the notoriety attached to her action of eloping with Paris.[29]

Perhaps surprising audiences familiar with dark-haired Podestà's beach scenes in *Rosanna* (dir. Emilio Fernández, 1953) and as Nausicaa in *Ulysses*, in *Helen of Troy* Podestà projects Helen as the (stereo-)typical 1950s image of female beauty that idealizes Nordic physical features: fair skin and blonde hair (Fig. 1.1). As if to underscore this stereotypical projection, Wise had Podestà dye her dark hair blonde for the role (likewise for Sernas as Paris), which she had not wanted to do.[30] From Korda's 1927 Helen to Harrison's and Petersen's more recent screen portrayals, and with the striking exception of Cacoyannis' Helen discussed below, the cinematic Helens have been blonde, which rests on a

Figure 1.1 Helen (Rossana Podestà) in *Helen of Troy*, dir. Robert Wise. Credit: [THE KOBAL COLLECTION].

[29] All interpreters note the stress on a moral Helen in Wise's, Harrison's, and Petersen's productions; Winkler (2009: 212) notes the requirement in American cinema for redemption of wayward protagonists.

[30] With rare exceptions, Podestà maintained her dark hair colour throughout her long film career.

weak linguistic basis.[31] The ancient Greek word often presumed to describe Helen's hair colour is *xanthos* which Liddell and Scott translates as '*yellow*, of various shades, freq. with a tinge of red, *brown*, *auburn*'— the three italicized words (in the original) all designating the colour range of *xanthos*. In Homer the masculine form describes Menelaus almost exclusively; the feminine forms are used for Demeter (as also in her Homeric Hymn) and various mortal women, but not Helen, or for the hair of Achilles. In the Archaic period Sappho (E. Diehl, *Supp. Lyr.* 13.5) and Ibycus (282a.5 PMG) both use *xanthos* once to describe Helen. Although the word is generally translated as 'blonde', it is rendered as 'tawny' when referring to lions, and 'red-haired' when describing Menelaus. In modern Greek it connotes light chestnut brown rather than Nordic blonde. Scholars have long recognized that ancient Greek colour terms referred less to hue than to the quality of light. In this respect, *xanthos* should more properly be rendered as 'shimmering', or perhaps 'golden' hair colour.[32] While the ancient literature suggests some privileging of the fair-haired, it tends to leave physical details to the imagination of the viewer (cf. the frequent observation about Homer's lack of a physical description of Helen). This combination of ambiguity in ancient colour terms and of lack of specific physical descriptions of Helen underscores the modern ideologies operating in casting the ancient Greek icon of beauty as a fair-skinned blonde.

This privileging of a blonde ethnic type as the ideal of beauty in the portrayal of Helen has several implications. Foremost is the constricting of a powerful mythic icon into an actual physical appearance, which severely limits her iconic stature.[33] Visually, blonde stars are seen as representing more distant, abstract concepts of beauty than those with darker hair and complexions, which the film's frequent displays of a statue-like Helen as the ideal beauty seems to confirm.[34] Stephen Gundle asserts that since the 1930s 'bottle blonde' female American stars functioned as Hollywood's projection of 'virtue, honesty and acceptability',[35] exemplified by the 1950s wholesome, cheerful, all-American girl next door portrayals of Doris Day and Betty Grable.[36] Moreover, the typical 'dumb-blonde' persona renders female sexuality unthreatening and the woman herself as child-like and vulnerable.[37] Pointedly contrasted to the manufactured look of blonde American stars is the 'natural', earthy appearance of the dark-haired, olive-skinned, and large-breasted Italian actresses, notably Silvana Mangano, Gina Lollobrigida,

[31] Contra Roisman (2008: 147). [32] Lyons (1999: 54–7).
[33] Roisman (2008: 147). [34] Gundle (2007: 159). [35] Gundle (2007: 159).
[36] Quart and Auster (2002: 230), Gundle (2007: 109).
[37] Quart and Auster (2002: 229).

and Sophia Loren, who openly exude a Mediterranean sensuality while still maintaining an aura of respectability approved by the Catholic Church and Italian audiences. In the hierarchy of ethnic-type privileging, the European background of the Italian actresses, despite their darker Mediterranean colouring, made them acceptable to American audiences, for whom women with darker features were associated with exotic and lascivious sexual behaviour.[38] Imported into these racially charged portrayals, the darker Mediterranean actresses serve to mediate between the 'purity' of the blonde stars and the unredeemable 'depravity' projected onto their darker hued sisters of African or Asian origin. While casting an Italian actress as Helen might evoke acceptable cinematic images of female sensuality, casting the heroine as an idealized blonde American archetype with small, pointed breasts serves several purposes: it contains Helen's legendary sensuality within a de-sensualized frame; it accentuates her fundamental respectability, key to the film's portrayal of a morally acceptable Helen; and it enables the heroine to appeal to a more upscale American audience, who, Gundle claims, associate large breasts with the lower class.[39]

The film's opening characterizations of Helen in three distinct settings—the beach, her nurse's modest abode, and the Spartan palace—portray Helen as an icon of beauty, haughty queen, and a woman of good morals.[40] The visual imagery of Helen's hairstyles and costumes sometimes converges, but at other times seems at odds, with her words and demeanour, adding a complexity to her portrayal. From the outset Wise's portrayal of Helen illustrates, primarily, the first meaning of the gaze: Helen functions as a symbol of her own iconic status, who nevertheless has moments of deep self-reflection while the camera displays her idealized beauty for the spectators' gaze. Before Helen ever appears onscreen, Paris' enchanted gaze upon her as he lies on the beach by the mast, a rope across his waist, prepares the audience for its first view of this iconic figure as she slowly grows before the camera striding forward in the surf. This romantic focus on Helen's figure slowly growing before the spectators' eyes underscores the desirous aspect of the spectator's gaze. Once in full view, the camera pauses on Helen who looks curiously down at Paris who, still enchanted, is looking up at her. The positioning of Helen and Paris in this scene reverses traditional gender

[38] See Kaplan (1997: 67, 74, 80–8). Gundle does not address how preference for sexy, sensual Italian actresses fits into the racism of female portrayals in American films.

[39] Gundle (2007: 156).

[40] For film synopsis, see Paglia (1997: 187–93, with her characteristic caustic comments), and Winkler (2009: 225–9).

roles. The woman is shown higher; she is the rescuer who actively looks down upon the man, who is portrayed as a shipwreck victim at a lower level, looked upon as much as he gazes upon Helen.[41] The cumulative effect is that Helen's stature is here enhanced doubly: appearing larger than life, she is a divine apparition like the goddess Paris envisions, and she appears of higher social status than Paris, a social differentiation the film will further explore.

As Helen emerges from the sea in her opening shot, curly bangs ring her forehead, her long hair framing her neck on both sides from the back. She wears a mid-thigh, peach-coloured sleeveless tunic fastened at her right shoulder, leaving her left shoulder and arms bare, an image that emulates 1940s–50s American pin-up models. Her somewhat authentic costume imitates the *chiton exomis*, a short racing tunic Spartan girls wore, which—if a sixth-century bronze figurine from Dodona, northern Greece, reflects actual wear—exposes the right breast and shoulder.[42] Helen's costume in Wise's film resemanticizes the ancient clothing, transferring its sensationalism to serve the desiring eye of the cinematic male gaze. To highlight Helen's status as iconic beauty, with one exception, she is the only major female character in the film to wear her tunic sleeveless and leaving one shoulder bare. Her costume serves a dual purpose: it is sexy, a soft fabric thinly draping her perky lifted breasts and a wet cloth clinging around her legs; she is, nevertheless, modestly covered from breasts to mid-thigh, and her tunic's soft pastel colour signals Helen's good character. Clad in this outfit for her first seven minutes onscreen, this portrayal fixes this blonde pixie-like image of Helen's mythical beauty in the minds of the audience as the basis for her subsequent portrayal in the film. Repeatedly the camera focuses on these images of Helen as idealized blonde beauty, while Paris, Cassandra, Priam, and Hecuba affirm the visual clues, each remarking on Helen's outstanding beauty on several occasions in the film.

While repeated views of this blonde Helen remind the audience of her status as an American icon of beauty, the film does not dwell on her beauty, but strives to show her moral acceptability. To do so, Wise first presents, then diminishes the impact of several stereotypical qualities of Helen, including her beauty, divine aspects, royal status, and sensuality. The film presents Helen's divine heritage as interwoven with her notable

[41] Camera angles that are the reverse of this positioning are characteristic of the peplum films, in which the muscle-bound hero is shot from below in order to enhance his stature. See, e.g., Günsberg (2005: 111).

[42] See Pomeroy (2002: 31–2) for description of the clothing. The figure is the British Museum GR208; see Pomeroy (2002: cover and fig. 1, p. 13) for the image.

beauty. Because Paris first sees Helen in the semi-dazed state of partially awakening on the shore, his calling her Aphrodite compellingly encourages the audience to appreciate her divine qualities as legitimately informing the mortal character being portrayed on the screen.[43] Paris, as well as Cassandra and Hecuba, reiterate this idea of Helen as divine beauty incarnate throughout the movie. Helen, however, either deflects Paris' divine comparisons humorously or she answers simply 'I'm only Helen', deflating her status as a divine icon of beauty and rendering herself as a more sympathetic, ordinary woman. Despite its frequent shots of the beautiful Helen, the film emphasizes a romanticized wholesomeness rather than the destructive potential of Helen's beauty.

While Podestà's Helen dismisses Paris' praise of her beauty and divine comparisons, she does assume the royal prerogatives of a queen of Sparta who knows her powers and uses them commandingly and regally. Even while dressed in her skimpy tunic, Helen imperiously asserts her royal authority over the palace soldiers, commanding their obedience; their embarrassed glances signal their discomfort at seeing their queen so attired. At the same time, she addresses Paris haughtily on several occasions and she regally introduces herself to the Trojans as 'Helen, Queen of Sparta'. While her demeanour and treatment by others repeatedly highlight Helen's royal status, from the outset the film suggests a more familiar, ordinary image. In the opening scenes Helen often behaves regally, while dressed in a manner that suggests the opposite. For example, she wears the long, one-shoulder tunic when visiting her childhood nurse's humble home, where mutual respect characterizes their interactions and where Helen readily performs ordinary domestic tasks. Moreover, her dress aligns her with the other characters regularly clad in one-shoulder bare outfits, mostly slaves, both female and male. Contrasting with her occasional regal bearing, Helen's pretense to slave rather than royal status throughout her early interactions with Paris underscores this alternate image and portends her ultimate societal position: underneath the royal trappings she is an ordinary woman, imprisoned like other women by her circumstances, an image which serves to render Helen sympathetic to the audience. Interestingly, rather than the goddess Helen, as Paris lies dying, he sees Helen as 'that little slave girl', a final reminder of the entrapping circumstances that exonerate her actions. Her dress continues to emphasize her ordinary status: on

[43] Scholars usually claim that Cacoyannis, Wise, and Petersen eliminated the Greek gods from their films: e.g., McDonald and MacKinnon (1983: 224, 228), McDonald (2001: 95), Pomeroy (2008: 67), Winkler (2009: 217), Bakogianni and Blondell (both this volume). As I show, the ancient world appears in many subtle ways.

the boat passage to Troy, she is wrapped in a heavy coarse brown cloak, covering her head and body, which she holds together at her neck. At the very time she is embarking on her adulterous affair, Helen is dressed like a Christian penitent whose crossing of the sea symbolically cleanses her of any moral failings. Both she and Paris are modestly and unostentatiously dressed on entering Troy: Paris in a short brown tunic covering his torso and that only slightly falls off his right shoulder, while Helen wears a white scarf that covers her head and shoulders over a floor-length plain brown dress that she wears through the next scene. Only before she reveals her name does she turn to quickly display a thigh-high slit in her skirt, echoing the thigh revealing skirts of Spartan women.[44] Although she twice wears the alluring, off one-shoulder, body-revealing tunic, in most of her scenes in Troy Helen is modestly attired in soft, muted colours. The stereotypical Hollywood scenario has turned the ancient tale of female power, betrayal, war, and glory into a romantic tale about the power of love.[45] Her total disinterest in ruling power and the film's build-up of her laudatory ethical traits accentuate the vulnerable woman beneath the royal trappings, imprinting this sympathetic image of Helen in the audience's mind.[46]

Finally, since displays of female sensuality are intrinsically interwoven with probative moral standards, the film strongly attenuates Helen's sensuality. In contrast to the full-bodied, sensuous 1950s female Italian stars whose sensuality dripped off the screen, Podestà's hints at passion, in keeping with her Americanized, blonde, 'good girl' image, are highly restrained. Helen's and Paris' few onscreen kisses, very mild by today's cinematic standards, display the proper 1950s limits of passion, their faces only engaged, eyes and mouths closed, no bodies wriggling or heated moans.[47] While they have one earlier kiss when Helen interrupts Paris' mission into Sparta, their most passionate moments occur not by design, but by a plot twist that throws them together hiding in the underbrush. In contrast, Hector and Andromache share only one

[44] Ibycus 339 PMG; Pomeroy (2002: 25 and n. 99).

[45] Roisman (2008: 133, 141), Winkler (2009: 219).

[46] Günsberg (2005: 121) notes that in the peplum films queens (especially Orientalized ones) generally signal danger, but Helen's disinterest in power defuses her potential threat.

[47] At 26.00, 47.00–28, 48.16–25, 1.21.08, 1.22.10–30; at 1.04.20, Helen lovingly kisses Paris' hand in subservient-like devotion, and at 1.58.46 gives a final closed-mouth kiss just before Paris dies. Some of this restraint is surely due to the limits imposed by the Hays code, in effect from 1934–62, when the current MPAA (Motion Picture Association of America) rating system began (Doherty, 1999: 336–67, Day and Nikoloutsos both this volume). However, Deborah Kerr's and Burt Lancaster's long, wet kiss with almost nude bodies wriggling prone in the surf in *From Here to Eternity* (more below) must surely have strained the letter of that code.

two-second kiss before he rides out to his death. The film further displaces the portrayal of a sensual Helen into an onscreen depiction of a sensual Paris, whose frequently displayed sensuous poses appear less problematic to the film-going audience.[48] From his first scene, Paris is on display, young, athletic and buff, revealing a bare, oiled muscular torso for almost eight minutes following his shipwreck and elsewhere throughout the movie. Extending Homer's poetic focus on pretty boy Paris (*Il.* 3.16–20), like the heroes of the later peplums, Wise puts Paris' mostly nude, muscle-bound body on display for much of the film, with little moral fallout with either the internal or external audiences.

Although Paris cinematically carries much of Helen's presumed sensuality, like her he is morally upstanding. Internally, after Aeneas has calmed the Trojans' outrage by getting them to turn their anger aimed 'at one Spartan woman against all the Spartans', Paris tells Helen that he has won a moral victory in that the Trojans will not pursue their anger against him or Helen. Externally, Jacques Sernas, as the very attractive Paris, wins over the audience by his heroic, all-American good looks and by his moral conduct. The film foremost displays Paris as a romantic hero, 'hopelessly devoted to a virtuous Helen'[49] whose moral and heroic actions include nobly rescuing Helen, not seducing her[50] and refusing to fight the Spartans until provoked.[51] He is a valiant fighter who despite the danger climbed the ship's mast during a storm[52] and he takes up 'Hector's good points as a statesman and patriot'.[53] Helen's loveless marriage, Menelaus' brutish ways, Agamemnon's blatant greed and power grabs are the villains that impel both Helen and Paris on their adulterous course and that, together with their true, Hollywood romantic love, excuse them from moral culpability.[54]

Visually complicating the film's presentation of a morally redeemed Helen are suggestive comparisons with Medusa, the mythical Greek figure, whose sight turned men to stone.[55] In ancient mythology and

[48] Günsberg (2005: 97–132); but see also MacKinnon (2002), Turner (2009). In *Troy*, Petersen completely displaces Helen's sensuality onto Briseis (Winkler, 2009: 224) or onto Achilles and Briseis, alone or together (Blondell, this volume).

[49] Nisbet (2006: 33); see also Winkler (2009: 219).

[50] Winkler (2009: 219).

[51] Pomeroy (2008: 50).

[52] Roisman (2008: 134).

[53] Nisbet (2006: 34).

[54] Roisman (2008: 141), Winkler (2009: 219–20).

[55] See, Gantz (1993: 303–10), Hirschberger (2000), Wilk (2000), Topper (2007).

art Medusa was portrayed as both very beautiful and horrendously fearsome. Athena wore Medusa's severed head on her aegis (the mantle across her chest) and emblazoned on her shield as an apotropaic device, an image to ward off evil, known as a Gorgoneion. Often portrayed bearded, with open mouth, protruding tongue, and a forehead framed by ringleted curls, the effect created a fearsome visage. The full body Medusa images showed several strands of braids hanging down across each shoulder and snakes emanating from the neck or wrapped around the waist. About the same time 'beautiful Medusa' images appeared in art and continued much longer than the fearsome Gorgoneia, though the Hellenistic and later images often depicted these beautiful Medusas with snakes for hair, the later mark of her visual iconography.[56]

Several film images first raise thoughts of Medusa and then invite comparisons between Medusa and Helen. For the first five and a half minutes, while the overture is playing, the screen displays a still image of an elaborate interior hallway, the spectator gazing down its centre. Relief griffin sculptures adorn both inner walls, while through a broad open doorway, on a raised platform, three Doric columns recede along each side. The camera angle reinforces the vanishing point perspective integral to western viewing since the Renaissance.[57] The camera's perspective converges on a strange sculpture in the back, which Camille Paglia calls an inappropriately Hindu-like image (1997: 189), and which might suggest to some audience members the Trojan priest Laocoon's struggle with snakes sent by the gods. The double-looped, snake-like emanations on each side of the figure might also evoke Medusa, a potentially ominous evocation at the film's outset. Interestingly, when Greek chieftains later enter through this hallway, this snaky sculpture is no longer there.[58]

Other images invite comparisons between Medusa and Helen. While Paris' opening enchanted look at Helen highlights the desirous quality of his gaze, it may also suggest the danger imminent in gazing upon Helen's beauty. Paris' fixed stare at a figure whose face, while beautiful, ringed as it is by tight curls with braids hanging down her breasts, might suggest Medusa's petrifying power. Helen's coiffure when she first enters the palace megaron (great room) evokes ancient Medusa images, with her hair in two thick braids hanging down the front of each shoulder, curls around her

[56] See Topper (2007) on beautiful Medusa vase paintings and on the affinities between the beautiful Gorgon and abducted maidens, such as Persephone, Thetis, and Helen.

[57] Berger (1972: 16); see also Winkler (2009: 7).

[58] So we learn the hallway belongs to the Spartan palace, but the audience would not know that earlier.

temples, and a long multiple braid in the back.[59] She does not enter ceremoniously through the double doors like the chieftains, but through the side, hinting at herself as a living embodiment of the Medusa-like statue that has disappeared. Her actions appear dangerously duplicitous. She cries out on Paris' behalf when he is fighting, causing Menelaus' suspicion, but she addresses Paris haughtily, offending him, but hardly assuaging her husband's suspicion. Clinching this comparison are the shots of the images on the lower part of the large, bronze double doors of Helen's boudoir: Gorgoneia. They are periodically visible behind Helen's and Menelaus' silhouettes in her chambers, where he almost chokes her while each of their heads covers a Gorgoneion, perhaps suggesting a Medusa-like decapitation. But as in the ancient tales, Menelaus does not kill Helen.

Wise seems to evoke these comparisons with Medusa only to differentiate Helen from her. While the 'horrible' Medusa gets killed, her face becoming an apotropaic device on temples, Athena's aegis, and warriors' shields, the beautiful Helen is saved, to lead a charmed, fortunate life. Mitigating these direct comparisons of Helen with Medusa, we quickly see the Gorgoneion images on other doors of the Spartan palace, including the exterior of Helen's room, and the room in which Paris is being guarded. This visual association of Paris with the Gorgoneion may disperse Medusa's destructive nature between Helen and Paris, auguring the great destruction they are seen to cause.[60]

If the Medusa comparisons suggest the destructive potential in gazing upon Helen, the power of Helen's own gaze is severely curtailed. She often has a dreamy, schoolgirl-like gleam when she is looking at Paris, and her wistful gazes express a similar illusionary desire: on the boat, when faced with the uneasy prospect of their upcoming life in Troy, Helen first gazes off into the distance, then into Paris' eyes, wishing to escape with Paris to an island ironically named Pelagos (Sea), where they can be insulated from the world. Shortly after realizing the conflicts they have brought to Troy, with the camera focused on her face from behind Paris'

[59] This hairstyle might more simply represent the hairstyles on archaic Greek female statues often depicted with multiple braids hanging down their fronts and a broad, braided panel down the back. But the other Medusa hints might concurrently extend to colour the interpretation of Helen's coiffure here. On snaky hair designs, see Day and Nikoloutsos (this volume).

[60] Later in the film, the Gorgoneion appears on Agamemnon's shield, war standard, and is painted on the prow of his ship; Cassandra and Andromache have similar ringleted, braided hairstyles. All these images lessen the impact of any Medusa-like qualities implied for Helen.

right shoulder for eighteen seconds, Helen has a similar dreamy look, as she wishes she could live with Paris on an island where they are untouched by the world's problems; she repeats this wistful look later as the horse is being wheeled in. In contrast to an earlier scene where Helen interjects a note of reality into Paris' fantasy wishes, in the two former instances Paris asserts his real obligations, thus delivering a final symbolic blow to Helen's stature. Rather than possessing a gaze emblematic of her inner power, Helen's gaze in Wise's film is illusionary and immaterial, while her power is trivialized.[61]

However strong these opening Medusa evocations may be, they quickly just fade away. Just as it minimizes Helen's divine, royal, and sensual aspects, the rest of the film's portrayal counters any hints of Helen's destructive potential by depicting her as a sympathetic, ordinary woman, whose actions stress her moral acceptability.[62] Initially, Helen's awareness of her position shows her struggling with the idea of having an affair with Paris. Only after the film reveals Helen's and Menelaus' loveless marriage, in which Helen is trapped with a husband she despises, does she yield to Paris.[63] Likewise, rather than Helen choosing to elope with Paris, another plot device forces her to escape with him to Troy, which further absolves her of guilt.[64] Despite initial execrations by members of the royal family or by the Trojan peoples crowded within the city walls, the film completely exonerates Helen from any culpability for the war, to the point where the Trojans hail her as they are wheeling in the horse. Helen shows her concern for those dying around her by willingly returning to Menelaus in order to put an end to the war, a gesture that backfires when the Greeks demand reparations and annual tribute, and Paris rushes in to drive Helen back to Troy, advancing the familiar exigencies of the plot by killing Patroclus en route. The entire Trojan royal family absolves this sweet Helen from any blame, seeing only the goodness in her. Most notably, Hecuba and Cassandra echo the absolving words that Homer assigns to Priam, 'Not you, but the gods are to blame for this war' (*Il.* 3.164), and the film's Priam both seeks Helen's forgiveness for misjudging her, and names her 'a princess of Troy'. This new Helen is always sweet, gracious, and smiling. The fact that the two highest-ranking Trojan royal women absolve her epitomizes the

[61] All interpreters find that Helen's power in *Troy* has been completely elided and trivialized. See, e.g., Roisman (2008: 144–5), Blondell (this volume).

[62] Winkler (2009) analyses Wise's projection of a moral Helen via the conduct and actions of Menelaus and their marriage; see also Roisman (2008).

[63] Roisman (2008: 141).

[64] Winkler (2009: 229).

fulfilment of Helen's desire since Homer—to be accepted by the Trojan women. And so Helen is, deemed blameless by both the internal and external audiences.

For all her similarities to 1950s blonde American stars, the film adds depth to Helen's character by imaginatively echoing a theme central to Euripides' play *Helen*: her dual identities. In the film Paris and Helen separately evoke the phantom of Helen and the split it connotes between her two selves. During her slave pretence, Wise's Helen calls herself a shadow of the real Helen and voices wistfully that she does not 'believe anyone knows queen Helen very well'. More pointedly as she and Paris embark for Troy, Helen tells him that the girl he thought he 'knew is quite nameless and without reality', thus implying that a radically different woman is departing with him for Troy. Hardly a mindless, cardboard icon, these remarks show Helen as an intelligent, thinking individual who reflects upon her situation in life.[65] As in Euripides' play, this idea of two Helens more readily allows for dismissal of the 'bad' Helen and emphasis on the 'good' one. Echoing Teucer's words in Euripides' play who distinguishes the good sense of the stage character before him as opposed to the destructive legendary Helen (*Hel.* 160–3), in the film Paris tells Helen that she is two Helens, both of them wise and good, while she is the one to insert caution here to Paris' fantasy spins. Despite her later momentary flights of fancy, this portrayal of Helen's thoughtful traits adds grit to her character, so that even as she resigns herself to returning to Menelaus, both during the voluntary exchange and at the film's end, she does so not as an empty-headed object, but with dignity and personal determination. Helen may be forced into a life not of her own choosing, but she fulfils her role with grace and awareness. This dimension renders Helen a more complex model for female identity than her stereotyped blonde image at first suggests.

A pertinent model for Helen's blonde image and good character traits in Wise's film might be Deborah Kerr, a leading blonde actress who as Karen Holmes in *From Here to Eternity* (dir. Fred Zinnemann, 1953) engages in extra-marital affairs. Holmes' revelation of her husband's repeated infidelities and alcoholism that resulted in her miscarriage and hysterectomy that precludes her having any children minimizes her adulteries and asserts her 'good girl' image in the view of the audience and of her lover Milton Warden (Burt Lancaster). Helen encountering Paris on the beach might well evoke Kerr's and Lancaster's

[65] Roisman (2008: 143) also finds Wise's Helen to be an intelligent woman, as well as independent, spirited, regal, commanding, and courageous.

steamy lovemaking in the surf. Despite their affairs, each film ends with the heroine on a boat returning home to life with her husband, in whatever imagined scenario of marital unbliss.[66] Podestà's blonde Helen even resembles Kerr's pale blondeness in her film, which might still evoke in some spectators' minds Kerr's portrayal as the indomitable Lygia in *Quo Vadis?* (1951), or as the ultimate symbol of white purity as a very pale looking Sister Clodagh dressed in a white habit in *Black Narcissus* (dir. Michael Powell, The Archers, 1946).[67] Even as Wise chose to portray an ancient tale of sex and adultery on the big screen, he did so in a way that would satisfy and appease contemporary American tastes and mores. In contrast to the biblically inspired epics framing the 1950s, completed by *Ben Hur* (dir. William Wyler, 1959), and rather than a story of Christian spiritual redemption, Wise portrays the prototypical story of sex, adultery, and betrayal in the western tradition. While this subject may well balance out the intense religious moralism of the decade's biblical epics, casting the legendary ethically dubious heroine as a blonde all-American girl ensures her placement among sympathetic American heroines, even those who may go astray, rather than among the Italian heroines whose more openly sensual portrayals suggest greater moral ambivalence to the puritanically minded American audiences of the 1950s. Through this 'whitewashing' of Helen's myth, as Winkler remarks,[68] the writers and directors can have it both ways: they can thrill the audience with a titillating tale of a beautiful vamp while staying on the side of right and morality.

Wise's stated purpose in producing *Helen of Troy* may have been to make an epic film. However, the very fact that he finally made a film, whose focus on Helen's story with only one major battle sequence probably situates it among 'chick flicks' rather than male-oriented action movies,[69] raises questions about the film's portrayal of concepts of female gender identity and women's roles in the 1950s. As portrayed by the young, innocent-looking leading blonde actors, the story is transformed from one of archetypal sensuality and desire to a bourgeois tale of

[66] Thus both films accord with the cinematic stress, characteristic of pepla, on the return to domestic heterosexuality at the film's end (Günsberg, 2005: 100).

[67] See Kaplan (1997: 86).

[68] Winkler (2009: 212).

[69] Winkler, in a personal communication, does not believe that having only one major battle relegates the film to 'chick flick' status. However, its focus on the hero's romantic interest in his beloved rather than in fighting with his male comrades assures its greater appeal to female viewers. Likewise, Solomon thinks that the film focuses too much on Helen's amorous pursuits and not enough on the male heroes of the Trojan saga (2001a: 103).

true love doomed by the precedence of a loveless marriage and cruel circumstances. Like so many romance novels and movies,[70] from Helen's and Paris' first embraces in Sparta, the film highlights this fantasy, romantic escape world of its protagonists, whose joy rings ominous in their extraordinarily carefree bliss as the horse is being wheeled into Troy. Although the final scene shows Helen's forcible return to Sparta after Paris' death, thereby emphasizing her dutiful fulfilment of her societal role through her return to her wifely duties and her first and legitimately married husband, it also underscores the durability of Helen's and Paris' true romantic love. Echoing a question she had asked earlier in the film, Helen's voice again asks, 'It can't be lost, Paris, can it? What has been lived and shared is never lost!' Paris' voice then exclaims, 'Never, Helen', both affirm that they will 'always be together'. As Helen's face fades out, the words, *The End* in red above the WB logo are superimposed over the ship sailing off into the distance.

Because this romantic fantasy image of Helen is drawn from a mythical icon, this portrayal valorizes women fantasizing their ideal love life; they may even indulge in extra-marital affairs during wartime, as no doubt some women did, but come war's end, marital duty and propriety must prevail. Helen's image provides an exciting alternative to the housewives and spinsters populating most 1950s American films.[71] Thus the film's and leading actress's characterization of Helen, quietly yet assuredly, affirms the overwhelming 1950s media emphasis on women happily returning to some putative traditional role that has them contentedly acquiescing to a position of wifely obedience and societal inferiority and that contains their sexual, sensual, and personal identities within a bland, non-threatening framework.[72] Moreover, this emphasis, in this and other 1950s films, on an acceptably docile (white) female image accords with the global self-portrayal in various US media, most notably in films, of the 'good', 'pure', male Anglo-Saxon hegemony that US foreign policy was advancing to the rest of the

[70] Harlequin romances began burgeoning in the 1950s (Avis Yarborough, 'Harlequin: The Business of Romance in the 1950s'), <http://www.loti.com/fifties_history/Harlequin_The_Business_of_Romance.htm> (accessed 1 October 2012).

[71] Quart and Auster (2002: 230). Quart and Auster note that *From Here to Eternity* was one of the few 1950s films to criticize openly the complacency and conformity of the Eisenhower years (231). For 1950s gender stereotypes in films set in classical antiquity see Nikoloutsos, Paul, and Pomeroy (all this volume).

[72] For the process of containment in both US–Soviet relations and in notions of female possibilities in the 1950s, see Blondell and Nikoloutsos (both this volume). See also Nikoloutsos (2013: 278–80).

world.[73] Politically, this film at this time would publicly counteract the House Unamerican Activities Committee's investigation of Jack Warner for supposed Communist leanings in a 1943 Warner Brothers film.[74] What safer way to deliver a political message than through a romantic tale? Although her actions spark a ten-year war and cause the destruction of Troy, Wise's film portrays a 'good', 'pure' Helen who was just trying to live her own life and who is held free of any responsibility for the carnage. By having Helen uphold proper female moral standards, even if her heart may romantically, truly love another, the film firmly reinscribes the 1950s idealization of women's domestic roles. Helen returns with dignity, walking proudly, still regally and defiantly to the ship after Paris' death. That the film's final image is of her dreaming of Paris as the ship sails back to Sparta projects the idea that women can fulfil what might be unsatisfying domestic roles with grace and dignity and that they can still find fulfilment in their romantic fantasies. The 1960s shifts in sexual, political, social, and cultural dynamics demonstrate how well—or not—such 1950s media projections of women's roles succeeded.

MICHAEL CACOYANNIS' *THE TROJAN WOMEN*

Michael Cacoyannis' 1971 cinematic dramatization of Euripides' play about the immediate aftermath of the conquest of Troy, *The Trojan Women*, fashions Helen from a radically different perspective than Wise's *Helen of Troy*. Consequently, it delivers a vastly different message about Helen's modern signification.[75] As opposed to Warner Brothers commissioning Wise to direct his epic film, *The Trojan Women* was the second of Cacoyannis' three cinematic homages to Euripides, which he produced and directed and for which he wrote the English screenplay, based on Edith Hamilton's translation. The other two were Greek

[73] See Russell (2007: 31–41) on the political dimensions, whether overt or veiled, of 1950s epic films, with imperial ambitions forming a key subject for historical epic films (217); Ross (2002) discusses the political dimensions of cinema from a historic perspective both to support imperialist and tyrannical aims and to resist them. Feminist film theorists usually see what Kaplan calls a 'collusion of the [white] male and imperial gaze' (1997: 67), including American audiences' denial of American imperialism (93). Negra discusses the role of film stars in advancing these cinematic nationalistic aims (2002: 375–7).

[74] President Franklin Roosevelt commissioned *Mission to Moscow* (1943) during World War II to show the Soviets as worthy allies, but it was used by HUAC to portray the Roosevelt administration as pro-Soviet (Ross: 2002: 203).

[75] For a synopsis of the Helen episode, see McDonald (1983: 204–10).

productions, *Electra* (1962) and *Iphigenia* (1977).[76] Filmed in Spain and distributed by Cinerama Releasing, *The Trojan Women* was produced at the height of the Vietnam War, while Cacoyannis himself was exiled by the military dictatorship then ruling Greece.[77] More overtly than Wise's film, *The Trojan Women* fits Steve Neale's characterization of films anchored in antiquity as marked by 'a dramatic and thematic concern with political and military power... rule, and... struggle'.[78] In good thematic company, *The Trojan Women* was released on the heels of Costa Gavras' *Z*, a 1969 French-language indictment of the Greek ruling junta (in which Irene Papas plays Hélène, the Deputy's wife), and just after a 1970 tidal wave of major war-centred films, including *Catch-22*, *Little Big Man*, *M*A*S*H* (Best Comedy, Golden Globe and Palme d'Or), *Patton* (Best Picture, Academy Awards), *Soldier Blue*, and *Tora! Tora! Tora!* Together these films provided a gritty palliative to the year's highest grossing film and Golden Globe winner for best drama, *Love Story*. Like the Italian Holocaust film released in the same year, *The Garden of the Finzi-Continis* (Best Foreign Language Film 1971, Academy Awards), and true to Euripides' purpose in his ancient play, Cacoyannis' film offers a major condemnation of war as seen through the sufferings of elite women: a crazed Cassandra (Genévième Bujold), a terror-stricken Andromache (Vanessa Redgrave), whose son will be torn from her to be cast off the fortification walls of Troy, and the disempowered Trojan queen Hecuba (Katherine Hepburn), who, now that her husband and sons are murdered, presides over ruins and ashes, not a prospering city. As such, the film foreshadows what James Russell calls the dark, violent, and pessimistic visions of the past in 1970s 'revisionist epics'.[79] The film's portrayal of Helen, however, suggests a different interpretation of her role.

Cacoyannis' film illustrates all three meanings of the gaze: 1) camera shots of Papas' face and body predominate in her scene, continuously displaying her as an object to excite the male spectator; 2) heeding Hecuba's warning, male characters hesitate to look at Helen, fearing some ruinous consequence; and 3) Cacoyannis sensationally dramatizes the power of Helen's own gaze through repeated focus on Papas' eyes.[80]

[76] On Cacoyannis' Euripidean trilogy, see MacKinnon (1986: 74–94). On *Iphigenia*, see Bakogianni with further bibliography (this volume).

[77] MacKinnon (1986: 80–1) discusses the political climate when Cacoyannis was filming *The Trojan Women*.

[78] Neale (2000: 85).

[79] Russell (2007: 46).

[80] McDonald (2001) analyses Cacoyannis' cinematic focus on characters' eyes in his *Iphigenia* as the vehicle to convey a range of emotions including suffering, pity, love, and death (98). McDonald asserts that the ancient Greeks expressed their concept of self

I will discuss these in the order 1, 3, 2; the second, as we shall see, is closely connected to the third.

Instead of shying away from depicting 'the most beautiful woman in the [ancient] world', Cacoyannis' vision as dramatized by Irene Papas displays the mythic Helen in all her divinely inspired sensuality and regal power. In pointed contrast to the more prevalent blonde American stars, the dark-haired, olive-skinned Greek actress exudes the dynamic sensuality that ancient Helen embodied and that many female Italian stars of the 1950s–1960s represented. The poster for the film visually underscores Papas' distinction as the only dark-complexioned star among the American and western European actresses who play the other leading female characters: Papas stands alone on the right, opposite the other female stars.[81] Far from projecting a static and morally proper notion of Helen's beauty, Papas' palpably sensual Helen exudes eroticism. Her character confidently knows how to use her female eroticism and deploys it at every moment on the screen.

In part the opening portrayal of Helen in her scene quintessentially epitomizes Mulvey's image of the woman objectified to delight the male gaze. The audience first views Helen's body through the gaps of the horizontal logs of the hut where she is being held. With just her voice, the command of someone so iconic, Helen easily gets the guard to pass her a basin of water in which she dips first her feet, spilling precious water out on the ground, a sign of her scorn for the thirsty Trojan women who howl shrilly at her actions. Provocatively viewed through the logs of the enclosure, Helen lets her robe fall and kneels naked into the basin—the erotic highpoint of the scene, while the audience gets only a fleeting glance of her breasts. The fact that she is never fully exposed to the viewer increases her desirability, as do her few moments of vulnerability, when she quickly recedes within the hut as the Trojan women pelt the enclosure with rocks. This voyeuristic scene presents Helen's fundamental qualities of beauty, sensuality, and eroticism as the dynamic, even empowering features of a real, living woman.[82] Except for her final moments of vulnerability, like Podestà in her opening skimpy tunic, this Helen maintains her regal bearing even while completely nude and imprisoned.

through their eyes. Constantinidou (1994: 2) notes that eyes are the Homeric non-verbal media for communicating ways of thinking and feeling.

[81] http://www.moviegoods.com/movie_poster/trojan_women_the_1971.htm, 28 August 2011.

[82] McDonald and MacKinnon (1983: 229) regard this scene as emphasizing Helen's beauty and power as a femme fatale.

Briefly extending the analogy with Wise's portrayal of Helen, in *The Trojan Women* Helen's appearance shifts from the opening nude, calendar-girl image to a regally outfitted queen with elaborate coiffure. Her dress identifies her royal stature, which she fully displays in her demeanour.[83] Reminiscent of the ceremonial robes of priestesses in Minoan frescoes, her robe communicates power. After several minutes the camera reveals the deeply plunging 'V' in the robe's back, exposing Helen's naked back. The robe's design might evoke elite Minoan women's dress, only transposing the topless bodices of the ancient to the back of the modern attire to satisfy modern social and cinematic conventions. With a similar transposition, it might also evoke the stories of Menelaus' dropping his sword upon seeing Helen's naked breasts, as his reaction to her naked back strongly suggests. Coincident with her regally arrogant bearing, the camera maintains an almost constant focus on Helen's face, eyes, and body, especially her naked back, to display to the spectators' gaze. The film thus privileges as the primary viewing lens for all audience members the male-framed gaze at the woman projected as the ultimate object of men's desirous gaze. With dark eyes and jet-black hair, Papas still represents ideals of beauty for Americans, in ways perhaps even more titillating to the male spectator in that she does not have to convey the all-American girl goodness projected onto the fair-skinned, blonde actresses.[84]

However, while the opening scene of Helen nude in the hut establishes the foundation of Helen's iconic beauty and sensuality through the conventional, normative, and expected lens of the male gaze, Cacoyannis frames even this opening voyeuristic viewing and the rest of Helen's scene through the lens of another gaze, that of Helen's eyes. For two minutes before we catch our first glimpse of Helen's body, the camera displays six separate shots of her eyes. Each shot is distinctive, contributing to a lively dynamic quality: her eyes peering through the horizontal logs of her temporary jail at the Trojan women jeering at her; her eyes following the guard as he moves to the left, then looking back right; Helen moving behind the slats, the camera following her eyes as she moves left; her two eyes moving slightly right; only one eye watching;

[83] They also share opening associations with a modest dwelling, but with greatly contrasting significations: Wise's Helen chooses to dwell for a time in her nurse's modest abode, which reflects their comfortable relationship, while Cacoyannis' Helen is imprisoned in her makeshift, temporary enclosure. Further distinguishing the two, Wise's Helen brings water to the recovering Paris in her nurse's home, while Cacoyannis' Helen demands water from the guard, which she selfishly uses for herself.

[84] Although produced by a Spanish studio with a largely international cast and crew, the fact that the film was made in English with an American star headliner supports my use of a notional American male audience for this analysis.

both eyes forward again as she whispers, 'Water!'. On one level, this camera focus on Helen's eyes contributes to the opening emphasis on her sensuality: her eyes dark and sensuously made up, teasing the audience and whetting their anticipation for finally seeing Helen herself. This build-up plays with the (male) audience's expectations about seeing the legendary beauty.[85]

But two short moments in this opening sequence, confirmed by Helen's comportment throughout the rest of her scene, suggest a different image. Just before the final shot of Helen's eyes, the camera displays another's eyes, those of the soldier guarding Helen. His eyes are seen not from the same camera angle the audience views Helen's eyes, but from the perspective of Helen looking at this soldier. We, via the camera, look at the soldier through Helen's eyes. Although Helen is technically inferior as a war prisoner, the soldier's response to Helen's gaze is to cast his own eyes down and look away, a gesture signifying his inferior status and perhaps, too, his apprehension at gazing at the powerful Helen. Immediately afterwards, Helen's eyes gaze directly forward at the camera through the hut's logs. Though imprisoned, the power that Helen's gaze entails is one that no ordinary soldier—i.e., a male—can match. Helen may be an archetypal object of the male gaze, but the gaze that she herself wields carries a far greater power.[86] Though not immediately apparent, the fact that Helen looks directly at the camera just before the audience views her body serves to give her gaze some power over the camera viewing her. The spectator may view Helen's body through the eye of the camera, but the lasting imprint of her powerful gaze means that she is watching the spectator watching her, a position disorienting to the voyeuristic spectator by reversing the positions of power he thought were in his (unseen) control.[87]

The power of Helen's gaze, both the effect of men looking at her and her own subjective gaze, shape Helen's scene with Menelaus. Just as Paris' enchanted gaze sets up the audience's view of Helen in Wise's film, so too Hecuba's attempt to forestall Menelaus' male gaze at Helen prepares for her entrance in both Euripides' play and Cacoyannis' film:

> But shun her, do not look on her. Desire for her will seize you; for through men's eyes she gets them in her power. She ruins them, and ruins cities too. (Hecuba, at 1.12.50–4 of the film)

[85] McDonald (1983: 240) asserts that in this scene 'Helen's beauty...is objectively conveyed by her expressive eyes and flawless body'.

[86] McDonald (1983: 239–40) also notes Helen's power over the guard and Menelaus.

[87] Kaplan (1997: 68) notes that the 'eye of authority' in early American films belongs to white men.

As object of the male gaze, Helen poses danger, for the effect of seeing her robs men of their power. Whatever gratification seeing her may provide is overwhelmed by the profound sense of loss and devastation that forms the price of this viewing. Cacoyannis expands this dangerous effect of the male gaze upon the female to show the power of the female gaze aimed at the very men who would look at her. Shortly after Hecuba's warning, Menelaus runs from the Trojan queen and looking up the hill towards Helen's enclosure orders the guards to drag her out. The camera then shifts quickly from seeing Helen's eyes peering through the hut's logs one last time to Menelaus looking away towards Hecuba, in a gesture reminiscent of the guard looking away from Helen's gaze, already signalling his comparably weakened position. But ignoring Hecuba's warning, as Helen is brought out, Menelaus looks back up the hill to be undone by his own stare. Not Menelaus' but Helen's gaze will dominate this scene, as was the case when the soldier was guarding her.

By inserting the female gaze into this cinematic nexus, Cacoyannis complicates the doubled construct of the male gaze. Helen's ability to project her own gaze includes the ability to turn her sexual objectification to her own purposes. In dramatizing Hecuba's words, Cacoyannis depicts a Helen whose effect upon men's gaze is emasculating, by portraying Helen as transforming her image from the expected passive object of the male gaze to the active gazer who wields her power effortlessly through her eyes and her own gaze.

The camera displays this power of Helen's gaze during her scene with Menelaus foremost by often zooming in on her face, twice revealing only her eyes. Their intensity is displayed to the camera framed by Menelaus' back. The scene illustrates Marianne McDonald's observations about Cacoyannis' *Iphigenia*: Cacoyannis' men are static and avoid looking at women's eyes; his women move about while their eyes 'stare, blaze, blame, or threaten'.[88] Helen demonstrates this power she wields through her eyes from her first words to her Spartan husband. She knows what words will catch him. She walks up close to him, telling him almost immediately that the guards have forced her out of her room and have laid their hands on her. Her words cause Menelaus to walk away quickly. Through all this, Helen maintains her gaze on her erstwhile husband, the camera held on her intent eyes. Her next use of her eyes clinches their power and reveals its sexual dimension. Changing her

[88] McDonald (1991: 98). Helen in *Helen of Troy* averts her eyes when Priam accuses her of occasioning the Greek invasion; likewise in the bedroom scene in *Troy* Helen avoids Paris' eyes, whereas when Helen sews his thigh after being wounded by Menelaus, Paris avoids looking at her (Cyrino, 2007b: 134, 144).

tone, Helen addresses Menelaus in the soft, enticing voice of a tender, loving wife. 'You haven't changed,' she cajoles him, and smiling confidently, eyes him up and down in a manner typical of men's eyeing women up and down to assess their sexual potential. Helen controls Menelaus, and s/he knows it. The camera has focused on Helen's eyes and face both in setting up this long-awaited reunion scene between former husband and wife and during it. Helen demonstrates her knowledge and use of the power she has over Menelaus through her gaze, and particularly by using it to express her dominance in a manner characteristic of male-dominating looks. Helen's subjective gaze shapes and dominates this scene.

The rest of the scene elaborates Helen's dominance through the very same qualities that Wise's film sought to diminish: her beauty/sensuality, eroticism, and royalty. Although when Helen exits the hut for her encounter with Menelaus she is dressed in a robe of power, the repeated shots of her naked back in the robe's deeply plunging V keeps her fundamental sensuality always in the mind of both internal and external audiences. Hecuba interprets Helen's revealing attire (Fig. 1.2) as a sign of the latter's irredeemable and censurable eroticism, which serves as an affront

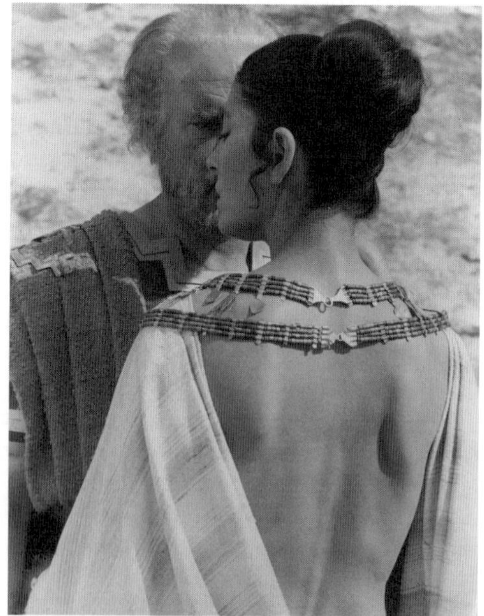

Figure 1.2 Helen (Irene Papas) with Menelaus (Patrick Magee) in *The Trojan Women*, dir. Michael Cacoyannis. Credit: [THE KOBAL COLLECTION].

to the abject situation of the captured Trojan women. The costumes of Helen and the Trojan women present stark visual contrasts: Helen in white, Hecuba and the chorus in black; Helen's dress revealing, the women completely covered.

Menelaus is clearly stricken by the sight of his wife's naked back and all the eroticism it implies. This shows the danger men risk by gazing at Helen. These displays also demonstrate how easily Helen's sensuality overpowers Menelaus. To her status as quintessential epitome of female sensuality and eroticism, Menelaus provides the archetype of the male who is easily subdued by this female power. Helen often gazes intently at Menelaus; he rarely looks directly at her; more often he glances and looks away quickly as if to avoid looking at the woman who can so readily overpower him. The camera's focus on Helen's face, eyes, and sensual displays satisfies the audience's expected delight in appealing to the desire of the male gaze. Helen's ability to use these qualities for her own benefit, and which the storyline, ancient and modern, sees as concomitantly destructive to the male gazer, dramatizes the seductive process by which the power of female eroticism entrances its object. Papas' Helen clearly understands this power of her own sensuality and unabashedly uses it for her own benefit.

Helen's regal command focalizes the dominance that her gaze expresses. Walking haughtily out of the hut to meet Menelaus, she passes the jeering Trojan women with head held high, a scornful smile on her face, and never glancing in their direction. She maintains this stance throughout most of the scene, outmaneuvering Hecuba and outwitting Menelaus with all her sensual and regal charms. If her kneeling supplication of Menelaus is genuine, she may nevertheless be using the appeal—in both meanings of the word—in her ploy to secure her survival and regain Menelaus to her side. Her knowing smile when Menelaus ardently snatches the dagger from her hand and forcefully tosses it aside,[89] and then orders her to the ship, reveals the confident knowledge that she once again is in command. By contrast, her Spartan husband is wrapped around her finger, a result clear to both Hecuba and the audience. The film emphasizes this powerful royal portrayal by its final image of Helen's face on the ship sailing home smiling smugly at Menelaus, then turning to gaze off into the distance, still smiling smugly. Despite its visual similarity to *Helen of Troy*'s ending image of Helen's face on the ship returning home, this image leaves a drastically different impact.[90]

[89] This is a Cacoyannis addition, not a detail in Euripides' play.

[90] Cf. the similar shot of Papas' face on the ship at the end of Cacoyannis' *Iphigenia*, where her eyes are blazing with anger at Agamemnon's murder of their daughter. McDonald compares this shot to the destructive gaze of the Gorgon (2001: 98).

Papas' portrayal of Helen in Cacoyannis' film offers a very different message about female identity and sensuality than does Podestà's in Wise's film. Now following the 'sexual revolution' of the 1960s in which women get recognized as sensual beings without the moral condemnation or dilution of the 1950s (at least in some circles)—and which some of the films of the late 1960s began to portray, notably *The Graduate* and *Woodstock*—female sensuality can be both valued and depicted cinematically. While Italian films popular in the West have a longer tradition of positively displaying female sensuality, in Cacoyannis' film this display is set within the effects of war, which emerge as especially devastating to women. On one level this display of Helen's sensuality reveals the film's affinities with the *Iliad*, where the centrality of female sensuality to the plot of male warfare is made explicit in the scene of Hera's seduction of Zeus (*Il.* 14.153–353). From beginning to end of that epic poem, male desire for the female is seen as both the cause for conflict among men and the reason men believe they must continue their bloody combats. However, this connection between women and warfare is far more tenuous for modern audiences. The effect of Helen's overtly proud sensuality in Cacoyannis' film suggests rather that it functions as part of the film's message of resistance to society's expectations of gendered, sexual, or political activities. In presenting a challenge to societal stereotypes that aim to repress female sexuality, Helen's defiant attitude concurrently challenges the concepts of normative feminine behaviour and the repressive inflexibilities of military and dictatorial regimes. It is in women's sexuality, sensuality, and even vulnerability that the keys to the resistance to oppression reside. As the movie poster proclaimed, 'THE STRENGTH OF MANKIND HAS ALWAYS BEEN ITS WOMEN.'[91]

In this regard the portrayal of Helen in Cacoyannis' film draws deeply from the ancient fundamental fertilizing power of a divine Helen rooted in a productive vegetative earth deity. Humans celebrate this beneficent power of such a divine Helen, and the stories of her repeated abductions and sexual liaisons evoke the disappearance and re-emergence of these female vegetative deities, which Persephone's story widely epitomizes for the ancient Greeks. Thus Papas' darker Mediterranean colouring serves to underscore her character's both sensual and divine earthy qualities, which the more abstracted construction of the white female American stars could not convey. This bedrock of Helen's earthy, fertilizing

[91] As a common Native American saying goes, 'No nation goes down until the hearts of its women are on the ground'.

divinity undergirds the proud confidence Helen displays in both her sensuality and her regal authority, and it infuses these onscreen characteristics with complex, polysemous dimensions. At root, such elemental qualities are not to be denied, a concept recognized in some cultures' mythic tales. Thus, the Laguna Pueblo tales of Kochinenako, Yellow Woman, tell of the female fertility deity's adulteries as essential to her role in providing abundance to the community.[92] Within the tales, her husband, father, and the entire community accept her adulteries since they result in community benefits that far outweigh any moral censure that might accrue to her personal or familial improprieties.[93] What the Laguna myths express openly become subsumed in Helen's tales—the moral strictures by which the mortal character in the tales must abide elide out her multiple divinized fertilizing properties.[94] Nevertheless, the salutary effects of such an elementally sustaining divine Helen appear to continue strongly enough to permit the stories' mortal Helen to return home to Sparta, unscathed by the great devastation her beauty was seen to cause. It is this depth of female power rooted in female earthiness, sexuality, and eroticism that Papas' Helen displays in Cacoyannis' film.

In Cacoyannis' film, as in Euripides' play, Helen uses her beauty and sensual appeal not to win a man, the expected social function of these qualities, but to argue and attain her own position socially and politically. This representation transforms her employment of these features into a social challenge. Far from simply adhering to societal expectations of the function of female beauty and sensuality, Helen's use of these qualities trumps these expectations by enacting radically different notions of female identity. In the voice of a self-confident woman, these conventional markers of female identity can serve purposes other than the expected societal prescriptions that limit the meaning of these female features to surface dimensions that serve men's desires.[95] What Helen's demeanour and actions show is that a woman's beauty and sensuality do not exist simply for male pleasure. While Helen depends on Menelaus' support in order to return home alive, her treatment of him shows that she assures this support for herself by displaying the full force of her eroticized female powers. Menelaus may accept or reject her, but it will be on her own grounds as a powerful woman who draws confidently upon her female powers, even (or especially) when she performs as most

[92] Allen (1986: 277).

[93] Allen (1986: 234).

[94] See Vivante (2014).

[95] See Blondell (this volume) on Helen's eloquence in the Homeric poems as a significant marker of her identity; see also Worman (2001).

vulnerable. This powerful image of female identity, rooted in ancient concepts of female powers that are sharply differentiated from female images constructed according to modern western male projections, radically challenges conventional, patriarchically-constructed ideas about acceptable femininity.[96]

Moreover, the film suggests the political implications arising from this challenge to the social construction of female identity. Helen's scene is situated within a film making a fiercely anti-war statement. In particular, it is sandwiched between the scene showing Astyanax being taken from his mother and the one showing him being walked up the fort's steps to be cast off its walls. Thus contextualized, it is worth asking if the cinematic emphasis on Helen's beauty and sensuality also serves this political message.[97] If Helen can employ these features to serve her own and not another's, specifically a man's, desires, she can also use them for political ends. In a landscape of devastation, she alone not only survives, but survives gloriously, visualized by her gleaming white robe, elaborate make up, and coifed hair compared to the other women's dark garments, dishevelled hair and plain stricken faces. Within the film Hecuba accuses Helen of collaborating with whichever side was most expedient, and Helen certainly appears to survive as the greatest prize of the war given to the conquering Greeks. Likewise, her survival, because of her outstanding beauty and archetypal sensuality, may suggest a cynical view of the use which a woman herself or others may make of her alluring qualities. Helen's beauty and royal position in Sparta together guarantee her passage home. Yet here, too, the political message might be more complex. If we extend the analysis of Helen's self-empowering use of her charming physical characteristics to political ends, her actions can be seen as showing a female resilience that, steeped in concepts of ancient erotic, abundance-providing female earth deities, triumphs over whatever ruling powers have established their control. Consequently, the film's portrayal of Helen's snub of the Trojan women, of Hecuba, and of Menelaus radiates on several levels that complicate the surface dramatic narrative. Far from being simply a beautiful sexed pawn in the schemes that others design, Helen's supreme control of her beauty and royal position challenge conventional ideas of female and feminine

[96] One sign of the depth of this radical use of feminine beauty is that mainstream feminist speakers or writers, whose discourse is almost universally framed in patriarchal social constructs, do not generally appreciate its empowering potential. See Zweig (1993b).

[97] McDonald (1983: 241) states that seeing Helen's smiling face on the ship just before Astyanax is hurled from the wall graphically displays Helen's power and the effects of that power.

identity. While Helen's extraordinary beauty and royal status may distance her from representing an 'Everywoman' for women generally, her use of her female powers, which the Helen in Cacoyannis' film like her ancient mythic prototype projects as shared female characteristics, transcends this gap of physical appearance and social status to model for women profound notions of their identity and how they might successfully employ their own powers for beneficial ends.

CONCLUSION

These two films, consequently, though drawn ostensibly upon the same ancient figure, end up presenting highly contrasted depictions of the ancient figure. Produced in the mid-1950s, during Eisenhower's presidency when fending off the unpatriotic assaults of the House Unamerican Activities Committee and supporting the United States' post-war ascendancy in the cold war struggle against the Soviet Union prevailed in Hollywood, Wise's *Helen of Troy* portrays a stereotypical, blonde American star (despite her Italian nationality) who is blameless for the war raging supposedly on her account, and who, despite her beauty and royal standing, ultimately shows herself to be the dutiful wife widely projected of women in 1950s media. In this apparent accord with the prevailing zeitgeist of its decade, this film and its portrayal of its female protagonist appear to reinforce the gender, social, and political conventions of its time, through an epic narrative that seeks to benefit from the popularity of the period's biblical blockbusters. The film, however, in the words of at least one reviewer, was one of the decade's failures at epic cinema.[98] As a result, its social and political messages may also have fallen flat. In contrast, Cacoyannis' *The Trojan Women*, produced in a more highly charged political climate by a director more intimately tied to turbulent political events, overtly contests multiple aspects of social and political conventions. The Helen in Cacoyannis' film proudly displays the female powers of her ancient mythic avatar upon which she draws more deeply. This portrayal itself of a woman who acts upon her identity defined in female-rooted powers and visible markers, seen most dramatically through the camera's focus on and the use Papas makes of her eyes, functions as a radical challenge to accepted notions of femininity,

[98] However, besides myself, Nisbet (2006) and Roisman (2008) express their admiration for this film.

especially as portrayed in 1950s and 1960s cinema. Moreover, it is possible to read this gender and social challenge in political terms as well. The lush sensuality of the Helen scene serves as a dynamic voice for political resistance in a film that otherwise recounts the devastating ravages of war. Regardless of one's actual station in life, this Helen is worth emulating for her sense of herself as a woman, her knowledge of her female powers, her ability to use her powers, and the resulting demeanour of self-knowledge, self-confidence, and empowerment she displays. It is this image of a powerful Helen on multiple levels that Wise and especially Cacoyannis distinctively dramatize. She successfully conveys to a modern audience how and why it is that in the ancient Greek mythology a single woman, Helen, could be 'the face that launched a thousand ships', igniting a ten-year international war.

2

'Third Cheerleader from the Left': From Homer's Helen to *Helen of Troy*

Ruby Blondell

Female power poses notorious problems for ancient Greek culture. Because Greek ideology and cultural practice both place severe restrictions on female agency, it is difficult for women to exercise power without transgressing the norms constituted to regulate their behaviour. Since the control of female sexuality lies at the heart of these norms, sex—more specifically, the active female pursuit of an object of desire—is typically implicated in women's transgressions and hence in the danger posed by the female as such. Insofar as female danger is wrapped up with sexual transgression, then, so is female power. And insofar as sex is bound up with beauty, Helen of Troy—by definition the most beautiful woman of all time—is also the most dangerous of women. Her godlike beauty grants her supreme erotic power over men, a power that resulted in what was, in Greek eyes, the most devastating war of all time. Other women, such as Helen's half-sister Clytemnestra, may be more violent, but none is more destructive.

Helen's destructive power matches that of Achilles, the mightiest of the Greek warriors at Troy, with whom she is linked as a (potential) sexual partner in several strands of the tradition.[1] The connection is a fitting one, for these two represent the gendered body at its most glorious: they are the apogee of female beauty and male strength, respectively.[2]

* This paper is reprinted from *Classical Receptions Journal* 1 (2009) 4–22, by kind permission of the press. It is unchanged, except for formatting, correction of a few typographical errors, and updating of URLs in the bibliography.

I would like to thank Alison Futrell, Douglas Roach, and especially Sandra Joshel for various kinds of assistance in researching this paper. I am also grateful to the Simpson Center for the Humanities for funding, and to a number of audiences for their comments on oral versions.

[1] For the evidence, see Schmidt (1996: 29–30).

[2] Achilles is also the most beautiful of the Greek warriors (*Il.* 2.673–4, Pl., *Symp.* 180a), but he is not eroticized in Homer (in contrast to Paris).

This complementarity also allies them in a more sinister fashion. Helen is often coupled with Achilles as a cause of the enormous destruction of the Trojan War.[3] Achilles is the principal agent of the slaughter, and Helen its principal—or at least its official—reason, each employing the mode of destruction appropriate to their iconically and symmetrically gendered status: her beauty is as deadly as his physical strength, her body as deadly as his body. The supreme expression of masculinity is predicated on the supreme expression of the feminine. At the same time, Helen's transgression provides a fig leaf to shield Achilles and the rest of the Achaeans from blame for their violence, transmuting invasion into justice and slaughter into heroism.

Having constructed female beauty as dangerous, and imagined an absolute standard of beauty fulfilled by a single extraordinary woman in whom such danger culminates, Greek culture devotes considerable energy to attempting to control or deny the power of its own creation. Blaming Helen is the most obvious way to contain her, by subjecting her to social control while still enabling her to serve as a convenient scapegoat for the Trojan War.[4] Yet, a remarkable number of Greek texts excuse or palliate Helen's behaviour.[5] In their own way, however, these defences too are strategies of containment. Blame is an acknowledgement of power, both because it implies agency in its object and because it recognizes that object as sufficiently threatening to require humiliation in order to constrain the irresponsible exercise of power. In declaring her not guilty, Helen's ancient defenders neutralize her by erasing her identity as a transgressive, dangerous woman. The long history of defences of Helen makes sense as an attempt to disarm her.

Such strategies of containment are arguably more effective than the more obvious discourse of blame, since they attempt to erase the transgressive Helen rather than merely chastising her. Yet, they still depend on the problem of her dangerous power. Significantly, no ancient Greek account simply eliminates Helen or her beauty from the tale of Troy, or denies that the war took place at all. Through all the story's permutations over time, what makes the Trojan War distinctive and gives it its peculiar character as a foundation narrative for Greek identity is the fact that it is always caused, somehow, by Helen as the supreme embodiment of female beauty—regardless of her presence or

[3] See esp. *Cypria* fr. I with Mayer (1996).

[4] Blame of Helen is most prominent in lyric poetry and tragedy. See Homeyer (1977: 13–36) and cf. Graver (1995: 53, 55–7). The theme of Helen as scapegoat informs the approach of Suzuki (1989).

[5] E.g. Gorg. *Hel.;* Eur. *Hel.*; Isoc., *Hel.*; Dio Chrys. *Or.* 11.14, 43–53 (cf. also *Or.* 2.13).

absence at Troy, her enthusiasm or reluctance to get involved. It is Helen's role that makes the war recognizable as the Trojan War, and not some other war or foundational adventure. And insofar as she is conceptually essential to the Trojan War, she is also essential to ancient Greek constructions of Greek identity—more specifically, masculine identity. That identity, it seems, inextricably predicates the achievement(s) of manhood on the danger of female beauty and its containment. Greek warriors *must* fight in deed to control the person of Helen or its phantasmic representations, and Greek authors *must* fight in word to contain her power by manipulating her story. Achilles is predicated upon Helen.

Despite the enormous distances—in time, space, culture—that divide Hollywood from the ancient Greeks, Helen remains an object of fascination and a site for the exploration of contemporary identities. This paper aims to show that process at work in Warner Brothers' *Troy* (2004), directed by Wolfgang Petersen from a script by David Benioff, as it transforms the Helen of the *Iliad*.[6] *Troy*, I shall argue, advances the Greek project of disempowering Helen. Despite a veneer of feminism, the movie does not celebrate the dangerous power of female beauty but denies it by means of an array of strategies, some of which echo ancient texts and some of which are specific to contemporary ideology and the cinematic medium.

The Iliadic Helen is simultaneously dangerous and sympathetic. The sympathy depends on a substantial eclipse of the danger, yet her power still glimmers round the edges.[7] In Homer, she and her surroundings gleam with a light suggestive of divinity.[8] The poet notoriously avoids dwelling on the specifics of her transcendent beauty. She appears swathed in shimmering garments, ambiguous, elusive and liminal.[9] Her impact is conveyed not through detailed description of her body but through the reactions of the internal audience, especially the Trojan elders, who say she is 'terribly like an immortal goddess' (3.158), and Paris, who declares—after ten (or even twenty) years—that he desires her

[6] The script draws on a variety of legendary sources for Helen's story, but the *Iliad* seems to have been Benioff's only source for her character. (Winkler 2007a: 4) gives reasons for viewing *Troy* as fundamentally Petersen's work (as opposed to the scriptwriter's or the studio's). On Petersen's involvement in the script see e.g. Cohen (2004: 40); Goldsmith (2004: 56). Unfortunately, space prohibits me from analysing the contributions of the rest of the production team.

[7] See Clader (1976: Ch. 2). The account of Helen in the *Iliad* that follows is based on Blondell (2010), which should be consulted for detailed argument and documentation.

[8] See Clader (1976: 25–6, 29–30, 57–62).

[9] On Helen's elusiveness in the *Iliad*, see esp. Worman (1997: 151–67).

now more than ever (3.442–46).[10] Veiled as it is, her beauty makes her both the ultimate object of desire and an emblem of the heroic enterprise as such. She is not the only reason for the Trojan War, but she is a real one, and as such indispensable.[11] The Greek warriors are, of course, driven by lust for glory and plunder, yet the location of Greek male honour in its women gives real cultural weight to Paris and Helen's transgression. By seducing another man's wife and violating the sacred laws of hospitality, Paris really does threaten the fabric of society and the institution of the household on which it is based. Though Helen may serve as a pretext, she is not *merely* a pretext.

Yet Helen's own culpability is muted. Men on both sides speak of her as an object that was 'taken' (e.g. 3.48, 13.626–7) and Paris even talks of having 'seized' her (3.444). No Greek blames her for her transgression. As for the Trojans, Helen tells us she fears, or is subject to, shame and reproach from various people (e.g. 3.410–12, 24.768–75), but no such blame is voiced by any speaking character and Priam notoriously declares that the gods are responsible, not Helen herself (3.164–5). This occurs in the same famous scene in which we witness her impact on the Trojan elders. Her effect upon men, which both explains and justifies the war, makes it impossible for the poet to show Helen blamed face-to-face. Her 'face' is, after all, the cause of the trouble—it both captivates and disarms.[12] Reports of blame are therefore removed to the margins of the narrative, where their dissonance is muted. Yet, this avoidance of blame also disempowers Helen, since it denies her any responsibility for causing the war and thus any agency in her own elopement.

As has often been observed, the only direct abuse of Helen in the *Iliad* comes from Helen herself.[13] Her repeated, and powerful, self-reproaches make it clear that she is to blame, in her own eyes, for betraying her husband to run away with Paris. If Helen herself avows her guilt then who are we—or Priam—to disagree? Yet, this avowal also frees the poet to present the Achaeans and Trojans fighting heroically for an object that is uncontaminated by their own disparagement. Since she blames herself so stringently, they are freed from the necessity of doing so.[14] It is Helen's

[10] Helen speaks of twenty years at 24.765–7, but the passage is anomalous.

[11] On the reasons for the war, see Collins (1988: 41–2). Helen does not exhaust those reasons, but she symbolizes them. If Menelaus dies, she will no longer serve as *casus belli*, so the war is over (cf. 4.169–74).

[12] Cf. the story that Menelaus planned to kill her after the war but dropped his sword at the sight of her, a scene often portrayed in art (Hedreen 1996).

[13] See esp. Graver (1995).

[14] Cf. Worman (2001: 27–9), (2002: 53–4).

self-blame that allows Priam to save face for her by attributing responsibility to the gods. It likewise permits the poet to evade the problem of whether a guilty Helen was 'really' worth it,[15] by assuring her guilt while allowing her to retain her splendour as an object of supreme value in the eyes of others. She has—conveniently—put herself in her place, so that they do not have to. Moreover, her remorse helps to characterize her positively in a specifically gendered fashion. Self-deprecation is a form of self-disempowerment characteristic of the Greek male portrayal of 'good' women, who often denigrate their sex in general and themselves in particular as inferior to men.[16] Blame of Helen by men, which would debase her value, is suppressed or eclipsed by the bright light of her beauty, but self-blame enhances her value as a woman, and hence, indirectly, the legitimacy of the heroic struggle to (re)claim her.

The Iliadic Helen also misses Menelaus (3.139–40, 3.173–6), and expresses acute contempt for Paris, whom she castigates as far inferior to her former husband, both as a warrior (3.428–36) and (by implication) in moral sense (sensitivity to shame) and integrity (stable φρένες) (6.350–3). This preference for Menelaus amounts to a confession that her elopement with Paris was wrong, not just ethically, but as a decision affecting her own happiness. In modern parlance, it shows the folly of 'romantic' matchmaking in comparison with functional, sensible 'arranged' marriages of the kind with which a 'good' woman is content (a message to be reversed in *Troy*, as we shall see). The point is reinforced by the fact that she also misses her parents, relatives, and friends (3.140, 3.163, 3.174–5, 3.180, 3.236–42). Her regrets endorse from her own lips the linchpin of Greek gender ideology whereby women's desires are excessive, unstable, and unhealthy, and lead only to trouble. In the *Odyssey*, we see the consequences of the re-established status quo: an elegant if uneasy and passionless[17] alliance between husband and wife, accompanied by an extraordinary level of affluence and comfort. All things considered, Menelaus seems to have been worth coming home to.

Helen's self-reproaches thus serve her interests by situating her as a 'good' woman who has learned her lesson. But they also provide her with a space in which to assert her own subjectivity and reclaim the agency

[15] Cf. Collins (1988: 51, 57–8); Ebbott (1999: 19–20).

[16] See e.g. Xen. *Oec.* 7.14, 39; Eur. *Med.* 407–9, *Or.* 605–6, *IA* 1393–4, *Andr.* 269–73; Soph. *Ant.* 61–2.

[17] Menelaus and Helen sleep side by side (4.304–5, 15.57–8). While this does not preclude sex (which is often implied by 'lying with', e.g. at *Il.* 2.355, 3.448, 16.184, *Od.* 8.342, 18.213), sex is not explicitly mentioned and there is no mention of φιλότης, or affection (on φιλότης as sex see Clader 1976: 36). Contrast the φιλότης that Penelope ascribes to Helen's relationship with Paris (*Od.* 23.219).

denied to her by men. As an assertion of past agency, her self-blame may be viewed as an attempt to retain a trace of the subjectivity of her original transgression. Where others blame only Paris, Helen links them as jointly responsible, implicitly placing their agency on an equal footing (6.356–8). She is the only person to use active verbs for her part in the elopement, saying that she 'followed' Paris after 'leaving' her former family (ἑπόμην . . . λιποῦσα) (3.174), 'went' and 'departed' from her homeland to Troy (ἔβην, ἐλήλυθα) (24.766). Though these verbs do not prove willing agency (one may 'go' under duress), they stand out in light of the fact that no one else uses active verbs for Helen's role. She clearly retains a sense of her own agency regarding the elopement and its disastrous consequences. The abusive language she uses of herself reinforces this, both by implicitly claiming agency and by conjuring her as a menacing, destructive figure.[18] The discourse of Greek misogyny is a transparent expression of male fears regarding female power. By appropriating that discourse Helen implies that she owns such power. Her self-blame is, in its way, an act of defiance.

Helen also remains powerful in Homer in a different way. Many Greek texts make it clear that the threat of women's beauty is intimately bound up with female control of discourse and its manipulative power.[19] Helen's use of self-blame and the discourse of 'good' womanhood are integral to a verbal self-presentation that proves highly effective in winning over the most powerful men in Troy. This verbal skill is complicit with her beauty in disarming external blame.[20] Moreover, speech is the poet's own medium, and there are well-known indications that the poet of the *Iliad* equates Helen's voice with his own. When we first encounter her she is weaving a tapestry that represents the armies fighting over her (3.125–8). This role as weaver of the Trojan War aligns her both with the poet and with Zeus himself, whose plan is fulfilled through that war.[21] Homer's Helen is also a mistress of language, using many modes of discourse to manipulate her audience, like the poet and the rhapsode who perform her.[22] And she is well aware that the stories she tells will live on through the medium of epic poetry (cf. 6.357–8). Her self-presentation is smuggled into the masculine narrative of the war as a

[18] Her diction associates her with strife, fear, war and death (Clader 1976: 17–23).

[19] See e.g. *Il.* 14.214–17, Hes. *Theog.* 201–6, *Hom. Hymn* 5.249–51.

[20] Similarly in the *Odyssey*, Helen's seductiveness is conveyed through both her discourse and her magic drug (Bergren 1981). On the manipulative language of both Homeric Helens, see Worman (2001).

[21] On Helen as a weaver/bard, see Clader (1976: 6–12), Bergren (1979, 1983: 79) and Worman (2002: 89–90); for Zeus as weaver, see Scheid and Svenbro (1996: 63–5).

[22] On the variety of genres that Helen appropriates, see Worman (2001).

whole, ensuring the survival of her voice as long as the epic itself survives. Over the millennia that voice has successfully disarmed not only the men of Troy, but the epic's putatively male external audience.[23]

Despite the fascination of the Iliadic Helen, and her pivotal role as cause of the Trojan War, Achilles usurps what might have been her story. The *Iliad* does not pretend otherwise: it is the tale of the wrath of Achilles. *Troy*, in contrast, though 'inspired' by Homer's *Iliad*, and focusing primarily on the tale of two male heroes, purports to tell 'the Trojan War myth in its entirety', including 'the story of Helen's love for Paris' (Benioff n.d.). Like most recent treatments of the tale, it proceeds from that initial romance to the final destruction of Troy in a way that the *Iliad* pointedly does not.[24] In keeping with classical Hollywood style, the film also gives heterosexual 'love' a prominence that it lacks in the *Iliad*.[25] 'Love' is part of the movie's epic agenda, as announced in the preliminary voice-over, and heterosexual pair-bonding becomes a tenet of the heroic code, as enunciated by the unimpeachably admirable Hector ('Honor the gods. Love your woman. And defend your country').[26]

Even the famous prophecy of Achilles' two fates—he may choose between a short life full of heroic glory and a long but undistinguished one—is recast in *Troy* to include a wife and children as part of the life he eschews. And even he ends up endorsing heterosexual romance. This is the story not of his wrath, but of his conversion to 'love'. He does briefly subordinate romance to revenge for Patroclus, remaining deaf to Briseis's pleas to refrain from fighting; but in the end he sees the error of his homosocial ways, subordinating military comradeship to the ultimate goal of heterosexual romance. He abandons the quest for glory through conquest, using his supreme strength only to seek out Briseis amid the blazing ruins and actually killing men on his own side who are molesting her. In a climactic *liebestod*, Achilles accepts his own death not because he has had his revenge on Hector, but because, so he tells Briseis, 'You gave me peace in a lifetime of war' [transcribed].

[23] Helen's voice has won over most readers of the poem. A rare exception is Ryan, who finds her 'wanton, self-centered, deceitful', and yet so 'irresistibly beautiful and charming' that 'we perhaps forgive her everything' (1965: 117).

[24] Homer is criticized on this point as early as Dio Chrysostom (*Or.* 11.28–29). For the contrast between the structure of *Troy* and that of the *Iliad*, see Mendelsohn (2004).

[25] For the centrality of heterosexual romance to 'Hollywood style', see Bordwell et al. (1985: 16–17). On Petersen's self-conscious adoption of an 'Old Hollywood' style for *Troy*, see Shahabudin (2007).

[26] Except where otherwise indicated, quotations from *Troy* are from the online script (Benioff 2003). In a few cases, where script and film diverge, I have transcribed the dialogue myself.

All this emphasis on heterosexual pair-bonding might lead us to expect some development of Helen's role. That expectation is not met. Rather, her significance is diminished.[27] An important mechanism in this process is the film's pervasive romantic ideology. *Troy* is heavily influenced by notions of heroism that posit the 'hero' and 'heroine' not primarily as embodiments of power or danger but as romantic victims both doomed and redeemed by 'love'.[28] The elopement of Helen and Paris is presented as a single foolish mis-step, both caused and excused by 'love'—as endorsed by none other than Priam, and even Hector. To be sure, Hector initially scolds Paris, declaring that he knows 'nothing about love'; but once the die is cast he actually prevents Helen from returning to the Greeks, on the grounds that 'My brother needs you tonight'. Priam asks only 'Do you love her?' Paris responds by equating his love for Helen with the aged king's love of his country. Priam accepts this tacit equivalence of Helen with the city of Troy, even though it calls for the latter to be sacrificed to the former, adding 'I've fought many wars in my time. Some were fought for land, some for power, some for glory. I suppose fighting for love makes more sense than all the rest.' *Why* it makes sense is not explained. Unlike, for example, the sophist Gorgias' argument that *eros* is an irresistible force that exempts its victims from moral judgement, romantic love is apparently self-justifying.

In stark contrast to many of the most prominent ancient Greek heroes, the romantic hero and heroine must be likeable. They may have minor flaws, but these must not be of a kind that risks undermining the sympathies of the audience. More serious defects may be present initially, but only if they are later shed under the influence of 'love', which typically transforms its victims for the better (quite unlike the typically devastating impact of Greek *eros*). (In *Troy*, 'love' has this effect on both Achilles and Paris.) Also unlike Homeric heroes, romantic heroes need not be powerful. In fact, power is something of a drawback, since it tends to undermine sympathy, at least according to the sensibilities of modern audiences who expect even their warrior heroes to be temporarily down—if not quite out—before they rise to ultimate victory. Power is particularly threatening to romantic sympathy, insofar as such sympathy

[27] All the most substantial female roles in the *Iliad* are reduced in *Troy*: Helen, Andromache, Hecuba (who is omitted entirely) and Thetis (cf. Cyrino 2005: 10).

[28] On the romantic plot(s) of *Troy*, see Futrell (2005). Romantic treatment of the Paris/Helen plot has classical roots (cf. Solomon 2007: 98), became popular in the Middle Ages (Scherer 1967), and is central to most pop-cultural representations, including Robert Wise's *Helen of Troy* (Warner Brothers 1955) and the USA Network's 2003 TV mini-series *Helen of Troy* (cf. Winkler 2009: Ch. 5).

is predicated on the powerlessness of the romantic dyad in the face of hostile forces arrayed against them (and often against 'love' itself). Accordingly, in service to the romantic validation of Helen's affair with Paris, *Troy* strips her of her ancient power even more thoroughly than does the *Iliad*. This Helen's reluctance to yield to her desire for Paris and her passive, unthreatening demeanour both capture important aspects of her Homeric persona; but the film goes further, completely eliminating the dark undercurrents that swirl around the bright figure of the Homeric Helen, and the hints of her veiled power.

An easy way to make Paris and Helen innocent victims in the eyes of a modern movie audience would be to portray them as puppets of the gods—Helen merely a gift to Paris from Aphrodite in consideration of services rendered. This would reflect the common view among non-specialists that the Greek gods use humans as mere puppets, depriving them of 'free will', choice, and responsibility.[29] But there are no divine characters in this movie.[30] Their presence would violate Petersen's notion of 'realism', an aspect of the film on which he laid considerable stress.[31] This refers not to 'realistic' recreation of the ancient world, but to the representation of the way people 'really' are. As the scriptwriter David Benioff put it, he wanted to 'see the human thing' (Faraci May 2004b). This purportedly transhistorical human nature turns out, of course, to look remarkably modern. Like most epic films, *Troy* fetishizes certain aspects of 'realism' or 'authenticity', but does so in order to address contemporary concerns using a highly stylized and historically arbitrary rendition of ancient times.[32] The ancients are exotic and alien, as marked by iconic details of script, costume, and set, but emotionally and ideologically, the Greeks are us.

The gods are therefore ruled out as a vehicle with which to engineer sympathy for the romantic dyad. Benioff's Helen is not, as he believes she is in Greek mythology, 'the victim of circumstances'; rather, the removal of the gods means 'her will is free, the choice is her own, and

[29] This view of the Greek gods has long been discredited by scholars. The classic treatment is Dodds (1951: Ch. 1). For a succinct statement of the case regarding Helen, see Edwards (1987: 318).

[30] The only exception is the ageing Thetis (Julie Christie), who shows no hint of special power or status. And of course she is not an Olympian, not one of the 'Greek gods' with whom many of the movie's audience would be familiar.

[31] Petersen (n.d.); see further Futrell (2005); Winkler (2007b: 456–60). Petersen claimed 'people would laugh today if you had God entering the scene and fighting and helping out. It's hard to even imagine that' (Russell May 2004)—a claim that seems quite extraordinary in a period when popular film and television are replete with the supernatural in myriad forms.

[32] Cf. Futrell (2005); and also Sobchak (2003).

the consequences on her own conscience' (Benioff n.d.). This gives the impression of empowering Helen by freeing her from divine control. Yet ironically, it *lessens* her power from an ancient perspective. In Greek myth, her semi-divine parentage and her intimate connection with Aphrodite are marks of exceptional status, which enhance, rather than detract from, the significance of her actions. The medium of film supplies many creative possibilities for such effects.[33] Petersen's conception of 'realism', in contrast, undermines the notion of Helen as someone whose godlike beauty makes her a creature of the imagination, not fully of this world. It leaves no room for her divine traces, for any suggestion that her beauty is other-worldly, transcendently desirable, or sinister in its power.

Eliminating the gods means that some other way must be found to sustain our sympathy for Helen, by minimizing, if not excusing, her transgression. Benioff claims that his script 'doesn't judge her for the choice' but merely shows its devastating consequences (Benioff n.d.).[34] But in fact, both the script and its realization on screen do everything possible to judge her, and to find her not guilty.

To start with, key aspects of the Greek story are altered in Helen's favour. She leaves no daughter behind her in Sparta—a standard feature of the ancient story (including the *Iliad*), and a standard cause for reproach by herself and others.[35] A Helen who abandoned her child would lose the sympathy of modern American popular culture, which values only parenthood above romantic coupledom. Nor does Benioff's Helen suffer any reproach from the Trojan women or her new family, even from Hecuba, the carping mother-in-law of the *Iliad* (24.770), who has disappeared from the script altogether. Like Homer's Helen she does blame herself for her actions, but far less repeatedly and severely, and, most importantly, not for the same things. She does not chastise herself as a moral or sexual transgressor, regretting only the consequences of a pursuit of 'love' that would otherwise clearly be fully justified. This characterization is arguably less effective than Homer's in eliciting sympathy for Helen, since her remorse is grounded not in her own weakness

[33] Thus, in the television mini-series *Helen of Troy* (USA Network 2003) the action is frozen around Menelaus when he sees Helen on the ramparts, effectively endowing this Helen (Sienna Guillory) with an impact that transcends her girlish looks. In *Troy*, cinematic special effects (e.g. slow-motion) are used to enhance Achilles' heroic splendour (cf. Scully 2007: 129), but not Helen's.

[34] More generally, it is hard to give serious credence to his claim that 'both sides have good and evil mixed among them' (Cohen 2004: 38)—a notion reiterated by Petersen, who claimed that the film 'refuses to take sides' (Russell May 2004), and bought by a remarkable number of critics and reviewers.

[35] Cf. *Il.* 3.174–5, *Od.* 4.263; Sappho 16 LP; Alc. 283 LP.

but in consequences that anyone could have foreseen—and that Paris actually predicts when he seduces her ('Men will hunt us and the gods will curse us').

In contrast to her Homeric counterpart, this Helen shows no trace of ambivalence towards Paris, even after he provides an excruciating display of cowardice in his duel with Menelaus. The romantic defense would be shattered if she declared, as she does in the *Iliad*, that Menelaus is a 'better man' and she should never have left him. When *Troy's* Paris says 'I'm a coward', Helen not only applauds his courage for facing Menelaus in the first place, but consoles him by claiming that he ran away not to save his skin, but 'for love'. She does call Menelaus a brave man (in implied contrast to Paris), and a 'great warrior' who 'lived for fighting',[36] but such prowess is no longer intrinsically admirable. Helen continues, 'I don't want a hero, my love. I want a man to grow old with.' The fantasy of a happy ending for their romance is left open by keeping Paris alive at the end of the movie, thus pre-empting the awkward mythological tradition that Helen remarried at Troy after his death in battle.[37] And of course Menelaus is dead, so the distinctly unromantic shadow of re-imposed domesticity at Sparta no longer looms over her.

Besides making Helen and Paris as innocent as possible under the circumstances, *Troy* shores up our sympathy for the romantic dyad by pitting them against the powerful and unequivocally wicked Agamemnon. In contrast to the *Iliad*—where the Greeks want to destroy Troy and then go home—this Agamemnon is a naked imperialist. For him, Helen's departure is no more than a convenient excuse.[38] As he tells Menelaus, 'I didn't come here for your pretty wife. I came for Troy.' He calls Helen 'a foolish woman' who has nevertheless 'proven to be very useful'. In the *Iliad* it is implied that the rationale for war would die with Menelaus (4.169–74); in *Troy* he does die, but that does not put an end to the war. The most beautiful woman in the world, desired by every man in the world (including Agamemnon),[39] has become the merest 'pretty' pretext for a war that is really being fought, in Hector's words, 'for one man's

[36] In the *Iliad*, in contrast, Menelaus is a 'soft' warrior (17.587–8), whom Agamemnon deems too weak to battle Hector (7.104–19).

[37] Benioff's original script had Paris escaping alive with Helen. The movie leaves his fate uncertain, but he assures Helen that they will always be together, whether 'in this world or the next'.

[38] On *Troy's* 'realist' power politics, see Rabel (2007).

[39] Helen is sometimes allowed to choose her own husband; on one account this is to curtail the threat she poses to other men's marriages, specifically Agamemnon's to Clytemnestra (Hyg. *Fab.* 78; cf. Gantz 1993: 566).

greed'. If Helen had not provided Agamemnon with the excuse he needed, he would have found another.

If the Trojan War has nothing to do with Helen then she did not start it, and she cannot end it. Accordingly, it is insisted that even her return to Menelaus would not stop the war. Hector prevents her from leaving Troy, saying that her departure would accomplish nothing, because for the Greeks 'this is about power. Not love'. The Trojans under Priam are willing to fight on behalf of 'love', yet Hector at the same time realizes that the war is 'not about love' and not about Helen, thus simultaneously giving a Trojan seal of approval to the romantic plot and exculpating Helen through Hector's understanding of the real nature of Greek imperialism. Hector's endorsement of the love between Paris and Helen is thus at the same time a denial of its significance, and more specifically of Helen's significance. If she did not cause the war, and cannot end it, then by implication she is not 'worth it'—not an adequate *casus belli* with power to wreak havoc among men. As we saw earlier, Helen does serve in Greek tradition as an ideological fig leaf for the glorification of male violence. But that is not all she is. At the end of the day, the Iliadic Helen *must* be worth it, if only to justify the glorious heroic enterprise of which she is the emblem. In *Troy*, however, the entire complex of motives for the war is replaced by an imperialism that is truly naked. The film removes the fig leaf, leaving the phallus exposed to view. This exposure requires a hapless, child-like, victimized Helen. She *must* be *not* worth it.

The move that supports Helen's innocence by rendering her transgression irrelevant thus requires her trivialization and disempowerment. It also permits the film to strip the Greek Helen of her very identity as the supreme embodiment of female beauty. If Helen is no more than a pretext for the war, there is no need to grant her beauty intrinsic power or value. There is consequently no need for *Troy* to protect the idea of her value by conveying the awesome power that the sight of her exercises over men. When she first rides into Troy a group of women stare and point in apparent puzzlement, but there is no sign that the onlookers are awestruck at her looks. As in the *Iliad*, Priam is clearly charmed by Helen, and he does compliment her on her beauty. But no one besides Paris seems dazzled by it—no group of Trojan elders gazes at her in uneasy awe. Nor do we see her exercising her charm over men through discourse—the script strips away her Homeric eloquence. The erotic danger that the Greek Helen embodies is domesticated by confining its overwhelming impact to a single mate.

The romantic defence is reinforced by the faux-feminist strategy of presenting any transgressive woman as a victim who would not have so acted if men had just treated her right. This makes Helen reactive, a refugee from Greek male oppression, not active in asserting her own desire or taking responsibility for her own transgression, as she does in the *Iliad*. Diane Kruger, who played Helen, tried to make the character 'youthful, vulnerable...sad...tragic' (Fischer May 2004). When an interviewer asked her to address the moral issue of Helen's departure, by asking why Helen went with Paris if she knew there was going to be war, Kruger did not answer the question directly but replied with a description of a 'sad', 'young' Helen who is 'married to a man she hates', adding, 'I just hope that people will look and see and believe in that hope of love, that hope of freedom, even if it was just for a limited time'—a freedom that a courageous Helen 'dared' to grasp (Fischer May 2004).[40] This feminism lite justifies the representation of Helen as a disempowered victim by claiming it as a feminist gesture. But if this is a species of feminism it is an uncommonly comfortable one. In marked contrast to the Greek original, Helen's defection is neither culturally nor ethically disturbing because it offers no threat to the prevailing ideology of the target audience.[41]

Unlike ancient Greek texts, art, and even theatre (with its stylized costumes, masks and male actors), the medium of live action film—despite its own myriad forms of stylization—requires the director to choose a particular flesh-and-blood woman to embody Helen's legendary beauty. The script of *Troy*, along with Petersen's notion of 'realism', calls not for a figure of awe-inspiring beauty but for an innocent, hapless everygirl. She must be attractive enough to be seen as a victim of her looks, but at the same time both childlike and ordinary, not charismatic or threatening in her sexual power. She must be not a heroic presence but a 'girl next door' who poses no threat to the male viewership, and with whom any (putatively youthful) female viewer may identify and sympathize. She must be pretty rather than beautiful.

'Pretty', the very word used of Helen by the patronizing Agamemnon, suggests triviality, innocence, and girlishness. This dismissive judgement of Diane Kruger's Helen rang true to the ear of countless movie critics. Reviewers were almost unanimous in finding her insufficiently 'fabulous-looking' (McGrath 2004: 38). A website that assembles the 'nastiest' critics' quotes on the subject conveys an overwhelming ordinariness: she resembles 'dozens of young women you might see at the mall', or

[40] Benioff also evades the moral issue. He says that Helen's elopement is 'beyond good and evil', that she does it because 'she has to survive' (Cohen 2004: 39).

[41] On vulnerability and victimhood as constituents of female desirability in Hollywood, see Dyer (2004: 42–6).

'the third cheerleader from the left at a basketball game', and has a 'bland sweetness' that makes her 'Helen of Abercrombie & Fitch' or 'Helen of Troy, N.Y.' (Anonymous n.d.).[42] The most euphoric account of her looks that I have found appears on a very pink website, 'written and edited by girls and teens', under the title, 'Diane Kruger: Gorgeous Girl Next Door' (Lynn B. 2004).

Though Kruger is 5'7" tall, according to the Internet Movie Database (IMDb), and gained 15 lbs to play this role, she remains slender and waiflike, lacking maturity, dignity and the statuesque quality so highly valued by the ancient Greeks.[43] She is also devoid of the spice of danger whose fragrance lingers around the Homeric Helen. There is, as Cyrino puts it, 'something insubstantial about her, a diminutive or adolescent quality that fails to capture the sexual magnetism of this legendary beauty' (2005: 10). Kruger's former careers—ballet dancer and successful model—speak volumes about the type of beauty Petersen chose for his Helen: not that of an actor, trained to express herself through her voice as well as her body, but that of a silent object depending for self-expression on the body alone, and in the case of modelling, presenting static images for the consumer's gaze.[44] We are worlds away from the Iliadic Helen, whose voice is a vital component of her seductive power, one that she uses to inscribe herself in history. Nor are Kruger's mediocre acting skills irrelevant.[45] Helen as an object does not need to act, but simply to be viewed. In acting/agency lies her danger. This is more than word play. The power of the Homeric Helen resides partly in her potential for agency. No woman's features alone can make her a Helen. In fact, the specifics of her looks are almost irrelevant, if she can *act* the part.

Perhaps Petersen thought that in order for Helen to serve as a blank slate for the projection of male heterosexual desire as such—a daunting role, it must be said—she should be deficient in any striking qualities of her own. Though this might seem to have a certain logic, it is fatally

[42] The word 'bland' recurs repeatedly (e.g. in Travers May 2004). Cf. also French (May 2004) and Mendelsohn (2004: 46). An exception is Stuttaford (June 2004), who rates Kruger at 1000 ships even though he hates almost everything else about the film.

[43] The word 'statuesque' is used advisedly, given the Greek propensity to liken beautiful people to statues (see esp. Steiner 2001). For height and physical substance as components of the Greek ideal of female beauty, see e.g. *Od.* 18.192–6. Even Wise's Helen, Rossana Podestà, who is three inches shorter than Kruger (according to the IMDb), appears to have more physical substance.

[44] Kruger's personal enthusiasm for acting, compared to modelling, seems distinctly lukewarm (Weinberg 2004: 148).

[45] As Green cruelly puts it (alluding to the ancient tradition of a phantom Helen or *eidolon*), Kruger's acting makes her 'the next best thing' to an *eidolon* (2004: 183). Admittedly the script gives her almost nothing to work with.

mistaken. A verbal description may successfully appeal to the imagination by leaving beauty under-described or generic, leaving fantasy to flesh out the picture. The same is true, in a different way, for highly stylized forms of visual representation such as Greek vase painting or tragedy. But mainstream cinema is characterized by a strong, if naive, conception of realism,[46] which relies in part on audience knowledge that 'real' people lie behind its images. In these circumstances, blankness is neither sexy nor the stuff of fantasy.

If an empty screen is desired, it might have been more effective to follow Homer's example by presenting a Helen veiled in mystery and using the reactions of the internal audience, combined with her concealed body, to provoke the imagination of the external audience and triangulate their desire.[47] But *Troy* takes the opposite tack. By stripping Helen naked early in the movie, Petersen also strips her of the mystery that might make this unknown actress's hidden body an effective site for fantasy. Nudity might seem to provide a more substantive view of Helen's ineffable beauty, but paradoxically it reduces the impact of that beauty by making it all too effable. By thwarting the gaze, clothing insists on the mystery that lies beneath.[48] To remove Helen's clothes is to locate her allure in the surface of her body, erasing the fascination and danger of that mystery by exposing her as a naked object to be assessed and evaluated in all her particularity. Such a 'realistic' Helen erases the 'real' Helen of Greek myth, insofar as the latter is phantasmal in her very essence.

Any actor playing Helen invites comparison not only with the viewer's personal fantasy but with the idea of physical perfection as such—a standard by which she is bound to fail. The Greeks seem to have conceived of beauty as something that can be measured objectively,[49] a conception that allows Helen by definition to reign supreme, and which indeed makes Helen possible in the first place. But current ideology

[46] For the 'realism' of Hollywood style, see Bordwell et al. (1985: 37) and cf. Ellis (1992: 57–61). For the illusion of unmediated 'historical' realism provided by film, see e.g. Lowenthal (1985: 367–8).

[47] On 'triangular' desire see Girard (1965). These strategies are brilliantly employed in Michael Cacoyannis' presentation of Irene Papas as Helen—the most powerful Helen on screen of which I am aware—in *The Trojan Women* (Kino Video 1972). Even in Wise's playful treatment the audience is invited by Paris's repeated comparisons of Helen to Aphrodite to see her beauty as transcending that of ordinary mortals.

[48] In Greek mythology, the story of Pandora (Hes. *Theog.* 570–612, *Op.* 57–105) suggests that female beauty is itself constructed through clothing and adornment, leaving the interior mysterious or empty (see esp. Loraux 1993: Ch. 2; Zeitlin 1996: Ch. 2).

[49] Cf. Pollitt (1974: 12–23); Steiner (2001: 32–44).

locates beauty in the eye of the beholder.[50] This conception of beauty is a natural companion to the romantic view of love as a subjective, personal phenomenon uniting two people who are uniquely and exclusively 'meant' for each other. But it makes the exemplification of perfect beauty literally impossible. A particular actor can only be *a* beautiful woman, not *the most* beautiful. We are *unable* to conceive of a Helen in the Greek sense, one who just *is* the most beautiful of all women. Once again, Petersen could have evaded this problem by focussing not on Helen's features as such, but instead on her effect on those around her. But as we have seen, he resists empowering her through the impact of her beauty, leaving Kruger exposed as merely one man's erotic ideal (whether that man be Paris or Wolfgang Petersen).

The selection of Diane Kruger to play this impossible part erases the ancient Helen's power in yet another, and distinctively cinematic, fashion. As we saw earlier, the ancient Helen is a female analogue of Achilles. Each dangerous in his or her own way, they are both demigods whose awe-inspiring, divinely bestowed gifts raise them above the common run of mortals. As such they are iconic and glamorous figures, comparable, in certain respects, with movie stars. Despite the obvious yawning contextual differences, there are ways in which ancient mythic heroes and film stars perform similar cultural work. Like stars, such heroes are charismatic, quasi-divine figures who embody specific qualities (such as strength or beauty) to a maximal degree; they reach us mediated by repeated verbal and visual representations; their images are iconic yet remain open to endless manipulation and reinterpretation; they are used as cultural ideals or models for behaviour, especially where gender is concerned.[51] *Troy*'s representation of Achilles as charismatic, self-aware, and effortlessly powerful was therefore enhanced by the deft choice of Brad Pitt for the role, which effected a plausible cultural translation of ancient heroic glory into an approximate modern equivalent. Like the glory (κλέος) of the ancient hero, passed down over generations in song and story, such casting brings with it the actor's glamour and renown, the resonance of his previous roles, of the tributary media and

[50] This may be traced back at least to Shakespeare (*Love's Labour's Lost* II.i.14: 'Beauty is bought by judgment of the eye'). It does, of course, coexist with more 'objective' assessments of beauty e.g. through beauty pageants, though these have long incorporated elements other than physical charm and are now on the wane, in large part displaced by designations of the world's 'sexiest' women (and men) in magazines and websites.

[51] On stars as models for human behaviour, see Stacey (1994); for Greek heroes, see Blondell (2002: 80–5).

off-screen gossip.[52] The casting is reflexive: Achilles, as reviewers noted, resembles a sulky movie star, his 'celebrity status' rendering him 'remote and unapproachable' (McGrath 2004: 38);[53] Pitt, in turn, is described by Petersen as a 'dark, edgy... tortured soul'—just like Achilles.[54] The script also gives him moody reflections on fame, which fit the modern star as well as the ancient hero.

No legendary figure radiates more star power than Helen. As the most beautiful woman of all time, she exercises supreme erotic power through her blinding impact on men's eyes. She exists to be viewed. Yet even in ancient tales this impact is often mediated by her images, whether verbal or pictorial. Like a screen star she is not only beautiful, but seductive, evasive, and available for fantasy and appropriation by fans and admirers, who may fall in love with her without ever having seen her in the flesh.[55] In the story of the wooing of Helen, most of her suitors know of her beauty only by repute. They court her sight unseen, based on her renown (κλέος).[56] Given the symbiosis between stardom and beauty—especially female beauty—one might imagine that Helen of Troy, the most beautiful woman in the world, would represent the ultimate role for the female star. Ironically, however, in the making of *Troy* this kind of casting was reserved for the male roles (notably Pitt). Despite rumours that various high-voltage stars were being considered to play Helen,[57] the final choice was a German with little movie experience and no public visibility in the USA.[58] Eschewing better-known actors, Petersen was looking for 'someone who was unknown, a new face, a fresh face', in explicit contrast to his desire to cast Achilles as a 'superstar' (van Beekus 2004: 20–1).[59]

[52] Petersen chose Pitt because Achilles was 'a pop star of those days' (Spelling 2004: 72–3). In his childhood, he saw Achilles as 'like James Dean or Marlon Brando' (van Beekus 2004: 19). 'Tributary media' is Smith's useful expression (1993: *passim*).

[53] Cf. also Scott (2004a: 16). This kind of equation of actor and role is central to the functioning of the star system.

[54] Flynn (2004: 28); cf. Bennetts (2004: 171, 211).

[55] For the 'complicated game of desires that plays out around the figure of the star', see Ellis (1992: 98).

[56] [Hes.] *Cat.* 199.2–3 MW, 199.9 MW. Idomeneus is an exception: he wants to see her in advance (204.60–3 MW).

[57] These rumours were fostered by the film makers (Lowe 2005). One rumoured candidate was Angelina Jolie, on whom see further below. A number of models were also considered, including sultry super-model Kemp Muhl, who was rejected because she was too young (Turner May 2004).

[58] She had appeared in one English-language TV movie and three French-language films.

[59] The pattern echoes Wise's choice of Podestà, who was 'the requisite "unknown" outside Italy' (Hayes: n.d.).

Petersen adopted this casting strategy because he wanted his Helen to have 'no baggage', but to be just 'Helen from Sparta', since 'no one had ever seen her . . . hidden in Sparta' (van Beekus 2004: 22).[60] His film thus elides the traditional wooing of Helen, and with it the renown that brought heroes from all over the Greek world to seek her hand.[61] Perhaps he thought the familiar features of a major star would obstruct Helen's function as an empty space for the projection of male desire.[62] But the choice of an 'unknown' actor only exacerbates the kind of problem that is (as I argued earlier) inherent in using any specific actress to play this role 'realistically'. To embody Helen successfully an actor must be not individual, but iconic; and an unknown is liable to come across as less iconic because more ordinary—or more 'real' in Petersen's sense—and thus, paradoxically, more individual than a star. Star-appeal itself depends in part on a carefully constructed 'ordinariness'; but this is complemented by a cultural circulation that makes the star simultaneously extraordinary.[63] The exposure of stardom makes an actor a public signifier, allowing audiences to draw on the collective desire that is produced and reproduced through ceaseless circulation of their images and the concomitant triangulation of desire. This kind of iconic energy is concentrated in the sex-goddesses of a culture's collective fantasy—the Marilyn Monroes—who carry a burden of erotic signification that far outstrips their identity as individual actors.[64] Angelina Jolie, Esquire magazine's 2004 'sexiest woman alive', might have been able to channel this kind of erotic

[60] Conversely, his idea that everyone knew what Achilles looked like seems to be based on the kind of exposure offered by film and TV (contrast the need for even the most famous warriors to be identified, by none other than Helen, in *Iliad* 3).

[61] In the film, her parents sent her to Sparta at the age of sixteen to marry a Menelaus who apparently lived there already. There is no indication of where she was sent from, and nothing about a competition for her hand, or the oath (Agamemnon assembles the Greek army through conquest).

[62] Such a view was expressed by the casting director, Lucinda Syson (Turner May 2004). According to the IMDb trivia page (which I have not been able to authenticate), 'Wolfgang Petersen originally didn't want Helen to appear in the movie. He felt that an actress couldn't live up to the audience's expectations, but the producers insisted she appear. Petersen went with an unknown actress for the same reason.'

[63] On stars as at once extraordinary and ordinary, see esp. Dyer (1998 and 2004).

[64] For the way Monroe embodied the sexual preoccupations of the 1950s, so that she 'conforms to, and is part of the construction of, what constitutes desirability in women', see Dyer (2004: Ch. 1; the quote is from p. 40). Among those who have played Helen on screen, Elizabeth Taylor in *Doctor Faustus* best exemplifies this kind of use of star-power (directed by Richard Burton and Nevill Coghill, Columbia Pictures 1967). Taylor 'stands for the type "star"—the most expensive, the most beautiful, and the most married and divorced being in the world' (Dyer 1998: 43, summarizing Walker 1966: Ch. 7). Cf. also Wyke (1997: 101–9) and Sobchak (2003: 309–10) on Taylor as Cleopatra.

energy into the role of Helen. Indeed, with hindsight that choice seems irresistible, since she and Pitt were poised to become Hollywood's most glamorous couple.[65] There is, as we saw, an undercurrent in Greek tradition suggesting that Helen's 'true' partner is Achilles. On the screen, however, as in ancient myth, Helen and Achilles were fated to remain apart.

In *Troy*, Achilles is not Helen's male counterpart but her replacement. Despite the lustre of Orlando Bloom's then-emerging idol status among teenage girls,[66] Brad Pitt, with his blazing star power and overwhelming sexual appeal, is clearly the primary erotic focus of this film. In Greek myth, Paris, like Helen, is the favourite of Aphrodite; as such he belongs in the bedroom, as opposed to the battlefield, where Achilles reigns supreme. In *Troy*, however, he is no competition for Achilles even in bed. Both men are womanizers until they meet the 'right' unique love-object, but in Paris's case this is reported sentimentally by his father ('Women have always loved Paris and he's loved them back'), whereas Achilles is presented to our gaze in a nude erotic tableau with two women. As critics realized,[67] it is Achilles who is *Troy's* supreme object of desire, supplanting not just Paris but Helen herself as the truly glorious sex-object in this film. Brad Pitt was at that time 'the most desired male in the world',[68] the only man ever to have been twice (1994 and 2000) named *People Magazine*'s 'sexiest man alive', whose gorgeous physique and celebrity status made him a male Helen for the turn of the twenty-first century.

The first appearance of Achilles is also the first erotic image in the film. We see him initially through the eyes of a nervous child, awestruck by the hero's reputation. Yet he is presented as the naked object of our gaze, asleep, passive, and apparently vulnerable. The departure from the standard Hollywood fetishizing of the naked female is quite striking.[69] But this objectification turns out to be no impediment to vigorous action; in a startling gesture, the sleeping Achilles suddenly grabs the child who has been sent to fetch him. He proceeds directly from this presumably heroic

[65] Her scandalous image at the time would have been an added bonus. She was involved in a high-profile divorce and would soon be accused of 'breaking up' Brad Pitt's marriage to Jennifer Aniston.

[66] Cf. van Beekus (2004: 24), Flynn (2004: 27), and Faraci (May 2004a).

[67] For example, Baine (2004), Burr (2004), and Edelstein (May 2004).

[68] Anonymous (2005). Vanity Fair called him 'the face that launched a thousand tabloids... who's perennially at the top of the world's sexiest-man-alive lists' (Bennetts 2004: 166). Advance publicity for *Troy* made abundant use of the exposure of Pitt's body.

[69] McCarthy (2004) notes that Pitt is 'lavished with elaborate photographic attention' of the kind usually reserved for female stars like Greta Garbo and Marlene Dietrich.

night of sex—with multiple women—to the heroic military conquest of a giant opponent. Throughout the film, his body remains the site of supreme masculine power, displayed, and eroticized, on the battlefield as well as in the bedroom. He finally dies almost like St Sebastian, wearing only a cuirass and short leather skirt, as his magnificent body takes one arrow after another from Paris' bow (not just a single ignominious shot to the ankle).

The disrobing of Helen is treated very differently. She is seen first from Paris' point of view, as she removes her jewellery (apparently unaware of his presence), then facing into the camera in close-up as he fondles her throat from behind (a shot conveying extreme vulnerability). She then unpins her dress before Paris' gaze and embraces him, in her only moment of erotic agency. Both are visible only from the waist up. The spectacle of Kruger's naked breasts pressed against Paris' armoured torso does not inspire awe. Rather, it continues to convey Helen's vulnerability.[70] No further sexual activity is shown (during their putative sex act, the film cuts away to Menelaus' dalliance with a dancing girl). Afterwards, we see the nude Helen from behind, reclining in a pose reminiscent of Velázquez's Rokeby Venus, while Paris looks down at her, now naked from the waist up.[71] They are not seen in bed together again. Instead, erotic attention shifts to Achilles and Briseis.

The substitution of Pitt's body for Kruger's is conveyed cinematically by trumping Kruger's only sex scene, early in the film, with Pitt's first such scene with Briseis. The latter starts with a shot of Achilles' sleeping face, again passive and apparently vulnerable, while Briseis stands over him with a knife at his throat. But once again his passivity is deceptive. He turns out to be well aware of her presence and soon turns the tables, rolling, buck-naked, on top of the fully clothed Briseis and actively initiating sexual intercourse. His naked body is a signifier of active eroticism, rather than a vulnerable object of display.[72] Petersen thus allows Pitt to supplant Kruger not only in charisma, star-power, dramatic and emotional significance, but also as both the subject and object of desire. As in the *Iliad*—though in quite a different way—Helen's centrality to the Trojan War story is usurped by Achilles.

[70] We have Kruger's word for her sense of vulnerability in this scene (Fischer May 2004). The effect was not lost on reviewers (for example, Stanley 2004).

[71] Both Kruger in this scene and Pitt in the scene described below reveal another inch or so of skin in the Director's Cut (2007), but without significantly affecting the contrast that concerns me here. The difference in Pitt's first nude scene is more striking, since the camera angle is changed to provide a fuller view of the two naked women behind him.

[72] Cf. Dyer's discussion of the difference between male and female pin-ups, where the former are distinguished from the latter by hard muscularity and activity (1992).

Like Helen in myth—as opposed to the movie—Achilles is presented as an object of desire to multiple sexual partners. Chief among these is Briseis, whose role as romantic heroine further displaces Helen from the erotic epicentre of the story.[73] Briseis, played by another little-known actor, the Australian Rose Byrne, is a 'feisty' heroine, in obedience to modern romantic conventions and the requirements of feminism lite.[74] Her counterpart in the *Iliad* is in some ways Helen's analogue—a woman at both the margins and the centre of the narrative, whose theft is the catalyst for a catastrophic dispute between men. But her role remains a tiny one.[75] Subsequent accounts, even in antiquity, enhanced her role as a love-interest for Achilles (King 1987: 172–4). Following in this tradition, *Troy* places their relationship centre stage.

Benioff conceived of Briseis as a powerful female presence.[76] As such, she supplants Helen to become the true focus of the pivotal story of abduction, seduction, and passion, serving among other things to make the Greeks, not the Trojans, the 'real' rapists and abductors of women. At the same time she is something of an anti-Helen. She is dark-haired, not blonde, and devoid of royal elegance or rich costume. Her lively manner underlines Helen's passivity and powerlessness. She resists victimization, chooses to return home rather than stay with the man she loves, and explicitly eschews a Helenic role ('I don't want anyone dying for me'). An effect—if not a cause—of this promotion of Briseis is the further erasure of Helen. Helen of Troy herself is no longer the most powerful female character (or the most powerful *as* a character) in the story of the Trojan War.[77]

The relationship between Achilles and Briseis trumps the childish romance between Paris and Helen in both erotic and emotional power. The personal connection between Achilles and Briseis is deeper, their sex scenes more numerous, more sexually explicit, more passionate,[78] and

[73] For the undermining of the Paris/Helen love trope cf. Futrell (2005).

[74] On Briseis as a formulaic 'feisty' heroine, see McGrath (2004: 38).

[75] Her only speech is her lament for Patroclus (19.282–300).

[76] Her character incorporates not only her namesake in Homer—much developed—but elements of the ancient Cassandra, Polyxena, Chryseis, Clytemnestra, and even Athena (see Allen 2007: 156–62; Danek 2007: 80–1). The script asserts that 'despite her torn robes, her noble bearing and authoritative tone command respect'.

[77] *Troy* exceeds even the requirements of the romantic plot in making Helen a passive victim. Wise's treatment is equally romantic, but gives Helen a much more assertive (and 'feisty') role.

[78] Briseis' knife in their first sex scene is a trope for violent, risky, destructive passion. Note too the swelling background music, which is absent from Paris and Helen's sex scene.

more intimate,[79] and their conversations much longer and more substantive. Judged by the standard visual codes of Hollywood, Byrne's Briseis is not stunningly beautiful, yet Achilles sees in her a beauty that shines through dirt, blood, and wounds ('You will never be lovelier than you are right now'). Her beauty is thus marked as 'natural', in contrast to the refinement and elegance of Helen, who never has a hair out of place. Achilles' attraction to his grimy captive also suggests that beauty is in the eye of the beholder. This accords with the romantic principle that there exists just one uniquely well-matched love-object for each human being, in contrast to the Greek assumption that beauty can be objectively measured—an assumption that underpins the very notion of Helen, as we have seen. This trumping of Helen as an ideal standard of beauty, and hence of her supreme erotic power, is a new twist not only in the story of the Trojan War but in the side-lining of Helen within that story.

It might seem surprising that contemporary popular culture—which typically pays at least lip-service to female empowerment—should not only embrace the ancient disempowerment of Helen but find new ways to express it. For the makers of *Troy*, however, as for Greek authors and for Agamemnon in this very movie, such a Helen is 'useful'. A powerful, wilful and transgressive Helen would undermine both the film's romanticism and its political ideology, both of which depend on making her a pretext rather than a cause, a victim rather than an agent, a vulnerable girl rather than an erotically powerful woman. Greek authors, including Homer, react to the threat of Helen by limiting her power, often in the guise of defending her. *Troy* does the same thing in a different way, by casting her as an adolescent everygirl, contrasting her with the feisty Briseis, and displacing her beauty in favour of the star-power and charisma of Brad Pitt's spectacular body. These contemporary modes of trivialization strip Helen of power and danger more effectively than any ancient text. By using her name and story the movie-makers are able to claim their tale as an ancient and (therefore) 'timeless' representation of 'the human thing'; but this prevents them acknowledging that their 'reality' leaves no conceptual or ideological space for the 'real' Greek Helen.

[79] We see them spooning, engaging in pillow-talk, and waking up in the morning with their naked bodies entwined.

Part II

MEDEA

3

Medea's Erotic Text in *Jason and the Argonauts* (1963)

Kirk Ormand

> 'There's a picture opposite me
> of my primitive ancestry
> which stood on rocky shores
> and kept the beaches shipwreck-free.
> Though I respect that a lot
> I'd be fired if that were my job
> After killing Jason off
> and countless screaming Argonauts.'
>
> —They Might Be Giants, 'Birdhouse in Your Soul'

> 'A heroine without a maxim, like a rebel without a cause, is destined to be misunderstood. And she is.'
>
> —Nancy K. Miller, 'Emphasis Added: *Plots and Plausibilities in Women's Fiction*'

In the 1963 movie version of *Jason and the Argonauts*, produced by Harry Schneer, directed by Don Chaffey, and written by Beverley Cross and Jan Read,[1] Jason meets Medea by saving her from drowning. The Argo has just made it through the Symplegades (a long and tiresome scene), when the sailors see some floating wreckage from an unknown boat, destroyed earlier in the sequence. Jason leaps into the water and, swimming a heroic and manly sidestroke, rescues Medea and brings her on board the ship. Once Medea has recovered, she and Jason gaze searchingly at one another, the camera alternating between them while they exchange information: Medea, we learn, is a priestess of Hecate;

[1] Because this paper deals with issues of gender, and relies on an article dealing with fiction written by women, I should point out that both Cross and Read were men, despite gender-ambiguous first names.

Jason reveals nothing more than his name. The sun is bright, the water sparkles, and light erotic feelings suffuse the scene. Shortly thereafter, however, a fight breaks out between Jason and a curiously prominent villain, Acastus (here the son of the evil king Pelias), who wounds Jason. On the following day, Jason and Medea retire to land, where Medea uses the root of Prometheus to magically cure the fairly minimal scratch on Jason's arm. Finally, Medea tells Jason how to reach Colchis: 'Follow the road to the east.' Jason asks, 'You're not coming further?' to which Medea replies, 'I go another way.' She turns and walks away, barefoot; the screen fades in an abrupt cut to the next scene.

'I go another way.' Indeed, in this movie, Medea seems to go 'another way' all the time. The movie, which is largely driven by the special effects created by the master of stop-action animation Ray Harryhausen, takes numerous liberties with the plot of Apollonius' well-known epic. I am not concerned to list and categorize them all; nor do I want to grant artistic primacy to Apollonius' version, which is itself replete with intertextual references to Homer, Pindar, Euripides, and to the epic tradition generally.[2] In any case, it is almost impossible to imagine how an epic movie could have been made in 1963 about Jason, if it tried to stay true to Apollonius' depiction of the oddly passive, frequently unimpressive project-manager of the Argonauts.[3] Instead, I intend to focus particularly on the greatly diminished role of Medea in this blockbuster film. In so doing, I do not intend merely to note that Apollonius' leading female character is considerably stronger, more active, and less of a dancing girl than Chaffey's (though all of that is certainly true). Rather, I want to look at some of the rifts and discontinuities in the text that the movie creates by transforming Medea into a passive erotic object without clear motivation. In particular, these discontinuities point to another narrative that lurks in the movie—a suppressed narrative of Medea's experience and deadly potential. 'Another way', as it were.

The movie produces these moments of discontinuity at particular moments of interaction with the text of Apollonius. That is, in several

[2] See, for example, Hunter (1993a) *passim*; Pavlock (1990: 61–7) is particularly strong on the ways that the character of Medea takes on the characteristics of an epic hero. Clack (1973) shows how Apollonius transforms similes from a Homeric model and systematically changes their context and meaning. Paul (2013: 93–132) discusses the ways that the *Argonautica* myth was used to challenge and push the boundaries of the epic genre in antiquity. I am grateful to Prof. Paul for allowing me to read a draft of her work prior to publication.

[3] Jason's characteristics as a hero have been extensively studied. Lawall (1966) defined the terms of the debate for the following several decades. For a more sympathetic view, see Clauss (1993: Ch. 1). Hunter (1993a: 11–17) points out that Jason is portrayed in ways that recall the transitional status of an ephebe, and notes the often remarked contrast between *amechanos* Jason and his predecessor, *polymechanos* Odysseus. Paul (2013: Ch.3) briefly discusses his 'inferior brand of heroism' as a deliberate questioning of the idea of an epic hero.

places the movie takes a scene in Apollonius' *Argonautica* in which Medea shows particular agency or *ambition*, and renders her instead a passive erotic object. Because the movie does not provide the motivation for these erotic texts, however (as Apollonius so famously does), the resulting romance evokes surprise and even laughter from the audience. In other words, the moments of heightened implausibility in *Jason and the Argonauts* can be read as nodes of particular stress in the intertext of movie and Hellenistic epic.

In producing this analysis, I am relying on the articulation of the 'ambitious' and 'erotic' texts that was made by feminist critic Nancy K. Miller in an important article nearly thirty years ago.[4] In her reading of the then-contemporary criticism of early women novelists, Miller argued that critics were operating under a masculinist paradigm that requires male protagonists to be ambitious, and female protagonists to see themselves as erotic objects. This clear gender split is not arbitrary, but represents a set of social expectations that we see clearly articulated in Sigmund Freud's interpretation of men's and women's daydreams.[5] Men, Freud explains, tend to have daydreams in which they are invulnerable heroes, and in which they accomplish whatever they want in the competitive worlds of business and adventure; in which, in other words, the usual impediments of the real world are easily overcome. This sort of ambitious daydream, Freud goes on to posit, also explains the structure of most heroic fiction. In Miller's paraphrase, 'The hero in this literature is continually exposed to danger, but we follow his perilous adventures with a sense of security, because we know that at each turn he will triumph.'[6] In this way, for male readers anyway, heroic fiction allows an easy identification with the protagonist by mirroring the reader's ambitious daydreams.

Women, however, are not thought to engage in the same kind of productive fantasy; in Freud's analysis, they see themselves, rather, in the curiously passive fantasy of the erotic:

> The impelling wishes vary according to the sex, character and circumstances of the creator; they may easily be divided, however, into two principal groups. Either they are ambitious wishes, serving to exalt the person creating them, or they are erotic. In young women erotic wishes

[4] Miller (1981).

[5] Miller relies on Freud's 1908 essay, 'The Relation of the Poet to Daydreaming'. My quotations of Freud come from Miller's citations.

[6] Miller (1981: 40). While we need not accept Freud's essentialist reading of the characteristics of men and women, his observations about the structure of most heroic fiction remain useful.

> dominate the phantasies almost exclusively, for their ambition is generally comprised in their erotic longings; in young men egoistic and ambitious wishes assert themselves plainly enough alongside their erotic desires.[7]

The crucial question that Miller asks, however, is how the relationship between fantasy and reality works in the case of women and their erotic texts. That is, if men dream of being impenetrable superheroes—say, of having the ability to yoke fire-breathing bulls and use them to plough a four-fold field—because the world normally prevents them from such accomplishment, what is the real-world frustration of desire that causes women to fantasize about being sexually objectified? Why do their 'ambitions' take that peculiar form? Indeed, Miller suggests, the 'implausibility' of much of women's fiction stems exactly from a refusal to accept this economy of desire.[8]

There is, moreover, a curious asymmetry in this bicameral division of dreams and fictional plots: while women's 'ambition is generally comprised in their erotic longings', which is to say that they have no ambition other than to be desired, men's ambitions exist easily 'alongside their erotic desires'. For them the erotic is at worst a distraction, at best, simply another ambitious conquest. And yet, female erotic desire also provides an important prop for male ambition. As Freud notes just a little later, 'in the greater number of ambitious daydreams... we can discover a woman in some corner, for whom the dreamer performs all his heroic deeds and at whose feet all his triumphs are to be laid.'[9] The male ambitious text relies on but simultaneously remains outside the bonds of female erotic desire. This model, as we will see, holds up remarkably well as an analysis of Jason in Apollonius' epic: from his point of view, to the extent that we are able to see it, Jason gets the fleece *and* the girl. Medea is a more complex character: she does exhibit erotic desires that render her a passive object, but as various critics have noted, she also demonstrates a dangerously masculine heroism—what I would call ambition. The 1963 movie, in transforming this epic-cum-romance into a typical heroic

[7] Freud (1908: 47–8), quoted in Miller (1981: 40).

[8] I should make it clear that my analysis is of a fundamentally different set of texts, and of different causes, than Miller's. Miller is concerned with the ways that works by early women novelists reject the masculinist paradigm of the erotic text, and in so doing are critiqued as 'implausible' by contemporary critics. *Jason and the Argonauts* was written and produced by men (as was Apollonius' *Argonautica*) and the implausibilities that I find in it are not, therefore, the result of a deliberately feminine mode of writing. Nonetheless, these implausibilities come to the fore when we look at the way that the movie manipulates the ambitious and erotic texts of its Hellenistic predecessor. The terms of Miller's critique, therefore, are useful for elucidating these moments of intertextual tension.

[9] Freud (1908: 48), quoted by Miller (1981: 40).

action story, flattens Medea's motivation and her character. But in the process, points of stress appear, and her ambition leaks out through the incongruities of her romance; Medea goes 'another way' in the intertext.

AMBITIOUS AND EROTIC IN APOLLONIUS' *ARGONAUTICA*

In order to carefully analyse the ways that the movie *Jason and the Argonauts* manipulates the erotic and ambitious texts of Apollonius' epic, it will be useful to briefly review the depiction of Jason and Medea in the earlier work. The bibliography on these two characters is extensive, and I do not intend here to provide an exhaustive analysis of their functions in the epic. Rather, I wish to highlight the complexity and ambivalence of motivation in Apollonius' text; it is the flattening of this complexity that results in the moments of incongruity in the 1963 film.

As Richard Hunter points out, in Apollonius we have less access to Jason's thoughts than to Medea's.[10] Indeed, the depiction of Medea as a young woman in love in Apollonius has long been held as a significant development in the history of Western literature, however much some critics have been concerned with what they perceive as psychological inconsistency.[11] Nonetheless, it does seem clear that Jason's motivation through most of the epic is an ambitious one: he wants to retrieve the golden fleece and return to Iolcus with it. This is not to say that he has no erotic experiences, but rather that from his perspective, those experiences are subsumed by his ambitious plot. His attraction to Medea (unlike her desire for him) is in the first instance motivated by business, and it remains unclear whether he is more devoted to her or to his beloved fleece.

Indeed, early on in the epic, we learn that *eros* has the potential to derail the quest for the fleece, unless properly managed. When the Argonauts land on the island of Lemnos, and are seduced by the Lemnian women, they dally:

[10] See Hunter (1993a: 15); Papadopoulou (1997: 657).

[11] Scholes and Kellog (1966: 181) give Apollonius considerable credit for his rendering of internal psychology. Phinney (1967) defends the portrait of Medea as psychologically sound against earlier readings such as that of Brooks Otis, who could not reconcile the inexperienced virgin of Book 3 with the cold opportunist of Book 4. See also Hunter (1987) for a defence of Medea's consistency of character. On the romance between Jason and Medea in general, see Beye (1982: 120–42).

Ἀμβολίη δ' εἰς ἦμαρ ἀεὶ ἐξ ἤματος ἦεν
ναυτιλίης. δηρὸν δ' ἂν ἐλίνυον αὖθι μένοντες,
εἰ μὴ ἀολλίσσας ἑτάρους ἀπάνευθε γυναικῶν
Ἡρακλέης τοίοισιν ἐνιπτάζων μετέειπεν·
«Δαιμόνιοι, πάτρης ἐμφύλιον αἷμ' ἀποέργει
ἡμέας, ἦε γάμων ἐπιδευέες ἐνθάδ' ἔβημεν
κεῖθεν, ὀνοσσάμενοι πολιήτιδας, αὖθι δ' ἕαδεν
ναίοντας λιπαρὴν ἄροσιν Λήμνοιο ταμέσθαι;
οὐ μάλ' ἐυκλειεῖς γε σὺν ὀθνείῃσι γυναιξίν
ἐσσόμεθ' ὧδ' ἐπὶ δηρὸν ἐελμένοι, οὐδὲ τὸ κῶας
αὐτόματον δώσει τις ἑλεῖν θεὸς εὐξαμένοισιν».

The sailing was now continually deferred from one day to the next. They would have wasted a great deal of time remaining there, had not Heracles summoned his comrades together, without the women, and reproached them as follows: 'Poor fools, does the shedding of kindred blood prevent us from returning home? Have we left our homes to come here in search of brides, scorning the women of our own cities? Do we want to live here and cut up the rich ploughland of Lemnos? We will not win glory shut up here interminably with foreign women. No god is going to hand over the fleece to us in answer to our prayers; we will have to work for it.' (1.861–71)[12]

This rousing speech motivates the men to leave Lemnos immediately, and to focus on the task at hand. Though Jason has evidently impregnated Hypsipyle, he leaves her with no great emotional display, and little more than instructions for the care of his future son; he is the first to re-board the Argo. The quest is set back on track, but more importantly, the conflict between heroic quest and erotic entanglement has been set. Wasting one's time with 'foreign women' is diametrically opposed to achieving his ambition. From here onward, Jason is a bit more careful about how and with whom he tumbles into bed.

The relationship that Jason begins with Medea, moreover, is marked from the beginning as one of ambition as much as desire. *Eros* may enter the story at the beginning of Book 3, but the invocation to the muses at line one tells us that this *eros* is in the service of the hero's quest: *Εἰ δ' ἄγε νῦν Ερατώ, παρ' ἔμ' ἵστασο καί μοι ἔνισπε/ἔνθεν ὅπως ἐς Ἰωλκὸν ἀνήγαγε κῶας/Ἰήσων Μηδείης ὑπ' ἔρωτι·* ('Come now, Erato, stand beside me and relate to me how it was that Jason brought the fleece from Colchis to Iolcus through the power of Medea's love.' 3.1–3) And indeed, it is because Medea falls madly in love with Jason that she aids him in the task of yoking her father's bulls and fighting the earth-born

[12] Translations of Apollonius are taken from the fine translation of Hunter in the Oxford World's Classics series (1993b).

men. Not coincidentally, the protection that Medea offers Jason in this famous scene corresponds precisely to the kind of protection that, as Freud suggests, characterizes the ambitious daydream and thus all novels. The hero is placed under the protection of a 'special providence', which convinces him of his own invulnerability: 'It seems to me . . . that this significant mark of invulnerability very clearly betrays His Majesty the Ego, the hero of all daydreams and all novels.'[13] At issue, then, is not only the hero's impenetrability, but his certain and fantastic knowledge of the same—which is exactly what happens to Jason when he anoints himself with Medea's Promethean drug:

. . . δῦ δέ μιν ἀλκή
σμερδαλέη ἄφατός τε καὶ ἄτρομος, αἱ δ' ἑκάτερθεν
χεῖρες ἐπερρώσαντο περὶ σθένεϊ σφριγόωσαι.
ὡς δ' ὅτ' ἀρήιος ἵππος, ἐελδόμενος πολέμοιο,
σκαρθμῷ ἐπιχρεμέθων κρούει πέδον, αὐτὰρ ὕπερθε
κυδιόων ὀρθοῖσιν ἐπ' οὔασιν αὐχέν' ἀείρει—
τοῖος ἄρ' Αἰσονίδης ἐπαγαίετο κάρτεϊ γυίων. . . .

Then Jason sprinkled the drug over himself: a mighty force entered him, inexpressible, without fear, and his two arms moved freely as they swelled with bursting strength. As a war-horse, longing for the fray, paws the ground prancing and neighing, its neck held up proudly and its ears forward, just so did the son of Aison exult in the strength of his limbs. . . . (3.1256–62)

As Miller observes, however, in the case of the masculine subject, '. . . the either/or antinomy, ambitious/erotic, is immediately collapsed to make coexistence possible in masculine fantasies . . .'.[14] And indeed, it seems that Jason sees his erotic encounter as a mode of heroism. As various commentators have noted, when Jason first meets Medea, the scene is written so that it recalls a Homeric epic *aristeia*; in particular, Jason is compared to the star Sirius, just as Diomedes is at the beginning of his *aristeia* in the *Iliad*.[15] Hunter notes, further, that the meeting owes much to the climactic battle of Hector and Achilles in *Iliad* 22.[16] But most important of all are the terms that Jason uses to address Medea. While she is busy melting in erotic desire, Jason is all business:

[13] Freud (1908: 51); cited in Miller (1981: 40). [14] Miller (1981: 40).

[15] See, for example, Beye (1982: 137).

[16] Hunter (1993a: 48). The scene also owes much, of course, to the interaction between Odysseus and Nausikaa in Book 6 of the *Odyssey*, another scene in which a clever older man uses his sex appeal to get material goods. See especially Pavlock (1990: 61–3).

> *. . . μηδέ με τερπνοῖς*
> *φηλώσῃς ἐπέεσσιν, ἐπεὶ τὸ πρῶτον ὑπέστης*
> *αὐτοκασιγνήτῃ μενοεικέα φάρμακα δώσειν . . .*
> *σοὶ δ' ἂν ἐγὼ τείσαιμι χάριν μετόπισθεν ἀρωγῆς*
> *ᾗ θέμις, ὡς ἐπέοικε διάνδιχα ναιετάοντας,*
> *οὔνομα καὶ καλὸν τεύχων κλέος.*

'Do not deceive me with sweet words, now that you have promised your sister to give me the drugs which will provide me with strength . . . In return for your help I shall show my gratitude to you in the future, as is right and appropriate for those who live a long way away, by spreading your name and your glorious repute.' (3.982–92)

Their conversation continues, of course, and eventually we are told that *τὸν δὲ καὶ αὐτὸν ὑπήιε δάκρυσι κούρης/οὖλος ἔρως, τοῖον δὲ παραβλήδην ἔπος ηὔδα·* ('. . . as the young girl wept, deadly love crept over Jason also', 1077–8), but this is the only moment in their exchange in which Jason's emotional state is revealed to the reader—in sharp contrast to the extensive description of Medea's virtual enslavement to desire (see below).[17] Even the terms that Jason offers Medea, namely an increase in her 'name and glorious repute' (*οὔνομα καὶ καλὸν τεύχων κλέος*) are the standard bargaining-chips of epic heroes.

Finally, it is worth noting that in so far as Jason demonstrates something like erotic desire, it seems to be addressed to the fleece as much as to Medea. When, after the speech quoted just above, Medea offers Jason the drug that will make him invincible, she takes it from her breast-band, clearly an erotic reference point. But Jason is more interested in the drug than in her:

> *προπρὸ δ' ἀφειδήσασα θυώδεος ἔξελε μίτρης*
> *φάρμακον· αὐτὰρ ὅγ' αἶψα χεροῖν ὑπέδεκτο γεγηθώς.*
> *καί νύ κέ οἱ καὶ πᾶσαν ἀπὸ στηθέων ἀρύσασα*
> *ψυχὴν ἐγγυάλιξεν ἀγαιομένη χατέοντι·*
> *τοῖος ἀπὸ ξανθοῖο καρήατος Αἰσονίδαο*
> *στράπτεν ἔρως ἡδεῖαν ἀπὸ φλόγα, τῆς δ' ἀμαρυγάς*
> *ὀφθαλμῶν ἥρπαζεν, ἰαίνετο δὲ φρένας εἴσω*
> *τηκομένη, οἷόν τε περὶ ῥοδέῃσιν ἐέρση*
> *τήκεται ἠῴοισιν ἰαινομένη φαέεσσιν.*

Without hesitation she took the drug from her fragrant breast-band, and his hands grasped it quickly and joyfully. She would have drawn off her whole soul from her chest and granted it to him in the thrill of his need for

[17] See Pavlock (1990: 64), 'Jason only very briefly feels erotic passion for Medea (3.1077–8). He is absorbed in the quest for the fleece and the task of returning home to Greece with his crew.'

> her; such was the love which flashed its sweet flame from his fair head and snatched the bright sparkle of her eyes. Her senses grew warm and she melted away as the dew of roses fades as it grows warm in the early rays. (3.1013–21)

Medea is the very picture of a young woman overwhelmed by desire, melting away like dew. Though Jason's shining head is grammatically the source of the *eros* that she feels, and that *eros* is said to 'snatch' the 'sparkle of her eyes', he seems to do nothing to evoke this reaction. When we are granted access to Jason's response, it is comparatively simple: Jason feels joy at the receipt of Medea's drug.

Similarly, when Medea does eventually help Jason obtain the golden fleece, he responds as erotically as anywhere in the epic—but his desire is directed towards the fleece.

> ὡς δὲ σεληναίης διχομήνιδα παρθένος αἴγλην
> ὑψόθεν ἐξανέχουσαν ὑπωροφίου θαλάμοιο
> λεπταλέῳ ἑανῷ ὑποΐσχεται, ἐν δέ οἱ ἦτορ
> χαίρει δερκομένης καλὸν σέλας—ὣς τότ' Ἰήσων
> γηθόσυνος μέγα κῶας ἑαῖς ἀναείρετο χερσίν,
> καί οἱ ἐπὶ ξανθῇσι παρηίσιν ἠδὲ μετώπῳ
> μαρμαρυγῇ ληνέων φλογὶ εἴκελον ἷζεν ἔρευθος.

> As when a young girl catches in her fine dress the gleam of the full moon hanging high over her bedroom under the roof, and her heart is delighted at the sight of the lovely radiance; just so then did Jason rejoice as he lifted the great fleece in his hands, and over his fair cheeks and forehead the sparkle of the wool threw a blush like flame. (4.167–73)

This is a remarkable simile. Not only is Jason implicitly feminized by the comparison; he also becomes a young, marriageable girl, much like the Medea of Book 3. His responses and reactions are explicitly those of the erotic text: he not only takes pleasure in his new possession, but also revels in himself as erotic object, in the desire that his appearance must evoke. As Hunter points out, moreover, the 'rejoicing' that Jason does here should be linked in our minds to his earlier 'rejoicing' when he received the drug from Medea (3.1014).[18] Even the red blush that spreads across his face is linked through the colour-word *ereuthos* to other erotically charged scenes in the epic.[19] For Jason, the erotic *is* ambitious, is either complementary to, or in some cases an element of, his heroic quest. As Hunter comments, 'Jason's motivating impulse—so different

[18] Hunter (1987: 132).

[19] See especially Pavlock (1990: 29–31).

from Medea's—is the need to complete the tasks imposed upon him by Pelias and Aeëtes and the desire to get home.'[20]

In the gendered world of the epic, Medea is obviously and famously motivated by erotic desire, though this motivation becomes complicated in Book 4 by a complementary, or perhaps competing, fear of her irrational father. In Book 3, however, she is ensnared deliberately with *eros*, through the machinations of the goddesses Hera and Athena. The resulting descriptions of her emotional state are among the most celebrated passages in the epic, particularly so for their apparent depiction of her inner psyche.[21] I would like to point out, in particular, that her character evokes exactly the idea that Freud puts forward about women's erotic fantasies: that is, what Medea finds especially attractive, indeed overwhelming, is to be in a position of being needed by the hero. In the passage discussed above (3.1014–21), which provides such a striking description of the transporting force of Medea's erotic desire, one phrase in particular leaps off the page: 'She would have drawn off her whole soul from her chest and granted it to him *in the thrill of his need for her*' (3.1015–16, emphasis mine). The Greek is, if anything, even more explicit than Hunter's fine rendering; a more literal translation is 'And then, drawing her whole soul from her breast she would have betrothed it to him, taking delight in him as he had need.'[22] It is not merely that Medea finds Jason striking and handsome—though she clearly does find him so—she also delights in the position of being *needed* (even if not necessarily erotically) by him.

Moreover, Medea is depicted as being willing, at least on a subconscious level, to believe that she, and not the fleece, is the real object of Jason's quest. After Medea has seen Jason, and been struck with the arrow of Eros, but before she has met with him, Medea has a remarkable dream:

> *Κούρην δ' ἐξ ἀχέων ἀδινὸς κατελώφεεν ὕπνος*
> *λέκτρῳ ἀνακλινθεῖσαν. ἄφαρ δέ μιν ἠπεροπῆες,*
> *οἷά τ' ἀκηχεμένην, ὀλοοὶ ἐρέθεσκον ὄνειροι·*
> *τὸν ξεῖνον δ' ἐδόκησεν ὑφεστάμεναι τὸν ἄεθλον*
> *οὔτι μάλ' ὁρμαίνοντα δέρος κριοῖο κομίσσαι,*

[20] Hunter (1993a: 62).

[21] Papadopoulou (1997) is particularly strong on the way that Apollonius manipulates Medea's self-presentation through 'interior monologues' in order to make her character more sympathetic to the reader. Beye (1982) sees her as more deliberately manipulative.

[22] The word I have translated 'would have betrothed' (*eggualizô*) literally means 'to place in another's hand' and clearly evokes the *egguê*, or 'betrothal' that preceded legal marriages in the Greek world. Even this unspoken wish, then, contains suggestions of the marriage that Medea desires.

οὐδέ τι τοῖο ἕκητι μετὰ πτόλιν Αἰήταο
ἐλθέμεν, ὄφρα δέ μιν σφέτερον δόμον εἰσαγάγοιτο
κουριδίην παράκοιτιν. ὀίετο δ' ἀμφὶ βόεσσιν
αὐτὴ ἀεθλεύουσα μάλ' εὐμαρέως πονέεσθαι·
σφωιτέρους δὲ τοκῆας ὑποσχεσίης ἀθερίζειν,
οὕνεκεν οὐ κούρῃ ζεῦξαι βόας ἀλλά οἱ αὐτῷ
προύθεσαν· ἐκ δ' ἄρα τοῦ νεῖκος πέλεν ἀμφήριστον
πατρί τε καὶ ξείνοις· αὐτῇ δ' ἐπιέτρεπον ἄμφω
τὼς ἔμεν ὥς κεν ἑῇσι μετὰ φρεσὶν ἰθύσειεν·
ἡ δ' ἄφνω τὸν ξεῖνον, ἀφειδήσασα τοκήων,
εἵλετο·

At once she was disturbed by deadly dreams, deceitful ones such as visit someone in distress. She imagined that the stranger undertook the challenge, not at all because he wanted to recover the fleece—it was not for that that he had come to Aietes' city—but to take her back to his own home as his properly wedded wife. In her dream she herself easily accomplished the challenge of the bulls, but her parents scorned their promise because they had challenged him, not their daughter, to yoke the bulls. From this arose a bitter dispute between her father and the strangers, and both allowed her to choose whatever outcome her mind desired. Without thought of her parents she immediately chose the stranger. (3.616–31)

As Papadopoulou points out, the dream is a clear expression of Medea's own wishes; the end of the narrative, in fact, has Medea in the position of being able to accomplish whatever she wishes, and she chooses Jason.[23] Even here, however, this wish is first expressed in the idea not that Medea would choose Jason, but that *he* has really come to Colchis to obtain *her*. Again, the fundamental form of female erotic desire is the wish to be desired. We should also note that the narrator specifically marks this dream as deceitful. To the extent that Medea thinks she is Jason's real object, at least from the narrator's perspective, she has missed the point.

At the same time, Medea's dream reveals another aspect of her motivation, one which troubles the neat dichotomy of erotic/ambitious. Medea, as readers of Book 4 have long noted, appears at times to have heroic ambitions and abilities of her own.[24] So, in her dream, she imagines herself being given the power to choose between parents and potential husband because she herself has completed the explicitly heroic task of yoking her father's fire-breathing bulls. Through her pharmacological magic, moreover, Medea plays an integral role in the fulfilment of

[23] See Papadopoulou (1997: 663).

[24] See, for example, Pavlock (1990: 67), Phinney (1967: 335, 339), Hunter (1993a: 59–61), Beye (1982: 135).

Jason's quest: she enchants the dragon that guards the golden fleece, keeping him asleep until Jason gives the word to go. In Book 4, towards the end of the epic, she again enchants the monster Talos, allowing the Argo to return home. Her active abilities are fully necessary for the successful fulfilment of Jason's ambition.

Medea's heroic side comes out most completely in Book 4, which is curiously short of descriptions of her erotic feelings.[25] As the Argonauts flee from Aeëtes and the Colchians, Medea becomes, briefly, an object of trade once again. Threatened by the Colchians, the Argonauts agree to entrust Medea to Artemis (a proper goddess for overseeing an unmarried girl) until a judge can decide to whom she belongs. Medea responds to this suggestion with a forceful speech recalling Medea's bitter reproach to Jason in Eurpides' *Medea* (492–519). She addresses him as an equal, reminding him of his responsibility to uphold his oaths and agreements.

That in itself is masculine enough; but Medea goes further. Jason tells her (truthfully or not, it is impossible to tell) that all of this is only a trick, by which the Argonauts plan to kill Medea's brother, Apsyrtus. Medea responds with chilling efficiency:

> *«τύνη μὲν κατὰ μῶλον ἀλέξεο δούρατα Κόλχων,*
> *αὐτὰρ ἐγὼ κεῖνόν γε τεὰς ἐς χεῖρας ἱκέσθαι*
> *μειλίξω· σὺ δέ μιν φαιδροῖς ἀγαπάζεο δώροις,*
> *εἴ κέν πως †κήρυκας ἀπερχομένους πεπίθοιμι†*
> *οἰόθεν οἶον ἐμοῖσι συναρθμῆσαι ἐπέεσσιν. . . .»*
> *Ὣς τώγε ξυμβάντε μέγαν δόλον ἠρτύναντο*
> *Ἀψύρτῳ. . . .*

> 'Your task is to ward off the Colchian spears in battle, but I shall cajole that man into coming into your hands. Soften him with splendid gifts, in the hope that I can persuade the heralds when they depart to make him come quite alone to hear what I have to say. . . .' So the two of them reached an agreement and prepared a terrible deceit against Apsyrtus. . . . (4.414–21)

Medea becomes a full partner in Jason's treacherous killing of her own brother; and in the event, her guilt is physically marked, as Apsyrtus stains Medea's veil and robe with his own blood as he dies. Though Medea cannot be said here to have a heroic quest that is the equivalent of Jason's, it is clear that she has moved beyond a purely erotic text. She

[25] Phinney (1967) sees Medea as a psychologically consistent character, motivated both by her love for Jason and her fear of her father. He grants, however, that the former is ascendant in Book 3, and the latter in Book 4.

refuses to be an object of commerce, a chit to be traded between powerful men, taking instead an active role in the pursuit of her relationship with Jason and positioning herself as his heroic partner.

Apollonius' epic, then, manipulates the ambitious and erotic texts of heroic fiction in ways that go beyond Freud's formulations. Jason's text is almost entirely ambitious, even when it comes to his love affair with Medea. At critical moments, however, his attraction to the object of his ambition becomes almost erotic, and for a brief moment, he becomes an eroticized subject, rejoicing in the play of light on his clothing. Medea goes still further; though she regularly interprets Jason's narrative in terms of an erotic text in which she is the highly prized object of his desire, she also steps out of this role, demonstrating abilities and ambitions of her own.

ABSENT AMBITION AND SUPPRESSED *EROS* IN *JASON AND THE ARGONAUTS*

Unlike the recent DVD and video re-release covers for the 1963 production of *Jason and the Argonauts*, most versions of the original poster for the movie do not depict Medea at all.[26] This is fitting, for one of the most remarkable aspects of the script is the diminished role that it gives to Medea in comparison to the ancient epic, particularly in terms of the ambitious plot pursued by Jason (played in the movie with bland stock heroism by Todd Armstrong). The character of Medea (played by Nancy Kovack) *does* almost nothing: she performs only two trivial acts of magic/pharmacology, she does not help Jason in his battle with the earth-born, does not help defeat the dragon as he grabs the fleece, is not present when he defeats Talos, and makes no mention of brothers or sisters, let alone taking part in the sacrifice of Apsyrtus.[27] No hint is given of the post-quest story familiar to us from Euripides' *Medea*.[28]

None of this is terribly surprising. *Jason and the Argonauts* was released in 1963, before the feminist movement gained full force in

[26] The recent video and DVD covers appear to have been taken from one of a set of eight 'lobby cards' that were produced at the time of the movie premier.

[27] Solomon (2001a: 113) suggests that Medea is played 'as a helpless, large-breasted, dancing Kewpie doll'. This is too harsh, and misses the hidden narrative that Medea creates for herself in this film; but the sentiment is not entirely off base.

[28] Paul (2013: 99) suggests that the mark of the cinematic Argonauticas is that they '. . . reject tragedy's incursion into their territory'. While I largely agree with this assessment, I believe that there are moments in the movie that invite an audience familiar with the myth to recall the tragedy that awaits the hero.

mainstream American culture. It is clear that the producers of the movie viewed it as a heroic feature, and it would hardly have done to represent the hero as entirely dependent on the woman he falls in love with. Nonetheless, the screenwriters clearly knew the tradition that they were working with, and in a few places Medea's agency is present, but diminished. One of the most remarkable of these instances is the scene described at the beginning of this paper. Jason has been wounded; the following day, Medea treats his wound with a local flower, and before our eyes the scratch (and it really is little more than a scratch) on Jason's shoulder disappears. A benign eroticism suffuses the scene, and we take it as an early moment in Jason and Medea's courtship.

It might seem too much to associate this scene with the drug that, in Apollonius, Medea gives Jason in order to make him invincible, were it not for a single detail. Jason asks Medea about the root that has magically cured him, and Medea replies, 'Some say it sprang from the blood of Prometheus.' This can only be a reference to the magic ointment that Medea provides Jason for his task of yoking Aeëtes' bulls in Apollonius, which, Medea tells us 'men say is called "the drug of Prometheus"' (3.846). The diminution of Medea's central act of pharmacology in Apollonius is little short of remarkable: no impenetrable shield to protect Jason from the fire-breathing bulls, Medea's Promethean magic has all the efficacy of a band-aid. The screenwriters, then, are well aware of the traditional portrayal of Medea, and have chosen deliberately to reduce the heroine's power. At the same time, the scene follows a pattern that I will argue is typical: it replaces a moment of Medea's powerful agency with one of bland, understated eroticism.[29]

Indeed, once nearly all of Medea's acts of pharmacology and aids to Jason have been removed from the plot, there is little for Medea to do in the movie other than to support the hero's vague romantic longings. But the movie is not, primarily, a Romance; the plot is directed fundamentally by Jason's quest for the fleece, and the focus rarely shifts to Medea. Singularly lacking, therefore, are the striking internal monologues that Apollonius' heroine delivers, in which she wrestles with her love for Jason and her devotion to father and fatherland (3.616–44; 3.772–80.). These pages of text in the epic are represented in a single brief scene in the movie, in which Medea prays to Hecate. She laments the fact that Jason is condemned to death and says, 'If I help him now in his quest for the fleece, I shall be a traitor to my country . . . and to you Hecate. And if

[29] Paul (2013: 98) states that 'Medea's narrative function is primarily as Jason's "love interest" (recasting Jason as a lover as much as a hero, as we will see later on), particularly in the 1963 film.'

not…to *myself.*' This is all the verbal access we are given to Medea's internal thoughts or feelings, and the result is that the plot of her romance with Jason, so carefully integral to Jason's success in Apollonius, is read as unnecessary and unmotivated in the movie. Like the heroines of the novels that Miller analyses, she becomes 'implausible'.

Nowhere is this more evident than in the scene in which Medea declares her love for Jason. The scene combines a number of moments from Apollonius, and also contains some densely intertextual dialogue; I analyse it here at a level of detail. In the somewhat contrived plot of the movie, Jason and his men, now resplendent in dress uniforms that have appeared from nowhere, have been imprisoned by Aeëtes. Aeëtes has been misled by Pelias' son Acastus (who turns out not to be dead), believing that they intend to steal the fleece. Medea arrives in the prison. We learn later that she has drugged the guards, or at least her father thinks she has, but we do not see her do so. It is night, and the scene visually recalls Medea's nocturnal, solitary desertion to the Argonauts at the beginning of Apollonius' Book 4.

Medea meets up with Jason, and tries to convince him to leave without the fleece. As in Apollonius, an equivalence is set up between Medea and the fleece as objects of Jason's desire. Here is the dialogue, which must be seen to be believed. Readers not familiar with the movie should imagine every line delivered with wooden deliberation on Jason's part, and languid sultriness on Medea's:

> J: Medea why did you come here? Was it Aeëtes who sent you?
> M: I came here to ask you to give up your quest and sail away with the Argonauts in peace…never to return.
> J: Never to think again of the golden fleece?
> M: Never to think of the fleece.
> J: Then it *was* Aeëtes. (*turning away, angrily*) You tell him I will fulfill the task the gods have sent me…and never betray the Argonauts—whatever he offers me. Even if it's Medea, high priestess of Hecate.

First, we note that Jason immediately and wrongly assumes that Aeëtes has sent Medea, and moreover that she is being offered to him in place of the fleece. Here, then, an equation is made between Jason's potential possession of Medea and the goal of his ambitious quest. But where in Apollonius it was Medea whose dream-state suggested such a substitution, in Cross and Read's version, it is Jason who angrily rejects such a trade. The idea, however, is not without import, for here as in Apollonius Jason reveals that he has a quasi-erotic relationship with the fleece itself. Medea urges Jason to go, and clearly struggles with the last phrase: '…never to return'. She is torn by her desire to save Jason and the thought that doing so means losing him. Jason misses this entirely: 'Never to think again of the golden fleece?' he asks. It is the most passionate thing that Jason has said to Medea so far, and he has the wrong erotic object.

The second half of the dialogue in this scene confirms the presence of the missing Apollonian subtext, and also results in the most implausible moment of Medea's self-expression:

> M: Please ... forget the golden fleece. I fear for your safety. If you're set on carrying it away, I must come with you.
>
> J: I'll go alone.
>
> M: No. I have to go with you. I have no country now. (*languidly closes, then opens her eyes*) And I love you. (*end of dialogue; Jason and Medea turn and leave the prison cell*)

Medea's declaration of love is an unmitigated failure as cinema. In the words of film critic Vadim Rizov, 'A love interest is inserted rather late into the film, to the derisive cheers of the audience....'[30] I have shown this movie to classes in Mythology several times, and can confirm that this scene always draws laughter. The audience simply has not been prepared for the strength of Medea's dedication to Jason. Adding to the sense of unintended comedy is Medea's delivery (spoken by Eva Haddon, who dubbed all of Nancy Kovack's lines in the movie): the words 'and I love you', are spoken in a hesitant, almost singsong voice, with a slight tonal inflection upward on the word 'love'. The declaration is almost, but not quite, a question.

There is more here, however. The logic of the scene is deficient, and this adds to the sense of incongruity. Why must Medea come with Jason *if* he is going to take the fleece? In Apollonius' version, Medea must remain with the Argonauts after this point in the plot specifically because she helps Jason to obtain the fleece, using her pharmacological skills to put the dragon to sleep. Her offer to go with Jason is, in fact, predicated on the idea that she will be useful to him in this way (4.83–91). Not coincidentally, Jason responds to this suggestion with a repetition of his earlier offer of marriage. The movie suppresses this moment of female agency, but retains Medea's conditional guilt. She has, we learn later, apparently drugged the guards in order to help Jason escape—but this is true whether he takes the fleece or not. In brief, then, the incongruity of Medea's erotic text masks another discourse, a lost story line in which Medea's help was neither so unmotivated nor so vague and passive.

[30] Review available at http://www.movie-vault.com/reviews/XMDENdtIMrlCiNLA. (accessed 17 December 2008.)

One further point remains to be made about Medea's declaration of love. In the phrase, 'I have no country now', Medea refers to the betrayal of her father and country that she has enacted by saving Jason. But it is a loaded phrase, and one with clear literary precedent. In Book 4 of Apollonius, when Jason is threatening to return Medea to Aeëtes so that he can escape freely with the fleece, Medea responds angrily:

> *«ποῦ τοι Διὸς Ἱκεσίοιο*
> *ὅρκια, ποῦ δὲ μελιχραὶ ὑποσχεσίαι βεβάασιν;*
> *ᾗς ἐγὼ οὐ κατὰ κόσμον ἀναιδήτῳ ἰότητ*
> *πάτρην τε κλέα τε μεγάρων αὐτούς τε τοκῆας*
> *νοσφισάμην, τά μοι ἦεν ὑπέρτατα, τηλόθι δ' οἴη*
> *λυγρῇσιν κατὰ πόντον ἅμ' ἀλκυόνεσσι φορεῦμαι,*
> *σῶν ἕνεκεν καμάτων, ἵνα μοι σόος ἀμφί τε βουσίν*
> *ἀμφί τε γηγενέεσσιν ἀναπλήσειας ἀέθλους·»*

> 'Where are your oaths by Zeus, protector of suppliants? Where have all the sweet promises gone? It was these which made me abandon my homeland, the reputation of my house, and even my parents, everything which was most important to me! This is not how I should have behaved—from shameless desire! Far from my home I drift alone over the sea with the gloomy halcyons, all because of your sufferings, because I wanted you in safety to complete the tasks of the bulls and the Earth-born.' (4.358–65)

This passage is itself loaded with literary history, recalling in several places Medea's speech to Jason in Euripides' *Medea* 502–19. The movie, however, has taken this moment of self-imposed exile and moved it. No longer an expression of Medea's anger at the way that Jason has repaid her services, it is simply absorbed into her expression of Medea's erotic desire. Ambition and agency becomes a passive eroticism on the part of the heroine.

In the scene immediately following, this phenomenon returns again. Jason and Medea arrive at the darkened grove where the dragon hides the golden fleece. Here the dragon is replaced by a seven-headed Hydra, which again gives Harryhausen an opportunity for virtuoso stop-action animation.[31] This is one of the most celebrated scenes in the movie, and it is certainly Jason's finest moment. He single-handedly fights off the Hydra with sword and shield; but again, the astonishing thing about this scene is what Medea does: nothing. Or rather, not quite nothing. She watches, becoming the 'woman in some corner, for whom the dreamer

[31] Konstantinos Nikoloutsos suggests that this substitution may have been made in order to liken Jason to Hercules, a cinematic hero already familiar to American audiences through many Italian *peplum* films made in the period 1958–65. I am grateful to Prof. Nikoloutsos for this suggestion.

performs all his heroic deeds and at whose feet all his triumphs are to be laid', of Freud's ambitious daydream. Medea's looks of evident concern are skilfully interspliced into scenes of Jason doing battle, directing the gaze and response of the movie's viewers, and fully heroizing Jason.

There is more than concern in Medea's looks, however. As Jason battles on with the Hydra, Medea's facial expressions become increasingly eroticized. The pupils of her eyes are dilated, her breathing is shallow as if excited. As the fight goes on, and Jason appears to be in peril, her mouth opens slightly. At one point, shortly before Jason stabs the Hydra in the trunk (apparently enough to kill this version of the monster) we see a close-up of Medea's face, lips parted, and she slowly closes, then opens her eyes. (Fig. 3.1) It all looks surprisingly like a scene of sexual excitement, and this is exactly the point. Here, as every reader of Apollonius knows, is Medea's single greatest moment: she enchants the dragon and thus allows Jason to obtain the fleece and complete his quest. The movie, denying that agency, compensates by presenting an unstated, barely suppressed moment of erotic intercourse. As Miller comments, discussing the apparent arbitrariness of some women's fiction, '... the refusal of the demands of one economy may mask the inscription of another'.[32] Medea's ambition has become a fully erotic text, in which she is the eroticized object of the audience's gaze; we watch her watching the heroic Jason in a state of sexual excitement.

Figure 3.1 Close-up of Medea as she watches Jason battle the Hydra in *Jason and the Argonauts*, dir. Don Chaffey.

[32] Miller (1981: 38).

I began this paper with a description of the final moments of Medea and Jason's first encounter in this movie. Medea tells Jason to take the road to the East to get to Colchis, but that she 'goes another way'. Immediately after this statement, Medea turns, and walks away; the screen fades, and we see her again in the next moment, in Colchis, heavily made up, lavishly dressed, the leader of an exoticized and ecstatic dance at the temple of Hecate. No explanation is given for her alternate route home, evidently faster than the one used by Jason, who arrives as a witness to the Hecate-ritual. Jason watches the dance and moment of religious ecstasy from behind an unnamed Colchian, aligning himself with the movie's audience as a voyeur; with him, our gaze is on Medea as a provocative, vaguely orientalized dancer. Even Jason appears thoroughly mystified by the discontinuity of the narrative.

In the scene that follows, that discontinuity marks the presence of Medea's text, a text of which Jason is dangerously unaware. After Medea finishes her dance, she puts on a ceremonial robe, a throne is brought out for King Aeëtes, trumpets play, and the royal court is in session. The first action of the court is that Medea pronounces a prophecy, which she suggests she gleaned from her ecstatic communion with Hecate: 'There will be one among us today, from the ends of the world. His name is Jason; any man of whom he asks his way, shall say this: "Aeëtes, King of Colchis, awaits him in the temple of Hecate." And that is all any man shall say to him.' As a prophecy, this is somewhat confusing. We know, with Jason, that Medea knows about Jason because she has already met him; for the Colchians, however, Medea's knowledge is presented as god-given.

At this moment, Jason presents himself, stepping out from behind the crowd. Aeëtes welcomes him, and tells him that his 'heroism is well-known'. He invites Jason to retrieve his men and return to the palace for a feast that night. At this moment, Jason expresses his confusion: 'Thank you my lord. But I do not understand.' He pauses, exchanging glances with Medea, who keeps her head directed straight ahead, glancing only with her eyes. Jason finally turns his head slightly, and says 'Medea....' Medea cuts him off, with a firm, 'Welcome...to Colchis.' This interchange takes only seconds on the screen; I have described it at some length because it demonstrates again the incongruity of Medea's relationship with Jason. Jason is confused, and how could he not be? He left a fairly normal Medea this morning, only to meet her as exotic priestess of Hecate this afternoon. He tries to talk to her; she pretends not to know him, and cuts him off.

What the scene shows is that there is another story here, a story that Jason, intent on his quest, is not aware of and nearly destroys. In

Apollonius' version, when Medea goes out with her attendants to meet Jason, she must pretend that it is an accident: Ὦ *φίλαι, ἦ μέγα δή τι παρήλιτον, οὐδ' ἐνόησα/μὴ ἴμεν ἀλλοδαποῖσι μετ' ἀνδράσιν, οἵ τ' ἐπὶ γαῖαν/ἡμετέρην στρωφῶσιν*.... ('I have made a terrible mistake, dear friends, and I did not realize that I should not go out among the foreign men who roam our land....' 3.891–3) Similarly, here, Medea evidently has reasons for not wanting to declare before her father and the Colchian court that she has already met Jason, in fact has dressed his wound. She must, instead, preserve the appearance of modesty. With this motivation in mind, her 'prophecy' becomes clear: not knowing that Jason is watching, she directs the Colchians to send Jason to her father without engaging in conversation with him ('And that is all any man shall say to him.') Medea is carefully controlling the discourse, so that the brief and unstated romance that we watched earlier is not exposed in public.

But this other story, this erotic text of Medea, is only present through its suppression, not only by Medea herself (as here) but also by the narrative frame of the camera. It is so carefully controlled that Jason nearly gives the game away; and indeed, so carefully controlled that many moviegoers miss it altogether. It presents itself only in moments of discontinuity, and particularly in moments that suppress the heroic agency demonstrated by Medea in the movie's immediate predecessor, the *Argonautica* of Apollonius. It is through these queer moments of apparently unmotivated eroticism that Medea's version of the *Argonautica* comes to the fore; an *Argonautica* that centres around her love for Jason and her abandonment of country to be with him, not around a god-given quest for a golden fleece. There is another narrative here, and it has left its mark, arriving in Colchis before us.

The very end of the movie drags the audience back to Jason's ambitious text, but again the movie seems at odds with tradition and with itself. We are taken to Olympus, the scene of numerous moments of divine machinery during the film, and we watch Zeus conversing with Hera about the film that we have just seen. Zeus says, 'For the moment, let them enjoy a calm sea, a fresh breeze, and each other. The girl is pretty and I was always sentimental. But for Jason, there are other adventures; I have not yet finished with Jason. Let us continue the game, another day.' On the surface, Zeus' words would seem to unequivocally support the ambitious text: Jason has further adventures in store, and Medea—not even named—is just a 'pretty girl' whom he can 'enjoy'. But Zeus, 'for the moment' hints at the transitory nature of this romantic ending. As these words are spoken, we watch Jason and Medea kissing, and some of us know what 'further adventures' Jason has in store. Medea will not be relegated to being an 'adventure'; her ambitious text will find its way out, and Jason's quest will become a tragedy.

4

Pasolini's *Medea*: A Twentieth-Century Tragedy

Susan O. Shapiro

'For me, nothing is natural, not even nature.' Pier Paolo Pasolini[1]

Medea (1969) is the second of Pier Paolo Pasolini's three adaptations of Greek tragedy for film.[2] The second half of the film focuses on Medea's character, but the first half of the film is all about Jason. We see him as a small boy, being raised by the Centaur, and then as a young man of twenty leaving the Centaur's hut to reclaim his father's throne. Finally, we see Jason's uncle Pelias, who had usurped the throne, promise to relinquish it if Jason will sail to Colchis to bring back the Golden Fleece.[3] Only after we have watched Jason grow to maturity does the scene shift to Colchis, Medea's homeland. There we see the Colchians, portrayed as an isolated and primitive culture, steeped in religious ritual (with Medea as high priestess), living a simple but peaceful existence before Jason and the Argonauts arrive to alter their civilization irrevocably. After seducing Medea and stealing the Golden Fleece (the Colchians' only valuable possession), Jason brings Medea back to Greece and lives with her for ten years, only to abandon her when she is no longer useful.

[1] De Giusti (1990: 110).

[2] Pasolini's *Edipo re* (*Oedipus Rex*) was released in 1967. His *Appunti per un'Orestiade Africana* (*Notes for an African Oresteia*) was filmed between March and October of 1969, during the pre- and post-production phases of *Medea*, but was not released in Italy until shortly after Pasolini's untimely death, in November of 1975. The *Medea* was filmed during June and July of 1969 and was released on December 27, 1969.

[3] Although the story of Jason and the Argonauts is not retold in Euripides' *Medea* (on which Pasolini's film is based), it is referenced at the beginning of the play (lines 1–15) and provides crucial background for it. The story was well known in the ancient world; Jason's ship, the Argo, is called 'famous to all' at *Odyssey* 12.70. For a discussion of the legend's early history see Green (1997:21–30). For the history of the Medea myth, see Graf (1997), Giannini (2000), and Isler-Kerényi (2000).

Medea, in a jealous rage, murders their two sons in retaliation for his callous treatment.

Recent scholarship on the film has stressed its anti-colonialist message. Jason is seen as a Western colonial power, while Medea represents an indigenous people, vulnerable to conquest and exploitation, symbolized by the theft of the Fleece. On this view, Medea's murder of her two children represents her revenge against the colonial power.[4] While this interpretation is partly correct (and is, in fact, supported by Pasolini's own analysis), when too narrowly applied, it represents a reductionist view of a complex and multi-layered film.[5] Among other difficulties, a narrowly political interpretation is unable to answer a central question posed by the film: how can Medea be portrayed sympathetically, the victim of Jason's imperialist designs, when she responds to this exploitation by killing her own two sons? Pasolini raises this question by ending the film with a close camera shot of a wild and distracted Medea—clothes askew and eyes raging with madness—in the middle of a raging fire that she herself has set. How can Medea be presented as both innocent victim and vengeful witch?

Ivar Kvistad has recently suggested that Medea's infanticide—in part because it resembles a traditional fertility ritual that she once performed in Colchis—is portrayed as a reasonable response to Jason's exploitation.[6] But such an interpretation is belied by several scenes in the film (including the final one, described above) that depict Medea and her actions in a strongly negative light. In this chapter I will take a different approach, arguing first, that although Medea and the Colchians are shown as victims of Jason's imperialist designs, the portrayal of Medea's character is more nuanced (and more critical) than scholars have generally acknowledged. Second, I will argue that Medea cannot be understood apart from Jason and the Centaur; the relationship between these three characters provides the framework for the film, and no one of them can be understood in isolation from the other two. Finally, I will show how Pasolini's film, informed by some of the most influential ideologies of the twentieth century, remains a powerful reflection of the intellectual crosscurrents of its time. In a review of Kvistad's article, Richard Hardin notes that 'some readers may resist [Kvistad's] yoking of Marx with [Sir James] Frazer',[7] but the unsettling combination of

[4] Bondanella (1983: 279); Greene (1990: 159); Fusillo (1996: 18); Kvistad (2010).

[5] Pasolini discusses the film in anti-colonialist terms in his interview with Jean Duflot (Duflot 1970: 112), discussed below.

[6] Kvistad (2010). Ryan-Scheutz (2007: 73) also suggests that Medea's infanticide can be justified because it is the only way that Medea can preserve her children's innocence and her own 'sacrality and cultural authority' in Jason's corrupt and desacralized world.

[7] Hardin (2011).

these two thinkers belongs to Pasolini himself. Influenced in the making of this film not only by Marx and Frazer, but also by Mircea Eliade, Antonio Gramsci, and other nineteenth and early twentieth-century thinkers, Pasolini synthesized their diverse ideologies into a deeply felt and highly original point of view. Whether Pasolini was able to fully integrate these widely divergent viewpoints may be questioned, but his *Medea* certainly presents a thoughtful and original response to some of the most compelling religious, social, and political problems of the twentieth century.

JASON AND THE CENTAUR

The development of Medea's character and the film's ideological influences can best be understood through a close examination of key scenes from the film. As the *Medea* opens, Jason is a boy of five and the Centaur (who is shown naked with a horse's body from the waist down) attempts to tell him about his family history and his need to reclaim his father's throne one day. The Centaur's recitation of Jason's complex genealogical history is clearly overwhelming for the boy, who seems (at this point in his life) to understand little or none of it. The next scene occurs a few years later, when Jason is thirteen. We see the Centaur, standing outside his thatched-roof hut in a lush natural landscape of grass, trees, and water, teaching Jason about his world:

> All is sacred, all is sacred, all is sacred! There is nothing natural in Nature, my lad, remember that. The day Nature seems natural to you, it means the end, and the beginning of something else. Farewell sky, farewell sea... Doesn't it seem that a small piece of that sky is quite unnatural and possessed by a god?... Wherever your eye roams, a god is hidden. And if by chance he be not there, the signs of his sacred presence are: silence or the smell of grass, or the freshness of cool water. Yes, everything is holy, but holiness is also a malediction. The gods that love, at the same time hate.[8]

The claim that there is nothing natural in nature sounds like a contradiction, but on closer examination we can understand the Centaur's poetic speech. For the Centaur, there is nothing natural in nature because

[8] All quotations from Pasolini's *Medea* are taken from the film (Pasolini 1969), cross-checked with the published transcript (Pasolini 1970: 89–108). In rendering the English translations of the spoken dialogue, I have generally followed the English subtitles, although in a few cases I have made minor alterations.

nature is itself divine, the god made manifest. The gods animate and 'possess' the visible sky and 'lie hidden' behind nature's beauty. But with the words, 'farewell sky, farewell, sea', the Centaur acknowledges that Jason will one day grow up and leave this mythic realm with its intensely lived experience of the natural world. In the rational world of adulthood, the sea and sky are nothing more than they appear to be. And yet this loss of intensity may also bring some stability for Jason. The Centaur's final words hint darkly that the gods of nature can cause sorrow as well as joy.

In his preliminary treatment for the film, titled 'Visions of the *Medea*', and published along with the verbatim transcript,[9] Pasolini inserts another scene at this point: Demeter, 'the Goddess of the Earth', suddenly appears and draws young Jason to her breast.[10] Although this scene does not actually appear in the film (and was probably never shot), it can help us understand the religious concept behind the Centaur's cryptic reference to the gods' destructive impulses. The image of Demeter holding young Jason may be reminiscent of the Christian Madonna, but Demeter is the ancient Greek goddess of grain, who can provide a bountiful harvest but also cause a punishing drought.[11] In this respect Demeter is no different from the other Greek nature deities: Zeus brings fertilizing rain but also destructive lightning, and Poseidon can keep sailors safe at sea but also bring storms upon them.[12] Pasolini's Centaur, while extolling the beauty of a natural world that is 'full of gods', understands that these same gods can also destroy.[13]

In the next scene, Jason is a young man of twenty, and the Centaur, without explanation, now appears fully clothed and in a completely human form. As he sends Jason off to reclaim the throne from his Uncle Pelias, the Centaur foresees that Pelias will send Jason to Colchis to bring back the Golden Fleece, and he tries to prepare him for this journey:

> For ancient man, all myths and rituals are real experiences, which he understands as part of his daily, physical existence. For him, reality is an entity so perfect, that the emotion he experiences, in the stillness of a summer sky, is equal to the most profound, personal experience of modern man... You will go to a distant land across the sea. There you will find a

[9] Pasolini (1970: 25–88). The transcript runs from pages 89–108.

[10] Pasolini (1970: 30). The English translations of Pasolini's notes are my own.

[11] *Homeric Hymn to Demeter* 302–9 and 467–73.

[12] For Poseidon, see for example the *Homeric Hymn to Poseidon* #22, and *Odyssey* 4.499–511 and 5.291–379. For Zeus, see *Odyssey* 5.303–5, 9.109–111 and 9.357–8. For Zeus' use of lightning and thunder, see Hesiod, *Theogony* 687–99 and *Odyssey* 24.539–40.

[13] According to Aristotle (*de Anima* 411a7–8), the pre-Socratic philosopher Thales believed that 'everything is full of gods'.

> world whose use of reason is different from our own. Life there is very realistic... That which man, discovering agriculture, saw in grain... that which he understood from the example of seeds that lose their form beneath the earth to be born again, all this has come to be the final lesson. The Resurrection, my lad. But now that final lesson is no longer valid... All this for you no longer has any meaning, like an old memory that doesn't concern you any more. In fact, there is no God.[14]

The Centaur is trying to give Jason some parting words of advice, but it is not at all clear exactly what he is trying to say. Why has the Centaur changed to a fully human form? Why does he speak (anachronistically) about Christ's resurrection and make a Nietzschean pronouncement about the non-existence of God?[15] And what does ancient man or the discovery of agriculture have to do with Jason's quest? Pasolini's preliminary notes to this scene provide some clues:

> [In Jason's eyes]... the Centaur is [now] a man, a simple man, who has lost his mythical form. This fatal landing in rationality and realism implies a turning away from the Centaur's education for young Jason: from now on he begins to rationalize and to desacralize everything that had originally been given to him as ontological and sacred (cf. the theories of Eliade, etc.).[16]

The Centaur has changed his form for Jason (and for us) because Jason has now turned away from the Centaur's mythic world, where a creature that is half man and half horse can actually exist, and toward a more prosaic, adult world of reason, action and manipulation. Just how much Jason has changed since the Centaur spoke to him of nature's sacredness will soon become clear; at King Pelias' court he smiles seductively at Pelias' many daughters, flaunting his masculinity.

Pasolini's reference in this passage to Eliade's theories is revealing. Pasolini also refers to the religious historian, Mircea Eliade, in a series of interviews with the French journalist, Jean Duflot, published shortly after the *Medea* was released.[17] As several scholars have noted, Eliade's theories—particularly those expressed in the *Myth of the Eternal Return*—had a profound influence on the film.[18] Because Eliade's

[14] Pasolini (1970: 93–4).

[15] 'God is dead. God remains dead. And we have killed him. How shall we comfort ourselves, the murderers of all murderers?' Nietzsche, *The Gay Science* [Kaufman (1974: 181)].

[16] Pasolini (1970: 30–1).

[17] Duflot (1970: 64, 87, and 111). See also Pasolini's review of Eliade's *Myth and Reality*, reprinted in Pasolini (1979: 367–71).

[18] See, for example, Bondanella (1983: 277); Greene (1990: 167); Schwartz (1992: 585); Ieranò (2000: 182); and Kvistad (2010: 236 n39).

religious theories had such a powerful effect on Pasolini, it will prove helpful to briefly outline some of Eliade's most relevant views.

For Eliade, traditional societies (which include the so-called 'primitive' societies of the modern world as well as ancient cultures), share a sacred, religious and mythic worldview, which Eliade sometimes refers to as an 'archaic ontology'.[19] Part of this worldview involves a cyclical concept of time, according to which the world is continually renewed through annual rituals, such as the celebration of the New Year or the rituals surrounding the planting and harvesting of crops.[20] Modern industrialized societies, by contrast, inhabit a profane or 'desacralized' cosmos; they have abandoned symbolic and mythic modes of thought and have embraced a linear, rational, and historical concept of time. Jason, now that he has grown to adulthood, represents this modern worldview in Pasolini's film.[21]

In dividing human consciousness into 'sacred' and 'profane' worldviews, and in assigning those distinct outlooks to 'archaic' or 'primitive', and 'industrialized' societies respectively, Eliade was strongly influenced by Carl G. Jung. Eliade spent more than ten years as a member of Jung's inner circle, and a Jungian sensibility permeates his thinking.[22] In particular, Eliade accepted Jung's view that every individual in a modern society re-enacts the development from a primitive and mythic worldview to a civilized and rational one as he grows from childhood to adulthood.[23] On this view, every modern man, no matter how secular, still carries that mythic worldview within himself, although it has been hidden and repressed. As Pasolini explains in his review of Eliade's *Myth and Reality*: '"archaic people" [are in a sense] ... contemporaneous to us, because it is clear that nothing in us is destroyed and everything coexists'.[24] Thus, although Jason has now become completely rational

[19] E.g. Eliade (1954: 92). Compare Pasolini's description of the Centaur's teachings as 'ontological and sacred' (quoted above).

[20] See, for example, Eliade (1954: 3, 35, 38, 76, 98, and 142) and Eliade (1959: 15–17, 72, *et passim*).

[21] Duflot (1970: 111).

[22] McGuire (1982: 150–2); Wasserstrom (1999: 3–36).

[23] Jung (1933a: 126).

[24] Pasolini (1979: 369–70). In addition to being exposed to Jungian thought through Eliade, Pasolini was also directly influenced by Jung's writings (Mimoso-Ruiz [1996: 260]). See, for example, Pasolini's statement that he chose Maria Callas to play the role of Medea 'because I believe that in the soul of Maria Callas there are the same archetypes of which Jung spoke' (Pasolini: 1975). See also Pasolini's quotation (in Italian) from Jung's essay, 'Relations Between the Ego and the Unconscious', as an epigraph to the collection of poems he wrote while working on the *Medea*: Pasolini (1970: 110). For the quotation in context, see Jung (1971: 78).

and secular and has forgotten the Centaur's teachings (as the Centaur said, for Jason, now, 'there is no God'), the Centaur's words still lie buried, deep within his psyche.

According to Eliade, ancient man saw the natural world as sacred:

> For religious man, nature is never 'only natural'; it is always fraught with religious value. This is easy to understand, for the cosmos is a divine creation; coming from the hands of the gods, the world is impregnated with sacredness.[25]

Thus, for archaic, religious man (as for Pasolini's Centaur), the natural world has reality and meaning because it is a manifestation of the sacred. Eliade also believed that sacred objects or places (such as sanctuaries and temples) can 'acquire a value and thus become real because they participate . . . in a [divine] reality that transcends them'.[26] Certain human actions can also acquire a heightened reality when they repeat or imitate divine actions, such as the creation of the cosmos. According to Eliade, this desire to imitate divine action is the origin of religious ritual.[27] By engaging in such rituals, archaic man re-enacts (and thus re-actualizes) ancient mythic events. The New Year festival, for example, re-enacts the cosmogony, or the 'passage from chaos to cosmos'.[28] By performing these recurring rituals at specified intervals, archaic man continually re-sacralizes and thus renews his life. For him, time is cyclical (measured by recurring events) rather than linear and historical. The world is renewed with each New Year celebration and nature is both physically and spiritually reborn with the coming of spring. These rituals connect archaic man to a transcendent reality and give his life meaning and purpose.[29] This is the primitive and sacred worldview that Jason will encounter when he meets the Colchians. Religious rituals and sacred objects (such as the Golden Fleece) form the centre of their world.

Eliade believed that, with the emergence of Judaism and Christianity, man began to acquire a more rational worldview and a more linear sense of time. Nonetheless, the mystical or miraculous aspects of these historically minded religions (such as Moses' burning bush or Christ's resurrection) can still transport believers into a transcendent and mythic reality.[30] This is the meaning of the Centaur's cryptic reference to the resurrection (quoted above). The miracle of Christ's crucifixion and

[25] Eliade (1959: 116). [26] Eliade (1954: 3–5).

[27] Eliade (1959: 11–16). For the influence of Sir James Frazer and the Cambridge Ritualists on Eliade, see Ackerman (2002: 193). Eliade frequently refers to Frazer's works, e.g. Eliade (1954: 53, 57 n7, 64 n20, 65 n29, 73 n41).

[28] Eliade (1954: 54).

[29] Eliade (1954: 3–5, 27–8); Eliade (1959: 68–9). [30] Eliade (1959: 11–12, 72).

rebirth is a symbolic repetition of the original miracle of the dissolution of the planted seed and its rebirth as a new life. For the completely secular modern man, however, that is, for 'a man who rejects the sacrality of the world, who accepts only a profane existence, divested of all religious presuppositions', for such a man, physical 'space is homogeneous and neutral'; sacred objects, such as 'the Golden Fleece, the Golden Apples, [and] the Herb of Life', have no meaning, and one calendar day is the same as any other.[31]

As noted above, Eliade believed that even the most non-religious men have not fully abandoned the archaic point of view; they have simply repressed it:

> There are, for example, privileged places, qualitatively different from all others—a man's birthplace, or the scenes of his first love... Even for the most frankly nonreligious man, all these places still retain an exceptional, a unique quality; they are the 'holy places' of his private universe, as if it were in such spots that he had received the revelation of a reality *other* than that in which he participates through his ordinary life. This example of crypto-religious behavior on profane man's part is worth noting.[32]

Modern secular man still retains this sense that particular places (as well as certain special objects and events) can acquire a heightened meaning through their participation in a larger-than-life reality, but his understanding of this experience has been lost and the experience itself has been drained of its full significance.[33] In fact, it is modern man's complete rejection of the religious point of view, with its recurring sacred rituals and its cyclical concept of time, and his unequivocal affirmation of linear, desacralized, historical time, that is the chief cause of his 'spiritual problems', i.e., his feelings of anxiety, nihilism, relativism, and existential hopelessness.[34] According to both Eliade and Jung, it is only by reconnecting with this archaic worldview (on a symbolic level), that modern man has any hope of regaining his lost sense of belonging in the world.[35] Thus, while Jason now represents the rational outlook and technological achievements of the modern world, he also represents its spiritual bankruptcy.[36]

[31] Eliade (1959: 22–3); Eliade (1954: 18).
[32] Eliade (1959: 24). The italics are Eliade's.
[33] Eliade (1959: 23); see also Eliade (1954: 21–5, 30, 38–44 and 51–4).
[34] Eliade (1954: 141–59); Eliade (1959: 201–13). See also Jung (1933b).
[35] See, for example, Jung (1933c: 113) and Eliade (1960: 231–45).
[36] Pasolini refers to Jason as an 'emotionless technocrat' in Duflot (1970: 111), discussed below.

THE ARGONAUTS IN COLCHIS

As Jason bids good-bye to the Centaur, the scene suddenly shifts to Colchis, a land of desolate landscapes, people wearing outlandish clothing, and primitive dwellings carved into cone-like rock formations. The scenes in Colchis were filmed in Cappadocia in central Turkey.[37] Cappadocia is known for its spectacular rock pinnacles (caused by the natural erosion of wind and rain into the soft volcanic rock), its rough underground dwellings (possibly dating back to the third century), and for more than seventy Byzantine cave churches (some with painted frescoes), most of which were carved into the rock during the ninth to eleventh centuries.[38] The landscape thus combines exotic natural features with primitive dwellings and sacred structures—the perfect location for Pasolini's archaic Colchians.

As the camera slowly pans across this otherworldly landscape, a gruesome fertility ritual unfolds. To the accompaniment of a monotonous, drone-like chant (no words are spoken, as in an actual ritual), a young man is tied to a cross-like structure, ritually daubed with paint, and then strangled.[39] Although at first the youth seems to relish the attention, he becomes more and more agitated as he begins to realize what is about to happen to him. But his struggles prove useless. After he has been killed, his body is cut to pieces and the Colchians eagerly smear his blood on the leaves of the young plants growing in the field. The youth's heart and other internal organs are distributed among the people, who quickly bury them in the fertile fields. Medea, as high priestess, supervises the ritual and utters the only words of this seemingly endless scene: 'Give life to the seed and be reborn with the seed.'[40] In his preliminary treatment of the film, Pasolini calls for this scene to be filmed 'objectively, as in a documentary',[41] and in fact this segment has the documentary look and feel of an ethnographic film, that is, a film attempting to document the activities of an exotic people, such as Robert Flaherty's *Nanook of the North* (1922) or John Marshall's *The Hunters* (1958).[42]

[37] Schwartz (1992: 554–6); Stack (1969: 173).

[38] Rodley (1985: 1–9); Kostof (1989: 3–50).

[39] Pasolini used an eclectic mix of sacred music from several traditions for the scenes in Colchis. To accompany the sacrificial ritual, he chose a Tibetan chant; Solomon (2001b: 332).

[40] Pasolini (1970: 94).

[41] Pasolini (1970: 31).

[42] For a brief and readable history of ethnographic film that includes a discussion of such thorny issues as accuracy, objectivity, and commercial influences, see Ruby (2000: 1–39).

This sacrifice and fertility ritual is an attempt to recreate on film Sir James Frazer's theory of the primitive vegetation god, whose annual 'death and resurrection' is both 'a dramatic representation of the decay and revival of plant life', and a ritual whose performance ensures that the cycle will continue.[43] The influence of Frazer's theories on Pasolini's *Medea* has been widely recognized.[44] Pasolini himself notes that the film 'rests on a theoretical foundation of the history of religions: M. Eliade, Frazer, Lévy-Brühl; works of modern ethnology and anthropology'.[45] In particular, Frazer's theory that 'in early times' this vegetation god 'was sometimes impersonated by a living man who died a violent death in the character of the god', is vividly portrayed in this scene.[46]

Because the fertility ritual is filmed as if it were a documentary, it looks realistic and thus has a powerful effect on the audience. But Pasolini's ethnographic approach also encourages his viewers to consider the ritual within the context of Colchian society. Anthropologists of the mid-twentieth century insisted that human activity could only be understood in relation to its cultural context. As one anthropologist notes, the principle of 'cultural relativity' means that every human action 'gains its cultural significance by its place in the whole [society] and cannot retain its integrity in a different situation'.[47] Clyde Kluckhohn explains:

> The principle of cultural relativity does not mean that because members of some savage tribe are allowed to behave in a certain way that this fact gives intellectual warrant for such behavior in all groups. Cultural relativity means, on the contrary, that the appropriateness of any positive or negative custom must be evaluated with regard to how this habit fits with other group habits. Having several wives makes sense among herders, not among hunters.[48]

Thus, although the human sacrifice and fertility ritual that we witness in this film is deeply shocking, we understand that it is a sacred, communal ceremony among the Colchians and an important part of their traditional culture.[49] It is qualitatively different from a murder that is

[43] Frazer (1922: 337–9); see also Ackerman (2002: 60–3).

[44] See, for example, MacKinnon (1986: 147); Schwartz (1992: 558); Fusillo (1996: 20); Biancofiore (2007: 88); and Kvistad (2010: 227).

[45] Pasolini in Duflot (1970: 111).

[46] Frazer (1922: 339; see also 353–6).

[47] Heyer (1948: 164). For an earlier articulation of this view, see Boas (1887) in Stocking (1974: 61–2).

[48] Kluckhohn (1949: 41).

[49] Pasolini (1970: 32).

motivated by individual passion or personal vendetta. The Colchians clearly believe that such a sacrifice is necessary to ensure a bountiful harvest and that the victim will participate in the larger cycle of life, that he will—in some sense—be 'reborn with the seed'. The Colchians' deep religiosity is evident, even though their savagery is shocking.

Into this mythic, isolated and pre-rational world, Jason and the Argonauts suddenly descend. Although ancient accounts of Jason and the Argonauts describe the Argo as a magnificent ship whose construction was supervised by Athena herself,[50] Pasolini departs from this heroic tradition; his Argo is nothing more than an oversized raft and his Argonauts are scruffy, rude adolescents, who break into the Colchians' primitive dwellings and take whatever they please.[51] In one scene, the Argonauts force their way into a simple hut belonging to one of the priests. They carry a chest filled with gold coins out of the house, and shove the priest aside when he tries to protest. The money in this chest is clearly the only thing of value that he possesses. As they leave with the chest, Jason tosses a single coin back to the priest, who is now lying in the dust, with the words: 'Take this. Pray for us.'[52] In this, as in all their actions, the Argonauts display a crass, self-centred attitude of privilege and entitlement. Jason's words convey his utter disrespect for the Colchians' religious culture.

As mentioned above, scholars have noted the anti-colonialist message implied in Jason and the Argonauts' disrespectful treatment of the Colchians. The Argonauts' looting of the Colchians' possessions and their imminent theft of the Golden Fleece will eventually lead to the destruction of the Colchians' society and culture, as a chorus of Colchian women foretells.[53] But Pasolini's cultural criticism is even more pointed than has previously been recognized. As the Argonauts are clowning around among themselves, the camera zooms in on two of them, the Dioscuri, twin sons of Zeus. Pasolini describes them as 'two twins with the air of two young criminals; handsome, but barely civilized, like animals'.[54] But *visually*, these two Argonauts look remarkably like the

[50] Apollonius, *Argonautica* 1.109–114. [51] McDonald (1983: 9).

[52] Pasolini (1970: 95).

[53] The female chorus is actually a recording of Balkan women's choral music, with fictitious subtitles purporting to translate the Colchian women's prophetic words; Pasolini (1970: 95); Solomon (2001b: 332). Here, too, the pseudo-documentary style of filmmaking has a powerful effect on the audience.

[54] Pasolini (1970: 40). Several ancient sources mention that Castor and Pollux (the Dioscuri) were members of the Argonauts' expedition (e.g. Apollonius 1.146–50 and Apollodorus 1.9.16).

Figure 4.1 The Dioscuri in *Medea*, dir. Pier Paolo Pasolini.

Beatles (Fig. 4.1). In fact, this is exactly how the Beatles looked in their most recent movie, the *Yellow Submarine*, which had been released in 1968 and had swept the world by storm. By the summer of 1969, when Pasolini's *Medea* was being filmed, music from the *Yellow Submarine* had saturated the air waves in Europe, and the cartoon-like art style made famous by the film—referred to at the time as Yellow Submarine Art—was being used to sell everything from biscuits to typewriters.[55] Conflating the Argonauts on the Argo with the Beatles on the Yellow Submarine is a stunning visual pun, but it also conveys a political message. Just as Jason and the Argonauts represent a modern industrialized power, which, as it colonizes traditional societies also destroys them, so the Beatles represent the cultural imperialism of a mass consumer culture that, because of its economic dominance, destroys whatever indigenous cultures may lie in its path. As Pasolini told Duflot: 'I consider the tyranny of the mass media a form of dictatorship, to which I refuse to make the least concession.'[56]

Pasolini's criticism of a mass media-driven consumer culture owes much to the influence of the Italian political theorist, Antonio Gramsci (1891–1937), and his theory of cultural hegemony. According to Gramsci, a dominant group can exercise indirect control over others by convincing them to accept the values and culture of the dominant group as their own.[57] Writing during the Fascist era, Gramsci was well aware that mass media—such as theatre, films, newspapers, and journals—can magnify and intensify this process.[58] By identifying the

[55] Sloane (1969). [56] Duflot (1970: 58).
[57] Adamson (1980: 170–9). [58] Landy (1994: 18–42).

Argonauts in this scene with the Beatles, Pasolini was criticizing the increasing impoverishment of twentieth-century culture through its acceptance of mass-produced and pre-packaged art forms as a substitute for creative expression.[59]

MEDEA AND JASON

As Jason and the Argonauts are harassing the Colchians on the outskirts of town, Medea, sensing that something is wrong, asks her attendants to help her prepare to pray in the temple.[60] After Medea is dressed in sacred vestments and undergoes a fiery purification ritual, she makes her way to the temple, at the centre of which stands the Golden Fleece. Suspended from a cross-like structure exactly like that on which the sacrificial victim had been hanged, and housed in its own temple, the Golden Fleece is clearly the centre of the Colchians' universe. As Pasolini explains:

> The Tree [on which the Golden Fleece hangs] is the Center, the *axis mundi*, which repeats on a small scale, in Colchis, the archetypal beginning of the foundation of the world... Alone, Medea approaches the place—the Center, the Omphalos—where the Tree of the Golden Fleece is located... Medea seems filled with the spirit of her land—of the gentle sun—of Antiquity... She falls to her knees before the small tree, humble and sublime, on which hangs the Fleece, symbol of the continuity and the absolute value of the human condition: and she prays.[61]

Pasolini's description draws heavily on Eliade's theories. According to Eliade, the creation of the world (i.e., the transformation from chaos to cosmos) took place at the centre of the world (the *axis mundi* or *omphalos*).[62] Archaic man feels the need to live his life in relation to this mythic centre. Thus, whenever the members of a traditional society establish a new city, town, or even a temporary settlement, they construct a symbolic centre (frequently a temple, but sometimes only a sacred tree, pole, or rock), which mythically replicates the original Centre, the meeting place of heaven and earth.[63] This symbolic centre becomes 'the central axis for all future orientation', and gives meaning to their lives by placing them in a direct relationship to the divine.[64] According to

[59] For the influence of Gramsci on Pasolini, see Sillanpoa (1981); Pasolini (1982); Bondanella (1983: 178–80); Greene (1990: 54–8); and Kvistad (2010: 228 and 236 n27).

[60] Pasolini (1970: 95).

[61] Pasolini (1970: 33 and 43–4).

[62] *Axis mundi*: Eliade (1954: 12); (1959: 38); (1960: 60). Navel of the earth: Eliade (1959: 45). *Omphalos*: Eliade (1954: 13); (1959: 47).

[63] Eliade (1954: 10–12); (1959: 32–6).

[64] Eliade (1954: 21).

Eliade, the primary function of a shaman, priest, or priestess is to constantly maintain his or her own communion with this sacred centre and thus facilitate that connection for others.[65]

Up until now, Medea has fulfilled precisely this function for her people, but on this occasion, when she finishes her prayer to the Golden Fleece, she catches sight of Jason lurking about in the temple. Their eyes meet and Jason gives Medea a seductive smile, the same manipulative gesture that he previously made to several of Pelias' daughters. But Jason's idle flirtation has a profound effect on Medea. Transfixed by his gaze,

> Medea tries to rise, to go towards him, to ask who he is . . . but the apparition [of Jason], as suddenly as it had appeared, disappears. An expression of sorrow and profound delusion imprints itself on Medea's face: she tries to search for him, to follow him . . . Instead she falls, suddenly, collapsing onto the earth, deprived of her senses.[66]

As Medea falls hopelessly in love with Jason, she loses her sense of connection to her people, her religion, and to herself.[67]

When Medea wakens from her trance, everything is different. She is no longer imbued with a sense of the holy; she is alienated from her gods and no longer cares about her religious responsibilities:

> Medea moves, observing around her all the things that had once held for her such a great, profound and vital significance. They do not respond to her glance. They are as if having fallen away into insignificance: they are dead things.[68]

Just as the Centaur had once told Jason: 'In fact, there is no God', the Golden Fleece is now meaningless for Medea, along with its sacrificial ritual and life-giving powers. She gently kicks away a bowl of offerings with her foot.

In her desire to make herself more attractive to Jason, Medea decides to steal the Fleece and present it to him as a gift. But since she is not strong enough to remove the Fleece from its stand, she awakens her younger brother, Apsyrtus. Apsyrtus is 'fascinated with his sister, and, like all adolescents, ready for all things new and adventurous'.[69] Medea easily convinces her brother to help her steal the Fleece; they then flee to

[65] Eliade (1960: 61–6). [66] Pasolini (1970: 45).

[67] In Apollonius' *Argonautica*, the god Eros shoots an arrow into Medea to make her fall hopelessly in love with Jason (3.275–98). In view of the way that Pasolini's Medea suddenly falls to the ground as soon as her eyes meet Jason's, it is tempting to surmise that Pasolini was also thinking of Eros' arrow here.

[68] Pasolini (1970: 45). [69] Pasolini (1970: 47).

Jason in a chariot. As Jason lovingly caresses the Fleece, Medea gazes longingly at Jason. Jason smiles seductively at both brother and sister (this seems to be his trademark *modus operandi*), and soon they are all in the chariot, driving across the barren landscape, racing to get back to the Argo before the Colchians discover their loss.

When the Colchians realize that the Fleece is gone, a wailing arises throughout the city. King Aeëtes and his soldiers organize a mounted posse to retrieve it. Just as the riders are about to catch up with the fleeing chariot, Medea takes an axe and savagely murders her brother. She then hacks up his body and throws the pieces out of the chariot, one by one (beginning with the head). She knows the Colchians will stop to pick up the pieces, allowing her and Jason just enough time to escape. Jason seems shocked by Medea's actions, but he does not protest. As Medea carries out this brutal murder, we hear again the unforgettable chant that had accompanied the Colchians' human sacrifice and fertility ritual. In Medea's deranged and lovesick mind, the authorization to sacrifice a human life as part of a religious ritual could be extended to the sacrifice of her brother's life in the service of her own erotic passion. But Pasolini makes it clear that Medea's actions are an anathema to the people she once called her own. When King Aeëtes and his soldiers see Apsyrtus' head on the sand they are struck with an immeasurable sorrow. A funeral dirge begins to sound as they lovingly collect, first the head and then each successive body part and carefully wrap it in a cloak. After collecting all of Apsyrtus' bloody remains, the Colchians return home, abandoning their pursuit of Medea and the Fleece. When the Queen and the Colchian people see what has happened, their sadness is indescribable. Because Prince Apsyrtus is the only heir to the throne, his death means the end of their kingdom and the destruction of their future. As they mourn collectively, 'tears and cries of sorrow arise from the city'.[70]

Medea, crazed with love and alienated from her society and its gods, is now willing to do anything to help Jason and tie him more closely to her. As Pasolini notes, Medea sees her brother's murder as 'a ritual act out of her religion and this removes the horror (for her) of the murder'.[71] But the murder of Apsyrtus is depicted in the film as a horrendous, unspeakable act that—no less than the theft of the Golden Fleece—spells doom for Colchian society. For this reason, the argument that Medea's later infanticide is condoned in the film because of its connection (in Medea's own mind) to the ritual of human sacrifice must be rejected. Apsyrtus' murder is even more closely associated with the sacrificial ritual than the

[70] Pasolini (1970: 50). [71] Schwartz (1992: 560).

infanticide, and it is depicted in a completely negative light. When Apsyrtus' murder is considered in accordance with the principle of cultural relativity (the idea that every human action receives its meaning from its function in its own society), the point becomes clear: the Colchians' profound communal sorrow at the death of Apsyrtus is proof that Medea's murder of her brother must be condemned.[72] Medea has now become alienated from her society, its religion, and its values; unless she can find a new point of reference to serve as a moral compass, she will continue to become more and more unhinged.

Medea's spiritual crisis is soon made explicit. After a full day at sea, the Argonauts land on a coast not far from Pelias' kingdom.[73] As the Argonauts pitch their tents along the shore, Medea becomes frenzied. She runs through the camp, shouting:

> You are not praying to God to bless your tents! You are not repeating the first act of God! You are not seeking the center, not marking the center! No! Search for a tree, a pole, a rock! Ahh![74]

Medea's exhortation thus embodies Eliade's theories of a sacred centre, the primary orientation point in every new settlement, marked by a sacred tree, pole, or rock that establishes a community's connection to their gods. The Argonauts, however, ignore Medea's cries; they have no understanding of her emotional disorientation and feel no empathy for her distress. Medea wanders off and tries to communicate with the gods that she has unwittingly abandoned:

> Speak to me, earth; let me hear your voice! I no longer remember your voice! Speak to me, sun! Where is the place where I can hear your voice?... Perhaps you are losing your way forever?... Earth, where is your meaning? Where can I find you again? Where is the bond that ties you to the sun? I touch the earth with my feet and do not recognize it.[75]

As Medea undergoes her spiritual crisis, the Argonauts build a campfire and take their evening meal. But when night falls, Jason gently carries Medea to his tent and smiles at her protectively; he lovingly undresses her, and they make love. As Pasolini explains:

> In this moment Jason's virility prevails. Medea... finds in love, suddenly (and in a humanizing way) a substitute for her lost religiosity; in the sensual experience she rediscovers her lost sacred relationship with reality. In this

[72] Kvistad, who has argued most vigorously that Medea's infanticide is given a positive interpretation in the film, does not adequately discuss the murder of Apsyrtus in his essay.

[73] Pasolini (1970: 51 and 96).

[74] Pasolini (1970: 96–7). [75] Pasolini (1970: 97).

way the world, the future, the good, the significance of things, suddenly reconstitute themselves before her.[76]

Medea has now become reconnected to the world through her love for Jason. The problem with her new orientation, however, is that Jason now constitutes Medea's entire world. She has abandoned everything she once considered certain—including her identity as a priestess and her relationship with her gods—and now lives her life for Jason alone.

When Jason arrives in Greece and presents the Fleece to Pelias, the king refuses to give up the throne. He states bluntly: 'Understand that kings are not always obligated to keep their promises.' Jason replies, 'Very well, I understand', (as if this answer was not unexpected), but he mocks Pelias' characterization of the Fleece as 'a symbol of the eternal nature of power and order', adding: 'I will tell you what in my opinion is the truth: this ram's fleece has no significance outside of its own country.'[77] And in fact the Fleece, now lying on the floor, looks no more extraordinary than a handsome rug. Jason's insight is closely connected to the principle of cultural relativity. Just as human actions acquire meaning through their place within society, so the power of a religious symbol lies in its significance to a community of believers. Pasolini's point here is that a cultural artefact has no meaning in itself; when a society is destroyed, its religion and culture die with it.

Because Pelias refuses to relinquish the throne, Jason takes Medea to the city of Corinth. Although they never formally marry, Jason lives with Medea for ten years, and she bears him two sons. Eventually, however, Jason decides to make a politically advantageous marriage to Glauce, the daughter of Creon, King of Corinth. Pasolini explains that Jason's betrayal of Medea represents not only the clash between ancient and modern civilizations, but also the colonization of the pre-industrialized world by modern industrialized powers:

> *Medea* is the confrontation of the archaic universe, which is hieratic and religious, with the world of Jason, which is, on the contrary, rational and pragmatic. Jason is the hero of the present . . . the emotionless 'technocrat' whose search is directed solely toward success . . . [But the story of Medea could] just as well be a history of the people of the Third World, of an African people, for example, who know the same catastrophe of contact with Western, materialistic civilization.[78]

Thus, for Pasolini, Jason and Medea's relationship functions on several symbolic levels. First, there is the confrontation of the archaic and

[76] Pasolini (1970: 54–5). [77] Pasolini (1970: 97). [78] Duflot (1970: 111–12).

religious point of view with the modern and secular one. Medea's religious worldview, with its close relationship to the gods, succumbs to Jason's utilitarian pragmatism and is eventually destroyed by it. Jason, for his part, motivated solely by a desire to advance to a position of power and influence (symbolized first by his quest for the Golden Fleece and then by his marriage to Glauce) feels no qualms about rejecting Medea and her traditional ways once she becomes an impediment to his progress. But Jason's spiritual domination of Medea and his appropriation of her people's wealth also symbolize the colonization of the developing world by the industrialized powers. In this sense, Jason's abandonment of Medea, once he has benefited from her love, symbolizes the politically sanctioned economic plunder that has characterized the colonization process. The cultural dominance that accompanies this economic exploitation, and the more general problem of the commodification of culture, is represented by the brief, visual reference to the Beatles.

But, in addition to the religious, economic, and cultural aspects of the clash of civilizations that Jason and Medea represent, there is also a psychological aspect. The psychological aspect of Jason's relationship to Medea is made clear in a vision that Jason has shortly before the wedding.[79] While standing in Creon's palace, Jason notices the Centaur, whom he has not seen in many years, a short distance away.[80] But as Jason runs up to greet the Centaur he becomes confused: he now sees *two* Centaurs standing before him (Fig. 4.2). One, the 'mythic Centaur', is the half-man half-horse he knew as a child; the other, 'rational Centaur', has the fully human form he saw as a young man of twenty.[81] The rational Centaur informs Jason that both he and the mythic Centaur still exist inside of him. He explains that the mythic Centaur can no longer speak to Jason ('because his logic is so different from ours'), but that he, the rational Centaur, can speak for both of them. The Centaur tells Jason that it is because of the continuing influence of the sacred, mythic Centaur still inside him, that

> despite your calculations and your interpretations—in reality, you love Medea . . . and you understand her spiritual catastrophe . . . the disorientation of an archaic woman in a world that does not believe in any of the things she always believed in.[82]

[79] There is a strong suggestion that this scene, which has a dreamlike quality, is meant to be a dream or vision, rather than an actual event; Pasolini (1970: 62).

[80] The interior scenes of Creon's palace were filmed in the Piazza dei Miracoli, next to the Renaissance cathedral in Pisa; Schwartz (1992: 555).

[81] For the names of the two Centaurs, see Pasolini (1970: 62).

[82] Pasolini: (1970: 62).

Figure 4.2 The Two Centaurs (Laurent Terzieff and Gerard Weiss) in *Medea*, dir. Pier Paolo Pasolini.

Jason, incredulous, asks, 'I love Medea?' And then he demands, 'What purpose does it serve me to know all this?... Why are you telling me this?'[83] But the Centaur is unable to answer such a utilitarian question, and Jason covers his eyes with his hands, blocking the Centaur from view.

In his interview with Duflot, Pasolini explains that Jason sees two Centaurs because, while firmly rooted in the modern world, he still retains the archaic worldview that the mythic Centaur represents:

> In the beginning, when Jason was a child, he saw in the Centaur a mythical animal, full of poetry; then, little by little, with age, the Centaur became rational and a sage; eventually, he became a man just like Jason. In the end, the superimposition of the two Centaurs does not destroy them. They are juxtaposed. The sense that one Centaur has surpassed the other is an illusion. Nothing is lost.[84]

In Pasolini's view, the earlier stages of a person's development are not destroyed when a new level of development is reached; the earlier stages are preserved (at a subconscious level) and continue to influence the personality. So Jason's mythic worldview, with all its meaning and magic, has remained deep within his psyche even as he developed into the modern, rational 'technocrat' who organized the Argonauts' expedition.[85] Jason's imminent marriage to Glauce (and the enhanced political

[83] Duflot (1970: 62–3). [84] Duflot (1970: 112).

[85] Compare Pasolini's view, quoted above, that 'nothing in us is destroyed and everything coexists'.

status that he hopes to achieve) represents his final ascent into the world of rational, scientific, industrialized society. That is the reason why Creon's palace is anachronistically located in the Piazza dei Miracoli, where Galileo is said to have laid the foundation of the modern scientific method by dropping two objects of unequal weight from the Leaning Tower of Pisa in 1589.[86] But because Jason's mythic worldview still continues to influence him, he does love Medea, just as the Centaur had claimed. The Centaur had been trying to warn Jason that, in rejecting Medea, he was also rejecting an essential part of himself; but Jason covered his eyes and walked away, dismissing the Centaur's advice.

CONCLUSION

The results of Jason's decision follow quickly. Medea re-establishes her connection with her ancestral god, who restores her magical powers. Medea then uses these powers to avenge herself for Jason's betrayal. After Glauce and her father have been burned alive, Medea completes her revenge against Jason by killing their two sons. At the end of the film, Jason begs Medea to allow him to caress, one last time, the lifeless bodies of his two young sons. But Medea, eyes blazing (Fig. 4.3), refuses his request, shouting: 'Nothing is possible any more.'[87]

By ending the film with an extended shot of Medea at her most irrational and destructive, Pasolini poses the question of how we are to understand her character: while we sympathize with her plight, her killing of her two sons (as well as her earlier murder of her brother), make her seem like a monster. Pasolini's answer to this conundrum can be found in his remarks on his film, *Appunti per un' Orestiade Africana* (*Notes for an African Oresteia)*, also filmed in 1969:

> Archaic civilization . . . must not be forgotten, despised and betrayed. But it must be integrated within the new civilization.[88]

In Aeschylus' *Oresteia*, the Erinyes (or Furies, ancient female spirits of vengeance) agree to transform themselves into the Eumenides (Kindly

[86] Schwartz (1992: 555). The story, widely considered apocryphal, is thoroughly discussed by Drake (1978: 18–21), who defends its authenticity (413–16). For Galileo's legendary status as the founder of modern science, see Segre (1998).

[87] Pasolini (1970: 108).

[88] On the nearly simultaneous production of these two films, see n 2 above. For the Italian, see De Giusti (1990: 115).

Figure 4.3 Medea (Maria Callas) in *Medea*, dir. Pier Paolo Pasolini.

Ones, protective and benevolent goddesses) through the efforts of Athena, who promises them that their ancient prerogatives will never be forgotten.[89] As Pasolini explains:

> The irrational, represented by the Erinyes, must not be dismissed (which would be impossible) but simply checked and dominated by reason, [by] a productive and fertile passion. Curses [*Maledizioni*] transform themselves into Blessings [*Benedizioni*].[90]

When they are ignored, belittled or betrayed, the ancient and pre-rational powers of vengeance can unleash a terrible destruction on those around them. But if these irrational powers are held in check by an understanding and compassionate reason, their destructive power can be transformed into a positive source of passion and creativity. Medea represents the same pre-rational powers in the *Medea* that the Erinyes represent in Pasolini's *Orestiade Africana*.[91]

In the *Medea*, the relationship between Jason and Medea might have produced such a positive transformation. If Jason had stayed with Medea and had restrained her most violent impulses through his love for her, she might have given 'the emotionless technocrat' some spiritual depth, just as she had tried to provide him with heirs. But Jason chose otherwise. Medea, scorned, betrayed, and unable to restrain herself, unleashes upon Jason the full destructive power of the archaic, irrational forces that she

[89] Aeschylus, *Eumenides* 988–1047.
[90] Schwartz (1992: 550–1). For the Italian, see Pasolini (1960: 3).
[91] Siciliano (1982: 332); Fusillo (1996: 17).

represents. The Centaur had once told Jason that 'holiness is also a malediction [*una maledizione*]'. Archaic curses (*maledizioni*) cannot be changed to blessings (*benedizioni*) without the transformative power of reason. A model for this 'passionate and productive' power is provided by the rational Centaur of Jason's vision, who speaks for the mythic Centaur and expresses the feelings that he inspires.[92] The fruitful harnessing of irrational forces by the constructive power of reason is an excellent metaphor for the creative process; some scholars believe that the Centaur figure is a stand-in for Pasolini himself.[93]

In conclusion, Medea is portrayed as both innocent victim and vengeful witch because she represents both the beneficent powers of nature and fertility and the destructive powers of vengeance and unreason. In Pasolini's view (as in the view of thinkers such as Frazer, Eliade, and Jung), such forces dominate the beliefs of archaic civilizations and also those of African nations, which were (at that time) considered primitive civilizations in the modern world. Thus, Medea not only represents the psychological forces of unreason and an archaic, religious point of view, she also represents the peoples of the pre-industrialized world. Jason, who represents the power of reason, also demonstrates the greedy and selfish actions of the colonial powers. Pasolini's message is that when the colonial powers had the opportunity to guide the underdeveloped nations productively and invest in their growth, they chose instead to expropriate their natural resources and destroy their social structures. While such a view seems naive and paternalistic from a twenty-first century standpoint, it represents a creative synthesis of several strands of progressive twentieth-century thought.[94] My analysis has also shown that Pasolini's Medea cannot be understood apart from Jason and the Centaur. Just as Medea represents the deep-seated power of unchecked emotion, and Jason represents the over-rationalized technocrat who thinks only of material success, the Centaur represents the idealized union of reason and emotion, the harmonious and fruitful relationship that Jason and Medea might have enjoyed.

[92] Pasolini (1970: 62–3). [93] Greene (1990: 159–60).

[94] See Viano (1993: 243) for a critical assessment of Pasolini's own 'cultural imperialism'.

5

Rebel and Martyr: The *Medea* of Lars von Trier[1]

Annette M. Baertschi

Lars von Trier is undoubtedly one of the most acclaimed, if also one of the most controversial film directors and screenwriters of contemporary European cinema. Since his first short film *Nocturne* (1980), he has produced an impressive number of feature films as well as several television series, music videos, and artistic installations, regularly provoking and polarizing his audiences. As one of the founders of Dogme 95, the back-to-basics movement renouncing elaborate special effects,[2] von Trier has restlessly and wilfully challenged cinematic conventions and cemented his reputation as iconoclast and taboo breaker. Moreover, in 1998 he drew headlines by having his production company Zentropa, established in 1992, be the first mainstream film company to produce hardcore pornographic films.[3] Finally, his very publicly staged and unashamedly self-constructed private persona has repeatedly caused irritation, whether he raised eyebrows because of his multiple phobias and eccentricities or alienated the media with his disturbing remarks on nazism while promoting his latest film *Melancholia* (2011) at the Cannes

[1] I would like to thank Konstantinos P. Nikoloutsos as well as the two anonymous OUP referees for their helpful suggestions and valuable advice. Moreover, I am deeply grateful to Mary-Kay Gamel, who encouraged me to contribute this essay to the present collection and generously shared her unpublished work on Lars von Trier's *Medea* with me. My analysis has benefitted greatly from her perceptive observations and comments. Finally, I would like to thank Diane Amoroso-O'Connor for her expert help with image-editing.

[2] On Dogme 95 see, e.g., Bainbridge (2007: 83–101) and Badley (2006: 80–94). See also Hjort and MacKenzie (2003) and Stevenson (2003).

[3] The laws against pornography were abolished in Denmark in 1967, and in 1969 Denmark became the first country in the world to legalize pornographic films and imagery.

film festival, leading to his being banned from the event by the Board of Directors.

At the same time, few viewers and critics would deny that Lars von Trier has created some of the most innovative and powerful films of the past two decades. Anyone who has seen his 1996 melodrama *Breaking the Waves*, his international breakthrough, or the even more harrowing *Dancer in the Dark* (2000), the third part of his 'Gold Heart' trilogy, is unlikely to forget the striking visual imagery and the emotional intensity of these films. Similarly, von Trier's ability to coax outstanding, career-best performances especially from his female protagonists on a regular basis deserves praise, even though his much publicized difficult relationship with actresses Björk and Nicole Kidman during the filming of *Dancer in the Dark* and *Dogville* (2003), respectively, the first part of his yet to be completed 'U-S-A—Land of Opportunities' trilogy, has earned him the additional negative epithet misogynist. It is thus safe to say that Lars von Trier's work has had a profound impact on the landscape of contemporary cinema, and it will be interesting to see which new projects he will—brilliantly, daringly, and provocatively as ever—pursue in the future.

In contrast to his celebrated feature films, which enjoyed wide theatrical release as well as critical and financial success despite all controversy surrounding them, von Trier's TV production *Medea* (1988) was only rarely seen and thus remained largely unknown until it was released on video in 2003. When it was first broadcast, it was poorly received by most critics, although it was awarded the Jean d'Arcy prize (Bourse Jean d'Arcy) for best international TV film in France in 1989. Von Trier himself, who generally is not on good terms with his earlier work with the exception of *Epidemic* (1987), said in an interview that he did not like *Medea* particularly, since he thought it was 'too insubstantial' and had 'too much of a papier-maché feeling'; he admitted, however, being fond of some scenes and also felt that the film contained some 'really stylish images'.[4]

This unfavourable personal assessment was matched by a prolonged period of neglect on the part of classical scholars who were primarily engaged with two other film versions of the Medea story: Pier Paolo Pasolini's *Medea* starring Maria Callas (1969), which fascinated its viewers with its complex synthesis of anthropological ritual, myth, political ideology, and psychoanalysis; and Jules Dassin's modern, programmatically feminist re-interpretation *A Dream of Passion* (1978). It was only after the release of von Trier's *Medea* on video and DVD that the imbalance began to be redressed and the film to be recognized as one of

[4] Björkman (2003: 115, 117).

the most eloquent and compelling adaptations of Euripides' famous play.[5]

This essay will first situate *Medea* within von Trier's cinematographic work and then provide a detailed analysis of the film, focusing especially on its 'theatricality'. I will argue that the setting and the prominent role attributed to nature and its sounds in *Medea* not only recall the conditions of ancient dramatic performances, but also greatly enhance our understanding of the emotional and psychological state of the main character, as von Trier recreates the Euripidean plot as a conflict between the elements. In addition, I will show that he reconfigures Medea both as a protofeminist and, more importantly, as a Christian martyr, thus transforming her story into a universal tale of female oppression and suffering.

MEDEA WITHIN THE CONTEXT OF LARS VON TRIER'S WORK

Although Euripides and Lars von Trier may seem like kindred spirits given both authors' propensity for challenging existing generic conventions and putting women centre stage, von Trier's starting-point was not the ancient tragedian. Rather, his *Medea* is based on the unrealized script of renowned Danish filmmaker Carl Theodor Dreyer (1889–1968), who had won worldwide acclaim with such landmark films as *The Passion of Joan of Arc* (1928), *Vampire—The Dream of Allan Gray* (1932), *Day of Wrath* (1943), *The Word* (1955), and *Gertrud* (1964), securing himself an important place in modern film history. According to von Trier, *Medea* was supposed to be Dreyer's first film in colour.[6] He had written the screenplay in collaboration with Preben Thomsen in the mid-sixties, loosely basing it on Euripides' play, and had reportedly already travelled to Paris in order to meet Maria Callas and offer her the title role,[7] when he suddenly died from pneumonia in spring 1968—just a year before the opera singer played the part of the Greek heroine in Pasolini's film.

[5] See Joseph and Johnson (2008), Forst (2002), Christie (2000), Rubino (2000); see also Stephan (2006), Müller (2000; [2]2002), and Forst (1998).

[6] Berthelius and Narbonne in Lumholdt (2003: 47).

[7] Apparently, the casting of Maria Callas as Medea was Dreyer's idea, although he has never been given credit for this. Drouzy (1986: 250), however, is sceptical about the veracity of this account, since there are no traces of such a plan in Dreyer's correspondence. He, therefore, does not rule out the possibility of the entire anecdote being purely fictitious, even though the choice of Maria Callas seems very natural given her Greek ancestry and,

Von Trier admires Dreyer more than any other film director and has frequently cited his work 'as the source of greatest influence in his approach to cinema'.[8] However, his decision to make a film of the script left by his idol was not entirely voluntary, since when asked by the Danish television theatre department in 1987 to adapt a play, von Trier originally suggested a version of *Romeo and Juliet*. It was only after the newly appointed head of television theatre, Brigitte Price, who had already produced the Euripidean *Medea* for the stage (with Kirsten Olesen, the Medea of Lars von Trier, in the leading role) and intended to transfer it to television using Dreyer's script, that he agreed to realize it himself. For he could not stand the idea of Price 'tampering' with the screenplay of the master of Danish cinema, as he later explained in an interview.[9]

At the beginning of *Medea*, von Trier explicitly pays homage to his illustrious predecessor by inserting two captions reminiscent of silent film practice. They read:

(1) 'This film is based on a script by Carl Th. Dreyer and Preben Thomsen from Euripides' drama *Medea*. Carl Th. Dreyer never managed to film his script.'

(2) 'This is not an attempt to reconstruct a Dreyer film, but an interpretation of the script, in respect and appreciation, and as such is a tribute to the master.'

The film indeed has an unmistakable Dreyeresque atmosphere and closely recalls the older Danish director's aesthetics, in particular the simplicity and sobriety of his visual style. In addition, Medea's clothing and her general appearance, as well as the many close-ups of her hands and face at the beginning and at the end of the film, refer back to the female protagonists of *The Passion of Joan of Arc* and *Day of Wrath*. Finally, von Trier used two of Dreyer's old actors in *Medea*, Preben Lerdorff-Rye (as the children's tutor) and Baard Owe (as Aegeus), just

more importantly, her worldwide success in Cherubini's revived opera *Medée*, which she performed at various international venues throughout the 1950s and early 1960s and also recorded on disc in 1957.

[8] Bainbridge (2007: 14).

[9] Björkman (2003: 114). In another interview von Trier said that 'it was nothing less than a case of blackmail' that made him accept the project, [...] 'because someone else would have taken it if I hadn't. And it would have been horrible for me if someone else had taken it—to have to see someone else doing it. So I did it.' See Björkman and Nyman in Lumholdt (2003: 101).

as he had worked with Dreyer's cinematographer in the Europa trilogy (1984–1991).

The fact that von Trier repeatedly engaged professionals who had collaborated with Dreyer underlines his fascination with his compatriot's unique way of directing. In particular, Dreyer's habit of continually revising and condensing his scripts in order to minimize dialogue appealed to von Trier, who adopted the same method when shooting *Breaking the Waves.*[10] For Dreyer distanced himself as much from psychological drama as he did from mere naturalism, as von Trier pointed out in an interview:

> There's nothing there that suggests everyday speech. They're like little captions thrown in here and there. Dreyer was more interested in creating an extremely beautiful and impressive stylization. There's no question of any realistic, psychological acting. The characters are almost icons. It's probably better to describe his films as visual art rather than cinema.

For Dreyer film was not just a medium for reproducing the world around him, but a means for creating a sublimation that reflected the (ephemeral) essence of its underlying truth. This he considered 'the ontological potential of artistic innovation in film'.[11] Consequently, his work concerned itself mostly with 'rather abstract but nevertheless universal themes such as justice, faith and the need for love in the quest for a rewarding life'.[12] Moreover, in Dreyer's narratives the story is usually set in the past and often involves an intimate circle of people, with the main focus being on the female protagonist and her suffering as a result of the group's cruelty.[13]

The parallels to von Trier's *oeuvre* are obvious, especially to his *Medea* as well as to both the 'Gold Heart' and the 'U-S-A—Land of Opportunities' trilogies, which similarly explore the feminine capacity for self-sacrifice and martyrdom. In addition, von Trier's films 'tend to be top-heavy on ideas and images, [and] sparse on narrative',[14] as one film critic put it, which further aligns them with Dreyer's artistic principles. Von

[10] Björkman (2003: 118).

[11] Björkman (1996: 6–7). On Carl Theodor Dreyer's work and cinematic art in general see Jensen (1988) and Drouzy (1982). In addition, see Jean and Dale D. Drum (2000). *My Only Great Passion: The Life and Films of Carl Theodor Dreyer*. Lanham, MD: Scarecrow Press; Raymond Carney (1989). *Speaking the Language of Desire: The Films of Carl Dreyer*. Cambridge: Cambridge University Press; David Bordwell (1981). *The Films of Carl Theodor Dreyer*. Berkeley: University of California Press [second edition 1995]; Tom Milne (1971). *The Cinema of Carl Dreyer*. New York: A. S. Barnes and Company; Claude Perrin (1969). *Carl Th. Dreyer*. Paris: Éditions Seghers; Eileen Bowser (1964). *The Films of Carl Dreyer*. New York: Museum of Modern Art.

[12] Bainbridge (2007: 14). [13] Ibid. [14] Rose in Lumholdt (2003: 87).

Trier's adaptation of Dreyer's *Medea* in particular stands out because of its symbolic and visually stunning imagery rather than the naturalistic portrayal of its characters (tellingly, von Trier used only a small portion of the dialogue found in his predecessor's script). It is thus quite likely that Carl Theodor Dreyer would have approved of the completed film, which so loyally paid tribute to his 'abstractionist' approach and the purity of his cinematographic language.

At the same time, von Trier's *Medea* clearly anticipates—formally, thematically, and stylistically—the trajectory of his later work. His Medea looks forward to the tormented female protagonists in his major feature films, such as Bess in *Breaking the Waves*, Selma in *Dancer in the Dark*, and Grace in *Dogville*, while simultaneously harkening back to Dreyer's Joan of Arc. Bess, for instance, a simple-minded girl, who lives in a strict Puritan community in Scotland in the early 1970s and childishly believes that she is able to communicate directly with God, resembles her mythical precursor in her immense capacity for suffering and self-denial. When an accident leaves her husband paralysed, she becomes a prostitute in order to fulfil his erotic desires and re-establish his will to live. Taking every sign of improvement on his part as an incentive to subject herself to ever more degrading promiscuity, she is as a result not only expelled from her church congregation, but also from her family, before eventually being brutally murdered.

Similarly, Selma, the main female character in *Dancer in the Dark*, is the embodiment of unconditional love and selflessness. An emigrant from Czechoslovakia, she works in a factory for kitchen equipment in a small town in the State of Washington in the mid-1960s, putting away as much money as she can for her twelve-year-old son, who has inherited her eye deficiency and will slowly go blind (as she is going to), unless he has an expensive surgery. After her neighbour Bill, who has lost his job but is hiding this from his wife, steals all her savings and refuses to return them to her, she shoots him in an act of self-defence during their subsequent fight. Since she is unwilling to reveal the true circumstances of the theft and therefore cannot prove that the money is hers, she is arrested, put on trial for robbery and murder, and finally hanged. Granted, Selma is much more naïve and idealistic than Medea, and she moves from one agonizing ordeal to the next precisely because she lives out her ideals. But once fallen victim to her own beliefs, she sacrifices herself completely for the sake of her son, just as Medea—at least in Dreyer's interpretation, as we will see—commits the ultimate sacrifice by killing her children.

Finally, in *Dogville*, Grace, another good-hearted, altruistic heroine, comes into conflict with the social order and because of her uncompromising emotional and moral absolutism sacrifices herself body and soul for love, this time not represented by a husband or a child, but by a town community that has granted her refuge and in exchange benefitted from her services. However, by eventually punishing the people who submitted her to increasingly cruel and inhuman treatment, Grace recalls Medea, who equally takes revenge for all the humiliation and injustice done to her.[15]

While the sympathetic portrayal of these women, who are all marginalized individuals just like their Greek predecessor, closely connects von Trier's *Medea* with his more recent feature films, this is not the only thing that they have in common. In fact, *Medea* also shares the Christian symbolism of *Breaking the Waves*, *Dancer in the Dark*, and *Dogville*, with each female protagonist—just like Dreyer's Joan of Arc before them—taking on Christ-like attributes and willingly enduring similar tribulations. It thus becomes evident that *Medea* is not just an isolated episode within von Trier's cinematographic work, but marks an important stage in his career and creative evolution as a film director.

Furthermore, von Trier has had a propensity for cinematic tricks and technical experimentation from the very beginning, seeking to explore the possibilities as well as limitations of a specific format or genre to the fullest. His *Medea*, too, 'was an attempt to make alternative television'[16] and to 'overstep the pre-established rules of traditional [. . .] narration'.[17] This was certainly part of the reason why the response of most television critics was so negative, if not downright spiteful, when the film was first broadcast in 1988. For instance, von Trier included numerous 'long and total shots obtained with a wide-angle-lens, techniques unusual for the small screen on which close-ups normally reign'.[18] Besides, he first shot the film on video tape, then re-adjusted colour and light and transferred it to film, and finally copied it back to video tape. He later reported, 'we toned down the colours in the first version in the laboratory, then ran the refilmed version through the lab a second time. We kept toning down the colours more and more.'[19] As a result, the images of *Medea* seem almost bleached of their original colour and on the verge of dissolving into graininess and monochrome murk.[20] The main goal of this process was

[15] For a detailed analysis of the similarities and differences between Medea's and Grace's vengeance see Richter (2008: 86–95).

[16] Andersen in Lumholdt (2003: 97).

[17] Lucantonio (2005: 4).

[18] Ibid.

[19] Björkman (2003: 119). Similarly, the dialogue and soundtrack were created afterwards in the soundstudio and added by post-synchronization.

[20] See Stevenson (2002: 54).

to give the film 'an almost archaic character, like an old silent film'[21] and to create a sort of mystical atmosphere.[22]

In what follows, I will examine, in greater detail, von Trier's unique visual style and his effective use of the medium of film in *Medea*, which is 'less dependent on "linear" narration than on the accumulation of meaning within and between images, in a developed form of Eisensteinian "montage"'.[23] Moreover, I shall explore how the 'new' master of Danish cinema, with the posthumous help of Carl Theodor Dreyer, engages with, and appropriates the Euripidean drama, paying particular attention to his 'improving' additions and departures from the original. I shall argue that von Trier in his adaptation puts special emphasis on the aspects of gender and politics that are likewise key issues of the ancient Greek play, whereas Pasolini in his version concentrated on such elements as myth, ritual, and spirituality.[24] Von Trier portrays Medea as a lonely and deeply wounded, yet strong woman, who faces an existential conflict in a patriarchal society and refuses to accept the role of victim that is expected from her.[25] At the same time, he combines this feminist approach with a Christian re-interpretation of the story, presenting Medea as the incarnation of the oppressed female, who takes on the misery and suffering of all women, before eventually liberating herself, albeit at the highest price possible. In so doing, von Trier manages both to capture the main message of Euripides' tragedy and to give a faithful interpretation of the version that Dreyer had distilled from it, all the while leaving his very own mark in terms of visual language and thematic focus.

VON TRIER'S RE-INTERPRETATION OF *MEDEA*

Von Trier's *Medea* begins with a prologue that immediately makes manifest the heroine's anguish and inner turmoil as well as the precariousness of her situation, just as the opening speech of the nurse in

[21] Tapper in Lumholdt (2003: 78).

[22] See Müller (2000: 154); see also Rubino (2000: 67): '[. . .] una patina livida si frappone costantemente a creare, tra la macchina da presa e la narrazione, una sorte di effeto-distanza rispetto al paesaggio e ai personaggi' ('[. . .] a livid patina tries constantly to create, between the camera and the narration, a kind of distancing effect on the landscape and the characters.')

[23] Christie (2000: 159).

[24] See Shapiro's contribution in this volume.

[25] See also Forst (1998: 64).

Euripides informs the audience about Medea's despair and helplessness after Jason has left her in order to marry Creon's daughter (*Med.* 1–48). An overhead shot shows Medea, dressed all in black and wearing a black skullcap, lying flat on the beach with her eyes closed and her arms stretched out on each side.[26] She sharply breathes in and digs her fingers into the sand as if to hold herself down, before the camera begins to rotate, first slowly, then faster and faster, signalling that her world has been turned upside down, making her lose all sense of direction.[27] When it stands still again, it shows the tide beginning to come in and gradually covering her. Next the viewer is confronted with a long-held shot of a large, deep expanse of water with Medea gone. It is only after a prolonged silence that she suddenly emerges from beneath, gasping for air and standing in the midst of the sea. Her re-appearance is staged as a slight shock effect or element of surprise,[28] since it makes one wonder how it is possible for a human being to stay under water for so long. More importantly, it illustrates that Medea will not allow herself to be submerged and washed away permanently (or even drown herself in her distress, as some critics have it).[29] Rather, she is determined to resist and 'respond actively to Jason's betrayal',[30] defending her place as well as her dignity.

This opening highlights a number of significant changes and innovations in von Trier's *Medea* vis-à-vis Dreyer's script (and Euripides' play, whose plot the film otherwise closely follows). First, von Trier eliminated the female chorus that Dreyer had planned to integrate, constructing his film along the traditional lines of Greek tragedy. Instead, von Trier included a second prologue after the film's logo, in which the earlier history of Jason and Medea—again in captions reminiscent of silent film practice—is briefly summarized. Granted, the attendants that surround the other major characters in the film, the servants of Creon's daughter Glauce, the entourage of the king himself, the ship-building crew of Jason, and the mourners following the funeral procession of Creon and Glauce, act as a kind of chorus commenting on, and reacting to, the events that are taking place.[31] However, this only emphasizes the total isolation and loneliness of Medea, who—as in the prologue—is mostly

[26] That this is Medea the viewer technically can only assume, for she is not properly identified until Aegeus calls her name in the subsequent scene.

[27] Her figure resembles a victim on a torture wheel, which highlights her intense pain, as Rubino (2000: 67) has suggested.

[28] Müller (2000: 167). [29] Rubino (2000: 67).

[30] Joseph and Johnson (2008: 117). [31] Ibid.

seen all by herself and can only rely on the support of the loyal nurse, which makes 'her abandonment seem all the more bitter'.[32]

Secondly, von Trier changed the original setting. Apparently, Dreyer had intended to shoot at least the introductory part of the film in Greece, even though he was primarily interested in demonstrating the modernity as well as universality of the human conflict portrayed in Euripides' play, and for this reason was eager to de-emphasize the exotic Greek element. In addition, a note at the beginning of his script indicates that his *Medea* was supposed to start in an amphitheatre.[33] Von Trier gave up both these ideas, transferring the drama from Greece to the coast of the North Sea and using the desolate, fog-bound marshlands of Southwestern Jutland as a natural set design frequently depicted in many outdoor shots.[34] In fact, the flat, windswept landscape of Jutland, in which land and sea seem to be engaged in an eternal struggle of the elements, plays a leading role in *Medea*. Moreover, von Trier made frequent use of the natural sounds of the region, such as waves, rain, wind, birds, and other animals, which are as eloquent as human speech, if not more so given the minimalist and often elliptic dialogue of the film. While Euripides proved to be an innovative playwright in his time by letting mythical characters speak in everyday language, von Trier revolutionized the conventions of contemporary TV drama in *Medea* by prioritizing the elemental sounds over the human voices.[35]

With his choice of location, von Trier distanced himself as much from Dreyer's vision as from Pasolini, who, similarly opting for a symbolic scenery, filmed the first, Colchian part of his adaptation in the arid, rocky mountains of Cappadocia and the second, set in Corinth, in picturesque,

[32] Joseph and Johnson (2008: 117). See also Richter (2008: 75–6). Medea's marginalization is further emphasized by the fact that she lives on the fringes of society and its main centre, Creon's castle, in a small, shabby hut close to the marshes.

[33] According to Drouzy, Dreyer had collected and studied a lot of material on the ancient Greek theatre, its architecture, scenic conventions, and religious context while working on the screenplay, despite the fact that he wanted 'to tell the true story that may have inspired the great Greek poet' and to highlight that a situation like Medea's could happen—and has happened—in our day, too, as he writes at the beginning of the script. See Drouzy (1986: 242).

[34] A lot of the filming also took place on the island Malø, see Björkman (2003: 116).

[35] See Müller (2000: 154). Forst (1998: 67) emphasizes in addition the many pauses and moments of complete silence that interrupt the specific soundtrack of the film and concludes (ibid., 78–9): 'Mit dem mutigen, oft provozierenden Einsatz solcher akustischer "Leerstellen", dem Dehnen von Zwischenräumen zwischen den gesprochenen Sätzen, steigert Lars von Trier die Spannung und die Konzentration einzelner Einstellungen.' ('By courageously [and] often provocatively inserting such "acoustic" blanks [and] expanding the intervals between the spoken sentences, Lars von Trier enhances the tension and concentration of particular shots.')

sun-lit Pisa. In short, '[von Triers] "Filmlandschaft" wirkt wie die feuchte und düstere Seite zu Pasolinis ausgedörrter und gleißend heller Wüstenkulisse' ('[von Trier's] "film landscape" appears like the watery and gloomy counterpart to Pasolini's torrid and glistening light desert setting').[36]

Finally, Medea herself seems to have special connections to water, as her ability to remain under the surface of the incoming tide for more than sixty seconds suggests. Later on, she also uses her intimate knowledge of the natural world to get the ingredients for the poison that she will smear on the wedding crown to kill Glauce. In contrast to Euripides, who minimizes Medea's supernatural powers and stresses her intelligence and rhetorical skills instead, von Trier's protagonist 'looks and acts amphibian, more comfortable in the water than [anywhere else]; she is a [. . .] figure for whom dry land is inimical'.[37]

Medea's powerful re-emergence out of the sea is followed by a first encounter with Aegeus, who sails by to consult the oracle and calls Medea by her name, thereby clearly identifying her for the viewers. This is an 'interpolation', so to speak, for the (one and only) meeting with the Athenian king in Euripides takes place after Medea's acrimonious agon with Jason (*Med.* 663–823). Aegeus' entry in the Greek tragedy has provoked criticism ever since Aristotle (*Poet.* 1461b 19–21), because it was regarded as implausible, and the entire scene has been condemned as an example of poor plot construction. Medea had just highlighted her need for a place of refuge before being able to take her revenge (*Med.* 386–91), and all of a sudden the required 'rescuer' arrives.[38] Von Trier in his *Medea* also inserts a meeting with Aegeus immediately after Medea's bitter debate with Jason, but he additionally has the Athenian king appear at the beginning and at the end of the film, thus not only accentuating Aegeus' significance, but also 'careful[ly] tightening [the] narrative causality' in his version of the story.[39]

In their first encounter, Aegeus asks Medea how things stand between her and Jason, but receives no answer to this question. Instead, she demands that Aegeus promise her that she will always be able to take

[36] Stephan (2006: 223).

[37] Joseph and Johnson (2008: 121). The importance that von Trier places on water in *Medea* may be a reference to the Russian film director Andrei Tarkovsky, whom he considers another predominant influence on his work and whose fascination with water imagery he shares. See Bainbridge (2007: 13).

[38] Allan (2002: 33–4). See also Pavlos Sfyroeras (1994). 'The irony of salvation: The Aegeus scene in Euripides' *Medea*', *Classical Journal*, 90: 125–42 (with a sample of past criticisms, 125–6).

[39] Christie (2000: 156).

sanctuary in his country, as if already suspecting her later banishment, and he twice guarantees this to her. In their second meeting, Aegeus needs Medea's help in interpreting the oracle's advice, and she assures him that she will be able to cure his childlessness, if he in turn will take her away, which he again confirms upon hearing about her expulsion. Moreover, he tells her that he will sail with the tide, thus also offering her an actual means of escape. Finally, after Medea has wrought her cruel vengeance, we see her waiting on Aegeus' ship and so have proof that he indeed kept his promise.

In the Euripidean play, Aegeus grants Medea refuge in his territory as well, but imposes the condition that she must make her own way to Athens (*Med.* 729–30). Therefore, the question that is repeatedly raised in the following scenes is how she will get there (*Med.* 729, 757, 771, 1122–3, 1237, 1294–7), which prepares the audience for her spectacular departure on Helios' serpent-drawn chariot at the end of the play.[40] In von Trier's film, by contrast, no such *coup de théâtre* is saved up. On the contrary, his re-ordering of the events makes it clear from the very beginning with whose help Medea will eventually get away. By having Aegeus appear at the beginning, in the middle, and at the end, von Trier turns him into an important, if unwitting, instrument of Medea's revenge, which, as a consequence, takes place with inexorable logic.[41]

Indeed, Aegeus' role in Medea's escape is further emphasized in the ensuing cut to the film's logo, as von Trier 'matches the upward cruciform shape of the mast of Aegeus' ship [...] with the central "D" [of Medea's name] forming the [crooked] tree', from which the dead bodies of her children are hanging (Fig. 5.1).[42] Von Trier's montage thus explicitly connects Medea's infanticide with her later flight from Corinth.

Just as Aegeus' repeated appearances strengthen the causal nexus of events in *Medea*, so does the frequent presence of Glauce, the daughter of Creon and Jason's young new bride. While she is kept off stage in the Euripidean tragedy and not even referred to by name, von Trier inserts a series of new scenes, in which she plays an important role, thus becoming a central character of the film. This is especially evident in the long wedding sequence that von Trier includes after the second prologue.

We first see Glauce standing in front of a mirror in her fire-lit room in Creon's castle, surrounded by a group of female servants, completely naked. The contrast to Medea's first appearance at the beginning of the film could hardly be starker. With her entire body being covered by her

[40] Allan (2002: 34). [41] Stephan (2006: 225); see also Christie (2000: 156).
[42] Joseph and Johnson (2008: 118).

Figure 5.1 Film logo, *Medea*, dir. Lars von Trier.

tight-fitting, black dress and her hair hidden underneath a black skullcap, Medea barely looks like a woman, but rather like a creature from the sea used to living in complete darkness. Glauce's skin, by contrast, is as white as can be, glowing in the warm, soft light of the fire. Her long, dark hair hangs free, adding to her ethereal beauty and 'signaling her youthful innocence and desirability. [...] [S]he is the epitome of the virgin, the young nymph every man in such stories wishes to marry.'[43] In fact, her shadow on the wall is enormous, indicating that with her beauty and sexuality she has eclipsed everything, in particular Medea, who used to be just like her when she first met Jason.[44]

Von Trier continues the visual symbolism described and the play with light and shadow in the following wedding night scene,[45] which again features Glauce mostly in the nude. Beforehand, however, he introduces the viewer to the two male protagonists, Creon and Jason. Creon knocks at his daughter's door to say that everybody is waiting and then descends through a dark, claustrophobic tunnel-system—the interior of his castle located on a hill—to a vast cavern deep below, stretching to the shore of the sea, where Jason is standing. Here he informs Jason that in recognition of his efforts to increase Corinth's prosperity more power and responsibility are being transferred to him. In addition, he offers him Glauce 'as a reward and a bond, to tie Jason to Corinth and its

[43] Joseph and Johnson (2008: 121–2).

[44] See Müller (2000: 160). See also Joseph and Johnson (2008: 119) and Boedeker (1997: 143).

[45] See the detailed interpretation in Müller (2000: 160–1); see also Forst (2002: 75) and Forst (1998: 68).

fortunes'.[46] While Creon's words reveal that the main purpose of this union is to secure the continuation of the royal dynasty and the succession to the throne, Glauce, who is both 'politicized' and 'eroticized' in von Trier's film,[47] does not play her part in the scheme. In the wedding night, she refuses to allow Jason to consummate their marriage, insisting that Medea has to be sent away first. This seems to imply that it was her who initiated Medea's banishment, which together with her 'apparently innate knowledge of sexual weaponry undermines her appearance of child-like innocence'.[48] At all events, her flaunting of her naked body, the silhouette of which Jason can see and feel through semi-transparent curtains that serve as room-dividers in their wedding tent, gives him a strong motive for expediting Medea's departure.

Jason's vain attempt to share Glauce's bed is matched to Medea lamenting her loneliness and the misfortune of being female, closely echoing the long monologue on the plight of womanhood at the beginning of Euripides' drama (*Med.* 214–66). She complains that a woman has no rights, whereas her husband is master over her body. Moreover, a man can find new friends, while she has just him to look to. The scene is a good example of the specific and highly suggestive montage technique that von Trier uses in *Medea*.[49] When Medea begins to speak, the camera is focused on her, while the background is only dimly illuminated and therefore not properly identifiable. As she continues her accusations against Jason, the image in the background becomes clearer and bigger—we recognize the faces of her sleeping children—and when she finally says 'I long for revenge', both sons are visible to her left and right in larger than life-size close-ups, thus unambiguously pointing to the instrument of her vengeance.

The next day Medea seems already quite set in her decision on how to carry out her revenge. When Creon comes looking for her, she leaves her house and walks into the foggy swamps, where she collects berries and seaweed that she will later use for the preparation of the poison. In doing so, she forces Creon and his entourage to follow her and confront her on her own territory. By his own admission, Creon is frightened of her and has difficulty locating her in the misty bog to tell her that she and her sons must leave the country.[50] Even though he is determined to prove his authority and expel Medea in order to protect his family, his threats sound empty, and when his servants put down the litter and he himself

[46] Christie (2000: 155). [47] Ibid. [48] Joseph and Johnson (2008: 120).

[49] Forst (2002: 75–6); see also Forst (1998: 69).

[50] This is another example of a 'non-communication' between two characters, which von Trier repeatedly stages in the film. See Richter (2008: 79).

steps into the marshy water to find Medea, the power dynamics have definitely shifted. For not only is he now reduced to the same level,[51] but he also grows increasingly fearful and disoriented being on unfamiliar turf, at some point even tripping over branches and bloodying his face, while Medea is perfectly at home in the watery world that surrounds her. It thus seems only natural that she succeeds in obtaining Creon's consent to her request that she may stay one additional day.

Her strong connections with nature are thrown into further relief in her subsequent encounter with Jason. In sharp contrast to the corresponding scene in Euripides, in which Medea angrily attacks Jason, denouncing his ingratitude and shamelessness, in von Trier's adaptation she simply states that he has not thought of his children, since otherwise he would not have betrayed them by marrying Glauce. Jason responds that he in fact has considered them claiming that not only women care about their offspring, before expressing his wish—exactly as in the Greek text (*Med.* 569–75; see also *Hipp.* 616–24)—that men could procreate without them. The conversation takes place at a big outdoor loom in the pouring rain, and while Jason, standing on the one side, is quickly soaked through, Medea, sitting on the other, seems impervious to the water and in total harmony with nature (Fig. 5.2). At first, a rainbow

Figure 5.2 Medea (Kirsten Olesen) and Jason (Udo Kier) in *Medea*, dir. Lars von Trier.

[51] On this point see also Rubino (2000: 71).

illuminates the scene, 'a sign of hope at least since Biblical times',[52] which seems to suggest the possibility of a reconciliation of the former spouses. Moreover, the arc of the rainbow directly points at Medea, thus recalling not only her once happy life in light and sunshine, but also her association with Helios so prominent in Euripides' tragedy and other (ancient) versions of the myth.

However, the fact that the couple talk to one another through the threads of the loom clearly marks their complete alienation and, more generally, the firm division of the sexes. The only thing that they still have in common are their sons. But when Jason in the course of their quarrel 'pushes his hand through the warp, angrily undoing the symbolic fabric of their family', it becomes evident that their lives that have been woven together must be separated once and for all, and that the children as the representatives of this joint life must be killed.[53]

In what follows, however, von Trier first makes the viewer witness the first part of Medea's vengeance, the murder of Glauce, which is another example of his specific montage technique. After Medea has met a second time with Jason pretending to seek reconciliation[54] and given him her poisoned wedding crown as a present for Glauce, the younger of the two boys, who accompany their father back to the castle, plays with it and accidentally wounds a white horse in Creon's stables. The next scene shows how the horse, as the poison begins to work, breaks loose from its tether and races blindly through the subterranean passages of the palace, before bursting outside and eventually collapsing on the beach, where it dies painfully on the wet sand. At the same time, we see Glauce putting on Medea's wedding crown in her room and admiring herself in the mirror, a glance that matches her first appearance in the film. Then she cuts one finger at the crown's sharp edges, and von Trier turns the camera to a flock of screeching black birds flying by her window, unmistakably announcing her imminent death.

By portraying Glauce's gruesome death only indirectly, if not less effectively, von Trier respected the conventions of Greek tragedy not to show brutal murders or other horrible crimes on stage. However, he did not adhere to the same principle for the second part of Medea's revenge, the killing of her sons. Rather, in radical departure from Euripides he made their murder 'the harrowing *visible* climax' of his film.[55]

[52] Joseph and Johnson (2008: 122). [53] Ibid. See also Müller (2000: 157).

[54] For an analysis of von Trier's technical and aesthetic experimentation in this scene see Forst (2002: 76–7) and Forst (1998: 70–1); see also Richter (2008: 78) and Müller (2000: 160).

[55] Christie (2000: 156).

Furthermore, he altered Dreyer's script, which called for Medea to give her children poisoned 'medicine' and then await their deaths in sleep while singing a lullaby, since stabbing them as in the Greek tragedy seemed too brutal. Von Trier decided to have them die by hanging instead, with the older boy assisting his mother in her horrific task. He justified his more shocking version in an interview as follows:

> Yes. Dreyer [. . .] thought it was too violent to have them knifed, which is what happens in the classical drama. He thought that was too bloody. He just wanted them to die in their sleep. I chose to make it more dramatic. I think there's more edge to my version as a whole. I thought it was better to hang the children. And more consequential. Either you kill them or you don't. The action ought to be presented as it is. There's no reason to tidy it up and make it look more innocent than it is.[56]

The scene takes place in bright daylight in the midst of a wheat field, but initially Medea is depicted at dawn—first from afar in a total shot, then up close—dragging something very heavy over the marshy plains and up to a hill. Von Trier parallels her journey with the events going on in Corinth, the cruel agony of Creon and the subsequent funeral procession for the dead king and his daughter, again using montage and superimposition to accelerate the action. Finally, Medea stops gasping, and the camera reveals that she has been carrying her sleeping children in a wooden cart, the younger of whom has woken up and needs to be comforted. The situation is highly evocative of Christ's walk up to Golgotha, an allusion that is further intensified by the appearance of the top of the hill, on which stands a lonely, crooked tree-trunk in the shape of a cross.[57] Medea here represents the whole of womankind, with the children being her burden both in the literal and figurative sense, her cross (or curse), implanted by the man to secure his progeny.[58] She is not pictured as a furious avenger or an evil magician with supernatural powers, but as a suffering creature, who has to bear her yoke through misery and pain to the bitter end.[59] In highlighting these aspects, von Trier stages Medea's rebellion not as a triumphant journey towards freedom and power like Euripides, but as a *passio* or *via dolorosa*, and it is certainly no coincidence that the film was first broadcast on Easter 1988.

[56] Björkman (2003: 118).

[57] As Richter has pointed out, the scenery also recalls the immolation of Isaac on Mount Morija (1. *Moses* 22). See Richter (2008: 98).

[58] Müller (2000: 157).

[59] Forst (2002: 77) and Forst (1998: 72).

In accordance with this distinctly human nature of Medea, her children are not simply the hapless victims of her vengeance as in most versions. On the contrary, the elder son understands his mother's intentions and tells her, after the sun has risen, 'I know what has to happen', aware of the necessity of his and his brother's death given his father's unfaithfulness. When Medea ties the rope she has brought around one dry branch of the tree and the younger boy playfully runs down the hill, he chases him, climbs back up and hands him over to his mother so that she can hang him. Once this task is accomplished, he asks Medea, who kneels traumatized in the grass, 'Help me, mother.' He then arranges his own noose and puts it around his neck, while Medea desperately holds him up in order to save his life, before her strength finally fails. Her extreme physical and emotional anguish in attempting 'to defer [at least] this "necessary" death'[60] is something that is undoubtedly burned into every viewer's memory and underscores that Medea's revenge in von Trier's adaptation is a horrifying act of self-denial and martyrdom.

After the infanticide, Medea sits calmly on Aegeus' ship, waiting for the tide to rise, while Jason, who had in vain pursued her after discovering the dead bodies of his sons, first rides around in a state of complete shock and then madly beats the fields and bushes around the tree-trunk with his sword. By contrast, Medea removes for the first time the black skullcap she has worn throughout the film, releasing a long mane of auburn hair (Fig. 5.3), 'a symbol of defiance [and] newly acquired freedom'.[61] At the beginning of the narrative she had been in danger of being drowned and washed away permanently by the sea, now she sails *on* the sea.[62] She has completed her vengeance and reclaimed her status by transgressing her conventional role, although her facial expression makes it clear that her suffering continues, and she gets no triumph, joy, or even relief, from carrying out her plan.

Von Trier allows himself one last theatrical gesture in this scene:[63] when the tide begins to come in, a sail is dropped and briefly flaps in front of the camera like the curtain at the end of an opera performance, thus obscuring Medea from view. When it goes up again, it reveals her in her new 'feminized' state, with her hair falling over her shoulders and her face, which had been almost completely motionless throughout the film, clearly exposing her feelings. Her loose locks signal that she is 'once again a nymph' and has 'regained her virginity [...],

[60] Christie (2000: 157).

[61] Joseph and Johnson (2008: 121). At the same time, the deep red colour of her hair is an unmistakable reminder of the murder she has committed. On loose hair as a symbol of a woman's freedom, see Bakogianni's contribution in this volume.

[62] Müller (2000: 167).

[63] See Joseph and Johnson (2008: 123).

Figure 5.3 Medea (Kirsten Olesen) after completing her revenge in *Medea*, dir. Lars von Trier.

[having] forced Glauce to trade places with her'.[64] Conversely, Jason has lost everything—a fact that could not become more evident than by the last image of the film, which shows him prostrate in the field in the very same position Medea was seen in at the start,[65] before this is superimposed by a picture of Aegeus' ship carrying Medea away from Corinth.

In conclusion, Lars von Trier's *Medea* offers a radically new interpretation of Euripides' play, while simultaneously adding to our understanding of its main themes, in particular the fate of a woman who revolts against the unjust power relations in which she lives and refuses to be victimized, no matter how high the price. Medea chooses revenge over motherhood, since her personal honour and dignity are more important to her than her children. Her conflict is mirrored in the film in the natural opposition of the elements, the eternal struggle between land and

[64] See Joseph and Johnson (2008: 123).

[65] See also Decker (1997: 22): '[Medea] löst ihr Haar; es fließt, wird zum wogenden Teppich, auf dem Jason [...], der Geliebte, der Mann, der Verräter sich windet, in dessen Brandung er umkommt. Der Ertrinkende—zuletzt ist es Jason, nicht Medea. Die Frau, immer ausersehen zum stellvertretenden Opfer der Gesellschaft an die Natur, hat es verweigert.' ('[Medea] loosens her hair; it flows, becomes a heaving carpet, on which Jason [...], the lover, the man, the traitor squirms [and] in the surge of which he perishes. The drowning person—at the end it is Jason, not Medea. The woman, always destined to be society's representative sacrifice to nature, she refuses to be the victim.')

sea. At the same time, von Trier portrays Medea's predicament and suffering as an unavoidable and perpetual condition of womankind, making her infanticide appear not as an unnatural, mad, or evil act, but as a desperate response to the extreme, irresolvable situation in which she finds herself, and the ultimate sacrifice possible.

Part III

Penelope

6

'Madonna and Whore': The Many Faces of Penelope in *Ulisse* (1954)

Joanna Paul

In 1954, the Italian production company Lux Film released *Ulisse* (*Ulysses*), a screen adaptation of Homer's *Odyssey*.[1] Despite Hollywood leading men starring in key roles—Kirk Douglas as the eponymous hero, Ulysses, and Anthony Quinn as Antinoos, leader of Penelope's suitors—the film has not enjoyed the same long-lasting, popular acclaim as the canonical Hollywood epics of this period, such as *Spartacus* (1960), in which Douglas himself starred a few years later. However, we should dismiss any temptation to disregard *Ulisse* as just a formulaic Italian genre film, a proto-peplum with little to recommend it.[2] The film did in fact have, and continues to have, a not inconsiderable impact on viewers. It occupied the number one box office slot in Italy for 1954, a commercial success which must have been at least partly due to the appeal and proven popularity of its cast and production team.[3] Douglas and Quinn lent a Hollywood cachet, but the big-name Italian producers, Dino De Laurentiis and Carlo Ponti, had also secured a leading director, Mario Camerini, previously best known for his romantic comedies. Alongside Douglas' Ulysses, and billed second only to him in the film's advertising, starred the Italian actress Silvana Mangano. Still only 24, she was already a well-known Italian film star; indeed, the box office top ten for 1954 contained two other films in which she appeared, *L'oro di*

[1] The film was only released in France and Italy by the end of 1954; the 1955 release date in other territories means that this film is often credited as *Ulysses* (1955).

[2] For a discussion of the peplum genre, see Günsberg (2005: 97–132), Pomeroy (2008: 29–59), and for further bibliography Nikoloutsos (2013: 265–6 n. 7), as well as Pomeroy in this volume. As Pomeroy shows, the peplum flourished from the late 1950s; in many ways, *Ulisse* can be seen as a proto-peplum, initiating key features of this strand of Italian filmmaking.

[3] Celli and Cottino-Jones (2007: 173).

Napoli (*The Gold of Naples*), at number five, and *Mambo*, ranked eighth.[4]

The initial commercial acclaim for *Ulisse* within Italy was not especially long-lived, or far reaching. Although it performed well in the US in comparison with other Italian productions, reviews were lukewarm: *Variety* lamented the fact that it had not been shot in CinemaScope (a new widescreen format first used for *The Robe* in 1953, in the hope of boosting cinema's spectacular appeal over that of television)[5] at the same time as observing that 'a lot, perhaps too much, money has gone into the making of "Ulysses"', whilst the *Monthly Film Bulletin* called it 'a long, dull let-down'.[6] However, in more recent critical discussion, *Ulisse* has been making up for these underwhelmed responses. Jon Solomon calls it 'the finest of all film versions of the Homeric poems', while Camille Paglia praises it as 'a model of well-paced, emotionally rich, and intelligent moviemaking about ancient culture'.[7] Chief among the reasons for this approval is the economy of the film's storytelling. Instead of trying to bring all the episodes of Ulysses' wanderings to the screen, the screenplay (notably credited to seven writers, and Homer!)[8] astutely restructures and recombines aspects of the original poem into a coherent film, 'one of the most entertaining and apothegmatic scripts of its kind', according to Solomon.[9] So, for example, there is no Telemachy (the first four books of Homer's *Odyssey*, in which Odysseus' son Telemachus sets out to find news of his father); nor does Ulysses visit the Laestrygonians, or encounter Scylla and Charybdis (amongst other omissions from his wanderings); nor does he actually visit the Underworld, or spend time with the nymph Calypso: instead, these two episodes are condensed into his stay with Circe, a narrative strategy which will be examined in detail in due course. Such 'liberties' with the Homeric poem might cause problems for some viewers, but most, like Solomon, have recognized how successful and *necessary* such a device is, in order to turn a long, episodic narrative into a dramatically satisfying film.

The fullest expression of *Ulisse*'s thoughtful narrative rearrangement is to be found in the casting of the central female roles: Silvana Mangano plays both Penelope, wife of Ulysses, and Circe, the enchantress who hinders his return to hearth and home. Any suspicion that this honour

[4] Ibid. [5] See Nikoloutsos (2013: 267).

[6] *Variety (Review)*, 8 December 1954; *Monthly Film Bulletin* 258: 22, July 1955.

[7] Solomon (2001a: 108); Paglia (1997: 187).

[8] Multi-authored scripts were a common feature of the peplum film; see Pomeroy (2008: 58).

[9] Solomon (2001a: 111).

was bestowed on Mangano as a favour from her husband—who just happened to be Dino De Laurentiis—is missing the point. Rather, her dual role cleverly introduces a visual and conceptual shorthand for the telling of the story, allowing us to address the theme of gender in the *Odyssey* in new and interesting ways, and bringing the film closer to the complexity of Homer's epic. Mangano's portrayal of these mythical women on screen, and audiences' responses to it, owes a great deal to the position she occupied within Italian filmmaking and popular culture more generally. *Ulisse*'s reception of Homeric women is inextricably linked to the public persona of Mangano (and her contemporaries), whom Stephen Gundle has described as 'representatives of a lifestyle that rested on clearly-defined gender roles, a dramatic, emotional mode of personal interaction, and some vaguely-defined idea of the good life in which leisure, food, personal appearance and sex all had a special place'.[10] It is not too far-fetched to see this gender typing referring almost as neatly to the *Odyssey*'s women as it does to Mangano et al. The mapping of gender roles in *Ulisse* is fascinating and complex, from both ancient and modern perspectives, and in fact goes beyond the provocative dichotomy proposed in this chapter's title, that of 'Madonna and whore'.[11]

'I WORE A WIDOW'S FACE': THE CINEMATIC PENELOPE

Carol Ann Duffy's poem 'Penelope', from which the above line is taken,[12] is just one example of a long tradition of receptions of Penelope, stretching from Homer to the present day. Although this chapter cannot provide a detailed account of this reception history, it is useful to be aware of how regularly Penelope has been thrust centre-stage and given a voice. Writers and artists have dissected her, examined her motives, queried her actions and emotions, and retold her story in her (their) own words. Creative artists in particular, perhaps responding more to the Latin literary tradition which 'embalms' Penelope as a 'unidimensional paradigm of virtue',[13] have either contributed to this embalming—as in Angelica Kauffmann's eighteenth-century paintings of a mournful

[10] Gundle (2007: 142). [11] Paglia (1997: 182). [12] Duffy (1999: 71).

[13] Jacobson (1974: 245). So, Propertius contrasts the unfaithful bride of his day (*hoc genus infidum nuptarum*) with the dutiful, true (*pia*) Penelope (3.13.23–4).

Penelope at her loom—or sought to rescue or reinvigorate her, even to the point of making her 'arrogant, vain, insecure, unsympathetic and sexually possessive', as Edith Hall sees Penelope in Margaret Atwood's novella *The Penelopiad* (2005).[14] It can easily be argued that Penelope has not needed rescuing, that her characterization in Homer is sufficiently interesting and strong by itself. But still, or perhaps because of this, scholarly discourse has debated Penelope as much as artists have. A particularly strong thread in recent criticism has examined the trustworthiness of her words, finding a strong 'indeterminacy' in the Homeric Penelope.[15] Although it may sometimes be appropriate to regard Penelope as the simple, stereotypical image of the faithful wife, it is important to recognize her multiplicity, whether in her ruse of weaving and unpicking Laertes' funeral shroud, so as to delay marriage to a suitor (and discussed in more detail below), or her various and shifting roles: a wife who grieves but is not a widow, a mother to a son on the brink of adulthood, the head of a household who is yet targeted by suitors.[16] Therefore, when Carol Ann Duffy has her acknowledge that she 'wore a widow's face', she is suggesting Penelope's ability to adopt different masks according to the situation—even, Duffy seems to imply, to *change her appearance* when necessary.

This is a particularly apt starting point for understanding Penelope (Fig 6.1), or rather Penelope/Circe in *Ulisse*. Superficially, this Penelope seems no different from the 'faithful wife' model that pervades many receptions: as we shall shortly see, there is much that is conventional and 'safe' in her cinematic characterization. But as the film unfolds, and the implications of Mangano's doubling become clear, we are offered a powerful vision of female potency and complexity, where neither Penelope nor Circe can be pinned down to one 'type', and the possibilities of these newly-imagined Homeric women are as rich as they have been shown to be in the *Odyssey* itself. It is, then, fitting that Penelope is the first character that we see when the film opens (after some brief, generic shots of a ship, behind the opening titles). A scrolling written prologue, reminiscent in many ways of the prologue to the *Odyssey*, ends with the words, 'It is the story of Ulysses, who dared defy the god and continued his journey to Ithaca, where his wife Penelope was waiting... and

[14] Hall (2008: 126). [15] Katz (1991); Felson-Rubin (1994).

[16] This is summed up particularly effectively by Nancy Felson-Rubin: 'The perspectives on Penelope as object create multiple images of her for the listener; yet only the image of the faithful wife survives to the end of the poem and enters into the post-Homeric tradition' (1994: 3).

Figure 6.1 Penelope (Silvana Mangano) in her bedchamber in *Ulisse*, dir. Mario Camerini. Credit: [LUX FILM/THE KOBAL COLLECTION]

waiting....'[17] Penelope is thus cued as a central component of the narrative,[18] and sure enough, the shot then dissolves (with the written titles persisting over the dissolve) to a shot of a silhouetted woman stood on the ramparts or terrace of a palace at dusk, her outline framed between two sculptural lions that recall, authentically, the Lion Gate at Mycenae. It is Penelope, and it is entirely appropriate that we see her in silhouette. Although one could argue that this shows Penelope as a blank, empty cipher, I would argue for a more positive reading. Mangano's silhouette represents instead Penelope as the female outline which can and will take on many different faces, 'the coy tease, the enchantress, the unreliable mother, the adulteress, the hard-hearted wife' as well as the faithful one:[19] all of these possibilities will be at least hinted at in *Ulisse*.

In the opening scenes, the situation in the palace at Ithaca is established: the suitors are carousing in the main hall, and being entertained by Phemius, the bard, who sings a song of Troy to them—a neat plot device which introduces the external audience to Ulysses for the first time, with Phemius' song motivating a lengthy flashback which recounts

[17] The film's written epilogue will be considered further later in this chapter; for a fuller discussion of the implications of the prologue and epilogue, see Paul (2013: 83–5).

[18] This reflects another critical trend which places Penelope as a principal agent of the *Odyssey*'s plot: see, for example, Finley (1978) and Heitman (2005).

[19] Felson-Rubin (1994: 3).

the events at the fall of Troy, and Ulysses's role in them. The maidservants, as in Homer, are misbehaving with the suitors, and Eurycleia, Ulysses' old nurse, is chastising them. The young Telemachus is also trying to assert his authority against the invaders of the palace, announcing his intention to leave Ithaca to try and find out what has become of his father. The chaos in Ithaca is reflected by Penelope's turbulent state of mind. Although our first glimpse of her in silhouette gave her the appearance of a calm, queenly poise, the next shot sees her rushing into the palace, excitedly announcing that she has seen a sign, a cloud forming the shape of a sail, at which Eurycleia tells her to stop desperately seeking omens and tormenting herself. Then, when Phemius sings his song, this tale of 'ancient memories' is clearly upsetting to Penelope, and when challenged for working too long on her tapestry (the famous weaving ruse, to which we will return in just a moment), she replies, 'It is the memory of Ulysses which prevents me from finishing it. It's my sorrow and tears, they cloud my eyes, and so my hands work slower.'

We are presented here with an emotional Penelope, and an apparently weak, passive one: when Telemachus threatens to leave, she is distraught—he is 'her strength' and she will not cope without him. At this early stage in the film, the signs are not promising for its presentation of interesting women, but there are glimpses of a more complex, stronger Penelope. In front of the suitors, at least, she attempts to assert her authority: even though they have extracted from her 'a promise she did not want to make', and Mentor chides them for taking advantage of 'the weakness of a woman', she reminds them that she is yet queen of Ithaca, and retains her composure in public at least. In the emotional conversation with Telemachus that follows, we are also offered a Penelope who is perhaps not so easy to read, something of the 'indeterminate Penelope', perhaps. Telemachus challenges Penelope to say that she doesn't really believe that Ulysses is alive, at all. 'What does it matter what I believe?', she replies. 'Ulysses is far off. This alone we know to be true. And that is why this tapestry increases each day, and is undone each night. And that is how I keep deceiving these suitors, who wait for me, while I wait for Ulysses.'

With the mention of the tapestry (as it is described in the English soundtrack to the film), *Ulisse* also presents us with one of the most compelling Homeric examples of Penelope's agency, and a *mētis* (cunning or intelligence) to match her husband's. As we learn in book two of the *Odyssey*, Penelope has shrewdly delayed a marriage to any of the suitors by saying that she must first finish weaving a funeral shroud for Odysseus' father, Laertes; but since she unpicks her weaving every night, the project is seemingly endless, and the marriage successfully kept at bay (*Od.* 2.93–110). The cinematic Penelope is employing the same *dolon*, or trick, and though we do not immediately learn the precise nature of the deceit, the significance of the weaving is foregrounded by the loom's prominence in the very first interior shot of the palace, where Eurycleia scolds the maids whilst stood in front of it. Indeed, the film uses the loom as the most obvious visual marker of Penelope's private space within the palace, as opposed to the hall which has been occupied by the suitors. Whenever she retreats to this area, which has little distinctive décor to speak of (the walls are mostly rough-hewn, and the colours sombre), the weaving dominates the *mise-en-scène*. Since this is the space in which Penelope gives vent to her emotions, whether in her early conversation with Telemachus, or her reunion with Ulysses at the end of the film, the significance of the weaving as a meaningful object seems clear.

The centrality of Penelope's weaving in the *Odyssey* is also unquestionable. Not only is it evidence of her capacity and willingness to do everything possible to preserve the *oikos*, even if it means deception, it also has a much deeper metaphoric significance, which has been examined in great detail by the many critics working on Penelope, and the issue of weaving more generally, over the past couple of decades. French feminist critics were the first to explore the equation of 'textile' and 'text' in mythic narratives, whereby the weaving of cloth affords a woman such as Arachne, Philomela, or Penelope, the (only) opportunity to tell and give form to her story.[20] So, early in the *Iliad*, we find Helen in her bedchamber at Troy:

> weaving a great web,
> a red folding robe, and working into it the numerous struggles
> of Trojans, breakers of horses, and bronze-armoured Achaians,
> struggles that they endured for her sake at the hands of the war god.
> (Il. 3.125–8, trans. Lattimore)

Helen is weaving the narrative of the Trojan war, and in telling its story in cloth, she is engaged in an activity analogous to that of Homer himself: the mythical woman becomes, in some sense, the epic poet too, and Helen brings *kleos* to the warriors by preserving their deeds in her weaving. The Homeric Penelope is a more complex case, though, for the simple fact that her woven shroud contains no images—at least, they are not described by Homer. Since she is not obviously telling a story, the analogy with the epic poet is less readily apparent, although it is not as

[20] Hall (2008: 121–2).

implausible as some have suggested.[21] Barbara Clayton maintains that this Penelope is a 'bardic figure', and argues that the Homeric weaving logically has to contain images, since a plain cloth would not work nearly so well for Penelope's trick; the fact that Homer remains silent about its content leaves us free to imagine that Penelope could in fact be weaving *anything*, thus making her potency as storyteller all the greater.[22] Moreover, we could see the repeated unweaving and reweaving of the shroud as symbolic of the oral nature of Homeric epic, in which narratives get made and remade over successive performances. Critics have also used Penelope's weaving as a template for understanding her wider significance in the poem, indeed her ability to shape its narrative: so for Felson-Rubin, Homer 'makes Penelope his accomplice in weaving plots and subterfuges. He places her firmly in a situation in which, to avoid disaster and survive, she must catch up several threads of plot simultaneously.'[23]

Given all of this, we would be quite justified in asking whether the prominence of the weaving in *Ulisse* carries similar meanings; and the issue becomes even more pressing when we consider the details of Penelope's 'tapestry'. For this is no blank shroud, but instead is vividly decorated with a small group of figures. Underneath a thick border consisting of a repeating anthemion motif, and on a plain white background, we see a man driving a plough, which is attached to a large ox; a small dog (or perhaps a cat) stands nearby, and the animals are framed on the right hand side of the scene by a tree with branches that loop over the cow. To the man's left is a woman holding a small baby. For most of the time that the loom is on screen—and certainly for most viewers—no further identification of the scene could be possible.[24] The iconography would simply seem to represent a generically 'ancient Greek' scene through its styling, which is unmistakably that of Greek vase painting. No actual source is to be found for this scene.[25] Instead, it seems to have

[21] Kruger (2001: 82), for example, claims that Penelope's 'work does not represent Homer's voice' as Helen's does (2001: 82), and takes the fact that no images are described by Homer as suggesting the relative unimportance of the shroud: as a 'blank text', it is symbolic of her body, on which nothing has been written in Odysseus' absence (unlike Helen's, which is inscribed by conflict and war, hence her representation of it on the tapestry [ibid., 84].)

[22] Clayton (2004: 34).

[23] Felson-Rubin (1994: 42).

[24] Compare with the TV movie of *The Odyssey* (1997), in which Penelope's weaving depicts Odysseus' ship.

[25] As Robin Osborne has pointed out, there are very few agricultural scenes represented on vases (1987: 18–20). The design of the plough and the shape of the ox in the woven scene, though, do bear a close resemblance to known vases which do depict such figures (such as a black-figure kylix that depicts agricultural scenes [Paris, Musée du Louvre, F77,

been designed as an amalgam of the styles and iconography of a wide variety of vases: the anthemion design at the top clearly reflects the use of this motif as a decoration of the neck of many pots, and the stark figures on a light background are taken from the white-ground painting technique. The dominant colour of the figures, though—a deep terracotta red—is in line with red-figure painting, whilst a design detail which persists in a band through the robes worn by the woman, the man, and into the ox itself, is clearly drawn from early geometric designs. This melange of details seems to have been consciously designed to evoke a general sense of 'Greekness' for the scene (hence the designer's decision to place it centre-stage in Penelope's rooms), which would be entirely in line with the visual strategies employed by most filmmakers who recreate antiquity, for whom accurate detail is far less important than the 'feel' of a scene.[26]

However, on close examination (which is most easily achieved when the weaving reappears at the end of the film), written inscriptions can be made out, labelling each figure (in Greek script) in the same arching manner that actual vases label their subjects. The man driving the plough is Odysseus and, unsurprisingly, the woman is Penelope, and the baby in her arms Telemachus. To be sure, most viewers of *Ulisse* will not be privy to these identifications (although it would not be too much of a leap to guess the woven figures' identities), but if we are looking for significance in Penelope's weaving, this cannot be ignored. What is the story she is telling through these images? Superficially, it is a story which speaks for the importance of the *oikos*, the family and household unit which she is trying to preserve through the act of weaving and unweaving (untelling and retelling) this very image: a pastoral image of household work (and the plough itself a symbol of fertility), faithful wife looking on, and baby representing the future.[27]

Beneath this 'safe' interpretation lurks something a little more complex, though, and that is the oblique reference it makes to a less well-known episode of the Odyssean myth, which tells what happens when

Beazley Archive 164] or a cup attributed to Nikosthenes [Berlin, Antikensammlung, F1806, Beazley 302815]), suggesting that they may well have been consulted by the film's designers.

[26] See, for example, Lane Fox (2004: 80) on the importance of 'a coherent "look" which will also feel right to the audience'.

[27] Moreover, the male baby Telemachus represents the successful continuation of a patriarchal society, underlining Penelope's conventional domesticity with an image which recurs in other similar films. Nikoloutsos' (in this volume) description of Gorgo in a similar scene in *The 300 Spartans* (1962) as 'a procreation vessel, a vehicle whereby primogenitary succession—the bedrock of patriarchy in Greek antiquity and western societies—continues uninterrupted' applies equally to Penelope here.

Odysseus was 'called up' to fight for Helen at Troy. Unwilling to go, he feigned madness by yoking a mismatched donkey and ox to a plough (and, in some versions, ploughing the beach and sowing salt into the furrows) until Palamedes, seeing through the deceit, placed the baby Telemachus in front of the plough (or held a sword to his throat), at which Odysseus was forced to intervene and thereby prove his sanity.[28] The implicit allusion to this episode is fascinating, deftly adding another layer to the story that Penelope is telling: it provides further evidence of Ulysses' own *mētis*, an apt subject matter for a cloth which is Penelope's own counterpart in cunning. Perhaps most importantly, not only does it bespeak the importance of 'family life' more generally, it also indicates the lengths to which Ulysses was prepared to go to protect it—and perhaps, therefore, serves to motivate the cinematic Penelope to persist in her own attempts to preserve the *oikos* for her husband's hoped-for return. And as Camille Paglia has noted, in the cultural context of *Ulisse*'s production, 'in ravaged postwar Italy', a matter to which we will return, 'the image seems to celebrate the return to love, family, fertility, and prosperity, made possible by peace.'[29]

No doubt because of the film's commitment to narrative economy, Penelope's weaving trick is soon discovered. After we have seen Ulysses on Scheria—where, suffering from amnesia, he is given good hospitality by the Phaeacians, participating in games and making quite an impression on the young Nausicaa—we return to Ithaca, and see Eurycleia whipping the slave girl who has revealed the secret to the suitors (as at *Od.* 2.108–9). Therefore, we have seen scarcely anything of Penelope actually weaving, or even unweaving, save some half-hearted picking at it toward the end of the first sequence on Ithaca; but still, the prominence of the weaving has offered some hope that Penelope can exert ownership of her own narrative, even by the very presence of the intriguing ploughing scene. That sense of agency in Penelope quickly dissipates with the arrival of Antinoos, though. Anthony Quinn's imposing, brash portrayal of the foremost of the suitors, who storms into the palace as if he already owns it, and enters Penelope's chambers with impunity, reinforces our earlier suspicions of a weaker Penelope. In their first encounter, she seems both fearful of him, and a little seduced by his arrogant statement that he has 'come to end your loneliness, Penelope'—a complaint that she made several times to Telemachus earlier. Later on,

[28] This myth was part of the epic cycle in Proclus' *Cypria*; see also Apollodorus, *Epit.* 3.6–7. There are no surviving visual representations, though Euphranor's representation of the story is attested in various sources.

[29] Paglia (1997: 187).

shortly before Ulysses' return, Antinoos declares his love for Penelope, and again seems to be on the point of winning her over with his promises to make her happy and feel like a woman again; in the midst of her emotional appeal to Antinoos that he protect Telemachus' life, to which the duplicitous suitor agrees, she allows him to embrace her, albeit reluctantly.

In the very next scene, though, Penelope is reunited with Ulysses, though she does not see through his beggarly disguise for some time. Again, we have a sense of Penelope's emotional turmoil and weakness. Clearly upset by the beggar reporting news of her husband—who had apparently spoken of the loom 'where you'd be waiting for him', emphasizing the link between Penelope and weaving once more—she reveals the full extent of her frustration to him: the length of time she has had to wait, her loneliness, her fears that he has met other women, that he has forgotten her, and her bitterness at his failure to return when the war ended. This is at least a Penelope who feels plausible, justified emotion. When the beggar sadly replies, 'You are right. It's possible for a man to come back too late', we recognize that Penelope's words are wounding. But her passivity is also clear. Telling the beggar that she is due to choose a new husband tomorrow, against her will, he replies 'perhaps you could free yourself?' 'I? How do you mean?', she replies. Ulysses then reminds her of the contest of the bow: the idea is planted, and Penelope regains some control by implementing it, but crucially, she has not conceived of it for herself, in the way that the Homeric Penelope does (*Od.* 19.576–80.)

The final sequence of *Ulisse* concerns the contest of the bow and its aftermath, Ulysses' slaughtering of the suitors. Penelope has little to do with this: when Ulysses reveals his identity, she appears shocked, but is quickly whisked away by her attendants, though we do then see brief shots of her watching the bloodshed, a look of anguish on her face, safely from a balcony over the hall. When it is over, and Ulysses laments having to bring bloodshed into his house on the day of his homecoming, Penelope too rushes to her private altar where she prays, 'Oh divine Athena, did his long road back to me have to be so bloodstained?' At this, Ulysses enters Penelope's—and his—bedchambers, with the words, 'my road had to be long and bloodstained. There was no other way to bring me back to you.' With a final bittersweet exchange, in which Ulysses promises to make up for her loneliness, they embrace, but the camera quickly pans away and focuses instead on the loom. The weaving is privileged once more, and over it rolls a closing epilogue, which ends with the words, '…and the epic poem that Homer sang of the hero's wanderings and of his yearning for home will live for all time'. The weaving that was always unfinished in earlier scenes (as it had to be, to suit the terms of the trick—it ended approximately three-quarters of the way down the figures' bodies) is now complete, as the Ithacan *oikos* is restored.

Does this final impression of Penelope do anything to mitigate her passivity? Again, the return to the weaving is important—as Penelope's creation, it suggests that the restoration of her family is at least partly achieved through her own bringing it into being in cloth. The reappearance of it under closing titles which specifically evoke Homer's epic also renews the possibility of seeing Penelope as akin to the epic poet. (It is interesting, in this respect, that although the images of the weaving are now complete, the weft yarns remain loose, hanging down at the bottom of the frame: the possibility that this woven story could be unpicked and told all over again is tantalizing—as indeed, we know it will be in the subsequent epic tradition.)[30] But for the most part, although the weaving in *Ulisse* gives some kind of voice to Penelope, we do not quite have 'the voice of a wife reinstated in an idealized marriage based on *homophrosunē* [harmonious likemindedness], a wife at once traditional and full of ingenuity and certainly the match of her polytropic husband.'[31] Though the portrayal of the cinematic Penelope is not without interest, by herself she does not do much to undermine the stereotype of the mourning, passive wife, or to suggest that she *is* Ulysses' match. But this Penelope does not exist only 'by herself'. We must now look to the other faces that the silhouette bears, in order to better appreciate how the Homeric Penelope 'of many ways' is matched by the cinematic one.

SIREN SONG: 'ARE YOU MY FAMILY?'[32]

In the *Odyssey*, Odysseus encounters the Sirens shortly after having left the island of Circe, retelling the story in his long analeptic narrative to the Phaeacians (12.165–200). Here, it is just one of a large number of episodes that Odysseus recounts: memorable, but of no overwhelming narrative significance, other than for the obvious danger that it presents (though no more so than most of his other encounters). In *Ulisse*,

[30] Crucially, this is also an ongoing epic tradition that now includes the film itself. See Paul (2013).

[31] Felson and Slatkin (2004: 112).

[32] The quotation is the first line of the track, 'Siren Song', from the album *Two Suns* (2009), by the British singer-songwriter Bat for Lashes.

though, the episode bears much more potent meaning in relation to the rest of the narrative. Importantly, we do not see the Sirens. This is in keeping partly with Homer, where they are not explicitly described either—Circe says only that they sit in a meadow (12.45)—and partly with the film's general reluctance to visualize divine beings or monsters.[33] The Sirens typically appear as bird-women hybrids in ancient art (most famously in the fifth-century red-figure *stamnos* in the British Museum), but this is left well alone here; the only visual clues are the bleached white skeletons on the rocks which alert Ulysses and his men to the encroaching danger.[34]

The precise nature of that danger becomes clear soon after the Sirens' song begins. In the *Odyssey,* they promise to sing of 'everything that the Argives and Trojans did and suffered in wide Troy through the gods' despite' (12.189–90, trans. Lattimore); this of course bears its own significance for Homer's narrative, as a demonstration of the extent of Odysseus' *kleos. Ulisse*'s 'Siren Song', always heard as a disembodied soundtrack whilst the camera focuses on Ulysses, tied to the mast, is very different: at first just an ethereal, female wailing, the lone female voice that cuts in quickly identifies itself:

> Ulysses... Ulysses... It is I, Penelope! Penelope the faithful! Your young bride when you sailed to Troy. Your journey is ended! You are back in Ithaca! I have waited for you a thousand nights for you to get tired of wandering, never resting beside me in your bed. You are home, Ulysses, home, in Ithaca at last!

Then a male voice joins in. It is Telemachus, lamenting that he has grown to be a man without knowing the face of his father, before Penelope interrupts: 'Come ashore to your son! You are home. Your kingdom, your waiting wife... I am waiting, Ulysses.' Ulysses, increasingly frantic, begs his men to stop rowing, and when they will not, he twists against his ropes, crying out 'Don't leave me!', as the wailing female vocals gain in intensity.

The notion of giving the Sirens the voices of Ulysses' family is ingenious. In myth, their song is meant to be the most entrancing, beautiful

[33] This is another reason for the general success of *Ulisse*'s adaptation, since it does not risk shattering viewers' belief in the narrative through poorly realized monsters (only Polyphemus appears, who is actually quite convincing). The agency of the gods is effectively conveyed using other visual strategies—for example, Poseidon only ever appears in the form of a statue; but the offence caused by Ulysses throwing this overboard is made clear through the immediate effects of storm and shipwreck.

[34] A detail reminiscent of a wall-painting from Pompeii, depicting Odysseus and the Sirens, in which skeletons litter the rocks in the foreground.

thing that a man can hear, able to lure him to his death without a moment's hesitation; in this scene, then, *Ulisse* shows us with great narrative economy that the thing that has most power over Ulysses—his heart's greatest desire—is indeed his wife and son. This is particularly necessary given that the opening third of the film has been mostly concerned with the families 'in waiting' that threaten to derail the reunification of Penelope and Ulysses: Antinoos has arrived in Ithaca in the preceding scene, and just before that, we have witnessed the 'courtship' of Ulysses and Nausicaa on Scheria. Penelope's yearning for Ulysses was not in doubt, but now we also witness the depth of Ulysses' pain as he is made to listen to the grief that his absence has caused his family. And for the film's audience, the anguish is intensified by our knowledge that were Ulysses to yield to this Siren song, it would surely end his chance of getting home.[35] It might also be noted that the film seems to take inspiration from another part of the *Odyssey* here. In the Telemachy, Telemachus learns from Menelaus that when the Trojan horse had been wheeled into the city, Helen circled it three times, calling out to the Achaians in their wives' voices (*Od.* 4.271–89). This was also a ruse to lure the men to their death (which Menelaus excuses by attributing it to a god's power over her), but Menelaus' retelling of the story is specifically to illustrate Odysseus' heroism. Whilst Menelaus and Diomedes wanted to get up or call out, only Odysseus realized the deceit and pulled them back. These two versions of the story may be slightly at odds with one another, and perhaps the Homeric version is more in tune with the cunning and astute Odysseus; but for Ulysses, the impact of this scene in the film as a demonstration of his devotion to wife and home is powerful, and could not be bettered.

'I AM THE PLACE WHERE ALL DESIRES ARE FULFILLED':[36] ULYSSES ON CIRCE'S ISLAND

Already, then, *Ulisse*'s 'Penelope' has been allowed to escape the confines of the Homeric character and make her presence felt, if only in voice, by appropriating another powerful female character, with the specific intention of emphasizing her own importance to Ulysses. This strategy

[35] 'That man who unsuspecting approaches them, and listens to the Sirens singing, has no prospect of coming home and delighting his wife and little children as they stand about him in greeting' (*Od.* 12.40–3, trans. Lattimore).

[36] From Margaret Atwood's 'Circe/Mud Poems' (1987: 220).

continues in an even more striking way in the very next scene. Having successfully escaped the Sirens, we see Ulysses and his men land on an island where lions roam along with the deer. Losing track of his men, Ulysses calls out for them, before a woman appears from the mists to tell him that they have gone. When asked who she is, she replies, 'Circe'. We then see the narrative largely follow Homer: after discovering that she has turned his men into pigs, Ulysses escapes that fate for himself (though not with the use of the mysterious flower *moly* here), but is instead seduced into staying with Circe, long after his crew have given up and gone home (Fig. 6.2).

In terms of *Ulisse*'s narrative, it seems appropriate that Circe should play an important role. As Judith Yarnall has shown, although Circe has had a number of different incarnations in her long post-Homeric history, she is essentially an archetypal figure; 'centuries of misogyny' have helped to fix that archetype as a dangerously sexual female, who is able to enslave Odysseus and keep him from his true goal of returning home.[37] As we have seen a mainly archetypal Penelope—the patient, faithful wife—so now we see the mysterious, magical temptress, representing the opposite pole of female behaviour (and thereby introducing

Figure 6.2 Circe (Silvana Mangano) and Ulysses (Kirk Douglas) in *Ulisse*, dir. Mario Camerini. Credit: [LUX FILM/THE KOBAL COLLECTION]

[37] Yarnall (1994: 194).

another key feature of the peplum genre, the dichotomization of female characters into 'good' wives and 'bad' mistresses).[38] However, the conventional 'madonna and whore' dichotomy does not go nearly far enough in explaining Circe's role in *Ulisse*. Yarnall clarifies the view of Circe as archetype with the following explanation, drawing on Jungian analytical psychology, and attempting to rid her of the negative accretions of her reception history:

> She is an image (and I follow Jung in this hypothesis) generated by a node of energy or a patterning process in our collective unconscious that demands expression. Circe offers an image of the strong woman who has power to give shape and form: someone we all experienced once, while we were waiting to be thrust out into this world. Because she acts upon adults, exclusively adult males, and not developing fetuses, she also acts as a dramatic reminder of our original, and in some sense constant, plasticity and helplessness. No matter what century or work Circe appears in, she is associated with our bodily vulnerability and has power over that—a power that is often presented as sexual allure.[39]

This description is clearly true of Circe in *Ulisse*: as in Homer, and most other versions of the myth, she uses her powers to physically change Ulysses' men into pigs (though she tells Ulysses that this was easier to do than he would think);[40] their plasticity, and Ulysses' helplessness (he is easily enchanted into staying with her) is clear. However, Circe's 'power to give shape and form' in the film extends beyond the men *to herself*. As was noted at the beginning of this chapter, Silvana Mangano plays Circe as well as Penelope: therefore it should be quite clear to all viewers, when Circe first appears to Ulysses, that this is in fact Circe/Penelope. Just as the Sirens appropriated Penelope's voice (or vice versa?), so too Circe has made herself appear to Ulysses as, in some sense, his wife.

To some extent, the film visually emphasizes the differences between Circe and Penelope. What we—and Ulysses—are then left to consider is the extent to which Circe and Penelope are one and the same, or distinctly different. Circe's hair is a suitably witchy greenish-blonde,

[38] See Nikoloutsos in this volume. [39] Yarnall (1994: 2).

[40] This references a recurrent interpretation of Circe's transformation of the men into pigs, which sees it as merely a revelation of their essential swine-like nature, that Circe 'actualises the swinishness in men' (Brilliant (1995: 168).) The American writer Katherine Anne Porter elaborated on this in her essay, 'In Defense of Circe', first published in the year that *Ulisse* was released: 'Not even a god, having once formed a man, can make a swine of him. That is for him to choose. Circe's honeyed food with the lulling drug in it caused them to reveal themselves' (Porter (1970: 135).) This somewhat undermines Yarnall's Jungian interpretation of Circe as a powerfully transforming archetype.

against the brunette Penelope;[41] her make-up is also much more defined, whereas Penelope wears little. Beyond this, though, the connection between the two women is made clear from the outset, and it goes further than the obvious facial resemblance: for example, Circe's dress, although much more glamorous with its beading and sequins, does recall Penelope's clothing, in that both use veils to frame the face, and emphasize the waist with corsets. The continuity between the two women is then made explicit in the following exchange between Ulysses and Circe. After lamenting her loneliness (as Penelope had done), Circe quickly draws Ulysses under her seductive spell. They embrace and he draws back her veil:

ULYSSES: Strange . . . same proud face . . . Same dark eyes as Penelope. Strange.
CIRCE: Why is it strange? Isn't the difference between one woman and another only in the mind of a man?
ULYSSES: No. The difference is Penelope would never let a stranger take her in his arms.
CIRCE: Not even a stranger like Ulysses?

Here we have a reminder of the nature of the faithful Penelope to which Ulysses is trying to return, but also a clear indication that Penelope is in fact in some sense already present for him, though differently embodied as Circe. (In the ancient tradition, too, Penelope and Circe may be connected through their beauty, and their iconographical attributes, in both art and literature—Circe is at the loom when first encountered at *Od.* 10.220f.)[42]

How are we to understand this amalgamation of Penelope and Circe, then? I would argue that it functions on several levels. Firstly, and most simply, it casts a new light on Ulysses' apparent betrayal of Penelope in spending so long with Circe. Although it can be argued that Odysseus' 'sexual adventures do not disrupt the *oikos*: the fact that he narrates these escapades to Penelope (as earlier to the Phaeacians) indicates that they do not constitute a violation of societal norms', it is not unusual for readers of Homer to struggle with the fact that Odysseus has to all intents and purposes committed adultery.[43] Conveniently, then, the film presents Ulysses as in fact merely sleeping with 'his wife'. Though the on-screen action is limited to chaste 1950s style clinches, the bed that Circe and Ulysses evidently share is a dominant feature of many shots, perhaps recalling the centrality of Penelope and Odysseus' marriage bed in

[41] Popular representations of witches have often used the colour green, as with the green-skinned Wicked Witch of the West in *The Wizard of Oz* (1939).
[42] Brilliant (1995: 170–1). [43] Felson and Slatkin (2004: 109).

Homer; interestingly, that bed is never shown in *Ulisse*'s Ithaca scenes, but perhaps that is because it has simply been transferred to Circe's island. Secondly, as well as potentially excusing Ulysses' behaviour, the Penelope/Circe amalgamation develops his characterization, using the same strategies of narrative economy that the Sirens episode had employed. Ulysses' readiness to lie with Circe, when Circe is visually one and the same with his wife, and her instant attraction to him, both reinforces Ulysses' masculinity and desirability, but also, again, indicates his deep-seated desire to return home.

In addition, the continuity of Penelope and Circe allows us to revisit our interpretation of Circe herself. In the film, Ulysses already questions her identity—when asking her to return his men to human form, he addresses her as 'goddess, demon, witch, whatever you are!'—and perhaps, just as Ulysses' behaviour is excused, so too Circe undergoes some rehabilitation here. Had another actress played her, we would have been much more likely to read her as again simply a bewitching adulterer, but with this casting, it is not so simple. Judith Yarnall argues that it is Circe's power over Ulysses that has led to centuries of misinterpretation of her as nothing more than a sexual predator; but just as Homer makes it a good deal more complex than just a matter of lust, so too the film is committed to showing Circe as possessing female power and agency that goes beyond the carnal. The Homeric Circe is the catalyst that facilitates Odysseus' journey home, showing him how to proceed, and warning him of the most dangerous obstacles that lie in wait; as such she 'embodies the power of the feminine in its primordial, highly ambivalent form', or even, in Jungian terms, the *anima*, a female figure that guards the gateway to man's collective unconscious.[44] This is well reflected in *Ulisse*. In another highly successful example of narrative economizing, Circe does not direct Ulysses to visit the Underworld on his own, but rather brings it to him, summoning the shades of the Achaians, his men, and (unexpectedly) his mother directly to him. This is in response to Ulysses' refusal of her gift of immortality[45]—saying that he would rather be mortal, she proposes 'then let the dead tell you how happy they are!' But Ulysses' convictions are not shaken: there are greater gifts than

[44] Yarnall (1994: 24). Yarnall is not totally committed to this element of Jungian rhetoric, though, seeing it as 'more clouding than clarifying'; it is better simply to think of Circe as an 'archetypal woman of power', she says (4–5).

[45] In Homer, this is the gift of the nymph Calypso, but the condensing of narrative means that Calypso is effectively subsumed into Circe in *Ulisse*. Interestingly, early media reports on the production said that Mangano would be playing a *triple* role—Penelope, Circe, and Calypso (undated *Daily Mail* report (possibly 1953?) in the BFI archives.)

immortality, he says, 'to be born, and to die, and in between to live like a man'. He 'accepts the inheritance' of mankind—its fragility—and is ready to die when the time comes. Ulysses' articulation of these words is powerful, and although it marks the moment when he wrests control of his own destiny back from Circe, it in no way lessens her power, for she, even if not the guardian of Ulysses' subconscious, is the one who has facilitated his access to it, to his inner sense of humanity. Now he is free to return to Penelope—but it is already Penelope, as Penelope/Circe, who has allowed him that opportunity.

We are moving towards a sense of Penelope and Circe as one and the same: the doubled object of desire for Ulysses which is also able to exert an essentially positive, creative power over him, drawing him towards home and the recreation of the *oikos* (Penelope) at the same time as eliciting his true identity as man (Circe). On this interpretation, Silvana Mangano's embodiment of both women indicates a kind of unity and 'one-ness' of female power.[46] Shifting perspective slightly, though, we must also allow that a *diversity* of female experience and behaviour is also communicated by this dual casting. Rather than seeing the archetypal Penelope and Circe as achieving holistic unity within Mangano, we could see them persisting as different, irreconcilable facets of woman; or, as Paglia would have it, 'the two faces of Eve, the ambiguous duality of woman that Western culture polarizes as Madonna and whore'.[47] Placing *Ulisse* in its cultural context brings this reading to the fore. Arthur Pomeroy points out the importance of the Second World War, where 'the exposure to new lands and customs of soldiers serving overseas in and after the Second World War' is reflected in the wanderings of Ulysses.[48] What he does not mention is that the female experience

[46] A recent interpretation of slightly earlier representations of both Circe and Penelope maps out very similar territory. The British painter J.W. Waterhouse famously depicted Circe as sorceress in two works (*Circe Offering the Cup to Ulysses*, 1891, and *Circe Invidiosa: Circe Poisoning the Sea*, 1892), followed by *Penelope and the Suitors* some two decades later (1912). At around the same time as the Penelope painting, Waterhouse was also working on sketches for a new Circe composition (never realized), this time showing her at a table, surrounded by, as Elizabeth Prettejohn describes it in the catalogue of a recent Waterhouse exhibition (Prettejohn et al. 2008), 'the paraphernalia of her magic arts' (182). In one of the oil sketches (cat. 57), a tapestry is shown in the background (albeit indistinctly), upon which appears Ulysses' encounter with the Sirens (itself the subject of an 1891 painting by Waterhouse), and the pose and appearance of Circe resembles that of Penelope in the 1912 painting. Therefore, as Prettejohn argues, 'the new composition... makes explicit the crucial role of Circe in directing Ulysses' voyages, as well as creating a new link between the learned sorceress and the "wise Penelope"' (ibid., 183). Some forty years before the film, then, we see another attempt to yoke Penelope and Circe together, even if fleetingly.

[47] Paglia (1997: 182).

[48] Pomeroy (2008: 66). We should also add the Korean War, here, which ended two months after *Ulisse* went into production on 18 May 1953.

of war is also given a clear voice in the film. We have already heard Penelope express her fears that, whilst Ulysses is away, he will have met other women—and so while Ulysses symbolizes the Allied soldier of the forties and fifties, roaming far from home, Silvana Mangano is *both* the wife patiently waiting at home *and*, more uncomfortably, the dangerous (foreign, other) woman who might steal that husband. The final dialogue between Penelope and Ulysses supports this view, since it could so easily refer to the experiences of separation that a large proportion of the contemporary audience would have undergone:

PENELOPE: (praying) Oh divine Athena, did his long road back to me have to be so bloodstained?
ULYSSES: (entering) My road had to be long and bloodstained. There was no other way to bring me back to you.
PENELOPE: (weeping) So many years wasted!
ULYSSES: So many years of our youth squandered in the savagery of war. Lost in confused wanderings.
PENELOPE: I was so lonely...
ULYSSES: I promise you, I'll make up for it, in the tranquil years that lie ahead.
PENELOPE: Yes, together!
ULYSSES: We'll make up for every bitter and lonely hour we both have known!

Still, the embodiment of Penelope and Circe in Mangano ought not to be reduced to a simple Madonna/whore dichotomy. By examining the film's cultural context more closely, we can see how the specific casting of this actress supports our reading of a more complex femininity in *Ulisse*. Mangano, one of the leading actresses in Italy at this time, first came to fame through her starring role in the 1949 film *Riso Amaro (Bitter Rice)*. Here, she played a young rice-worker, also called Silvana, in a role that would quickly make her world-famous, largely as a result of her youthful sexual appeal. As a press release from the *Italian Films Export* agency reminded viewers, the famous still shot of Silvana (taken by Robert Capa) 'without makeup, standing knee-deep in a flooded rice field and wearing a tattered sweater, shabby shorts and torn black stockings became one of the most famous pin-ups ever published and made her face and figure famous in every village and hamlet of the world'.[49] This was a particular vision of female sexuality that was being reflected in many other Italian films of the period: actresses such as Mangano,

[49] 5 November 1954, BFI Archives. Given the date, the press release could very likely have pre-empted the release of *Ulisse* in Britain.

Sophia Loren, and Gina Lollobrigida inhabited a number of *popolana* (peasant women) roles, in which 'their beauty... appeared to be raw and primitive, and more individual than the manufactured variety associated with Hollywood.... They seemed to embody the hopes of Italy, still a predominantly agricultural country, as it recovered from the war.'[50]

The screening of the teenage Mangano's rustic sexuality had a huge impact and brought her worldwide fame, but it was also significant for shaping her image as a 'star', and establishing the first layer of associations that she would bring to all subsequent roles. As Stephen Gundle reflects, Silvana in *Riso Amaro* is 'a creature of the earth, an archetype whose generous figure, overt sensuality and instinctive simplicity lent her a primitive, primeval quality'.[51] This assessment clearly resonates with the idea of Circe as archetype that we have just been examining, and so already we can see how Mangano's portrayal of the mythic women in *Ulisse* gains power from her earlier roles. Mangano starred in many other Italian films before *Ulisse*, each of them adding new layers. In the aftermath of *Riso Amaro*, Mangano, along with Loren and Lollobrigida, amongst others, came to exemplify a particular brand of Italian female character that would be called the *maggiorata fisica* (literally, the well-endowed physique), playing roles which emphasized their sexual allure, and their abundance of earthy sexual qualities.[52] So, when Mangano appeared in films such as *L'oro di Napoli*, where she played a prostitute, or *Mambo* (both 1954), where the impact of her captivating dance was such that it would be enshrined as an iconic scene of Italian cinema by *Cinema Paradiso* (1988), she was creating, on the surface at least, a heavily sexualized—but never simply whorish—persona.

Indeed, that persona was more complex than this simple sketch might suggest. Just as her dual role in *Ulisse* represented the multiple facets of female identity, Mangano was also actively seeking to stake out different territories in her public and private life. From the very beginning of her career, she swung between taking film roles to fulfil her contract with Lux Film, and her desire to be simply a mother; in fact, she repeatedly declared her retirement from film, beginning with the birth of her first daughter when she was only 20. Even when she was more resigned to pursuing a film career, Mangano—along with the other *maggiorate fisiche*—participated in a considerable revision of that initial model of Italian gender stereotypes, which involved 'a rejection of the canon of florid beauty... The actress very deliberately sought to achieve a refined

[50] Buckley (2008: 271). [51] Gundle (2007: 1450).

[52] Cf. Pomeroy's discussions of Sylva Koscino and Gianna Maria Canale, stars of the contemporary Italian film *Fatiche di Ercole*, in his contribution to this volume.

appearance after her first pregnancies and put herself beyond the type of beauty she had helped create on the screen. By 1960, she had evolved into an ethereal presence, more spirit than body, whose film roles bore no resemblance to those of her early career.'[53] Mangano changed her make-up, dieted to a more svelte appearance, and consciously distanced herself from her *popolana* persona, apparently to the extent of banning the famous images of herself in *Riso Amaro* from her home.[54] The effect of all of this was that even in public, Mangano was characterized as a complex, elusive woman:

> La storia di Silvana Mangano è la storia di una donna dalla personalità inconfondibile. Nata da madre inglese e da padre italiano, i due temperamenti, decisamente contrastanti, entrano spesso in conflitto e determinano una certa incostanza negli atteggiamenti di Silvana e nel suo carattere a volte pieno di contraddizioni.[55]

> The story of Silvana Mangano is the story of a woman with an unmistakable personality. Born of an English mother and Italian father, the two temperaments, decidedly mixed, often come into conflict and lead to a certain fickleness in Silvana's conduct, and a character at times full of contradictions.

There is perhaps a suggestion of misogyny in this characterization of Mangano as fickle, but from another perspective, we may also see it as her guarantee of complexity, and so authenticity as a woman. And if it was so much in evidence in her public persona, then it should be even more clear just how effective her dual casting in *Ulisse* was, allowing her to bring this pre-existing image of female intricacy and complexity to the role.

As Maggie Günsberg has shown, this idea of femininity is in fact a pervasive theme throughout Italian cinema of this era, and is not confined to Mangano;[56] elsewhere, the same actress may be used as a way of presenting repeated takes and retakes on various models of gender. Within the cinematic depiction of mythical women, the casting of Rossana Podestà, Nausicaa in *Ulisse*, as Helen in the following year's production of *Helen of Troy* is one example, and, as Arthur Pomeroy shows elsewhere in this volume, Jane Mansfield plays both Deianeira and the Queen of the Amazons in *Gli amori di Ercole* (1960). But for the most emphatic embodiment of this strategy, we can only look to Mangano

[53] Gundle (2007: 174). [54] Buckley (2008: 275).

[55] Uncredited and undated 'Biografia' of Silvana Mangano, BFI archives (my own translation).

[56] Günsberg (2005: 159–72).

again, whose examination of female identity would continue in her post-*Ulisse* career and culminate in her work with the Italian director Pier Paolo Pasolini. 1967 saw her star in Pasolini's version of the Oedipus myth, *Edipo Re*, this time as Jocasta. This role offered even more rich possibilities for female complexity, for Jocasta is, of course, both wife and mother to Oedipus, giver of life and its destroyer, nurturing female and dangerous sexual liaison: all the different female roles that were at least hinted at by her characters in *Ulisse* are here repeated. What is more, Mangano again plays *two* roles within this film: the mythical Jocasta, but also, in the film's explicitly Freudian framing narrative, the modern mother (who in fact represents Pasolini's own mother). Pasolini, it seems, was fully aware of Mangano's ability to embody the intricacies of female power and identity on screen, and he kept working with her. Again, she played a mother in his film of the following year, *Teorema*, before taking an uncredited role in 1971's *Il Decameron*—appropriately, perhaps, playing the Madonna. For an actress who was often reluctant to commit herself fully to the profession, we are fortunate that Silvana Mangano left behind such fascinating cinematic material: her film roles explored the complexities of female experience to great effect, and it was the templates of mythic women that offered the greatest opportunities to do so.

7

Why is Penelope Still Waiting? The Missing Feminist Reappraisal of the *Odyssey* in Cinema, 1963–2007

Edith Hall

PENELOPE IN KONCHALOVSKY'S *ODYSSEY*

In Wolfgang Petersen's *Troy* (2004), when Achilles (Brad Pitt) is too busy worrying about Briseis to devote himself to armed combat, Odysseus (Sean Bean) remarks cryptically to him, 'women have a way of complicating things'. Unfortunately, women scarcely complicate the plot of *Troy* at all. Hecuba does not feature, Helen possesses not one iota of mysterious power, and Briseis is amalgamated with both Chryseis and Cassandra. Yet alongside the reduction of the *Iliad's* already meagre female quotient, and the wholesale deletion of the authoritative and eloquent old queen of Troy, the movie does doff its cap in the direction of its emancipated third-millennial female audience members by allowing Briseis to stab Agamemnon in the neck. Her action is presented as a feisty post-feminist refusal to be complicit in her own victimhood, when the brutal patriarchal overlord is about to take her captive.

David Benioff's otherwise lacklustre screenplay here dared—however tentatively and briefly—to rewrite the Homeric poem in a way that does not diminish but enhances its presentation of female agency. It is an important moment from the perspective of anyone thinking about women in movies set in ancient Greece and Rome. The physical initiative taken by Briseis (Rose Byrne) in her own self-defence shows that even in Hollywood it is possible to think creatively about female roles in ancient Greece and in ancient Greek epic. It is a shame that the possibility that Homeric epic could be changed to make it less demeaning to women had never struck Andrei Konchalovsky and Chris Solimine when they adapted the *Odyssey* as a miniseries for NBC, first aired in 1997 and subsequently distributed as a film on VHS and DVD.

From the perspective of a female spectator, the movie (which Konchalovsky also directed) is perhaps the most depressing cinematic excursion into ancient Greece ever to have been made. Armand Assante, who played Odysseus, struggled manfully with the inadequate dialogue, but Greta Scacchi seems to have given up before she started. She is an intelligent actress, well known for her commitment to women's equality. She has turned down roles (including the predatory Alex Forrest played instead by Glenn Close in Adrian Lyne's gynophobic *Fatal Attraction* [1987]) precisely because they pandered to male fantasies. But she nevertheless seems to have been rendered powerless by the script and the directing style in Konchalovsky's *Odyssey*. She was prevented by them from displaying almost any of the emotions for which Penelope's situation cries out. Rage at abandonment? Grief at being denied further children? Pleasure at being in charge of her own Ithacan fiefdom? Boredom with her narrowly confined domestic environment? Desire for a 'suitor'? Retaliation against being sexually harassed on a daily level? Irritation with Telemachus for throwing his weight about with her? An urge to go and find out for herself what had happened to Odysseus? Hardly.

Her one plausible emotion given more than one scene (and one for which no explicit basis is to be found in Homer) is her sexual frustration, giving rise to the suspicion that Greta Scacchi was offered the part less because of her apt age (late thirties) than because of her rather racy reputation. This was not something she deserved, nor had courted, but a result of the perceived sensuality of her outstanding beauty when she was a very young woman. She was only offered roles entailing sex scenes and nudity, earning her the unwanted journalists' soubriquet 'Scorchy Scacchi'. Konchalovsky's conception of the role of Penelope interacts not with the actress's skills but with her reputation, since she is presented as a now ageing sex goddess. When, residing on Calypso's island, Odysseus dreams of Penelope, it is as the nubile girl he used to chase around the marital bedroom in sex games on Ithaca; in the concluding scene she is even made to beg Odysseus for reassurance that she has not aged too badly. Yet Scorchy Scacchi is not even assertive sexually. When not cooling off her groin in rippling sea waves and orgasmically murmuring the name 'Odysseus', she is actually required to spend almost the entire film on the verge of or actually in tears, and to exude a sense of utter fragility. Typically, she faints like a maiden in a Victorian novel after smiling too hard when she finally finds Odysseus in her bedroom.

This helpless note is struck in the opening sequence, when Penelope is not even allowed to give birth bravely or without Odysseus intervening. The very first shot shows Odysseus sprinting, bow in hand, across Ithaca to reach her. She is wincing in labour (although she looks far too slim to be nine months pregnant), and so he masterfully picks her up, carries her body to the house, tells her to imagine she is lying on a beach, and improbably commands 'give me the pain!' She moans pathetically while he expropriates the sole heroic role—producing a child—only a woman can play in nature, as the camera focuses on him pulling (rather than her pushing) the baby from her body. He then walks with the newborn round Ithaca, and it is he, not Penelope, who gloats in a voice-over, 'this day was the proudest day of my life!'

Odysseus is almost immediately taken off to war, informing us that he is Odysseus and (all too accurately) that 'this is *my* story' (emphasis added). He says long good-byes to his mother Anticleia (Irene Papas) and to a shrine of Athena, but to the again tearful Penelope he delivers an instruction that will shape her entire future (to remarry if he does not return—but only when Telemachus is grown to manhood). This she accepts, lugubriously, but without any demur or curiosity. From here onwards, the film could potentially have developed Penelope's stature, since (unlike the *Odyssey* for most of the wanderings) it does intercut Ithacan scenes with those of Odysseus' adventures. But in these Ithacan scenes Penelope's status as a character deteriorates from insipid to inane. She fails to stand up to Anticleia over the upbringing of Telemachus. She then fails to dissuade Anticleia from suicide. She indiscreetly tells Telemachus the secret of the olive-tree bedroom, and the film excises completely her careful testing of Odysseus' trustworthiness at the climax of the action. Since the film also ends with their bedroom reunion, and no sense whatsoever that Odysseus might have to leave Ithaca once again as predicted in Homer's poem, the complicated reactions Penelope might have experienced to this news are avoided—or evaded. Penelope has kept her legs together, and her virtue has apparently been sufficiently rewarded by a sex bout with Odysseus after two decades. There is no sense that this has ultimately cost her any sacrifice.

What are we to make of this dismal portrayal of one of antiquity's most famous heroines? I have heard the argument from some male scholars that the figure of Odysseus as quest-hero is a 'universal' psychological archetype with whom anyone, regardless of gender, can identify, certainly in such an intimate and psychologically compelling medium as cinema. But surely this argument was repudiated long ago by Laura Mulvey, when she explored how the female spectator in the cinema is coerced into looking at narrative through male eyes, being positioned between an idealized, active, powerful male ego and a passive, powerless one identified as female.[1] In more psychoanalytical terms, if women do enjoy adopting this masculine point of view as they identify with Odysseus-questers enjoying multiple sexual relationships or interesting travels, it is because as little girls they experienced a pre-Oedipal, phallic fantasy of omnipotence; nevertheless, the spectatorial position they take on in the cinema is temporary and 'transvestite': the recovery of the long lost aspect of their sexual identity can only be uncomfortable and partial, and they must always oscillate between identification with Odysseus and with Penelope.[2]

Alternatively, Konchalovsky's Penelope might hypothetically be defended on the ground that Penelope's chastity and patience are celebrated in the original *Odyssey*. This is, at the crudest level, true. But Konchalovsky was happy to interfere with the prototype when it suited him. More importantly, he has actually interfered with the poem in order to stress Penelope's libido and downgrade even further her agency and the extent of the depictions of her subjectivity. The Homeric Penelope has some great speeches and dream narratives which reveal some of her inner thoughts, and even she is a good deal tougher and more assertive than the figure produced in Konchalovsky's version. From the Renaissance onwards, numerous dramatists and opera composers responded to the Penelope they found in the Greek text by making her the centre of emotional stage works, from Giambattista della Porta's Counter-Reformation *Penelope* (1591) and the seminal *Il Ritorno d'Ulisse in Patria* (*The Return of Odysseus to his Homeland*) of Claudio Monteverdi and Giacomo Badoaro (1640) onwards.[3] Homer's Odysseus values Penelope's intelligence, and the poem celebrates the desirability of 'like-mindedness' within a marriage (*Od.* 6.181–4). It was Penelope to whom Odysseus delegated the responsibility for his household by making her his regent (*Od.* 18.259–70). The satisfactory outcome of the poem depends as much upon Penelope's qualities as on those of Odysseus. This makes her almost unique in Greek mythology, where clever women have a tendency to misbehave, and feminine docility is valued more than shrewdness. The Homeric Penelope is also more complex, mysterious, and nuanced than this screen substitute. She has developed interesting relationships that are left unexplored in the film. It is explicitly said in the poem, for example, that she preferred the company of one of the suitors to that of the others; moreover, the complexity of her relationship with Melantho, a 'disloyal daughter' figure on whom she lavished love as a child, has huge dramatic potential.

[1] Mulvey ([1975] 1989a: 20).
[2] Mulvey ([1981] 1989b: 37).
[3] See Hall (2008), chs. 3 and 9.

The problem of Penelope's tortured consciousness should be a screenplay writer's gift, offering a combination of intense moments of interiority combined with an almost detective-plot style mystery. She is so multi-layered and paradoxical that she has long frustrated scholars bent on tracing a consistency or unilinear development in her portrayal. The enigma begins when she summons the beggar, outraged at the suitors' treatment of him. This, she says, could never happen if Odysseus came back. At this point Telemachus sneezes *and Penelope laughs* (*Od.* 17.543–50). No such mysterious reaction, or underlying sense of humour, is suggested in the film. Before she has met the beggar, the Homeric Penelope tells the suitors to bring bridal gifts; the narrator comments, 'Odysseus saw with glee how she lured them to make presents to her, stealing their souls with persuasive words though her heart meanwhile was set elsewhere' (*Od.* 18.281–3). This raises the possibility that Penelope really believes that Odysseus is about to return, or even that she has seen through his disguise, neither of which is remotely suggested in Konchalovsky's version. The picture of Penelope built up subsequently in the Homeric poem is perplexing. Does the archery contest occur to her because she believes that the crisis must be resolved one way or another? Does her *subconscious* mind recognize Odysseus while her consciousness does not? Is she an irrational creature so emotionally confused that it is pointless to look for consistency of motive? Whichever way the Homeric story is read, it is certainly sexist: we are asked to collude with this woman's husband and son in scrutinizing her misery. Yet the narrative incontrovertibly offers a range of interesting interpretations of Penelope that have been entirely overlooked in the filmmaking process.

Indeed, the potential to make Penelope more interesting was not completely overlooked by earlier film writers and directors. It is disheartening to discover the extent to which the cinematic Penelope has actually regressed during the precise period when we might have expected her to emancipate herself somewhat from her patriarchal plotline. The Penelope of Mario Camerini's *Ulisse* (1954), played with such dignity and eloquence by Silvana Mangano,[4] has far more of a mind of her own than Konchalovsky's, even being allowed to show revulsion at the violent revenge taken by her husband. The movie relating to the *Odyssey* that has reached the widest audience, on account of the fame of its director, is Jean-Luc Godard's *Le Mépris* (*Contempt*, 1963); this film puts the Penelopean experience centre-stage. It centres on the making of a film of the *Odyssey*, of which the director is Fritz Lang, acted by himself. One of the

[4] See Joanna Paul's chapter in this volume.

snippets of the embedded film that is seen during the scrutiny of the rushes sequence offers a striking image of Penelope, standing against a bright yellow wall, adorned with heavy make-up suggesting Mycenaean frescoes.

Yet the important Penelopean figure here is Camille (Brigitte Bardot), the wife of the 'internal' screenwriter Paul Javal (Michel Piccoli), with whom she is becoming increasingly disenchanted. The film was adapted from Albert Moravia's novel *Il Disprezzo* (1954, usually translated as *A Ghost at Noon*), which is narrated by the Odysseus figure. But, for the film, Godard took the radical decision consistently to adopt, through subtle use of the camera and careful writing, the wife's perspective. This is particularly remarkable because, in casting the stunning Bardot, he ran such a high risk of completely pandering to the desiring male gaze. But instead he uses Bardot to signify the endlessly reversible nature of the cinematic image, which 'solicits our emotional involvement with the characters while at the same time making us see those characters as actors'.[5]

Camille does eventually get killed off, perhaps in a symbolic enactment of the providential destiny of unfaithful women in the Western cultural tradition, but she has been allowed a remarkable degree of moral autonomy and even commentary on the emerging narrative line. She runs, with a curious detachment, through a series of obscenities to see how her husband will react. She also reads a book arguing that it solves nothing to murder a sexual rival, which brings to mind not only her husband's jealousy of the love rival Prokosch, but also the carnage in *Odyssey* 22. The degree to which Godard rewrites Penelope's archetypal role is a result of his fascination with the process of translation itself—not only between languages and historical periods, but also between media. As Godard has himself insisted, written discourse 'automatically' changes when it is turned into film. *Le Mépris* is a radical adaptation of a novel which Godard despised (he described it as 'a vulgar and pretty trash novel [*roman de gare*], full of classic and outmoded feelings'), and, as Nicholas Paige has put it, Moravia's trite love triangle is 'systematically undermined by Bardot's Camille', through her incessant 'back-and-forth between love and contempt'.[6] Moravia's novel, moreover, itself 'translates' the ancient epic into a radically different idiom; this complicated process, of screening a novel that adapted a poem, resulted in a film which Godard claimed could actually have been entitled *In Search of Homer*. Since the *Odyssey* itself is irrecoverable, fragmented into an ever

5 Paige (2004: 15).   6 Paige (2004: 14).

increasing number of different retellings, what is the problem with retelling the experience of Penelope and Odysseus themselves? Both Camille and Paul are products of Godard's interrogation of the Western tradition which, it is discovered, cannot and will not answer back. But they are both victims of a modernist cultural anomie and interpersonal isolation.[7]

In the 1960s, then, it was possible to explore the ideas that Penelope was the most significant figure in the Odyssean plot, and that the negative experience of her marriage might be cinematically interesting. Three years after *Contempt*, as Jon Solomon has pointed out, there are Odyssean reverberations in Arthur Hiller's comedy *Penelope* (1966), starring Natalie Wood. Although by no stretch of the imagination a 'feminist' film, the star of the show was nevertheless a proactive woman who felt so neglected by her banker husband that she robbed his bank.[8] The slightly subversive undercurrent to this plot in economic as well as gender terms must have had something to do with the politics of the man whose novel was adapted for the screenplay: although writing under the pseudonym of E.V. Cunningham, he was none other than Howard Fast, the communist author of the novel *Spartacus*, and no stranger to classical material.

The portrayal of Penelope in Konchalovsky's movie could have learned much from Camerini, Godard, or indeed Fast's novel. This recent screen *Odyssey*'s reactionary sexual politics are all the more noticeable since it was made two decades after Feminism, at least in the West, had begun to win the public argument. Much of the crucial legislation was passed in the UK during the 1970s, which also saw the first International Festival of Women's Film, held in New York in 1972, and the International Women's Film Seminar in Berlin in 1974.[9] At the same time, feminist critiques of film began to circulate. But the figure of Penelope in Konchalovsky's movie has been entirely unaffected by, for example, Claire Johnston's foundational 1973 critique of the stereotypes of women in film, which drew on both Simone de Beauvoir's *The Second Sex* and Roland Barthes' semiotic theory to demonstrate how classical cinema produces the ideological sign 'woman' entirely in subsidiary relationship to the sign 'man'.[10] Konchalovsky's Penelope only reaffirms the audience stereotypes of the female psyche as masochistic and depressive or hysterical, a definitive typology which Mary Ann Doane has identified in the woman-centred melodramatic films of the 1940s.[11]

[7] Paige (2004: 8). [8] Solomon (1995–6: 126). [9] Rosenberg (1983).
[10] Johnston ([1973] 1991: 25–6). [11] Doane (1987).

Konchalovsky's audience scrutinizes Penelope's pain and sometimes her desire, rather than being allowed to explore her subjective experience of them; this is a telling instantiation of Teresa de Lauretis' hypothesis that women's subject position, as depicted in the cinema, is fundamentally in conflict with the life experience of female spectators who know that they are 'real', historically situated subjects.[12] Konchalovsky certainly has not heard the news, supposed by some overly optimistic film theorists to have been universally heard, that the white heterosexual male subject is in crisis in the cinema, with his masculinity becoming increasingly denaturalized and fragmented.[13]

There are major flaws, therefore, in the argument that the inbuilt sexism of the *Odyssey* gives the modern writer no choice but to make Penelope feeble. Not only earlier Odyssey-related films, but also Homer's own epic portrait as well as feminist film theory, have all been pointing for decades in other, more interesting directions. It is therefore time now to turn to the numerous well-known movies, in the more than thirty years since Barry Levinson's baseball epic *The Natural* (1984), whose plots and visual images explicitly make reference to the *Odyssey*, or which can be shown by external testimony to have been influenced by it. Indeed, the cultural penetration of the *Odyssey* and its status as the archetypal biography, romance, action-adventure story, quest story, and revenge narrative all in one produce regular allegations that parallels have been drawn between it and movies where the screenwriters may consciously have drawn none at all. Recent examples of films which were allegedly influenced by the *Odyssey* include both the original 1960 film *Little Shop of Horrors* and its 1986 remake, *Watership Down* (1978), *Waterworld* (1995), Zacharias Kunuk's devastating Inuit *Atanarjuat* (2001), *Captain Corelli's Mandolin* (also 2001, an adaptation of Louis de Bernières' novel, directed by John Madden), Tim Burton's *Big Fish* (2003), and even the maritime adventures in *The SpongeBob SquarePants Movie* (2004), which include monocular foes and an angry sea god.

One reason for the complexity of the relationship borne by the *Odyssey* to the film industry is that it has held a special place in aspiring screenwriters' lore since Christopher Vogler's bestselling handbook *The Writer's Journey* (1992). The formula for a successful screenplay that Vogler advises is structured around quotations and archetypal figures that he traces to the *Odyssey*—the wise elder figure (Mentor or Obi Wan Kenobi in George Lucas' 1977 *Star Wars*), the Herald figure (Hermes or

[12] de Lauretis (1987: 20). [13] Easthope (1986).

the telegraph clerk in Fred Zinnemann's *High Noon* [1952]), the Shapeshifter (Proteus and countless morphing superheroes and their adversaries), and so on. Another analysis of Hollywood plot structure emphasizes the importance of the 'classical storytelling technique' that involved two parallel (and invariably male) protagonists who pursue, simultaneously, different courses of action although they end up working together towards a shared goal.[14] This formula is exemplified in Richard Donner's *Lethal Weapon* (1987), but it could have been lifted straight from the *Odyssey*, with its separated father and son's parallel travels and eventual reunion. The important point is no longer whether any particular screenwriters have drawn on the *Odyssey*, or indeed ever read it, but that they would almost all self-consciously cite the *Odyssey* as a key text in the history of adventure narrative. This epic's status, at least in Hollywood, has once again—and in a new sense—become a matter of legend. Yet the films whose relationship to the *Odyssey* is difficult to prove need not detain us long here. This article is about the role of relatively direct cultural descendants of Penelope in modern cinema, and—bizarrely—in none of the films named in the previous paragraph does the male protagonist have a wife or even female love interest with anything like the importance of Penelope in the Homeric *Odyssey*.

Yet the same principle, astonishingly and regrettably, applies to the films in which the relationship with the *Odyssey* is indeed demonstrable. There is not a single film among these in which the figure based on Penelope has anything like the status of the Odyssean heroine, whatever criterion is used to measure that status—aesthetic, ethical, degree of psychic interiority, or simple number of minutes in which the camera considers her situation or replicates her gaze. This is despite the feminist reassessment of Penelope in contexts other than the movie industry. It was Helene Foley who as long ago as 1978 first showed how the *Odyssey* uses 'inverted sex role' similes to underline the tensions in the marriage and undermine patriarchy—for example, when Penelope finally accepts her husband and clings to him like shipwrecked men who grasp dry land (*Od.* 23.233–8).[15] It has now been than twenty years, moreover, since the feminist scholar Carolyn Heilbrun delivered her seminal lecture 'What was Penelope Unweaving?', which argued that women were actually trapped by the narratives in which their roles had been defined—which emphatically did not include the role of quest hero, or indeed of anything much other than object of desire or self-denying mother, always dependent on male authority and power. Heilbrun urged that women needed to

[14] Thompson (1999: 44–7). [15] Foley (1978).

produce new narratives which gave them role models with agency, a variety of experiences, intellectual range, and adventures independent of love and marriage. They needed to 'unweave' the old stories which underpinned patriarchy and reweave them in ways that nurtured in women, rather than discouraged, a sense of autonomy, independence and curiosity.[16]

Two years later, in 1987, Sheila Murnaghan's outstanding *Disguise and Recognition in the Odyssey* broke new ground within Classics by arguing that Penelope is construed as a heroic type who achieves her goals by cunning intelligence, only to be knocked down as such by an ideological imperative inimical to male-female equality. Marilyn Katz's *Penelope's Renown* (1991) is perhaps the first feminist study to make a virtue out of the ambiguity of Penelope's presentation, showing how the poem's audience is kept guessing about the type of wife that she will turn out to be—an adulterous Helen, a murderous Clytemnestra, or an exemplar of fidelity and virtue. Penelope, as the constantly evolving and least determinate figure in the poem, is thus the paramount symbol of its poetics. Three years later, Nancy Felson-Rubin acknowledged Penelope's power as a signifier of open-endedness, but focused on the engagement of the listener/reader with the unfolding of the story to ask whether subjective ways of identifying with the emotional vicissitudes in this text are in themselves irredeemably gendered. An excellent range of approaches to all the female figures in the *Odyssey*, not only Penelope, are presented in the 1995 collection of essays edited by Beth Cohen.

Had she lived, Heilbrun would no doubt have also been gratified to see that few Greek or Shakespearean heroines have not been the subject, over the last two decades, of feminist re-envisioning in creative media as well as academic circles: Clytemnestra has been justified, Jocasta transformed into a freethinker, Shakespeare's Kate from tamed shrew to rape victim, and Penelope has indeed been allowed, outside the cinema, to weave her own subjectivity. Just two years after Heilbrun's incendiary lecture, the first of several novels rewriting the *Odyssey* was published in Austria—Inge Merkel's *Odysseus and Penelope: An Ordinary Marriage.*[17] This rewrote the *Odyssey* from the perspective of the women left behind—above all Penelope, but Eurycleia is also upgraded. Merkel's novel demonstrates ways in which a modern film could make Penelope interesting. Her Penelope eventually finds her sexual starvation agonizing. She develops an eating disorder, varicose veins, and a plausible drink problem. She stops washing and resorts to black magic. She nearly has a

[16] Heilbrun ([1985] 1990). [17] Merkel ([1987] 2000).

lesbian affair; she climbs into bed with Amphinomus before getting cold feet; she flirts with Antinous. Merkel asks what constitutes a heroic ordeal: the torment of constant movement or of enforced confinement? Although denying that she is a feminist, Merkel owes much to the self-consciously feminist tradition of reading Greek myths instantiated in Christa Wolf's *Cassandra* (1975). She finds Homer's picture of his supposedly intelligent queen of Ithaca insulting. Her Penelope knows everything about Odysseus' affair with Calypso (an 'island tart'), and she is not hoodwinked by her husband's vagabond disguise. From a woman's perspective, this makes for a more emotionally satisfying read than the *Odyssey*, where Penelope is scrutinized for the effect men's actions are having on *her*, rather than *vice versa*.

Merkel's innovative book has received little attention in comparison with the two women-focused *Odyssey* novels published in 2005, Adèle Geras' *Ithaka*, told by an orphaned granddaughter of Eurycleia, and *The Penelopiad* by Margaret Atwood. Unlike Merkel, Atwood makes her Penelope as obnoxious as her Odysseus. She is arrogant, vain, insecure, unsympathetic, and sexually possessive. She is tyrannical with her slaves; it is she who orders the twelve 'disloyal' maids to hang around the suitors 'using whatever enticing arts they could invent'.[18] Penelope has here displaced Odysseus as an epic hero, as Atwood's title implies (at least one scholar, impressed by Penelope's prominence, long ago described the poem as the *Penelopeia*).[19] The novel has also formed the basis of a very successful stage version, in 2007, a collaborative production by the Royal Shakespeare Company in England and Canada's National Arts Centre, directed by Josette Bushell-Mingo. In this stage version Penelope is granted agency, intelligence, and gifts as a raconteur. She is not likeable, but she is certainly complicated, and a gift for an outstanding actress such as Penny Downie, whose realization of the role was simply stunning.

Other dramatists have updated the *Odyssey* in fascinating female-friendly ways. Derek Walcott's Penelope in *The Odyssey: A Stage Version* (1993) is appalled at the carnage wrought by Odysseus, rebukes him for turning the house into an 'abattoir', demands to know whether it was for such a scene that she kept her 'thighs crossed for twenty years', and forbids him to hang the maids. In Rachel Matthews' radio play *The City at Night* (broadcast on BBC Radio 4, 4th November 2004), Ulee is a former man who has undergone a sex change operation. She is now searching for her fiancé on the Newcastle quayside. *Current Nobody* by

[18] Atwood (2005: 115). [19] Finley (1978: 3–4).

Melissa James Gibson, performed at the 2006 Sundance Institute Theatre Laboratory, involves another kind of sex role inversion by having Penelope going away as a war photojournalist, leaving Odysseus at home with a teenage daughter, Tel, who grapples with the cost of her mother's epic ambition. There have also been innumerable Penelopes reassessed by women poets. Linda Pastan's seven-poem lyric cycle 'On Rereading the *Odyssey* in Middle Age' weaves into an imitation of the poem the responses of a mature reader.[20] Carolyn White's 'The voyage of Penelope' (1993) presents Penelope's heroic journey through her dream life and her textile;[21] 'Penelope serves Odysseus breakfast' (2000) by Karen Bjorneby has the wife of a prosperous businessman announce that *she* is going on a cruise. The focus of Louise Glück's lyric cycle *Meadowlands* (1996) is also a failing modern marriage in which Penelope's subjectivity is prominent.[22]

ECHOES OF PENELOPE IN OTHER FILMS

Yet despite the significance of Penelope in fiction, theatre, and poetry by women, no film has, to my knowledge, yet been made which both obviously adopts the *Odyssey* as archetype and also situates Odysseus' wife Penelope as an experiential subject of equal importance as her husband, let alone equal agency or equal right to control the narrative. Some of the films scarcely require further investigation. Eric de Kuyper's German-language gay soft porn movie *Pink Ulysses* (1990), designed to arouse men who desire sex with other men, offers a Penelope who combines a brothel madam's grinning seediness with a rather comforting maternal presence, but she is very much relegated to the background of the scenes of homoerotic mutual pleasuring. She wears striking Knossos-fresco make-up, but is not the centre of anyone's attention, sexual or otherwise, and certainly granted no hint of subjectivity.

If we turn the clocks back to 1984, the *Odyssey* underlay a more mainstream (indeed at the time popular) movie which won four Oscar nominations, including Best Actress for Glenn Close in the 'Penelope' role. But her acting skills were actually wasted since the film objectified her as an exemplar of shining Madonna-like selflessness. The film was Barry Levinson's *The Natural*, starring Robert Redford as Roy Hobbs, an

20 In Pastan (1988); see the excellent study by Murnaghan and Roberts (2002).

21 Reproduced in DeNicola (1999: 135–7).

22 See Murnaghan and Roberts (2002), especially 15–24.

ageing former baseball star who achieves a magnificent comeback. The movie also takes Hobbs back to his long-estranged fiancée Iris, and the son he had unwittingly sired sixteen years before. The prominent Odyssean references consolidate the film's mythic power. When the young Hobbs is first held fast in conversation by Harriet Bird, a combination of Calypso and the Sirens, she is pointedly made to ask him whether he has ever read the epics of Homer. For most of the film the self-controlled, tortured, and mysterious Odyssean persona of the fast-forwarded Hobbs, now in his late thirties, keeps the viewer guessing as to what he had being doing throughout his absence. In addition to Harriet, there is also another murderous seductress, 'Memo' Paris, who threatens Hobbs' memory of who he really is by appealing, Circe-like, to his animal desires. But the backlit figure of Iris (who always wears white and here seems to have acquired a halo), the patient farmer-fiancée named after one of the Homeric messengers of the gods, can inspire him to heroic deeds of sporting prowess.

The screenplay for the film version of *The Natural* was written by Robert Towne, adapting Bernard Malamud's synonymous 1952 novel, to which the *Odyssey* is both more and less important. The degree of alteration to the novel in the overall plotline of the movie is breathtaking, and actually makes it far more like the *Odyssey*. Iris' significance is enormously upgraded, and she has a grown son by Roy. But her increased significance is entirely in relation to her function as a redemptive influence on the long-absent father of her child; we learn nothing of how she has spent the intervening years—the emotions that seeing Roy again have aroused—or indeed of her life outside her role as their son's mother. Moreover, the new storyline in the movie evades the ethical complexity of the novel, since the couple and their son end up a happily reunited All-American nuclear family back home on their Midwestern farm. The movie ends with a scene of redemptive purity where Roy plays with his son in the golden light of a wheatfield.[23] The difference between the novel and the film versions of *The Natural* crystallizes the tension (outside the movies) in current reactions to Odysseus as a hero. In the novel it is precisely the masculine values of sexual appetite, competitive sport, and macho business culture that bring the story of Hobbs—who fails to make a lasting relationship with a woman—to a tragic conclusion; in the movie, it is Hobbs' identity as a decent Midwestern male, rooted in

[23] On the way lighting is used to emphasize Iris' near-divine purity, in contrast with the sordid Memo, see Brown (2002: 161–5).

his soil and his frontier values, that saves him and his docile, saintly woman.

If Iris is an irredeemably, indeed almost risibly two-dimensional fantasy figure serving only male ideological interests, then thankfully matters had advanced somewhat by the time that *Sommersby*, the next Hollywood film saturated in the *Odyssey*, was released in 1993. The background to the presentation in this film of the Penelope figure, Laurel, is however extremely complex, since the screenwriters were 'translating' the successful French movie *Le Retour de Martin Guerre* (*The Return of Martin Guerre*, 1982). This had used an original screenplay that reconstructed documents relating a real, historical court-case in sixteenth-century France. The female historian who acted as consultant on the film has pointed out that the screenplay was written by men, and that the picture of the wife in the old documents was entirely created by men; one of them commented on the resemblance she bore to the Homeric Penelope.[24] When it came to the American remake, which relocated the story to Tennessee during the reconstruction period, the screenplay writers went back to the *Odyssey* and thoroughly reinforced the echoes of the Homeric archetype, even down to making the Odysseus figure, Horace Townsend (Richard Gere), a Classics teacher who is fond of the Homeric epics.

But the role of the waiting wife in the new, Deep South *Odyssey* enacted in *Sommersby* had the potential to be completely rewritten to enhance its portrayal of the wife's perspective, just as the role of Joseph (Eumaeus) is given rich new resonances by making him a newly emancipated slave. There are indeed a few suggestions of how interesting a character the 'Penelope' type can be, especially in the expert hands of the peerlessly intelligent and poised actress Jodie Foster. But the screenplay scarcely gives her a chance. She plays along with Townsend rather passively, although suspecting and soon knowing that he is not her husband but an imposter, falls in love with him promptly (although screen chemistry between her and Gere was unfortunately lacking). Almost instantly, she becomes relegated to the role of accessory to his exciting moral quandaries: his fight with the rival suitor, the stand he takes against racist bullies of the former slaves, his vigorous attempts to create a new tobacco-based economy for the whole inter-racial community, and the court case which dominates the final section of the film. There is nothing particularly wrong with this film, but the role allocated to Laurel is nowhere near as complicated as that of Horace Townsend, Homer's Penelope, or the wife of Martin Guerre, Bertrande de Rols,

[24] Zemon Davis (1997).

played with such power and charm by Nathalie Beye. This was a remarkable achievement given the constant danger of being upstaged by the potent presence of Gerard Depardieu as the man claiming to be her husband.

The most promising 'Penelope' ever to have appeared on screen is surely the figure of Louise in Mike Leigh's *Naked*, made and financed in Britain, but released the same year as *Sommersby*. The film examines inner city decay and the poverty-stricken underbelly of the Thatcher years, but since its release has been linked by critics with the *Odyssey*. This is a result not of any statement by the director, nor any mention of such a parallel in the publicity literature. Indeed, the *intention* of such a parallel would be difficult to prove, since Mike Leigh's actors often improvise their own lines, a technique of scene development in which the skill of David Thewlis (who played Johnny, the wanderer figure) is legendary. Yet the undertext becomes almost impossible to avoid during the encounter between Johnny and the waitress. She takes him to the flat she is 'sitting' while its owners are away. The lounge is littered with Greek souvenirs, statuettes of gods and hoplites, and translations of Greek authors including a copy of E.V. Rieu's bestselling Penguin Classic translation of the *Odyssey*, which Johnny brandishes at his reluctant hostess. Of the owner of the flat Johnny enquires, mockingly, 'Is he a Homer-sexual, yeah?', and later comments that he does not want 'to sound Homer-phobic', before emphasizing that he likes the *Iliad* and the *Odyssey*, in particular Achilles, 'the wooden horse, Helen of Troy . . . the Cyclops'.

Once this intertextual allusion has been made, Johnny's violent past, his habitual wandering, his serial encounters with weird individuals, and the constant deferral of domestic closure with his Penelopean woman (Louise, memorably played by Lesley Sharp) cannot fail to remind any viewer acquainted at all with Greek mythology of the *Odyssey*. It is a modern version, however, where the monsters and villains are poverty, unemployment, and existential despair. Johnny is a knowing protagonist, and his references to philosophical questions or literary allusions create a collusive bond between him and the viewer. Thus after his attempt at dialogue with the foul-mouthed young Scot, Archie, he tells Archie's girlfriend Maggie that Archie has a wonderful way 'with Socratic debate'. All this is delivered in a stream of deadpan irony.

While waiting for Louise to come home from work, he has sex with the temporary lodger, Sophie, a goth drug addict sporting a Siren-like bird tattoo. She spends much of the movie trying to regain his sexual attention, frustrated by his deep emotional bond with Louise. She thus synthesizes Siren, lotus-eater, Circe, and Calypso. Johnny subsequently leaves the flat after an unsuccessful encounter with Louise, and wanders off into the night, a new member of the London homeless. Johnny's sex scenes are intercut with episodes involving the other male lead. Jeremy, an upper-class sadist, represents the worst aspects of the suitors. Indeed, he moves in to Louise's flat and extracts brutal sex from Sophie by pretending to be the landlord. Meanwhile Johnny, after being mugged, turns up at the flat. The scene is set for what should be the showdown in which Johnny discovers his inner hero and ousts the rival from his latter-day Penelope's residence. In Mike Leigh's universe, however, there is no such thing as a traditional male hero, and Johnny fails miserably. He suffers blows to the head, resulting in a fit, regresses into a childlike state, and is humiliated. It is the marvellous Louise whose raw courage and psychological cunning drive Jeremy away. But the tender reunion of Johnny and the resourceful, resilient Louise proves fleeting, because Johnny staggers off again at the film's conclusion, to life as a London vagrant.

In *Naked*, the Penelopean heroine suggests some ways in which an imaginative, sensitive screenwriter could develop the role of the Odyssean hero's patient woman. Mike Leigh is no sexist, and the film is in one sense an extended critique of masculinity, from the moment when it opens with Johnny apparently committing a rape in a Manchester side street. But Louise's role still remains extremely slight in comparison with the extended adventures and non-stop verbal pyrotechnics that constitute Johnny's role. The other *Odyssey*-related movie to have been made in Europe during the last two decades followed fast on the heels of *Naked*, and is equally in no way a sexist film, but scarcely offers an identifiable role for Penelope at all, Theodoros Angelopoulos' *Ulysses' Gaze*, released in Greece in 1995 as *To Vlemma tou Odyssea*, is well deserving of its title: the mental perspective throughout the film is emphatically that of its émigré Greek hero, a film director named just 'A' (Harvey Keitel), a modern Odysseus who returns from the USA to his homeland in search of three histories: his own, that of south-eastern Europe, and that of the medium in which he works.

Like Odysseus, 'A' 's personal psychic biography is defined by a series of women, including his mother and four younger women, all played by the same powerful Romanian actress, Maia Morgenstern. How wonderfully this titan of Romanian theatre might have played an intact, single Balkan waiting wife with an interesting story all of her own! Yet the (ultimately Freudian) merging of Odysseus' women has been a tradition in male-authored narratives since Joyce associated Leopold's Calypso and Penelope, and Camerini made Mangano play both Circe and Penelope; Angelopoulos clearly feels that it was appropriate to follow suit. The result is that although women, plural, are crucial to 'A' 's experiences and subjectivity, not one of them is an authentic subject in her own right. Indeed, 'woman' in the film is a construct which fragments, like coloured-glass beads refracted a hundred times in a kaleidoscope, in 'A' 's memory and filmic travelogue. His most serious old love interest, and therefore, perhaps, his potential Penelope, is the enigmatic woman he glimpses in the street in Florina, the town in north-western Greece where his film is being shown at the beginning of Angelopoulos' movie. But the sexual passion in the film is mostly directed towards Kali, a woman whom 'A' encounters in a museum and on a train; she is a Calypso figure, who shares his journey and becomes involved with him erotically, but whom, like Odysseus, he leaves in Konstantza, telling her that he cannot love her.

The third woman gazed upon by this Ulysses is another seductress, but this time Morgenstern plays a widow in Bulgaria in 1915. She tries to force 'A' into assuming the identity of her deceased husband by dressing him in her husband's clothes; she offers him her body as if, Circe-like, she can transform his inner soul and thus make him her captive by appealing to his physical appetites. But finally, Morgenstern appears as Noami, a modern version of Nausicaa, the daughter of the curator of the Sarajevo Film Archives at which 'A' arrives during the siege of the early 1990s. Noami dances with 'A' to a modern rock tune, but the music becomes transformed into a much older melody, perhaps from the 1950s, and Noami morphs into the mystery woman whom 'A' had left behind in Florina many years ago. Noami herself is gunned down, along with some children and her father, and the movie ends with the implication that she somehow represents all the women with whom 'A' has been involved. *Ulysses' Gaze* does not set out to offer a woman's perspective on history and memory, but the decision to make one woman play all 'A' 's lovers, however interesting from the perspective of his subconscious reactions to the world and women, made it quite impossible for any single, important female role to develop at all in the film as a whole.

If Penelope is written out of Angelopoulos' response to the *Odyssey* through fragmentation, she is written out of *Ulee's Gold* (1997) altogether by having died six years before the action even begins. This is an excellent film, directed by Victor Nuñez, which portrays a Florida Vietnam veteran (Ulee Jackson) struggling to keep his family together after his neglected son goes off the rails and receives a prison sentence. His daughter-in-law Helen has become a drug addict and run away with the lowlife criminals who enticed his son into crime, and Ulee has to act to save all his womenfolk, including his grand-daughter Penny, from these villains when they break into his house and take them captive. But the original Penelope, his wife, is dead. Curiously, in her absence, a sense of her indubitable importance to this family does come over rather better than in most films where the Penelopean woman is physically present. Her not being there actively causes Ulee's intense loneliness, the problem he has in taking a moral lead, and the pain of his son and grandchildren. She is, moreover, replaced by the significantly named Mrs Hope, the divorcee next door. Mrs Hope is portrayed sympathetically: her own perspective is represented by several camera shots as she becomes more and more impressed by Ulee's moral toughness, and she has her own tale of childlessness and love of the countryside to tell. Yet this film overwhelmingly belongs to Ulee (brilliantly acted by Peter Fonda), an uptight, ageing man who discovers in himself a capacity for true moral as well as physical heroism.

A far more commercial example of a movie with an obviously Odyssean plot is Anthony Minghella's *Cold Mountain* (2003), which portrays the most sanitized Odysseus and frustrating Penelope of all time. The movie is an adaptation of Charles Frazier's 1997 novel of the same name, in which the connection with the *Odyssey* is more explicit. It is set, like *Sommersby*, at the end of the Civil War, and a destitute soldier is returning, although this Odysseus, a carpenter called Inman (Jude Law), is no impostor. The state is not Tennessee but the town of Cold Mountain in North Carolina. Here the Penelope figure, Ada Monroe (Nicole Kidman), moves with her ageing preacher father. There is little moral complexity in the film's drawing of any of the 'good' characters (who hate violence) and the 'bad' ones (who use it constantly). There is only one suitor (Teague), and despite the appalling conduct shown by him and his gang, there is no sense of the emotional need for revenge on the part of either Ada or Inman. There is no neglected child and no testing of fidelity or identity.

The disappointment created by Kidman's Ada for anyone looking for an interesting cinematic Penelope is exacerbated because there are some moments when Ada *almost* springs into life as a complicated subject in her own right—for example, when she studies the pictures of the war dead posted in the town. The novel, moreover, divides the plot equally between Ada and Inman, and the film attempts to follow suit. It begins with Ada's voiceover reading a letter to Inman in which she expresses her fear that the war will change them both beyond their reckoning. The camera then cuts to Inman at war, and then back in time to the day when they met on Cold Mountain. But Kidman's looks are the dominant interest in the scenes relating to their courtship, especially in the sequence in which he gazes at her through a window as she plays the piano at a party. A totemic importance attaches to her objectified physical appearance, established when she gives him the photograph of herself before he leaves.

Part of the problem is the failure of the romance between Inman and Ada to light any sparks. If two people who hardly know each other and have only kissed once are to hang on to their fantasies and memories for five celibate years, then we need at least to feel some sexual chemistry, but the awkwardness of their early scenes together 'defies belief'.[25] Part of the problem is that this Penelope is young, coy, pert, posh, has not experienced either sexual intercourse or motherhood and is completely incompetent when required by sudden poverty to work as a peasant householder. Moreover, she is completely upstaged by the powerful, lively, glowing Renee Zellweger as Ruby Thewes, the tough-minded country girl who teaches her how to survive;[26] it is as if Frazier and Minghella have literally split the Homeric Penelope and put more than half of her in the lower-class woman. The Inman/Ada symmetry is entirely destabilized by the presence of this character.[27]

There is yet another character who actually steals all the rest of Ada's Penelopean thunder, and that is Sara, Natalie Portman's superb cameo portrayal of the young widow with whom Inman stays but does not make love. From the moment when he hears her sick baby son's cries from outside her house, the film becomes electric. Finally, we are faced with the real cost of the war to waiting women; her baby is suffering from a high fever and will not feed, and Sara's yearning for the safety a man's protection might bring her is achingly, painfully vivid. Inman's body is presented to the camera from her perspective, as she yearns for his benign physical proximity. When they are brutally awoken by Yankee soldiers, she is raped while the baby screams outside; the violence of the reactions of both Inman and Sara (he cuts down one of her persecutors with an axe, while she shoots another) suddenly put the viewer into terrifying touch with what women under threat in time of war must really feel like. This sequence in the film is important because it shows what a powerful effect could be made by a Civil War *Odyssey* that took Penelope seriously as anything much more than eye candy.

One recent film whose link with the *Odyssey* is speculative nevertheless warrants discussion here because, again, the woman who has been left behind by the restless Odyssean wanderer, however brief her role, suggests an interesting direction in which a modern cinematic Penelope could be developed. The film is the German director Wim Wenders' *Don't Come Knocking* (2005). It was immediately linked with the

[25] Romney (2003). [26] Berry (2003). [27] Ignatieff (2004).

Odyssey,[28] a poem whose evocation of landscape had been praised by Wenders in a speech delivered in 2003.[29] His obsession with the *Odyssey*'s poet was already apparent in the old storyteller, actually named Homer, in the Berlin of his *Der Himmel über Berlin* (1987, usually known outside Germany as *Wings of Desire*). Wenders' Homer 'is the representative and bearer of collective memory, the spirit of history. He is also the spirit of Berlin, who laments the vanishing of the city in the war.'[30] *Don't Come Knocking*, written by and starring Sam Shepard, seems to be ironically informed by the story pattern of the *Odyssey*. This Odysseus, an actor named Howard Spence, has fallen on hard times. A former star in Westerns, at the age of sixty he has only drugs, booze, and sex to help him face his declining career. After yet another debauched night in his trailer, he gallops away from the film set in his cowboy costume to rediscover his soul.

He gradually loses his movie star identity, acquiring the clothes of a ranch hand, and discovers he has a child in a depressed Montana ghost town. He tracks down his former lover (a waitress named Doreen, played by Jessica Lange, Shepard's real-life wife) and his grown-up son. Wenders' earlier collaboration with Shepard in *Paris, Texas* (1984) is widely regarded by cinema scholars as a dark take on the story of Odysseus and Penelope—Wenders' 'interpretation of Homer's saga of the man longing to find his lost home'.[31] But the details of the earlier part plot of this 'second idiosyncratic Western Odyssey', as *Don't Come Knocking* has been marketed, are in fact far closer to the ancient poem, since the son is now adult, and Doreen is middle-aged. Lange's hilarious performance rests on her conviction that 'What's wonderful about Doreen is she's actually a really happy woman. She has a son she adores, and she doesn't harbour any resentment until this guy shows up and won't leave her alone. That makes her a very interesting character to play.'[32] Here is a fully realized, middle-aged, independent woman who has managed perfectly well without the onetime lover who inseminated her. The only problem is that we see so little of her relative to him.

Jessica Lange, a great beauty who struggled in her early career to be offered parts that asked her to do anything more emancipated than scream as she was picked up in the mighty ape's fist in John Guillemin's *King Kong* (1976), relished the humour and complexity of her thoroughly grown-up and grounded Doreen. Although the role is very much a 'supporting' one, subsidiary in every way to Howard's, movie

28 See e.g. the review in *Frankfurter Allgemeine Zeitung*, for 24th August 2005.

29 Wenders (2003).

30 Kolker and Beicken (1993: 151).

31 Salles (2008: 22).

32 'Production notes' (2006).

roles of this calibre for middle-aged women are few and far between. Another intelligent actress who is also middle-aged and a mother is Holly Hunter, who recently complained that film actresses over the age of 38 only ever get offered a particular role type in Hollywood, 'cast opposite a big movie star. You're playing his wife, and he's cheating on you with someone else. The story doesn't depend upon your thoughts and actions.'[33] It is unlikely that she would include in this category of roles her appearance as Penny McGill in the Coen brothers' Odyssean comedy *O Brother Where Art Thou?* (2000). Yet the overall effect of Penny's contribution to the film is complicated. Its 'take' on the Homeric wife is certainly more open-minded and ideologically subversive than in any of the other examples which have been discussed here, and yet Penny is, in the manner of the films of the 1930s and 1940s that are being parodied, certainly trapped on screen as an exotic object for scrutiny in a particular male comedic idiom. The Coen brothers' Penelope points the way forward to new cinematic possibilities for reassessing the ancient heroine, while simultaneously distancing the audience from her emotionally in reading her marriage to Everett almost entirely from his perspective.

Penny has certainly not been faithful. In Everett's absence she has produced seven daughters, apparently all by different fathers. Moreover, she has told the girls that their official daddy is dead, having been hit by a train, and that she is planning to marry her fiancé, Vernon T. Waldrip, simply because he's 'got a job. Vernon's got prospects. He's bona fide!' This Penelope is an impoverished single mother struggling to look after her children in tough economic circumstances. In the contemporary world, it is indeed a prison sentence being given to their husbands that probably causes most modern Penelopes' predicaments, and the movie makes no bones about the unglamorous reason why Penny was deserted, nor about her need to choose a man who can support her financially.

Everett can't even stand up as a fighter to his rival for his wife's hand, being defeated in the fistfight with Vernon in Woolworth's. He is also given misogynist rhetoric that recalls Agamemnon's language in the *Nekyia* of the Homeric *Odyssey* (11.501–34), denouncing Penny as 'Deceitful! Two-faced! She-woman! Never trust a female, Delmar! Remember that one simple precept and your time with me will not have been ill spent!... Truth means nothin' to Woman, Delmar'.[34] But Everett does win Penny over by convincing her that he has financial prospects through the success of his song recording, and through

[33] Levine (2008). [34] Siegel (2007: 231).

accomplishing the quest for her wedding ring. The film ends with a suggestion that Everett is facing a life being bossed around by the controlling Penny, a denouement that is suspended vertiginously between empowering her as a female and playing along with the pernicious sexist stereotype of the hen-pecking wife.

CONCLUSION

On 16th October 2008, as the idea for this chapter was taking shape, the online edition of the entertainment weekly *Variety* broke the news of a planned collaboration between Warner Brothers and Brad Pitt's production company Plan B. They want to make a new futuristic movie version of the *Odyssey* which is set in outer space. Pitt, who of course starred as Achilles in Wolfgang Petersen's *Troy* (2004), is expected to portray Odysseus; the planned director is George Miller, famous for the *Mad Max* action adventure movies. None of the advance publicity has yet mentioned Penelope: we have to hope that this new extra-terrestrial *Odyssey* does not follow the precedent of the animated children's series *Ulysses 31* (originally broadcast 1981–2) in excising her from the fun but puerile thirty-first century Sci-Fi adventures of Ulysses and Telemachus altogether.

Perhaps there is hope of a powerful new Penelope from another quarter, since during the same week as the *Variety* article, a project was announced by Ridley Scott, apparently another variation on the 'Odysseus in space' theme. Scott described his proposed film *Forever War*, a screen adaptation of a 1974 novel by Joe Haldeman, as 'the *Odyssey* by way of *Blade Runner*'.[35] The Haldeman novel features a relatively adult partnership between the 'returning' hero William Mandella and his fellow soldier and wife Marygay; this offers a glimmer of hope that there may be an interesting 'Penelope' role in the Hollywood pipeline. Ridley Scott has, after all, been known to create films with strong roles for women out of genres traditionally dominated by men, such as the road movie *Thelma and Louise* (1991). But what we really need is a complete rethink of the Homeric epic in cinematic terms, written and directed by women. The Coen Brothers had the right instincts in their insouciant rewrite of the Penelope role and in casting Holly Hunter; all she needs is Margaret Atwood to provide the

[35] Akbar (2008).

screenplay and Jane Campion (as in *The Piano*, 1993) to direct. Another possibility would be Kathryn Bigelow, who directed the fascinating police woman Megan Turner, played by Jamie Lee Curtis in *Blue Steel* (1990). If creative modern women such as these once decided to put the record straight on Penelope, they might indeed, in the words of Sean Bean's Odysseus in *Troy*, 'have a way of complicating things'.

Part IV

Other Mythical Women

8

The Women of Ercole

Arthur J. Pomeroy

Filmed in the middle of 1957, released in Italy in February 1958 and in the UK and United States in the middle of 1959, the mythological fantasy *Le fatiche di Ercole* was an unlikely turning point in the history of Italian cinema. After it grossed a remarkable 900 million lire in Italy and became a box office success in India and Japan as well as in France and Germany, the American entrepreneur Joe E. Levine acquired the rights, redubbed the film, now simply titled *Hercules*, and after a Barnum-and-Bailey style publicity campaign gained box office takings of over five million dollars.[1]

The release of director Pietro Francisci's film inaugurated a trend in Italy to make adventure films set in the past that was to last until 1965 and encompassed numerous other Hercules titles.[2] When dubbed into English and released by American producers (most notably Levine's Embassy Pictures Corporation, the Woolner brothers, and Nicholson and Arkoff's American International Pictures), these films also attracted considerable audiences outside Italy. The financial gains from overseas sales in turn enabled the survival of the general Italian film industry. Although the output of *sandaloni* did not garner the prestige that went to the Art House films of Fellini, Antonioni, De Sica and other well-regarded Italian directors of the period, it did provide regular employment for local actors and their film crews. Just as *Hercules: The Legendary*

[1] Takings: IMDb; Cammarota (1987: 209–10): third among peplum movies for box-office success, just behind *Ercole e la regina di Lidia* (1959) and the most successful of these films in Italy, the Aldrich-Leone directed *Sodom and Gomorrah* (1962). Joe E. Levine and publicity: Pomeroy (2008: 37–8); Lucas (2007: 206–7). For a recent account to the significance of Ercole, see Blanshard and Shahabudin (2011: 58–76).

[2] Cammarota (1987: 61–5) lists 22 Hercules films from this period. This count does not include various Maciste films, for instance, relabelled with the Hercules brand in foreign markets (cf. Nisbet [2006] 51–2).

Journeys and its spin-off *Xena: Warrior Princess* in the 1990s were to provide employment and training for New Zealand actors and crews that would be invaluable for larger projects such as Peter Jackson's *Lord of the Rings* trilogy, the string of Italian films set in times past (historical or mythological) from the 1950s and 1960s allowed both older professionals, such as scriptwriter Ennio De Concini and scenarist and cameraman Mario Bava, and newcomers, such as Sergio Leone and Sergio Corbucci, to advance their careers significantly in the following decade.[3]

The phenomenon was of particular interest to French film critics. It appears that one of the members of the film club at Lyons coined the term 'peplum' for such movies, while Jacques Siclier, writing in *Cahiers du cinema* in 1962, saw the style as offering a native European alternative to Hollywood fantasy films centred around characters such as Tarzan and Superman. Less cerebrally, but with some justification, the French critic and later film director Luc Moullet viewed works that could entertain a general audience, such as Cottafavi's *The Vengeance of Hercules,* as a welcome alternative to Italian neo-realist tedium (in this case, in a sharp comparison with Visconti's *Rocco and his Brothers*, which had won the Fipresci Award at the 1960 Venice Film Festival).[4]

None of this could have been readily foreseen when Francisci and his crew were filming *Le Fatiche di Ercole*. It is likely that Galatea, the Italian

[3] Sorlin (2008: 93–6) argues that the traditional belief that the peplum saved Italian film (an argument based on a frequently cited remark by Mario Bava about the importance of Francisci's *Le fatiche di Ercole*) is thinly supported by the box-office takings of the *filone*. Instead changes in regulations that favoured Italian film after 1956 may have been more significant for the industry's survival. Sorlin is right to warn against over-estimation of the *filone* (in Italy as elsewhere, romantic and comic films continued to dominate at the box office), but may pay insufficient attention to the effect of foreign sales on the economic return of such films. Giordano (1998: 23–5) also considers the possible effect of attempts to reduce communist influence in Italy from 1954 onward, particularly directed against the leading directors of neo-realist films, that may have encouraged the production of fantasy films.

[4] In general on the term 'peplum' and its history: Pomeroy (2008: 46–8); Spina (2008: 62). Moullet's 1961 review for *Cahiers de cinema* is reprinted in Loffreda (2001: 124–5). There has been some resistance to the use of the term 'peplum' among American classicists (e.g. Briggs [2010: 158]), but although this does not correspond to any classical genre, this *filone* in Italian film preceding similar trends in Italian western and *giallo* is undeniable. Günsberg (2005: 97) gives a figure of three hundred Italian films that can be labelled 'peplum' in this period. Aubert (2008: 196) offers striking graphs that indicate two major phases of production of films about antiquity, one centring on 1913–14 where up to eighty-five films were made in a single year, and another (Italian) peak ca. 1959–65. For American reactions to these films, see Lucanio (1994).

The contrast that Moullet draws between Italian neorealist film-making and the popular tradition of adventure films centred on Cinecittà rather buys into the self-mythologizing of neorealism—as Steimatsky (2009) brilliantly shows, Visconti, De Sica, and Antonioni had their own mythology of 'Italy Year Zero' that actually ignored many of the realities of post-war Italy.

production company behind the film, hoped for something in the style of the Kirk Douglas vehicle, *Ulysses* (1954) or *Helen of Troy* (1956).[5] Those films were, however, joint American-Italian productions.[6] *Le Fatiche* was scripted by Ennio De Concini (who had been one of the group of writers for *Ulysses*) and filmed by an entirely Italian crew. An American 'star' was imported for the title role, but Steve Reeves had been almost unknown in cinema except for a bit part as a body-builder in the Jane Powell and Debbie Reynolds musical, *Athena* (1954).

While as an ex-Mr Universe, Reeves was an understandable selection to play the character of Hercules, choosing a strong man from Greek mythology to be a film subject was in itself a notable decision. Early in Italian silent film history body builders had played important roles. These included Bruto Castellari as Ursus in *Quo Vadis* (1912) and Mario Guaita-Ausonia as Spartacus, the leader of the slave revolt against Rome (*Spartaco*, 1913).[7] Most famous of all was Bartolemeo Pagano's Maciste, who first appeared in a supporting role in Pastrone's *Cabiria* (1914), but went on to star in his own right in at least twenty-five more films through to 1927. By the 1950s, however, following Mussolini's portrayal of himself as the muscular saviour of his country, such Roman[8] strong men had been tainted by an association with Fascism. Hence director Francisci's decision to choose a Greek hero and have him played by an American. Hercules' generally cheerful disposition and willingness to play a secondary role to those in power clearly dissociates the hero from ideas of might equalling right.[9] The first half of the story

[5] On these films, see Paul and Vivante in this volume, respectively.

[6] A brief history of Italian cinema after the fall of fascism reveals the gradual restoration of its film industry. Cinecittà, the film studio created by Mussolini, was converted into a refugee camp from 1945–50, and Admiral Ellery Stone, the chief of the Allied Control Commission, declared his firm intention to suppress any Italian film-making in the future (Steimatsky 2009: 34). The effect (and probably intention) was to flood the Italian market with American film imports. The interventions of Giulio Andreotti from 1947 on led to the restoration of Cinecittà for filmmaking and a restriction on repatriation of film profits to America. This, in turn, led American companies to spend these profits by filming in Rome and making use of Italian skill in creating colossal extravaganzas (e.g. Mervyn LeRoy's *Quo Vadis*, filmed at Cinecittà in 1949).

[7] On Guaita, see Wyke (1997: 44–5). He went on to direct one of the earliest Hercules films, *La cintura delle amazzoni* (1920), about which I have no further information. Nearly two hundred muscleman films were produced in Italian cinema between 1913 and 1926: Günsberg (2005: 217 n. 3).

[8] Even Spartacus had been portrayed as a Roman, rather than a foreigner, in Italian cinema—for instance, in Riccardo Freda's *Spartaco* (1953) he is a soldier sentenced to slavery for refusing to participate in Roman atrocities in Thrace.

[9] Both De Concini and Francisci have at times claimed the credit for inventing the treatment of Hercules in *Fatiche*. See Lucas (2007: 193), citing Franca Faldini and Goffredo

includes the obligatory depiction of Hercules at some of his mythological labours, dealing with the Nemean lion as an immortal and, as a mere human and so receiving visible wounds from the bout, the Cretan bull. But, while offering the hero the chance to flex his muscles, this part of the classical depiction of the hero was difficult to film convincingly in the days before CGI. To combat the episodic nature of Hercules' trials, De Concini added a romantic theme. The leading character discovers that his divine strength does not always win the approval of mortals and that he needs to win the heart of a lady by other manifestations of personal worth.[10] Hercules renounces his immortality and proceeds to take part with Jason in the quest for the Golden Fleece. Returning successfully to Iolcus, he overcomes the machinations of the wicked Eurystheus and raises Jason to the throne, before leaving with his new bride, Iole, for further adventures.[11]

De Concini is clearly playing with the depictions of Hercules in Greek literature: rather than progressing from human to divine (a theme favoured from the Hellenistic period onward, but uncomfortably reminiscent of fascism), his hero, originally burdened with excessive power, discovers his humanity through suffering. This treatment is much closer to the treatment of Hercules in classical Athenian tragedy, but with a much more upbeat ending for a modern audience. In De Concini's version, Eurystheus, the king of Tiryns, whom in mythology the hero is forced to serve by the trickery of Hera and who imposes various labours in an attempt to destroy the hero, is but a shadowy villain who has plotted to murder the former king of Iolcus and raise Pelias to the throne. The blame for the death of the ruler has been placed on the murdered king's son, Jason, and his instructor Chiron (here a human, not a centaur), who have fled after the murder and during their wanderings left the Golden Fleece, the symbol of royal power, in Colchis. When Hercules asserts their innocence, all are sent on a mission to return the Fleece to Iolcus. This is readily recognizable as a version of the story of Jason and the Argonauts, whose opening Greek setting is also Iolcus. But there is additional contamination from the story of Hercules' exploits in

Fofi, 'The Fofi Papers, Part Two: Maciste Rights the Wrongs', *Spaghetti Cinema* 74 (March 2003) 2–12.

[10] In effect, the same theme appears in Disney's *Hercules* (1997).

[11] Thus the English dub (from Titra Sound Company) that accompanies the Joe E. Levine release. It must be noted that this script varies considerably from the Italian and French dubs (all three are available in the Édition Prestige Peplum Collection DVD, *Les Travaux d'Hercule*) and from the English Language Dubbers Association (ELDA) version that originally accompanied the film. For a comparison of the two English versions, see Lucas (2007: 207–9).

Oechalia, as related by Sophocles in *The Women of Trachis*: in that drama, Hercules has killed Iphitus, the son of the king, in a drunken rage, and later returned and destroyed the city—all, it turns out, because he is in love with Eurytus' daughter, Iole. His arrival at Trachis with his new prisoner-bride in tow leads to the final tragedy of Hercules' wife Deianeira giving her husband the poisoned robe treacherously gifted to her by the centaur Nessus, in her belief that it would restore Hercules' love for her. In *Fatiche*, Hercules is only indirectly responsible for the fate of Iphitus, since the young man recklessly exposes himself to the Nemean lion and is killed trying to emulate the hero. Still the people of Iolcus, including Iphitus' sister Iole, are overcome with grief for the son of their king and blame Hercules for his death. At the close of the film, Hercules does destroy the king's palace, though here it is Pelias who is the ruler, not Eurytus/Eurystheus.[12] Furthermore he acts only in defence of Jason and the other Argonauts, and when the guilt-wracked king commits suicide, Hercules is exempted from any responsibility for his end. Indeed, *Fatiche* has as one of its themes the need to forgo vengeance. Jason's personal growth that marks him out as a future ruler is not only shown by his bravery in killing the dragon that guards the Golden Fleece, but also by his acceptance in the same scene of the message from the dead king Aeson written on the back of the fleece, advice already voiced by Chiron, that he should not seek revenge. At the close of the film Iole recognizes the sacrifices that Hercules has undertaken and, following her father's dying advice, offers herself to be his bride—a far cry from the Sophoclean version in the *Trachinian Women* of Hercules taking his women by force. The final scene of the pair sailing off together is a cinematic cliché that vastly differs from the tragic ending provided by Sophocles.

IOLE AND ANTEA

Iole has a much more substantial role in *Fatiche* than in Sophocles' tragedy, since she is the primary cause of Hercules' deeds, not merely the indirect cause of Deianeira's tragic actions. Playing opposite her, Steve Reeves at the beginning of the film provides a good-natured, if rather ingenuous, hero who learns through his experiences. Critics have

[12] De Concini seems to conflate the king of Oechalia with Hercules' traditional enemy, the king of Tiryns, and moves events to Iolcus, making Eurystheus the prime mover in Pelias' usurpation of the throne.

often noted that Reeves also possessed almost feminine good looks to go with his excessive musculature.[13] Unlike more recent Hollywood action stars such as Sylvester Stallone or Vin Diesel, he has a remarkably unthreatening presence on screen. Furthermore, having an American actor portray the protector of the weak would have accorded well with Italian experiences during World War II and accord with post-war images of the United States as a land of openness and opportunity.[14] Hercules' future partner also needed to contribute to the cinematic fantasy. The choice of Sylva Koscina to play Iole fully satisfied this need. Auburn-haired, tall, shapely, and elegant, Koscina was a relative newcomer to cinema;[15] she was discovered when a photograph of her greeting the winner of one of the stages of the Tour of Italy was published in the local newspapers.[16] As 'Miss Di Tappa', she thus followed a common pattern of post-war Italian actresses who had originally attracted attention in beauty competitions (which were themselves a symbol of freedom from the fascist emphasis on restricting female roles to the familial sphere). But Koscina did not look like a local: although some accounts speak of her as Slovenian, she was born in Zagreb to Greek and Polish parents, and moved at a young age to Italy.[17] Hence, she was able to combine exotic and Italian traits, a combination which served her very well in numerous comic roles thereafter. She was both voluptuous (a quality she shared with actresses such as Silvana Mangano,[18] Gina Lollobrigida, and Sophia Loren) and light-haired (in contrast to the typical dark-tressed and olive-skinned Mediterranean beauty of those actresses). Rossana Podestà, a striking brunette as Nausicaa in *Ulysses* (1954), had taken top billing as the blonde *Helen of Troy* (1956), but her restrained image probably accounts for why she never achieved anywhere near the success as a 'star' as did Koscina.[19]

[13] Lucas (2007: 197).

[14] America could also be seen as a land of rampant capitalism and worker exploitation—the two mythologies existed simultaneously after the liberation of Italy and were clearly dependent on political ideology (Christian Democrat versus Socialist and Communist) in the 1950s. See Landy (1996a).

[15] Her previous experience was in Pietro Germi's neo-realist *Il ferroviere* (1956) and a number of low-budget comedies that were restricted to local distribution.

[16] Achtner (1994).

[17] Lancia and Poppi (2003: 190). The Wikipedia article on Koscina suggests that she was genuinely Croatian, since her family name is attested in the Split area, and that her Polish-Greek heritage was an invention of her publicity agents. This latter claim is not, however, supported by evidence.

[18] For Silvana Mangano, see Paul in this volume.

[19] Stefanutto Rosa (2002). Height may also have been a factor: Podestà is listed as 5 foot 4 inches tall, six inches shorter than Koscina. For Podestà, see Vivante in this volume.

While male actors who actually were or might appear 'American'[20] appealed to Italian audiences, much less attention has been paid to their female counterparts. Koscina's light hair could suggest to an Italian viewer that she was an American-style, 'liberated' woman, as most obviously embodied on screen by Marilyn Monroe during the 1950s, or else from a higher class Italian background (since blondeness was a feature of northern Italy or the Frankish aristocracy of the south).[21] In short, she was not a typical Italian female. Koscina's divergence from the model can be seen from an event that occurred two years later. When in 1961 Franca Cattaneo became the first blonde to be chosen as Miss Italy, the magazines of the day felt the need to defend the judges' choice.[22] At the same time, Koscina's glamour admirably suited her for the role of a princess of royal blood. She was thus a perfect fit to play the part of the sophisticated beauty who wins the heart of the unrefined hero.

In *Fatiche*, Iole is first seen driving an out-of-control chariot along a dangerous cliff-top trail. She is rescued when Hercules, who happens to be picnicking at the spot, uproots an entire tree and throws it in front of the runaway horses. Once saved, Iole promptly faints, which enables Hercules to gently place her on the ground and admire this remarkable creature. Is she a goddess? Certainly her 'golden' hair and dress (a short *chiton*) might suggest an incarnation of the goddess Diana,[23] and Hercules' stare at this rare object of beauty reinforces the audience's appreciative gaze. Iole's admission when she discovers that her legs are still weak (a substitution for 'I'm still trembling' in the original dub) further focuses on the physical attributes of a woman fit to partner Hercules.[24]

[20] Aside from Steve Reeves, the role of Hercules in the peplum period was also played by the American body builders Ed Fury, Mark Forest, Mickey Hargitay, Brad Harris, Dan Vadis, and Gordon Scott. Exceptions are the English-born South African Reg Park and the Italians Sergio Ciani and Adriano Bellini acting under English stage names ('Alan Steel' and 'Kirk Morris').

[21] Since royal families in the Mediterranean countries had often been of northern European origin (the Greek royal family is a particularly striking example) or intermarried with northerners (cf. Princess Grace of Monaco), a light-haired princess of pale complexion probably well fitted common expectations.

[22] Gundle (2007: 173). The selection of a black Miss Italy in 1996 was even more alarming to some and resulted in the launching of a Miss Padania competition in 1997 by Berlusconi's Northern League (Gundle [2007: 224–32]).

[23] Although Hercules may have started life as a *Greek* hero, the divinities in the peplum tradition are regularly given their equivalent Roman names. Hence Diana, not Artemis; Jupiter and Jove, not Zeus.

[24] At 5 foot 10 inches, Koscina was tall enough not to be dwarfed by the 6 foot 1 inch Reeves and on screen her long legs are well displayed in short dresses. By contrast, some earlier embodiments of Italian beauty (such as Princess Margherita of Savoy) had sometimes been described as 'best seen seated' (Gundle [2007: 38–9]).

Hercules expresses his admiration, but in a way that suggests naiveté, rather than lasciviousness. 'You say it so very simply—as if you were speaking of a plant or an animal. I almost think you're sincere' is Iole's tactful response.

Still, while she is a suitable partner for Hercules in many respects, Iole is limited by the gender expectations of the period. If she may seem to resemble Diana outside the palace,[25] in domestic quarters Iole is likely to be wearing a full-length peplum of some pastel shade. Like Phaethon, she has not been able to control her chariot (a point, underlined in the Titra dub which gives her a new line in self-exculpation: 'Is it so strange that a girl couldn't manage those horses?'). She humours her saviour and also shows a tender-hearted side when, on the way back to the palace, she narrates the tale of the condemned murderer she and her family met on the road and her subsequent nightmare about his punishment. As she defends her father's reputation against suggestions that he might have been involved in Aeson's murder, Hercules detects more than a hint of doubt in her account. Deeply insecure as the daughter of guilt-ridden king Pelias and sister of Iphitus, whose excessive machismo suggests both physical and sexual uncertainties, Iole needs to be sheltered from the evils of the world by the love of a good man—a protection that is promised by Hercules. The physical courtship beginning with Hercules placing his mouth next to the place on the meat roast where the princess had taken a dainty bite, advancing to a near embrace as she leads him to his room in the palace, finally leads, after a superhuman throw of the discus, to a kiss for the Olympic victor from his admirer. Still the wry humour in this tale (is Hercules' discus still in orbit?) undercuts the cult of the body beautiful attached to the Olympic Games, particularly in the work of Leni Reifenstahl, and avoids the taint of eugenics that had been associated with Hellenic ideals in the first half of the twentieth century.[26]

This athletic idyll is interrupted by emotional doubt when Iole, along with the rest of the population of Iolcus, learns of the death of Iphitus and blames Hercules for not protecting her brother. Indirectly, she causes Hercules to question the value of his personal strength and to feel the need to prove his worth by acts of altruism. He gives up his

[25] Or perhaps the modern 'sporty' woman, whose engagement in leisure activities would be indicative of independence and affluence in Italy in the 1950s. Giordano (1998: 45) compares Koscina's dress to the *gonnellino* (mini-skirt) of female tennis players.

[26] The participation of Hercules in an Olympic-type contest in *Fatiche* (lightly mocked when Castor and Pollux stand next to him on different levels as if on the victors' dais) also recalls the aristocratic premises of modern athletic contests. That Hercules thus founds the *modern* Olympic Games is one of De Concini's frequent jokes at the expense of mythology in this film.

immortality in order to be able to feel human emotions and embarks on the quest for the Golden Fleece to prove the innocence of Jason and his dead friend Chiron. It is not accidental that Hercules promises that Iole will be safe once he has returned the Golden Fleece: the revelation that the villainous Eurystheus secretly desires the king's daughter makes this protection all the more essential. But Iole as object of desire has by now ceased to be a significant agent in the film's narrative. Her attempted rescue of Hercules in the dungeons of the palace proves futile when she and her maid are locked in, while the revived hero in his hurry to save Jason and the Argonauts simply rips the door down on his way out without saying a word to his beloved. In the second half of *Fatiche,* homosociality with its attendant adventures triumphs over the attractions of domestic bliss. Only after the fighting—and in accordance with the wishes of Iole's dying father—are the two reunited.

At the conclusion of the film, Iole and Hercules sail away into the sunset. The differences in the voice-over between the Italian and American versions are striking. In the original Italian, this is Jason's benediction:

> From great suffering, from blood, is often born the regenerative force of Love. That is why Hercules and Iole are today setting out toward happiness, like all do when Justice and Peace return. For these ideas are eternal, like the experience of life. Farewell Hercules. Farewell Iole. The life that awaits you will be happy and sad, dark or sunny, like that you have lived through. But you are together and that will be enough to carry on.

Contrast the Titra redub:

> Now there is justice and the clouds over Jolco[27] pass away. Out of great sorrow and spilled blood forces of good are sometimes born. Hercules and Iole are leaving now to find a new happiness. They will seek among the race of men where justice and peace will be with them again. Farewell Hercules. Farewell Iole. Life awaits you with all its glories and all its shadows. But even among the most difficult tasks the gods may prepare for you, you will have each other till the end of time.

What in the Italian original is almost a Christian marriage celebration, with the warning that, just as in the past, all will not be smooth sailing in life ahead, is changed in the American dub into the suggestion that Hercules and Iole are setting out on a life of adventure. Happiness is not dependent on the restoration of peace and justice (as in post-war

[27] The dub simply reproduces the Italian version of Iolcus; similarly, Eurystheus becomes Eurysteus from the Italian 'Euriteo'.

Italy), but is something that may be found somewhere else on earth (the likely reference to the United States is unmistakable). *Ercole e la regina di Lidia* had already had its Italian release before *The Labours of Hercules* had its first US screening, so Hercules' and Iole's honeymoon was to be no conclusion but only an interlude in the series. Hence the announcement of further tasks set by the gods (in line with traditional mythology, but in contrast with *Fatiche,* where the gods are remarkable for their absence)[28] and a declaration of the eternal nature of romantic love.

If Sylva Koscina is the embodiment of light and goodness in *Fatiche,*[29] and is usually filmed in outdoor scenes or in a sun-lit and glamorous boudoir, the casting of Gianna Maria Canale as Antea, the Queen of the Amazons on the island of Lemnos,[30] would appear to be equally deliberate. In contrast to the newcomer Koscina, Canale was a well-established actress in Italian cinema and her participation is given prominence in the credits and film posters for *Fatiche*. Her star quality was proven after her performances in the *femme fatale* roles of Sabina in Riccardo Freda's *Spartaco* (1953), Theodora in *Teodora Imperatrice di Bisanzio* (1954), and Giselle du Grand in *I Vampiri* (1957). Second in the Miss Italia competition of 1947 where Gina Lollobrigida took third place, Canale represented a more traditional 'south Italian' ideal of beauty, including natural wildness and passionate emotions, in contrast to the domesticated Koscina. As such, she is a dangerous foe for the Argonauts. The Queen of the Amazons makes an attractive partner to the youthful would-be monarch Jason as an older woman (although in fact only six years older than Koscina) who can teach a young man much.[31] The very choice of scenery in which the two female leads are placed highlights their contrast. Hercules, before leaving on the quest for the Golden Fleece, declares his love to Iole in front of a playing fountain (a scene of human taming of nature), while the Amazons live in a grotto

[28] The Sybil tells of the will of the gods and Hercules can take an oath by Jupiter, but there is no direct interference in human affairs. This 'Christianizing' of the Hercules films is most notable in *Hercules at the Centre of the Earth* (1961) where the deeply religious Reg Park actually invokes 'Jesus' on set. 'Jove' is then substituted in the dub. See Lucas (2007: 396).

[29] It can hardly be accidental that in Franju's 1963 remake of Feuillade's *Judex*, Koscina was chosen to play the blonde circus artist, Daisy, who, at the film's conclusion, engages in a Manichaean life-and-death battle on the rooftops of Paris with the dark-haired villainess, Diana Monti (Francine Bergé).

[30] The geographical specification of Lemnos, following Argonaut mythology, seems to be an addition to the American script: in the Italian/French versions, the Amazons live on a generic 'island'.

[31] See Gundle (2007: xxi) on the likelihood of an Italian male's first sexual experience being with an older, married woman or a prostitute; on the sexual attractions of Italian women to outsiders since the Grand Tour. See Gundle (2007: 3).

(unnaturally lit in shades of green, blue, and orange) amid verdant glades festooned with flowers.[32] Not unsurprisingly, such unrestrained abundance masks secret perils: the Argonauts are to be killed once they have fulfilled their function in mating with the women of the island. The threat is discovered by a young Ulysses, who informs Hercules. The hero, who is alone in not falling under the spell of the Amazons because of his love for Iole, is thus able to save his companions. As the Argo sails away, the Amazons attempt to lure the crew back in the fashion of the Sirens, but an operatic chorus of sailors under the direction of Orpheus drowns out their song. While in *Ulysses* (1954) the hero had to be tied to the mast to restrain him from swimming ashore and the sailors' ears blocked to keep out a song promising reunion with their loved ones, in *Fatiche* the bonds of male comradeship are shown as easily overpowering the individual enticements of female companionship.

IOLE VERSUS OMPHALE AND ANTINEA

A successful film almost demands a sequel and the Italian box office takings of *Fatiche* alone required the return of the main leads in another Francisci-directed production, *Ercole e la regina di Lidia* (1959, released in the UK and USA as *Hercules Unchained* in 1960). Instead of the tale of Hercules' labours, into which was inserted the quest for the Golden Fleece, this time scriptwriter De Concini has Hercules involved in the Seven Against Thebes saga, with Hercules' enslavement to Omphale inserted in the middle of the film.

Although Sylva Koscina returns as Iole, in *Regina* she serves mainly as the damsel in distress, having been left behind at Thebes (her husband's home town, portrayed as 'the big smoke' by its most famous inhabitant) while Hercules attempts to sort out the men's problems. Almost at the beginning of the film her change in status from Pelias' daughter to Hercules' wife is underlined. She is asked by Laertes to act as a surrogate mother to the young Ulysses, and Argos presents her with Orpheus' lute to be used to entertain the menfolk. The different behaviour expected of her husband, too, is indicated when Ulysses asks Hercules who is racing his wagon to slow down now that he is a married man (Iole is initially too

[32] See Lucas (2007: 204) for Mario Bava's trick photography that exaggerated the size of La Fontana, while masking buildings in the background; the home of the Amazons is the Cascate di Montegelato, a site close to Rome that has been a favourite background for pepla as well as other Italian films.

polite to criticize her husband's driving but thanks Ulysses for the reminder). In Doris Day fashion, she even sings a tune,[33] adding to the impression that the second Ercole film has become a domestic comedy. Only after some light workout, when Hercules defeats the half-giant Antaeus (played by the Italian champion ex-boxer, Primo Carnera) by throwing him into the sea and upends an impolite Argive officer who is blocking the party from taking shelter in a cave at the entrance to Hades, does the plot take a darker turn. The introduction of the quarrel between Polynices and Eteocles and the siege of the city by the Argive army provide opportunities to test Hercules' devotion to his wife, a trial that he nearly fails. After the hero, on his way to negotiate on behalf of the Thebans, drinks from the fountain of Lethe and is carried off to Lydia in a state of stupefaction, Iole is left to pass the time with her maids, working on a tapestry and pining for her husband (thus anticipating Penelope's future role in the *Odyssey*, although at this point Hercules is only three days absent).[34] Things take a turn for the worse when the insane tyrant Eteocles decides that Hercules has betrayed him and prepares to feed forlorn Iole to his tigers.[35] Iole's role as the frightened victim is foreshadowed when she screams at the death of a tiger trainer and reinforced by her fainting when her servants are thrown from the main gate of Thebes. She manages to escape from the city, but only to fall into the hands of the besieging army. Iole is only just saved from being raped by the enemy general when the duel between Eteocles and Polynices demands his immediate attention and Ulysses' counterattack from Thebes routs the Argive army. The film concludes with a funeral pyre for Oedipus' dead sons that will purify Thebes and its citizens, including Hercules and Iole who embrace on the walls of the city next to an archaic statue of Zeus. If the insane hatred of Oedipus and his sons has brought the wrath of the gods on the city, in death they have cleansed all Thebans. Hercules intones:

[33] The original song is *Con te per l'eternità*, a vocal version of the Ercole films' romantic theme, sung by Marisa Del Frate; in the English version, there is a new song, 'Evening Star' (words by the lyricist for Hoagy Carmichael's 'Stardust', Mitchell Parrish, sung by June Valli), expressing the feelings of a girl who has just been swept off her feet by her beau. See Lucas (2007: 235–6). The difference between the two once again illustrates different cultural expectations from romance.

[34] De Concini comically undermines this scene by having Iole's maid find a pair of metal cuffs and chains at the bottom of her box of keepsakes. The chains are a memento of Hercules' actions at the end of *Fatiche*, but might also suggest that Iole likes her man in restraints.

[35] Note the scene where the Theban prisoners gaze up through the bars of their prison at the tigers in the arena. The image is the stock portrayal of Christian martyrs awaiting their doom and is thus well designed to draw audience sympathy.

> How you have suffered, Iole. The gods have placed many obstacles against us and there will be others.

To which Iole replies:

> I hope we shall withstand them. Somehow the gods will be kind if we just love one another.[36]

The message that love may bring forgiveness is strong, but once again suggests that Iole now does little more than embody the joys of domesticity. Despite Hercules' reputation in the ancient world as a womanizer, among the later Ercole films only in the Mickey Hargitay and Jane Mansfield vehicle, *Gli amori di Ercole* (*Hercules and the Hydra*, 1960) does the hero (after the death of his wife, Megara) truly fall in love again—in this case both with Deianeira (Mansfield) and the Queen of the Amazons in the guise of Deianeira (also played by Mansfield).[37] In effect, it is not two-timing if Hercules' women all look the same. In the considerably superior Duccio Tessari-scripted[38] series of Hercules adventures, Hercules' wife Deianeira is twice played by blonde actress Eleonora Ruffo (in *La vedetta di Ercole* [*The Vengeance of Hercules*, 1960[39]] and *Ercole al centro della terra* [*Hercules in the Haunted World*, 1961]), but has almost no part to play except to be threatened by the likes of Christopher Lee. In the middle film of this trilogy, *Ercole alla conquista di Atlantide* [*Hercules and the Captive Women*, 1961] Deianeira has such an insignificant role as wife and mother that Ruffo can be replaced by Luciana Angiollilo without the audience apparently noticing. The romantic aspects of the

[36] All presently available versions of *Regina* are pan-and-scan 4:3 reproductions of the Joe E. Levine Warner Brothers' release. Clearly this reduces the effect of the original widescreen (2. 35:1) production. Comparison with the original script is also likely to reveal different emphases between the Italian and English versions.

[37] A doubling of the heroine probably inspired by the dual role of Silvana Mangano as Penelope and Circe in Camerini's *Ulisse* from 1954. See Paul in this volume.

[38] Other script credits include the directors Vittorio Cottafavi (*Vedetta* and *Atlantide*) and Mario Bava (*Centro*) and Alessandro Continenza (who had a hand in *Gli Amore di Ercole* and many other pepla). In interviews, individual participants often claim credit for particular treatments within the peplum movie. It is probably best to regard these films as joint efforts within which the stylistic approach of certain participants can often be detected. Tessari's comic advice on how to create such films is readily available in Winkler (2007b: 455–6).

[39] The official US release of this film by American International Pictures not only changes the name to *Goliath and the Dragon*, but also inserts sequences from an unfinished local Hercules production. Hyllus becomes Goliath's younger brother. Re-editing is common with the American releases of the pepla, but is particularly noticeable in the AIP releases. Still, the most egregious case of re-editing is not a foreign release, but Lucidi's *La sfida dei giganti* (*Hercules the Avenger*, 1965), a virtual cento composed from clips of *Hercules and the Captive Women* and *Hercules in the Haunted World*.

story are instead transferred to Hercules' younger companions: his son Hyllus (in *Vedetta* and *Atlantide*) or rambunctious friend Theseus (in *Centro*).

If, as a married man, Hercules is no longer looking for a partner, his fidelity may still be tested. In *Regina*, this role falls to Omphale, the Queen of Lydia, who uses and discards the prime masculine specimens that her soldiers have scoured the Mediterranean to bring back to her kingdom.[40] Her discarded lovers are killed and then made into statues, immortal trophies of her conquests. The part of this Asian[41] (and so, it is implied, decadent) queen is played by Sylvia Lopez, whose flaming red hair, ample figure, and implied wild sexuality make her closer to the ideal of Mediterranean beauty than Koscina's Iole. Although Lopez was actually Austrian by birth (born Tatjana Bernt, married to the French composer François Lopez), she gives the impression of having the fiery temperament of a Carmen. Her performance was so striking that she was often given a prominent position on posters for the film, while Koscina only earned participatory credits.[42] Still, Hercules when he recovers his senses starts to give the orders in the palace (a novelty which enchants the previously imperious queen) and when he leaves, she is reduced to clutching his leg as a suppliant, begging him to stay. When this fails, the love-struck queen commits suicide by throwing herself into the vat of embalming fluid.

In Cottafavi's *Ercole alla conquista di Atlantide*, bad queen (and even worse mother, since she has just tried to sacrifice her own daughter) Fay Spain as Antinea, the Queen of Atlantis, similarly attempts to seduce Hercules and make him her accomplice in her attempt to conquer the world through a race of supermen. But Hercules is not to be caught twice by such tricks. He quickly overpowers and rescues his brainwashed comrade Androcles when he attempts to murder him on the queen's

[40] Lydia is regarded as an island in the English dub: this may be a translation change modelled on the Lemnian episode of *Fatiche* (note the use of the Cascate di Montegelato once again in *Regina* as the setting for Omphale's palace) or a geographical modification (since Lydia is in reality part of Anatolia and so on the Asian mainland) already in the original script.

[41] The design of Omphale's realm is a strange mix of non-European forms: her soldiers appear to have Tartar helmets, her palace has towers similar to those of Angkor Wat, and her throne room and embalmers/sculptors are Egyptian. The resultant statues are, however, recognizably Greek types and the observant viewer may note that the name on the statue base intended for our hero is (in Greek letters) 'Herakles'.

[42] Lucas (2007): 232 (Italian poster: Lopez foregrounded over Koscina whose name is also obscured in the credits); 236 (lurid Turkish poster, showing only Hercules and Omphale); 237 (French poster, showing Hercules and the Queen of Lydia on each side, with Koscina given fourth billing after Primo Carnera!).

orders. Hercules is not to become one of the many embalmed lovers kept in Antinea's palace. Cottafavi here makes prominent one of the not-so-hidden sources for the Amazons in *Fatiche* and the Omphale episode in *Regina*, the popular French novel *L'Atlantide* (1919), which had by this time been filmed numerous times. Indeed the choice of the name Antea for the Amazon queen in *Fatiche* must already be seen as a homage to Benoit's book. In Cottafavi's version the queen's wiles are ineffective and Hercules, in James Bond style, destroys the villain's headquarters and saves the world. As a film, *Ercole alla conquista di Atlantide* is excellent entertainment, but it does suggest that the plotline of voluptuous vamp seducing the hero is close to being played out in this setting.[43] There is, however, an interesting innovation in providing Antinea with a daughter, a relationship absent in Benoit's novel. This not only allows Hercules to rescue her from the monster Proteus just as Perseus saves Andromeda, and provides a love interest for Hyllus, but also allows a comparison of the two families. Whereas Hercules is part of a stable nuclear family only complicated by the actions of his teenage son, Antinea has no male partner and is ready to sacrifice her daughter to ensure the success of a brood of unnatural male warriors. In effect, fascism is now defined not as the hyper-masculinity of Mussolini, but as a lack of masculinity that can be identified in the world-endangering threat of gynocracy.[44]

CONCLUSION

If Hercules can be considered an archetypal mortal with more than human strength and appetite, so can the villainesses he faces. While Hercules seeks to impose male-dominated civilization, these women threaten it by their ability to negate male civic values by concentrating on pleasure and thus emasculate and eventually annihilate their male

[43] On Cottafavi's film and its comic undertones, see Winkler (2007b: 466–9), Pomeroy (2008: 51–4), and Shahabudin (2009). Gianna Maria Canale had already reprised her role as Antea, the queen of the Amazons in the comedy peplum, *La regina delle Amazone* (1960), released in the US as *Colossus and the Amazon Queen*, although there is no 'Colossus' in the film. Her star turn in the first Hercules movie was also enough to gain Canale another vamp role as Astra in *Maciste contro il vampiro* (1961).

[44] Identifying fascism with a lack of confident masculinity can also be seen both in popular Italian films of the period (in *Se sei vivo spara* [*Django, kill . . . If you live shoot*, 1967] the hero has to overcome a band of black-shirted homosexual cowboys) and in the sexual politics of art-house productions (e.g. Bertolucci's *Il Conformista* [1970]).

partners.[45] As princess, Iole has a much less powerful role: she is the love object to be obtained by displays of masculine prowess, but once gained has little function except as one (a privileged one, for sure) of many claimants for the hero's attentions. As such, Deianeira can substitute for Iole without raising concern.[46] If anything, Hercules' wife represents the claims of domesticity from which he must be separated for the story to progress.[47]

All this is hardly controversial. But reception studies require that in addition to the recognition of prior themes in later forms, their cultural context should also be examined. A Hercules film can be read as a variation of the standard Hollywood movie.[48] At time of release, there would be different resonances for Asian or North American audiences, but the cinematic gaze on the body beautiful, both male and female, was likely to be universal.[49] However, I hope I have also been able to show that not only Steve Reeve's Hercules (as long recognized) but also Sylva Koscina's Iole acted as signifiers for a set of aspirations of the late 1950s that were specific to their initial Italian audiences. It is the fate of Iole that, although Hercules rejects the more vulgar temptations offered by the Mediterranean seductresses in the Ercole films, his union with a princess can only end in domesticity and cotidian duties. Iole's promises

[45] The queen of the Amazons in *Fatiche* simply kills her lovers. Omphale turns them into statues, while they become specimens in Antinea's trophy case. In *Gli amori* the Amazon queen turns her lovers into living, but blighted trees (one of which eventually strangles her as Hercules makes his escape).

[46] The reasons for this change in the Ercole cycle are unclear: Sylva Koscina may not have wished to reprise her role, but there was no difficulty in substituting other actors for Steve Reeve's Hercules. Given the inclusion of a nearly grown-up son in Hyllus in the scripts, Hercules' wife should now be considerably older, but Eleonora Ruffo was actually two years younger than Koscina.

[47] The same is true of Hercules' separation from Deianeira in *Hercules: The Legendary Journeys* telemovies (1994). See Blondell (2005: 76). In the television series (1995–9) Hercules' nuclear family is killed off by Hera, which considerably widens his opportunity for romantic adventures. Günsberg (2005: 115) suggests that Hercules' separation from his family in the peplum films may have had a special resonance for an Italian audience given the phenomenon of southern males migrating alone to obtain employment in the north during this period.

[48] So Clauss (2008), especially at 63, comparing Hercules' return to Thebes to servicemen returning from the Second World War and the Korean War. Perhaps more obvious for the original Italian audience was the realization that Polynices, by inviting the black-clothed Argives to engage in what was previously a domestic dispute in Thebes, is acting as the Italian fascists did by using German troops to maintain their power in Italy after 1943.

[49] Günsberg (2005: 131) rightly notes that as audiences cannot be classified by one fixed identity, so the gaze of the spectator in peplum films shifts between a variety of desires and cannot be readily labelled 'male' or 'female', 'youthful' or 'mature', 'working class' or 'educated'.

of freedom, status acquisition, and wealth resolve into traditional family patterns. Hence the readiness of the Duccio Tessari-scripted trilogy to poke gentle fun at these storylines.[50] Iole was to return in the 1990s in *Hercules: the Legendary Journeys*, but there her role as teenage temptress/ blonde bimbo was no threat to family man Hercules. The exotic actually appeared in the guise of the New Zealand-born actress, Lucy Lawless, whose dark tresses and unladylike behaviour prepared the way for her subversion of the genre in *Xena: Warrior Princess*. But that is another story.

[50] The anti-fascist, but also anti-nuclear message of *Ercole alla conquista di Atlantide* (1961) seems not to have been noticed in the English-speaking world at the time of its initial release. For the stone of Uranus and the effects of Uranium, see Winkler (2007b), Shahabudin (2009: 211–14), and Burke (2011: 38–46).

9

Annihilating Clytemnestra: The Severing of the Mother–Daughter Bond in Michael Cacoyannis' *Iphigenia* (1977)[1]

Anastasia Bakogianni

The Greek-Cypriot director Michael Cacoyannis (1921–2011) creatively adapted Euripides' play *Iphigenia at Aulis* in his film *Iphigenia* (1977). This was his third adaptation of a Greek tragedy for the silver screen, following *Electra* (1962) and *The Trojan Women* (1971).[2] Together the three films form Cacoyannis' Euripidean trilogy,[3] his testament to the modernity of Euripides, whom he considered the most relevant of

[1] This article is dedicated to the memory of Michael Cacoyannis who passed away on 25 July 2011. I will always be grateful for his interest in my work and for permission to reproduce the three photographs that appear in this article. Many thanks also to Gonda Van Steen and Lorna Hardwick for their many helpful suggestions. A particular debt of gratitude is owed to Konstantinos P. Nikoloutsos for his careful editing work and invaluable advice.

[2] Classical scholars have increasingly engaged with Cacoyannis' Euripidean trilogy. For his *Electra*, see Bakogianni (2008) and (2011); MacKinnon (1986: 75–80); McDonald (1983: 261–319). For *The Trojan Women*, Bakogianni (2009); MacKinnon (1986: 80–5); McDonald (1983: 192–259); and in this volume see Vivante's article on the portrayal of Helen. For *Iphigenia*, see Bakogianni (2013); Michelakis (2006a: 127–9) and (2006b: 223–4); McDonald (2001); MacKinnon (1986: 85–94); McDonald (1983: 128–91).

For the trilogy as a whole see: Solomon (2001a: 259–74, 263–6); McDonald and Winkler (2001). For more general studies in which Cacoyannis' oeuvre is mentioned, see also Michelakis (2004: 199) and Hardwick (2003: 81–2). For the modern Greek film criticism perspective, see Siafkos (2009: 120–34, 181–7, 210–16); Soldatos (2002a: 290–2), (2002b: 61–2 and 157–8); (2004: 482–4); Kolonias (1995).

[3] MacKinnon argues against labelling the three films as trilogy (1986: 74–5). I would counter that there are enough similarities and common themes running through all three films in order for them to deserve the title. Audiences and readers should be reminded of the advantages of viewing and discussing them as a unit, as well as singly.

the three ancient tragedians.[4] One of the director's strategies for making the ancient plays 'speak' to contemporary audiences is by focusing on the human relationships in them. One of the most important relationships in his *Iphigenia* is the bond between mother and daughter. Cacoyannis chose to explore it closely in his film as a means of demonstrating how war and irredentist ambitions lead to the destruction of the nuclear family.

Cacoyannis' approach to filming Greek tragedy was successful in both artistic and financial terms.[5] He was able to raise the necessary funding to complete the three films modelled on Euripides' plays. He received numerous honours for these adaptations. His *Iphigenia* was presented at the 18th Greek Film Festival and at Cannes.[6] It was also nominated for an Academy Award for Best Foreign Film in 1977. The reception of his trilogy has flourished in recent decades: it has been presented at various film festivals throughout the world and since its release on DVD it has continued to gain new audiences.[7] Its pedagogical value is demonstrated by its inclusion in school and university curricula.[8] Its 'afterlife' therefore appears to be assured.

The film has received some scholarly attention in classical reception studies. This paper seeks to place renewed emphasis on the artistic and sociopolitical context of the film in an attempt to shed light on Cacoyannis'

[4] During a conference held at Delphi in 1981 Cacoyannis stressed that he felt 'a special affinity for Euripides' because 'his whole attitude towards war, religion, towards human relationships is just that much closer to us today' (1984: 214). For a discussion of the modernity of Euripides, see also Walton (2010).

[5] *Electra*'s box office in 1962 was 76,846 drachmas. See Soldatos (2004: 400).

[6] Despite the honour that this represented, Cacoyannis' *Iphigenia* was less well received at the Festival in 1977 than his *Electra* fifteen years earlier. Soldatos (2002b: 148).

[7] Examples illustrating the continuing reception of Cacoyannis' Euripidean trilogy include: it was screened in London at the National Film Theatre in 1981 and again on 12 and 13 of May 2001 at the Barbican Theatre. It was also screened in Greece earlier that same month (4–16 May 2001). This presentation formed part of a series of events celebrating Cacoyannis' oeuvre with a screening of most of his films and an exhibition organized by the *demos* of Athens to celebrate his life's work. Another screening took place at the 14th Antipodes Greek Film Festival (20 September–8 October 2006) held in Melbourne. The films' inclusion in this Australian festival organized by the Greek community of the city testifies to the trilogy's continuing importance in the dialogue between past and present and the construction of modern Greek identity. *The Trojan Women* and *Iphigenia*, in particular, are screened every year, since 2009, at the National Library of Buenos Aires and other venues in the federal capital by the Hellenic Association *Nostos*.

The release of the trilogy on DVD was delayed due to long-drawn-out disputes over copyright. The films started to appear in the 2000s: *Electra* (MGM: 2002), *The Trojan Women* (Kino International Corp: 2004), and *Iphigenia* (MGM: 2007). A Collectors' Deluxe DVD edition of his Euripidean trilogy for the Greek market became available in 2006 (Audio Visual Enterprises).

[8] On the pedagogical value of cinematic adaptations, see Paul (2007: 304–5); McDonald (2008); Rose (2001).

departures from the source text and his appropriation of Euripidean tragedy as a powerful tool whereby to comment on contemporary events and address modern concerns and ideas. The severing of the mother-daughter relationship has also been overlooked in previous scholarship on the film. This paper seeks to fill this critical vacuum by means of a scene-by-scene analysis of the film and a close reading of the visuals. The scene-by-scene reading seeks to cast light on the film's power dynamics, which are underexplored in previous scholarship, and to explain why women occupy such a prominent place in this film in particular and in Cacoyannis' art in general.

Euripides' play offers us a very ambiguous account of these events and one that is permeable to a multiplicity of interpretations;[9] our understanding of the play is further complicated by the particularly problematic nature of the surviving source text itself.[10] It is this 'problematic' play, however, that served as the model for one of the most moving depictions of the mother-daughter relationship in the reception of Greek tragedy in the medium of film.

CACOYANNIS AND GREEK TRAGEDY

Hollywood meets European Art Cinema

Cacoyannis' stated aim was to bring Greek tragedy to large audiences by taking advantage of the popular appeal of the medium of cinema.[11] In order to accomplish this goal he successfully married elements of the Hollywood classical style with a European art cinema sensibility, thereby creating a hybrid style that was designed to be both mainstream and avant-garde.[12] In his adaptation of Euripides' *Iphigenia* he offers audiences a blend of what I have labelled 'popularized/filmic' and 'stylized/

[9] On the difficulties of interpreting the play, see Gamel (1999: 326–7).

[10] According to Kovacs 'the number of lines suspected by one scholar or another of being interpolated is far larger here than in any other Greek tragedy' (2002: 157). In Diggle's opinion the textual problems of this play meant that it could 'not be judged by ordinary critical standards' (1994: 49). See also Gurd (2005: 62–4) and Foley (1985: 67). I use David Kovacs' edition of the play (2002).

[11] Cacoyannis (1984: 225).

[12] The classical Hollywood style emerged in the years 1908–27, but its golden age was the three decades that followed. For an in-depth analysis of this dominant cinematic language and style see Bordwell, Staiger, and Thompson (1985). See also Kaplan (1998). Art cinema is characterized by greater variety, on which see Vincendeau (1998: 440–1). An important category in the scholarly discussion of art films is that of 'national' cinema. On European national cinema see Crofts (2006: 45–7); Aitken (2001); Sorlin (1991).

poetic' elements.[13] This fusion is what makes his reception of the tragedy so distinctive and acknowledges his debt both to the mass-entertainment cinema of Hollywood and to the more thoughtful and individualistic products of European art cinema.

The decision to film Greek tragedy was indicative of Cacoyannis' art cinema sensibilities, as well as of his education and background. Hollywood has so far shown no interest in Greek tragedy, preferring instead to focus on historical and/or mythic subjects from ancient Greece that have often provided the subject for spectacular action films of epic proportions.[14] Independent directors, on the other hand, have been fascinated by the possibilities of adopting ancient Greek drama for modern audiences.[15] Their output showcases the wealth of possibilities inherent in such endeavours.[16] They enjoy a reputation for being *auteur* directors. This type of director defines himself/herself as a filmmaker who is not a mere craftsman, but an artist. They reject filmic conventions and formulas. Instead they utilize the medium to develop and express a personal creativity that includes, but is not limited to ideological perspectives.[17] Independent directors choose Greek tragedy as a means of expressing personal and artistic ambitions.

Although Cacoyannis worked in Hollywood in the 1960s, he often spoke of his opposition to the Hollywood system.[18] His most successful collaboration with a Hollywood studio was *Zorba the Greek* (1964) made for Twentieth Century-Fox.[19] His next Hollywood project, *The Day the Fishes Came Out* (1967), was a failure, and Cacoyannis decided to return to making films independently. He preferred having more direct control over his films than Hollywood generally allowed filmmakers. He did

[13] Bakogianni (2009: 56). In discussing Cacoyannis' technique, McDonald has used the terms 'artificial' and 'natural' (1983: 248).

[14] For an exploration of ancient Greece in the popular mediums of film and television see: Elley (1984: 52–75), Solomon (2001a: 259–74), Nisbet (2006), Winker (2007b), Berti and García Morcillo (2008), Pomeroy (2008), Richards (2008: 133–41), James (2009), Potter (2009), Shahabudin (2009), Turner (2009), Winkler (2009: 70–153), and Blanshard and Shahabudin (2011).

Recent offerings in this genre include *Troy* (2004), *Alexander* (2004), *300* (2006), *Clash of the Titans* (2010), and *Immortals* (2011).

[15] On Greek tragedy on screen, see Michelakis (2001), (2004), (2006b), (2013). See also Nikoloutsos (2010) on the reception of Euripides' *Iphigenia at Aulis* in Argentine avant-garde cinema.

[16] Independent directors who have adapted Greek tragedy include Pier Paolo Pasolini, Lars von Trier, Jules Dassin, Miklós Jancsó, and Inés de Oliveira Cézar.

[17] (Stoddart 1995: 40). I am also indebted to Lorna Hardwick for her comments on this point.

[18] Cacoyannis (1995: 14).

[19] This is the film upon which Cacoyannis' international reputation rests. The Greek press, however, criticized it for presenting a stereotypical view of modern Greece. For this view of Cacoyannis' work, see Zacharia (2008: 330–7).

actually exert a great deal of control over the finished production. He wrote the screenplay, chose the actors, and directed all three adaptations of Euripides' tragedies. The theory of the dialectic of montage, formulated by the Russian filmmaker Sergei Eisenstein,[20] stresses the control that a director can exert over the ideological message of his/her film. I would argue that Cacoyannis approached the adaptation of Euripides' plays for the medium of film in this vein.

Contrary to other *auteur* directors, however, Cacoyannis chose to create a realistic, rational, and linear narrative for his cinematic receptions of Greek tragedy.[21] MacKinnon makes the point that the text of *Iphigenia at Aulis* is so problematic that a filmmaker is faced with the choice of either just accepting the textual difficulties or heavily adapting the source in order to 'make sense' of these problems.[22] Cacoyannis chose the latter approach. He based his screenplay on the surviving source text and rationalized it by making additions and changes wherever he felt them to be necessary. He reinterpreted Euripides' ambiguous characters, reduced the role of the chorus, and changed the *deus ex machina* ending—all elements that he felt would alienate modern viewers.

Euripides' dramatic personae are highly complex. In his adaptations, Cacoyannis tended to favour one side of the characters over the other. In *Iphigenia*, Clytemnestra is portrayed as a loving mother, Iphigenia as an innocent, young victim, and Achilles as the heroic, if rather proud young warrior, who falls in love with her. Ranged against them is a weak Agamemnon who cannot stand up to the pressure exerted by the army and other eponymous heroes. His fear and desire to maintain his grip on power lead him to dress up his daughter's sacrifice in a nationalistic rhetoric about dying for the benefit of Greece. The ugly truth is that the reason for Iphigenia's sacrifice in Cacoyannis' reception is not a divine command or 'necessity', but Calchas' desire to punish Agamemnon for the killing of Artemis' sacred deer. Calchas is supported by Odysseus who wants to

[20] Kolker (1998: 15–17).

[21] Pier Paolo Pasolini, on the other hand, preferred to emphasize the mythical and anthropological elements in his receptions of Greek tragedy *Edipo Re* (1967) and *Medea* (1970). In his interview with McDonald (2001: 81–2), Cacoyannis stated that he preferred a different approach to Pasolini's. According to him the Italian director was interested only in the mythical origins of the story and he raided Greek tragedy for the 'bare bones of a plot'. Other *auteur* directors like Jules Dassin preferred to transplant the plots of Greek tragedy into modern settings, as in his *Phaedra* (1962) and *A Dream of Passion* (1978) modelled on Euripides' *Medea*.

[22] MacKinnon (1986: 85–6).

accrue greater personal power and a higher standing within the Greek army.[23]

Another aspect of Cacoyannis' realistic treatment of *Iphigenia at Aulis* involves the role and function of the chorus. In his previous two adaptations of Euripides' plays, the director retained, to some degree at least, the chorus. In *Iphigenia*, however, he largely subsumed it into the narrative of his film, thereby eliminating one of the 'stylized/poetic' elements that characterized his other two film adaptations. In *Electra* and *The Trojan Women* he just shortened the chorals, gave the chorus members a more prominent role, and took care to portray them both individually and as members of a distinct group. In *Iphigenia* he went a step further. In the third film of the trilogy Cacoyannis radically reduced the role and function of the Greek chorus. He gave Iphigenia a group of attendants who are also her friends and support her throughout her ordeal. The distancing effect of having a chorus of women from Euboea is abandoned, as it would break the 'illusion' of realism that Cacoyannis was striving to achieve. In Cacoyannis' reception, it is the men who introduce conflict into the close-knit, harmonious, and nurturing world of the women.

In addition, Cacoyannis eliminated all but a few of the references to the gods in his films. There are no divine epiphanies, nor any *deus ex machina* endings.[24] The illusion of reality that makes the film more accessible to modern audiences is, therefore, never broken.[25] This decision has important implications for his adaptation of the problematic text of *Iphigenia at Aulis*. Cacoyannis eliminated the contested ending of the surviving text where a stag substitutes for Iphigenia by the grace of the goddess Artemis.[26] He also added over half an hour of additional material in order to stamp the drama with his personal interpretation of the story. It is in this prologue that the reasons for Iphigenia's sacrifice are made clear, Agamemnon's motivation is established, and the mother–daughter

[23] Bakogianni (2013).

[24] In his *Electra*, modelled on Euripides' play, Cacoyannis created a realistic ending for his protagonists. The siblings choose self-exile after they lose the support of the people by committing matricide. See Bakogianni (2008: 162–4). His *Trojan Women* opens without the distancing effect of Euripides' divine epiphany of Poseidon and Athena. Instead Cacoyannis sought to engage the sympathy of his audience by focusing on the mistreatment of the enslaved Trojan women. See Bakogianni (2009: 62–3).

[25] In Cacoyannis' own words: 'To show them on the screen would be alienating to modern audiences, who should identify with the characters and be moved as Euripides intended his audiences to be.' Quoted in Winkler (2009: 218).

[26] Scholars have debated the authenticity of the 'happy ending' of the text as it survives. Kovacs believes that the play ended with Iphigenia departing for the altar and that there was no last-minute rescue (2003: 77).

bond is movingly portrayed. Cacoyannis thus turned the problematic nature of the text as it survives into an advantage.

The sociopolitical context

Upon his return from London to Greece in 1953, Cacoyannis contributed to the renaissance of the Greek Film industry.[27] He specialized in the exploration of 'the fragile nature of human relations' in his cinematic oeuvre.[28] In Greece, his most popular film remains, unquestionably, *Stella* (*Στέλλα*, 1955), starring Melina Merkouri as a singer torn between two ways of life. Throughout the 1950s, Cacoyannis continued to direct films set in contemporary Greece with strong female leads that problematized the position of women in Greek society. His film *The Girl in Black* (*Το κορίτσι με τα μαύρα*, 1956) features Elli Lambeti in the role of Marina, a young woman scorned by the men of her island home of Hydra for her aloofness. In *A Matter of Dignity* (*Το τελευταίο ψέμμα*, 1958), Lambeti plays Chloe, a woman who has to choose between two suitors: Niko, a wealthy Greek-American who can help her family financially, and Galanos, the poor man she loves. Cacoyannis' interest in tragic stories with strong female protagonists is what attracted him to Euripides, famous since antiquity for his unorthodox portrayal of women. Cacoyannis believed that 'feminist concerns predominate in Euripides'.[29] Iphigenia's chauvinist rhetoric in *Iphigenia at Aulis* is therefore downplayed in the film.[30] In his Euripidean trilogy Cacoyannis largely focused on the female protagonists and their point of view. In the

[27] The Greek film industry produced low budget films, mostly comedies and melodramas, for the domestic market. One of the first attempts to capture on camera the revival of Greek drama in the modern state is Dimos Bratsanos' film of the performance of *Prometheus Bound* that was the highlight of the Delphic Festival organized by Angelos Sikelianos and his wife Eva Palmer in 1927. See Bakogianni (2008: 125) and Soldatos (2004: 13). The introduction of sound and the import of foreign movies led to the industry's decline which was further disrupted by World War II. It was only in the 1950s after Greece returned to a state of relative political and financial stability, that production flourished, and it was during this renaissance of the industry that Cacoyannis produced his *Electra*. On the Greek film industry in this period, see also Nikoloutsos in this volume.

[28] Pendergast (2000: 148). His first film was a comedy '*Κυριακάτικο Ξύπνημα*' translated into English as *Windfall in Athens* (1953), squarely aimed at the popular end of the contemporary Greek film market.

[29] MacDonald and Winkler (2001: 75).

[30] Particularly in lines 1393–4. Rabinowitz (1993: 51) detects in the play a 'general denigration of the feminine'.

second and third film he portrayed them as victims reacting to male ambition and lust for power, wealth, and conquest.

The director's perception of Euripides' plays as condemning war was in agreement with the view prevalent in the 1970s that sought to imbue Greek tragedy with a strong anti-war message.[31] This was a period during which the performance of Greek tragedy was rediscovered for its potential as an act of resistance to dominant ideology. Greek drama, because of its privileged status in the canon of Western culture, proved fertile ground for adaptations with a radical agenda. Cacoyannis, like many other modern Greek artists, went into exile when the junta seized control of the country. He shot his *Trojan Women* in Spain. In *Iphigenia* Cacoyannis' portrayal of the mother–daughter bond is an important component of his strategy to demonstrate Euripides' anti-war message.[32] It echoes his portrayal of Hecuba's relationship with her daughter Cassandra and her daughter-in-law Andromache in the earlier film. In *Iphigenia*, however, Cacoyannis gave his audience the chance to see mother and daughter together before their lives were fatally disrupted and their bond broken by death.

One of the reasons for Cacoyannis' perception of Euripides' *Iphigenia at Aulis* as an indictment of war[33] is that he viewed the play through the prism of political events in modern Greece and his native home island of Cyprus. The two decades in which he produced his three cinematic receptions of Euripides' plays saw political unrest, the breakdown of democracy, and a military junta in Greece, while Cyprus stumbled from

[31] The 1960s and 70s were turbulent decades and directors responded to this climate by producing increasingly more politically engaged films. See Cowie (2004) and Sorlin (1991: 139–49). On the contemporary theatre stage a similar trend can be observed, on which see Loraux (2002) and Hall (2004: 1). For a similar artistic phenomenon in Latin America in the same period, see Nikoloutsos (2012: 1–5). Classical scholarship also debated the anti-war message of Euripides' work in this period. A popular example of this trend was Philip Vellacott's revised translations of Euripides' plays for Penguin.

This is a trend that has proven popular in the subsequent performance history of Euripidean tragedy. Euripidean plays were performed on both sides of the Atlantic in protest against the recent wars in Afghanistan and Iraq. Two high profile examples of theatre productions that propagate the view that there is an inherent anti-war message in Euripidean tragedy are Katie Mitchell's *Iphigenia at Aulis* (2004) and *The Trojan Women* (2007) staged at the National Theatre (London).

[32] In her 2004 production of the play Mitchell also emphasized the strong bond between mother and daughter and the innocence of the latter in order to make them more sympathetic to contemporary audiences.

[33] Cacoyannis, in his phone interview with McDonald and Winkler (2001: 74), described Euripides as a 'pacifist'. For the political resonances of *Electra* and the modern Greek context, see Bakogianni (2008: 149–52). See also Chiasson (2013). For *The Trojan Women*, see Bakogianni (2009: 46, 53–5).

one crisis to another until the Turkish invasion that divided the island into two parts. The unrest in the Greek political arena, and more widely in society, in the period 1961–75 informs Cacoyannis' film. The director portrays the Greek camp in a very similar light, a place, that is, where the power dynamics are constantly shifting and the army is called to play an important role in determining the leadership contest.[34]

The legacy of the Greek Civil War (1946–9) was one of bitter hatred and entrenched divisions. A series of conservative governments dominated the political life of Greece in reaction to the communist unrest after the end of World War II. The election of 1961 was particularly bitterly contested. The leader of the conservative party and incumbent Prime Minister, Konstantinos Karamanlis (1907–98), defeated his opponent George Papandreou (1888–1968), who led a coalition of centre-left liberal forces. Karamanlis, however, was dogged by persistent rumours of election fraud.[35] The assassination of the centre-left politician Grigoris Lambrakis by right-wing extremists in May of 1963 exacerbated an already volatile situation. These troubles and his worsening relationship with the palace led Karamanlis to his resignation in June 1963.[36]

A period of instability followed. Two interim governments and a narrow-margin electoral victory by Papandreou that ultimately proved unsustainable eventually led to a working government after the elections of February 1964. Papandreou's government, however, was destabilized by the Aspida (Shield) scandal in which his own son and future Prime Minister, Andreas Papandreou (1919–96), was involved. At the heart of the conspiracy was a group of young officers with left-wing sympathies that opposed right-wing influences in the army. Public opinion, ever fearful of 'the communist threat', was alarmed by the allegations of foreign influences at work within the armed forces. Papandreou quarrelled with the palace about how to best handle the scandal and resigned.[37]

The political crisis that this second resignation precipitated raged on for nearly three years until elections were finally scheduled for May 1967. Fearing another victory by Papandreou, a group of army colonels staged a military coup on the morning of 21 April 1967. The triumvirate of Georgios Papadopoulos, Nikolaos Makarezos, and Stylianos Pattakos took

[34] For a more detailed account of how Cacoyannis adapted the politics of Euripidian tragedy to address contemporary political concerns, see Bakogianni (2013).

[35] Papandreou, a powerful and effective orator, accused Karamanlis of 'νοθεία' (fraud) and rallied the opposition forces for what he called his 'ανένδοτος αγώνας' (relentless fight) against corruption. Christopoulos and Bastias (2000: 204–5).

[36] See also Clogg (2002: 152–3).

[37] Christopoulos and Bastias (2000: 216–18) and Clogg (2002: 158).

advantage of the nation's disillusionment with the recent upheavals of the democratic system and the resulting apathy to consolidate the army's grip on power. There was surprisingly little resistance in 1967 and throughout the first few years of the dictatorship. It was the junta's persecution of anyone whom it considered a threat that gradually hardened opposition. By 1973 the dictatorship was losing its grip on power. The worsening state of the economy, a naval mutiny, and a student uprising in Athens weakened the regime. The hard-line Dimitrios Ioannidis, former head of the notorious security police, overthrew Papadopoulos and took control. It was he who fatally mishandled a crisis in Cyprus with lasting repercussions.

The crisis was precipitated by the discovery of oil off the coast of the island of Thassos (1973–4), which prompted a claim by Turkey for the rights to drill in the Aegean Sea.[38] Ioannidis' response was to interfere in the internal affairs of Cyprus. The junta followed this policy of intervention ever since it had assumed power. This served to alienate Turkey. Diplomatic relations between the two countries deteriorated throughout this period. The Greek dictatorship's aggressively irredentist policies put Archbishop Makarios, head of the Cypriot government, in an untenable position. Ioannidis tried to incite a coup on the island in July 1974 and an attempt was made on Makarios' life.[39] This was the beginning of the end for the short-lived independent republic of Cyprus. Turkey invaded on the 20th of July and occupied the northern part of the island. War between Greece and Turkey was only narrowly avoided, but the issue of Cyprus remains open to this day.

As a native of Cyprus, Cacoyannis was profoundly affected by these events and decided to return to the island in September 1974 in order to record events as they unfolded. His documentary *Attila 74* (1975)[40] captured the tragic fate suffered by many of his fellow Cypriots. In his documentary he examined the causes that led to the invasion, but the most powerful and moving scenes arose out of his visits to refugee camps. He recorded eye-witness testimonies of the experience of displacement and exile. Cacoyannis focused in particular on the suffering and pain of mothers and their children, a number of whom were missing

[38] Clogg (2002: 162–3). The dispute over who owned the rights to drill for the oil intensified and open hostilities nearly broke out in 1975–6. Christopoulos and Bastias (2000: 311–12). For the long history of the island's troubles, see Woodhouse (1984: 110–12, 269–81, 286–8).

[39] Koliopoulos and Veremis (2002: 301–5).

[40] Attila was the code name the Turks chose for the operation. It is also a reference to the brutality of Attila the Hun.

or were dead. In his documentary these figures became symbolic of the fate of Cyprus itself.

The correlations with *Iphigenia* made less than three years later are striking. Cacoyannis' second portrayal of Clytemnestra as a grieving mother whose child is sacrificed on the altar of the irredentist ambitions of corrupt politicians mirrors the real-life tragedy of his home island. The scenes where Clytemnestra laments the fate of her daughter are reminiscent of Cacoyannis' interviews with bereaved mothers in *Attila 74*. For Cacoyannis Iphigenia has come to symbolize Cyprus. In 1974 Cyprus was a very young nation, like the young girl sacrificed in the film. Clytemnestra's palpable anguish in the film echoes that of the mothers of Cyprus who lost their children. Cacoyannis reinforced and enhanced the political dimension of Euripides' drama by interpreting it as an indictment of irredentist ambitions and the suffering they cause. This is an aspect of the play that has been receiving increasing attention in classical scholarship. Carter, for example, characterized the play as 'a political drama in the purest modern sense of that word'.[41] By reinforcing the political dimension of the drama Cacoyannis invites a re-evaluation of these elements in the source text.

THE MOTHER-DAUGHTER BOND: CACOYANNIS RE-IMAGINES EURIPIDES

Iphigenia offered Cacoyannis the opportunity to revisit his earlier portrayal of Clytemnestra in his *Electra* and to make it more complex. This time he wanted to explore the reasons behind her decision to betray and murder her husband; not to portray her simply as a murderous woman incapable of love and cruel towards her daughter, as he did in his earlier film.[42] Instead he reveals to his audience how, and more crucially why, Clytemnestra, 'the mother', was destroyed and transformed into a cold, unfeeling 'monster' driven by hatred. On the visual level Clytemnestra's transformation into a monster is depicted at the end

[41] Carter (2007: 69). For Wilkins the play is 'pre-eminently "social" and "political"' (1990: 190). Luschnig described Agamemnon as a career politician (1988: 74). See also Kitto (1961: 361). McDonald (1983: 183) went so far as to agree with Cacoyannis' interpretation of the play as a condemnation of war. Kovacs, on the other hand, believes that we are meant to see Iphigenia's sacrifice as 'a necessary precondition for a necessary war' (2003: 101).

[42] For Cacoyannis' portrayal of Clytemnestra in *Electra*, see McDonald (1983: 300–2); Bakogianni (2008: 152–4 and 161).

of the film. She is shown on a wagon going back home, her gaze fixed on the Greek ships setting off from the coast. The wind blows her black, thick locks in front of her face, making them look like the coils of a snake. In this scene Clytemnestra resembles Medusa.[43]

In order to explore in full the relationship between Clytemnestra and Iphigenia, as he envisioned it, Cacoyannis added several scenes to the ones drawn directly from Euripides' play. The audience first encounters mother and daughter at home in the ruins of Mycenae.[44] Cacoyannis' first shot of Clytemnestra (Papas) is of her calling her daughter's name from inside the battlements. Iphigenia (Tatiana Papamoschou, who was only thirteen when the film was shot) is roaming the hills. In her first scene in the film, she waves her arms, while holding her white veil. Cacoyannis thus created an image of Iphigenia as a carefree young girl. The soft strains of her musical *leitmotif* are heard for the first time, reinforcing her youth and innocence.[45] The reason for Clytemnestra's summons is the arrival of a letter from Agamemnon (Kostas Kazakos) with the false news of Iphigenia's upcoming wedding to Achilles—the one that Agamemnon wishes to revoke in Euripides' prologue (*IA*, 98–162). The first thread in the fateful trap thus coils around the previously carefree young girl.

Throughout this scene Clytemnestra is represented in her role as 'mother'. The director attempted to portray Clytemnestra as an affectionate mother, a side of her that is erased or suppressed in classical literature, in tragedy as well as in the *Odyssey*, and in art (both ancient and modern) where she is stereotypically portrayed as a murderer of her husband and an adulteress.[46] Cacoyannis directed Papas to portray Clytemnestra as openly affectionate. In this scene, for example, after Iphigenia has finished reading the letter, her mother strokes her cheek and then they embrace. One of Iphigenia's younger sisters joins in this female display of affection and solidarity. This is perhaps the young

[43] Michelakis (2006a: 127). I am indebted for this suggestion to Konstantinos Nikoloutsos and for drawing my attention to this reference.

[44] Cacoyannis obtained permission to film in these famous ruins for both his *Electra* and *Iphigenia*. In these scenes, past and present are visually conflated: the classical past and modern Greece in 1961 and 1976 when Cacoyannis shot the two films, respectively. The fact that the archaic palace is in ruins signals that the movies belong to modern times, but filming there creates the illusion of a 'timeless' Greece (Michelakis 2001: 244) and adds a sense of authenticity to the films.

[45] Mikis Theodorakis composed the music for Cacoyannis' Euripidean trilogy. Iphigenia's theme is soft and lyrical. It is played smoothly by strings and woodwind instruments. It thus has a number of qualities that have been labelled as stereotypicaly 'female' in the history of film music. I am indebted to Stella Voskaridou for my discussion of the soundtrack, on which see Voskaridou (2013).

[46] For the reception of Clytemnestra, see Komar (2003).

Electra—an addition which makes this scene doubly ironic given that in his first cinematic adaptation of Euripidean tragedy Cacoyannis emphasized the hatred that Clytemnestra's second daughter feels for her mother. That night, as mother and daughter prepare for bed, Clytemnestra carries the young Orestes and puts him to sleep. She informs Iphigenia that she intends to disobey her father and accompany her to Aulis because like any mother she wants to prepare her daughter for marriage and dress her for the ceremony. The next morning they set out for Aulis after Clytemnestra kisses her younger two daughters goodbye. As in Euripides, Orestes accompanies them (*IA*, 621–2). In line 622, Clytemnestra describes Orestes as a 'νήπιος' (infant). In Cacoyannis' film he is a small boy of about two or three, as he is in some ancient receptions of the story.[47] The implied reason is that he is still too young to be left alone at home. His function in Cacoyannis is to serve as the other child on whom Clytemnestra lavishes her maternal affection for the rest of the film, particularly in the scenes of the journey to Aulis.[48] Thus the audience's first impression of Cacoyannis' Clytemnestra is that she is a devoted and loving mother.

The director depicted the journey of mother and daughter to Aulis in detail to shed light on the relationship between the two. Riding in open carriages amidst the Greek landscape, the connection between the earth and the women is emphasized—in particular the stark contrast between the tense atmosphere of the scenes in the army camp and the peace of the rural countryside through which the convoy rides.[49] The queen, her daughter, and their female entourage are accompanied by a few soldiers, but this is mostly a group of women. The landscape becomes more arid and brown the closer they get to the coast. This acts as a visual symbol of the crisis within the Greek army[50] and the contrast between the fertile and peaceful space occupied by the women and the male-dominated camp.[51]

[47] See Michelakis (2006a: 121).

[48] In Cacoyannis' film both Clytemnestra and Iphigenia make effective use of Orestes' presence in their attempts to change Agamemnon's mind. It is also significant that after Iphigenia's sacrifice he is not seen accompanying his mother on her return journey.

[49] For the importance of the landscape in Cacoyannis, see Michelakis (2001: 244–5).

[50] For Michelakis the barren landscapes in Cacoyannis' *Iphigenia* act as a visual metaphor for the troubles of the modern Greek state in the 1970s (2001: 248). The world of the women and the shady grove where the priests tend to their flocks are set up in stark contrast to the military world of the Greek army camp. This contrast makes the aridity of the male world of war all the more striking.

[51] Cacoyannis physically located the Greek army on a beach outside of Corinth and used actual Greek soldiers from the military camp at Haidari and others based in the Peloponnese (Siafkos 2009: 211).

The caravan stops to rest during the night. Clytemnestra's first priority is the comfort of her children. She stands over Orestes' cot to make sure he is comfortable. Iphigenia, who has trouble sleeping, is leaning against the door with her eyes closed.[52] Ironically, she says that she thought she felt a breath of wind. This way Cacoyannis inscribes his filmic text with various visual and aural markers that prefigure the tragic events at Aulis. In an effort to help Iphigenia sleep, Clytemnestra sings softly to her, as if she were a baby again. Her song, which resembles a prayer, asks that love be kind to her daughter rather than 'wild':

> *Αφροδίτη κάνε να νιώσω τη χαρά της αγάπης*
> *κι όχι το άγριο πάθος, ούτε την τρέλα της.*
>
> Aphrodite let me feel the joy of love
> And not its madness, and not even wild passion.[53]

Figure 9.1 Clytemnestra (Irene Papas) and Iphigenia (Tatiana Papamoschou) on the journey to Aulis in *Iphigenia*, dir. Michael Cacoyannis.

[52] Doors are symbols of transition and change. Iphigenia has arrived at just such a transitional phase in her life. She believes that she will leave behind her childhood and become a wife, but it is death that awaits her in Aulis.

[53] These first two lines are modelled on Euripides' choral (543–57). This translation appears in the subtitles of the film.

Cacoyannis once again stresses the close bond between mother and daughter. Costumes and props also play an important role in this scene.[54] Both Clytemnestra and Iphigenia are dressed in white (Fig. 9.1), while significantly Iphigenia lies down on a blood-red carpet that prefigures her death.

Just before they reach the army camp Clytemnestra sends a messenger ahead to inform Agamemnon of their imminent arrival. Iphigenia changes her clothes, just before they reach the camp, her modesty protected by a wall of blood-red fabric that her handmaidens erect around her. All these scenes between mother and daughter are Cacoyannis' additions inserted before the film rejoins the action of Euripides' play. These added scenes allowed Cacoyannis to depict in detail the mother–daughter bond before it comes under attack. The director emphasized the love and affection that existed between mother and daughter in order to imbue the events that follow with a greater sense of tragedy and thus to put his stamp on the ancient story.

As reported in Euripides, upon Iphigenia's arrival at the camp she is greeted by the army (*IA*, 425–34). The film further presents Odysseus (Christos Tsagas) as a menacing presence, watching mother and daughter from a hill. The Greek soldiers and the king of Ithaca will play a decisive role in the events that follow; therefore it is fitting that they are the first witnesses to their arrival. Clytemnestra, in yet another maternal gesture, holds the sleeping Orestes in her arms. Iphigenia is eager to be the first to greet her father. Clytemnestra, indulgently, remarks that of all his children Iphigenia is the one who feels a special bond with her father. In Euripides Clytemnestra only mentions that of all his children Iphigenia loved him most (*IA*, 638–9). The words 'ιδιαίτερη αδυναμία' (a special weakness) she uses in Cacoyannis are particularly fitting. In the film it is her father's reasoning that is the first inducement that leads eventually to Iphigenia's change of heart. It is because she loves her father so much that his words begin to work a change in her.

The scene between father and daughter that follows is both very moving and ironic; ironic, in the sense that Agamemnon knows what Iphigenia's fate will be, while she innocently thinks about the dangers he will face in battle. In this scene Cacoyannis once again effectively uses Theodorakis' theme for Iphigenia to emphasize her childish innocence. This torments Agamemnon who tries to hide his emotions by being gruff and withdrawn,[55] but this only leads Iphigenia

[54] Cacoyannis chose Dionysios Fotopoulos as his costume designer for *Iphigenia*.

[55] The nurse takes Orestes to his father so that he can greet his son, but Agamemnon ignores the young boy. His deliberate distancing from his family is his way of coping with

to suspect that there is something wrong. She knows her father well. Throughout this scene she keeps calling him 'πατέρα' (father),[56] emphasizing their strong bond.[57] Clytemnestra, on the other hand, is more reserved. She only clasps her husband's hand and is more interested in questioning him about the prospective groom. She attributes his withdrawal to his sadness at losing their daughter to marriage. Clytemnestra thus assumes that he shares her feelings as a parent who is about to place their first daughter in the care of a husband.

Clytemnestra's preoccupation that the ceremony be worthy of her daughter's status leads her to question the decision to hold the wedding ceremony in an army camp under the 'σκιά του πολέμου' (shadow of war). Agamemnon tries to impose his will by reminding her of his rights as her husband. He hopes to force Clytemnestra to return home, but she defies him, because as a mother she feels it is her right to be present at her daughter's wedding. As she says emphatically: *Εγώ τη γέννησα, εγώ θα την παντρέψω* (I was the one who gave birth to her, I will be the one to give her away in marriage).[58] Clytemnestra's blatant rejection of Agamemnon's orders demonstrates the troubled state of their marriage. Against her fierce resistance Agamemnon is powerless and forced to accede to her wishes. Clytemnestra continues to direct preparations for the supposed wedding.

Iphigenia's young attendants regale her with descriptions of the great Greek heroes they saw, a scene which draws its inspiration from the opening choral of Euripides' play as it survives (164–302). Instead of a description of Achilles, however, the hero himself appears. The real reason why Agamemnon summoned Iphigenia to Aulis is gradually revealed over the course of this scene. At first Clytemnestra, unaware

the emotional strain of this tragic reunion that he wishes he could have avoided. Cacoyannis thus builds a case for Clytemnestra adopting the same coping mechanism at the end of the film.

[56] Iphigenia calls Agamemnon 'πατέρα' instead of 'μπαμπά' (dad), which would be more appropriate for a young girl of her age. She thereby shows she can speak, and therefore think and act, like an adult, not like a child—as she is portrayed later in the film when she changes her mind and embraces her sacrifice. Given the political climate of the time, μπαμπά would not have been used by Cacoyannis, as it is derived from the Turkish *baba*.

[57] In Euripides in the scene between father and daughter (631–80), Iphigenia uses the word 'πατήρ' (father) and its derivatives nine times (two contested). Cacoyannis is thus following in the footsteps of the ancient tragedian. In modern Greek culture, however, the emotional appeal of the stereotype of the existence of a special bond between father and daughter is particularly strong.

[58] Cf. Euripides, *IA* 736: καλὸν τεκοῦσαν τἀμά μ' ἐκδοῦναι τέκνα. (It is only right that I should be the one to give my daughter away in marriage).

Cacoyannis once again emphasizes Clytemnestra's motherhood in his script.

of the truth, tries to treat Achilles as a son-in-law. At this point this is what comes most naturally to her. His rebuff leads her to discover that he knows nothing about the marriage to Iphigenia. His words disturb her deeply and she puts a protective hand on her stomach as she tells him: '*τα λόγια σου με σφάζουν*' (Your words slay me).[59] At this point in the ancient play Clytemnestra only expresses her amazement (*IA* 844), not the sense of dread that Cacoyannis' Clytemnestra feels. Her instinctive gesture of protecting her middle prefigures the loss of the first fruit of her womb, Iphigenia. Clytemnestra's fears are confirmed in the worst possible way when her slave reveals the truth to them. Cacoyannis placed this scene on the top of the wooden palisade that protects Agamemnon's enclosure in order to allow Iphigenia and her attendants to overhear her fate unbeknownst to Clytemnestra and Achilles. She is drawn there by her mother's scream of denial when she first hears the news. Cacoyannis effectively uses close-up shots to reveal the agony of mother and daughter.[60] Papas's physical acting style is particularly effective in this scene: she stifles her instinctive cries by using one of her veils. She falls against a wall, her whole body tense and unsteady. This effect is enhanced by Cacoyannis' deliberate use of shaky camerawork to draw attention to her emotional turmoil.

The supplication scene is also characterized by a highly physical style of acting, whose aim is the emotional engagement of the audience. The scant evidence that survives suggests that ancient Athenian tragic acting was more restrained and formal. Euripides, however, was amongst the innovators who sought to achieve a more realistic style.[61] Cacoyannis' aim was to invest Greek tragedy with real emotion to which contemporary audiences could respond.[62] That is why his characters display a 'Mediterranean fire'.[63] His Clytemnestra falls to her knees, clutches Achilles' tunic and then his arm as she begs for his help to save her daughter. He ends up nearly dragging her along the ground as she refuses to let go of him. Her desperation is palpable, and Iphigenia's desperation matches that of her mother. This is expressed in filmic terms in the scene where she tries to escape her fate by running away into the forest. Shaky camera work reinforces her turmoil in a mirror scene to that of Clytemnestra's agony upon first hearing the news. Cacoyannis grafted this scene

[59] Cf. Euripides, *IA* 844: *ἐμοὶ γὰρ θαύματ᾽ ἐστὶ τὰ παρὰ σοῦ* (What you say amazes me).

[60] On the difference between the ancient mask and the modern close-up, see McCart (2007: 248).

[61] For the surviving evidence, see Csapo and Slater (1994: 221–74).

[62] Cacoyannis (1984: 15).

[63] McDonald (1991: 138).

onto the fabric of Euripides' tragedy to reinforce Iphigenia's position as the victim of the story.[64] Her mother, too, is a victim at this point in the filmic narrative.

Clytemnestra does do her outmost to defend her daughter, by calling up her most powerful weapon, persuasion. She is determined to use all means at her disposal to try and change Agamemnon's mind. Her appeal is carefully stage managed. She appears with loose hair and wearing a dark robe over her dress, both signs of mourning.[65] She goes on the attack and impugns Agamemnon's manhood for not telling her the truth. At first he tries to deny it and resorts to a display of anger, but Clytemnestra frustrates his desire to escape her words by using her body to physically block his attempts to abandon the conversation. In Cacoyannis his silence not only condemns him; it is also a sign of his emotional cowardice. He cannot bear to face his wife, or the truth.

Papas makes effective use of the story evoked in the surviving text of the play that makes this Clytemnestra's second marriage.[66] She reminds Agamemnon that he killed her first husband, Tantalus, and forced her to marry him. She accuses him of being motivated not by love, but by the lust for the power and wealth he expected to gain by their alliance. She makes it clear that she submitted, but never loved him. Cacoyannis removed any mention of Agamemnon's murder of a baby by Tantalus. Its inclusion would interfere with the perception of Iphigenia's sacrifice as a unique event that destroyed Clytemnestra as a mother. Had a similar incident taken place in the past, this would have weakened his design. The climax of the scene is Clytemnestra's warning to her husband:

Αν γυρίσεις, θα σε περιμένω,
το μίσος μου σαν την οχιά!

If you return I will be waiting,
my hatred like a venomous snake.

[64] McDonald (1983: 146).

[65] Before Clytemnestra discovers the truth, she wears her hair in a high bun that emphasizes her royal status. As a married woman of high rank, she is expected to appear composed and regal. Once she learns of Agamemnon's plan to sacrifice their daughter, however, Clytemnestra breaks away from the strictures of patriarchal society and the expectation that she must submit to her husband's will. She chooses instead to fight for her daughter's life. In this scene onwards, she leaves her hair loose as a sign of her characterological transformation. I am indebted to Konstantinos Nikoloutsos for this suggestion.

[66] There are doubts about the authenticity of the text in which this passage appears (1148–84). Kovacs attributes it to the reviser and not to Euripides (2003: 96). Cacoyannis effectively manages to incorporate the story into his filmic narrative, using it to explain Clytemnestra's lack of affection for her husband.

She warns him that all that it will take to unleash her vengeance will be an excuse. For the knowledgeable members of Cacoyannis' audience this will be provided by the enslaved Cassandra, whom Agamemnon introduces into his *oikos* as a concubine.[67] Clytemnestra grabs the back of Agamemnon's tunic as he throws open the doors to the courtyard. She screams at him not to force her to become evil by his actions.[68] This *agon* lies at the heart of how Cacoyannis understood Clytemnestra's motivation for the murder of her husband upon his return from Troy. In Aeschylus' *Agamemnon* Clytemnestra justifies her actions to the chorus by invoking her husband's filicide (1521–9 and 1551–9). Cacoyannis adopted her point of view in *Iphigenia*. In his third Euripidean adaptation he refined his portrayal of Clytemnestra, by making her more humane. In his earlier *Electra* the director presented his audiences with an irredeemably evil Clytemnestra (played by Aleka Katseli), a greedy, cruel and arrogant woman. In this version the audience watch her helping Aegisthus to murder Agamemnon, and oppressing her daughter Electra (played by Irene Papas). In *Iphigenia* Cacoyannis wanted to explore Clytemnestra's motivation and explain her reasons for her hatred of Agamemnon. This time Cacoyannis is on the side of Clytemnestra. The audience is invited to sympathize with her plight as first Menelaus (Kostas Karras) and then Odysseus arrive to remind the king of his decision. She again attempts to prevent her husband from leaving, but this time she is unsuccessful. He shakes her off violently, shouting that there is nothing he can do to prevent the sacrifice.

Cacoyannis located Clytemnestra's attempts to change her husband's mind indoors, with only Orestes as an innocent witness to their quarrel. Once outside, however, she enjoys the support of the other women and the nurse. They have to physically hold her up when she hears the news that Iphigenia has been found. This is a female support group similar to the one that sustains Katherine Hepburn's Hecuba in *The Trojan Women*. Cacoyannis thus emphasizes the polarity between female solidarity that

[67] On the whole Cacoyannis tends to assume a non-knowledgeable audience: spectators not familiar with the mythical story and its reception in tragedy. His expository prologues demonstrate how he sought to bridge the gap between knowledgeable and non-knowledgeable members of the audience. In this particular instance, Clytemnestra's threat is more effective if it were left vague, as indeed it is in *Iphigenia*. Familiarity with *The Trojan Women*, where Cassandra is torn from her mother and taken to Agamemnon's ship, would suggest the shape of the excuse he provides his wife. However, since the film was banned in Greece at the time of its release, contemporary modern Greek audiences in the late 1970s are more likely to have been familiar with the ancient story rather than Cacoyannis' reception of it.

[68] According to Gamel, in the play Clytemnestra only turns evil 'when the system she has upheld betrays her' (1999: 317).

characterizes Clytemnestra and her attendants, and the bitter male divisions that characterize Agamemnon and the Greek army. With the exception of Achilles' support of their cause and Iphigenia's change of heart, women and men are stuck on opposite sides of an unbridgeable divide in this third film in Cacoyannis' Euripidean trilogy. Only the younger protagonists are able to momentarily bridge it, but with fatal consequences.

Aristotle criticized Iphigenia's change of mind in Euripides' play as an inconsistent characterization (*Poetics* 1454a 31–3),[69] but Cacoyannis took great care to show how and, more importantly, why the young girl changed her mind. Not present during her parents' quarrel,[70] she will mirror some of her mother's arguments when she, in turn, seeks to change her father's mind using words. Iphigenia, however, does not resort to threats. Instead, she tries to rouse his paternal feelings. When the soldiers drag her back to her father's encampment, she falls to her knees and begs him to spare her. In another highly emotional scene both father and daughter are moved to tears. Iphigenia, too, pleads with her father, using both words and hands. In this she unconsciously mirrors her mother again, but her tone is less aggressive, as befits her age. At first Agamemnon tries to break away from her and escape her words, as he did with Clytemnestra, but eventually maddened by guilt he reacts violently. He grabs Iphigenia and shouts that he has no choice, as he did with her mother earlier.

Agamemnon's justification is that the Greek army will turn against them all, if he halts her sacrifice. In this highly physical scene Iphigenia runs to her mother's embrace, while Agamemnon pursues her (Fig. 9.2). Iphigenia ends up prostrate on the earth. He stretches his hand to his daughter attempting to bridge the gulf that now separates them, but she closes her eyes. His argument that the forces ranged against them are formidable has, however, been made explicit by Cacoyannis: his prologue depicted the lust for war and gold that has maddened the army, whereas Euripides leaves room for ambiguity given that the audience never sees the army.[71] The threat it represents is implicit rather than explicit.

[69] Several scholars have challenged Aristotle's view, for example Gilbert (1995: 224) and Gregory (2005: 260).

[70] In Euripides Iphigenia is present during their quarrel. Her attempt to escape in Cacoyannis is another device meant to make her more sympathetic to the audience.

[71] See McDonald (1983: 144). In her production, McDonald used extras to give the impression of an army hovering in the wings.

Figure 9.2 Agamemnon (Kostas Kazakos) tries to separate mother and daughter in *Iphigenia*, dir. Michael Cacoyannis.

Agamemnon finally succeeds in leaving the compound, abandoning the task of escorting Iphigenia to the altar to his brother Menelaus, but he, too, cannot face the prospect. Male cowardice is once again contrasted with female strength.

Nowhere is this more powerfully demonstrated than in the scene where Iphigenia gradually arrives at the conclusion that she cannot avoid death, so the only thing to do is to face it bravely. After Agamemnon's departure, mother and daughter embrace (Fig. 9.3), and

Figure 9.3 Iphigenia in her mother's embrace in *Iphigenia*, dir. Michael Cacoyannis.

Clytemnestra sings Iphigenia a second song. This time it is a lament, an expression of her grief at the prospect of losing her daughter. It is also perhaps intended as a talisman meant to guard her from the power of death:

> *Ήλιε, που δίνεις στη ζωή το φως*
> *Κρύψου να μη μας βλέπει ο θάνατος, το δρόμο του να αλλάξει.*
>
> Sun, you that give light to life
> Hide so that death will not see us and will change paths.[72]

In Cacoyannis it is Achilles' intervention and his willingness to sacrifice his own life for the victims' protection that is the next crucial step in the process of Iphigenia's change of heart. In a radical departure from Euripides, Cacoyannis' young hero is genuinely committed to helping

[72] In the subtitles the second line reads 'Hide so that death will not find us'. I have modified it to stress Clytemnestra's desperate hope that death will not find them, present in the original modern Greek.

mother and daughter. The audience sees him try to change the army's mind about going ahead with the sacrifice. His own troops throw stones at him and refuse to obey him when he declares his intention to defend Iphigenia. This is another scene where Cacoyannis privileges his audience by showing them the off-stage spaces of Greek tragedy, which has an impact on how they view the events that follow.[73] Achilles is stained with blood when he arrives to let Clytemnestra know the outcome of his attempt to alter the course of events.[74] In Iphigenia's eyes he is the fearless protector she had cried out for earlier, without any real hope that one would appear. In Euripides he is less straightforwardly heroic.[75] In a significant scene the young protagonists slowly turn to face each other, and the shy Iphigenia raises her gaze and looks into Achilles' eyes. The action pauses for a bit as they fix their eyes on each other. Cacoyannis thus suggests that Iphigenia and Achilles experience an instant attraction.[76] This, coupled with the appearance of a group of soldiers led by Odysseus coming to take Iphigenia to the sacrificial altar, works a change of heart in the young protagonist.

It is out of love for her father and Achilles that Iphigenia concludes that it is better to die well, since she cannot avoid death. The visible presence of the army adds weight to Agamemnon's fears. His compound is surrounded by soldiers throughout the film. Their presence reinforces the danger they represent, should the Atreidae try to prevent Iphigenia's sacrifice.[77] Cacoyannis, however, opts to stress the strength of the emotional arguments that determine Iphigenia's change of heart. Ultimately, she changes her mind for love. The strength of her courage is underscored with the noble strains that Theodorakis composed for this scene.

[73] For the impact of the off-stage space on the characters in the play, see Gamel (1999: 323).

[74] Cacoyannis visualizes a scene that is only reported in the source. In Euripides Achilles informs Clytemnestra of this incident in a rapid exchange of *stichomythia* (1345–68) that is indicative of his agitation and the urgency of the situation. In the drama there is at least the possibility that Achilles has exaggerated the force of the opposition or that he mishandled the situation. In Cacoyannis' reception there is no such possibility. Michelini (1999–2000: 48) believes in the veracity of Achilles' report, as does Kovacs (2003: 97).

[75] McDonald (1983: 156).

[76] Rabinowitz (1993: 46–7) believes that Iphigenia falls in love with Achilles in the source text. Her feelings for him explain, in part at least, her change of heart. By making Achilles reciprocate her love, Cacoyannis imbues this scene with a romantic sensibility that the original lacks. Foley is also convinced that Achilles is struck by 'a genuine *eros* for his bride' (1985: 75).

[77] Some classical scholars agree with this assessment of the situation in the source text. The army would not allow Iphigenia to escape their camp now that she is among them. See Hose (2008: 225). For the view that Agamemnon's fear of the army is exaggerated, see Luschnig (1988: 119); Arrowsmith (1978: xi); Conacher (1967: 256).

She walks towards the soldiers sent to escort her to the altar, while both Clytemnestra and Achilles retreat before her. In that moment she is stronger than both of them. She calls for her veils and crown. Cacoyannis acknowledges Iphigenia's bravery, but he also undermines the Panhellenic rhetoric she uses as part of her justification: *Μιας και η Ελλάδα θέλει την ζωή μου της την δίνω* (since Greece demands my life I give it to her). She is echoing the rhetoric her father used in order to persuade her, but her naïve acceptance of it only serves to highlight her innocence.

Iphigenia's use of this type of rhetoric is more ambiguous in the source text. The rhetorical construction of the barbarians of the east as a threat dates back to the Persian Wars.[78] The Panhellenic rhetoric of Agamemnon and Menelaus, which Iphigenia also espouses, plays upon these ideological constructions of barbarians as the natural and rightful enemies of Greece. During the Peloponnesian War, Persia saw its chance to enhance its sphere of influence by encouraging the continuation of the conflict between the two premier city-states of Greece. As the war drew to its close, Panhellenic ideas resurfaced. In the fifth century BCE the concept of Panhellenism was understood as the unification of the many city-states of Greece against an external enemy, such as the Persian Empire.[79] At the Olympic Games of 408 BCE the sophist Gorgias gave a rousing Panhellenic speech urging the Greeks to forget their differences and to unite against their common enemy, the barbarian Persians.[80] The war against Troy provided the perfect model for such a Panhellenic expedition, so Euripides' exploration of this concept within its mythical framework is certainly topical. Cacoyannis, given his own historical and political context, chose to undermine its power and effectiveness by depicting it as nothing more than empty rhetoric used to deceive an innocent young girl and to justify her murder.[81]

[78] For an in depth discussion of this phenomenon, see Bridges, Hall, and Rhodes (2007).

[79] Michelini (1999–2000: 55).

[80] Dimock (1978: 4); Gamel (1999: 326).

[81] The proposed union of Cyprus with Greece was expressed in terms of Panhellenic rhetoric, while Turkey was represented as the barbarian East (its territory used to belong to the Persian empire that had threatened the city states of fifth-century Greece). However, Cacoyannis, in both *Attila 74* and *Iphigenia*, reveals the dangers inherent in this rhetoric. In his documentary, Cacoyannis argues that the price of such rhetoric, aggressively pursued by the junta, was a divided Cyprus. In the film the price of war is the sacrifice of an innocent girl motivated by the Greeks' greed for Trojan gold (Cacoyannis in Siafkos 2009: 213–15). In Cacoyannis' cinematic reception the Greek leaders are ruled by ambition and Cacoyannis explains Agamemnon's decision to sacrifice his daughter as being motivated by his desire to lead the army against Troy.

Zeitlin (1995: 190) argues that Euripides undercuts this type of Panhellenic rhetoric in the source text (1995: 190).

That is how Clytemnestra views her daughter's sacrifice. She is prepared to go to any length to try to prevent it. She even offers up her own life in order to save that of her daughter. Her impassioned response to Achilles' warning to hold onto Iphigenia at any cost is that they will have to cut off her arms before they can take her daughter. Iphigenia's change of heart is therefore a blow to her as a mother to which she responds with a deep, low groan to Iphigenia's pronouncement. Iphigenia tries to reconcile her to the idea of her death, which she has come to see as inevitable, by attempting to appeal to her maternal instincts. She reminds her mother that the Greek soldiers have mothers, too, and asks Clytemnestra to put herself in their place. This appeal demonstrates that Iphigenia knows that Clytemnestra is at her most vulnerable as a mother. She fails to understand, however, that her actions will destroy that side of Clytemnestra forever.

Cacoyannis created a poignant farewell scene between mother and daughter in order to stress their bond and the agony of its severance. Now it is Clytemnestra who cannot bear to look at Iphigenia. The daughter asks her mother to look after her sisters and Orestes, a promise that Clytemnestra will not keep. It is when Iphigenia asks her not to blame her father that Clytemnestra's true feelings are revealed.[82] She blames Agamemnon and she is determined to extract retribution. For her the sacrifice is nothing but a '*φόνος*' (murder), as she screams at the watching soldiers. Clytemnestra wants to accompany her daughter to the altar, but Iphigenia is equally determined to spare her mother that painful ordeal and asks her to stay behind. Clytemnestra embraces Iphigenia one last time, and as her daughter starts her fateful journey to the altar, she begs: *Μη φεύγεις, μην πας* (Don't leave, don't go). Clytemnestra thus rejects Agamemnon's arguments that arise out of his fear of the army and out of his ambition to be the leader of the Greeks in the war against Troy. His Panhellenic rhetoric does not hold any consolation for her, either. In the last shot of mother and daughter

[82] Kovacs is convinced that lines 1369–70 are not authentic (2003: n.72, 97) and he includes them in brackets in his edition (2002):

[τῶν ἐμῶν λόγων· μάτηρ γάρ σ'εἰσορῶ θυμουμένην
σῷ πόσει· τὰ δ'ἀδύναθ ἡμῖν καρτερεῖν οὐ ῥᾴδιον.]

which he translates as '. . . to what I have to say. For I see that you are angry at your husband to no purpose. It is not easy for us to endure beyond our limits'. Kovacs argues that it does not make sense for Iphigenia to try and persuade her mother that her anger is unjustified; he also argues that the last section of the quotation makes her sound self-contradictory.

Cacoyannis not only adopts these lines; he also expands on them in order to emphasize Iphigenia's love of her father, even at this point, and to contrast her feelings with those of her mother whose mind now turns towards revenge.

together Cacoyannis focuses his camera not on their faces, but on their clasped hands, symbolizing the strong bond the two of them have enjoyed. Slowly their hands unclasp and the bond is broken. Poignantly, Iphigenia's veil runs through her mother's fingers until even that last token of her presence is gone.

In his cinematic reception of Euripidean tragedy, Cacoyannis demonstrates that Iphigenia's sacrifice might have been a courageous act on her part, but it was also pointless. The much anticipated winds blow before the sacrifice is completed. His Iphigenia feels a touch of wind, as she climbs the hill to the altar where Calchas (Dimitris Aronis) awaits her. Agamemnon tries to call her back, while Clytemnestra, empathically connected to her daughter, rushes out of the encampment, but it is already too late. The film ends with Clytemnestra making her lonely way back to Argos in the growing dusk as the winds now blow fiercely and the Greek fleet begins its journey to Troy. Cacoyannis finishes his Euripidean trilogy with a powerful image: Clytemnestra gazing at the departing fleet as her black hair flutters wildly in the wind. Among the last shots in the film is one from Clytemnestra's perspective. The audience sees the departing fleet, its lamps bright in the growing twilight, partly obscured by her hair; the spectators thus literally 'see' the world through Clytemnestra's eyes. The freeze frame that concludes the film is a close-up of Clytemnestra's face, partly obscured by her loose black hair,[83] her eyes blazing with hatred. Clytemnestra the mother no longer exists. She has been destroyed. The new Clytemnestra has but one purpose in life: to avenge her daughter's 'cowardly' (άνανδρος), 'treacherous' (ύπουλος) murder.

CONCLUSION

Michael Cacoyannis truly deserves the title of 'a poet of the modern Greek cinema'.[84] In *Iphigenia* his moving portrayal of the mother–daughter relationship engages the cinematic audience's sympathy for Iphigenia and Clytemnestra. The young girl acts as the moral centre of

[83] Her hair is black, the colour most associated with death. All three protagonists, Iphigenia, Agamemnon, and Clytemnestra die in the mythical tradition. Iphigenia is sacrificed, Agamemnon is murdered by his wife and her paramour, and Clytemnestra herself is killed by her son Orestes. I am indebted to Konstantinos Nikoloutsos for this suggestion.

[84] Pendergast (2000: 148).

his re-interpretation of Euripides' drama as an indictment of the corrupt politics and irredentist ambitions that lead to war. Agamemnon's cowardice and lust for power bring about the annihilation of his family and eventually his own murder. By choosing to proceed with the sacrifice he destroys not only his daughter, but also her mother, his wife. Cacoyannis re-imagined Euripides' drama in such a way as to allow contemporary cinematic audiences to relate to it in modern terms. The director's adaptation of *Iphigenia at Aulis* is informed and enriched by contemporary events in modern Greece and Cyprus. It is a vivid reminder of the diachronic appeal of Greek tragedy. Cacoyannis succeeded in his aim of translating Euripidean drama into the modern medium of cinema, arguably most successfully in his third and final effort. He thus demonstrated the rich possibilities offered by the silver screen for the re-creation of Greek tragedy, as well as the impact and relevance of these ancient dramas in the modern world.

10

Mythic Women in Tony Harrison's *Prometheus*

Hallie Rebecca Marshall[1]

> But Zeus will destroy this race of speech-endowed human beings too, when at their birth the hair on their temples will be quite gray. Father will not be like-minded with sons, nor sons at all, nor guest with host, nor comrade with comrade, nor will the brother be dear as he once was.
>
> Hesiod, *Works and Days*, 180–4
>
> Translated by Glenn W. Most

The story of Prometheus in the Aeschylean *Prometheus Bound* is a masculine narrative of conflict between males of the old and new order, and of punishment for those who, although they are meant to be subservient, undermine the future vision of the new governing order. Yet female characters enter into this narrative from both the human and the divine realms. The chorus of Nereids enters offering sympathy to the bound Titan. Later Io enters frenzied in her bovine form, pursued by a gadfly, having done no wrong. She thus presents a darker vision of the new governing order, where intentions are concealed by turning the girl you have raped into a cow, so that evil deeds might seem innocuous and escape unnoticed. The stories of Prometheus and Io paint a picture of the Olympian order as tyranny, with no concern for the well-being of the larger community, of the older gods, or the much younger and more fragile humans. Those who offend any Olympian will be punished—severely. It is this narrative that lies beneath Tony Harrison's feature-length film/poem *Prometheus*, and while, like the Aeschylean play, the

[1] This work was supported by the Government of Canada through the Social Sciences and Humanities Research Council.

central narrative is male, Io and the chorus of Nereids also appear, providing a parallel female narrative of suffering and of bearing witness to suffering. This paper explores Harrison's use of the female narratives of *Prometheus Bound* in an attempt to capture the pervasive communal suffering experienced wherever and whenever tyrannical power is wielded.

Tony Harrison is known among Classicists for his translations and adaptations of ancient Greek drama for the theatre.[2] Harrison, however, writes poetry for a number of different media, from traditional volumes of poems, to verse drama, to poems for the news pages of *The Guardian*, to film poetry. He began working in film in the mid-1970s, when he worked on George Cukor's disastrous film *The Blue Bird*, and he continued producing film/poems for the next twenty years, increasingly taking creative control, just as he had with his work in the theatre.[3] The majority of his film/poems were intended for television, but in 1998 he produced his first and only feature-length film/poem *Prometheus*, which had a limited circulation. As Edith Hall put it, the film 'was screened at some esoteric venues, broadcast on UK Channel 4 television, and subsequently disappeared almost completely from public view'.[4] Nick Lowe has observed,

> A distinctly Harrisonian irony of the information age is that works created in recorded media can turn out to survive less well than works for the ephemeral stage and press, so that these printed versions bear something of the relationship to the filmed originals that the scripts of Greek plays hold to their original competitive performance event: an irreproducible experience of a one-off mass audience....[5]

In spite of the limited circulation of the film/poem as a cinematic experience, however, Hall has asserted that 'the eye of history will later view Harrison's *Prometheus* as the most important artistic reaction to the fall of the British working class as the twentieth century staggered to its close, a fall symptomatic of the international collapse of the socialist dream'.[6] The film/poem draws upon the well of Greek drama, as had much of his work in the theatre since 1981's *The Oresteia*. Like his earlier play *The Trackers of Oxyrhynchus*, it uses the model of Greek drama to criticize Thatcherite politics, and the consequences of the 1984 coal miner's

[2] These include: *The Oresteia* (1981); *Medea: a sex-war opera* (1985); *The Common Chorus* (1988); *The Trackers of Oxyrhynchus* (1990); *The Kaisers of Carnuntum* (1995); *The Labourers of Herakles* (1995); *Hecuba* (2005); and *Fram* (2008).

[3] On his experience of working on *The Blue Bird*, see Harrison (2007: xii–xxiv).

[4] Hall (2002: 129).

[5] Lowe (2007: 149–56, 151).

[6] Hall (2002: 129).

strike and the subsequent pit closures. Thereby the film/poem explores the Promethean legacy of the twentieth century more broadly.

THE SOCIO-HISTORICAL CONTEXT OF HARRISON'S *PROMETHEUS*

For the last quarter of the twentieth century the future of Britain's mining industry was an explosive political issue. On 9 January 1972 British coal miners went on strike for the first time since 1926, when one of their central demands had been the nationalization of the British coal mines—a demand belatedly met in 1946. The 1972 strike lasted for seven weeks. The resultant energy shortage forced the Conservative Prime Minister, Edward Heath, to reduce the working week to three days. In the face of the energy crisis the government ceded to the miners' demand for higher wages. Just over two years later, however, the miners again went on strike. This time the strike lasted four weeks. The miners' strike produced another national energy crisis that resulted in a state of emergency being called and the reintroduction of a three-day working week. Prime Minister Heath decided to call a general election hoping that the support of the voters at the ballot box would strengthen the government's attempts to deal with the striking miners. Heath ran under the slogan: 'Who runs the country—the miners or the government?' Heath and his Conservative party were defeated. The new Labour government, led by Harold Wilson, reached a deal with the miners shortly after coming to power. The British miners next went on strike ten years after they toppled Heath's government.

In 1984 the government was led by Conservative Prime Minister Margaret Thatcher and the coal industry was in a period of decline. In response to this decline the National Coal Board decided to close twenty mines, which would result in 20,000 miners losing their jobs. While the contract that had been negotiated as a result of the 1974 strike theoretically prevented the closure of the mines, the National Coal Board argued that the 1974 contract was no longer valid due to changes in the British economy. Not only was the National Coal Board unwilling to honour the contract, but the Conservative government, under Thatcher's guidance, was determined to curb the power and influence of the British Labour Unions, including, if not especially, the National Union of Mineworkers (NUM). NUM, under the leadership of Arthur Scargill, was equally hell-bent on asserting the power of the union and enforcing the terms of the 1974 contract, painting the looming conflict in apocalyptic terms. On 4 July 1983 Scargill addressed the delegates at the National Union of Mineworkers' Annual Conference, saying, 'We have two choices. We can give in, as many German people did in the 1930s, and allow the worst to happen—we can watch social destruction and repression on a truly horrific scale and wait for the inevitable holocaust. Or we can fight back.'[7] Ian MacGregor, chairman of the National Coal Board from 1983–6, characterized this statement as a declaration of war, and described Scargill and the National Union of Mineworkers as 'the enemies within'.[8]

While many would take issue with MacGregor's assertions regarding who declared war against whom in 1984, as well as his characterization of Scargill and NUM as enemies of the state, there can be no doubt that the conflict that surrounded the ensuing strike was bitter and violent and that it had massive social consequences which extended beyond the mines into the mining communities and into private domestic life. While Scargill's comparison of the fate of coalminers in Britain with the holocaust was excessive, his basic argument that, if the Tory government of Margaret Thatcher had its way coal miners and coal-mining communities would cease to exist in Britain, was accurate. The strike was for many coal miners and coal-mining communities a fight for their very existence. And while the strike is usually discussed in reference to its male participants (the miners, the police, the government ministers, and board chairman), with Margaret Thatcher being portrayed as a Clytemnestra-like woman in whose breast beat the heart of a man, the strike also had a devastating impact on the women whose lives were intimately interwoven with the strikers.

On 12 March Arthur Scargill called on the miners to strike, starting a strike that would last almost a year. Scargill did not call a ballot for the national strike action and as a result of a new law passed by the Conservative government, which required unions to ballot members on strike action, the strike was ruled to be illegal. NUM's assets were seized and miners were denied state benefits and their wages.[9] The government

[7] In the late 1990s, amidst yet further mine closures, the accuracy of Arthur Scargill's doomsday predictions was recognized. The headlines in the paper used to light the fire at the beginning of Harrison's *Prometheus* read, 'Last Yorkshire Pit to Close Tomorrow', underneath of which is the headline, 'Arthur's nightmare prophecy fulfilled'.

[8] MacGregor (1986: 11).

[9] Soup kitchens became commonplace in the mining communities as a means of providing food to the miners and their families who had no income with which to buy food or other necessities. For first person accounts of the hardships that many mining families endured during the strike, see Stead (1987: 31–8).

mobilized the police in huge numbers to deal with the picket lines, which were considered to be illegal public protests, barring access to a number of mines. During the course of the strike 11,291 people were arrested and 8,392 were charged with offences. In March 1985 NUM voted to return to work without a new agreement with the National Coal Board. Ultimately the strike allowed the government to accelerate the closure of a number of mines. In 1985 twenty-five pits were shut down. When Michael Heseltine became Trade and Industry Secretary in 1992, he oversaw a further round of mine closures. In the two decades since the strike one hundred and fifty-six mines have closed.[10] The few British coal mines that remain are privately managed. In the twenty-first century the National Coal Board no longer exists, and NUM has all but been destroyed.

THE COAL MINERS IN HARRISON'S *PROMETHEUS*

Harrison's film/poem *Prometheus* is set in the aftermath of the final miner's strike, when Scargill's apocalyptic vision of the future of coal mining in Britain had become a reality. The mining communities felt that the Conservative government under Margaret Thatcher nursed a hatred for them akin to the enduring hatred of Zeus towards Prometheus for the theft of fire. The unionized miners had done what at the turn of the twentieth century would have been unthinkable for the working class: they demanded, and received, compensation appropriate to the dirty, dangerous nature of their work. The strikes by which they had achieved those wages had brought the nation and its government to their knees and made them all aware of how dependent they were upon the working class. As Seabrook and Blackwell wrote of the mine closures in the *New Statesman*:

> It is perceived by the community as a story of political revenge: for 1974, even for 1945. Who knows what dark atavisms stir in the Tory breasts at the mere mention of miners, those heroes of Labour, those barely human creatures of the early industrial era, who toiled in their true element, the earth, whose villages were sooty blots on the landscape, and whose ways were alien and terrifying to the cultivated society that resented its dependency upon them.[11]

[10] BBC News (Friday 5 March 2004).

[11] Seabrook and Blackwell (1993).

Harrison picks up upon the image of the miners as rebellious heroes, creating a Promethean hero out of a grizzled old miner wearing long johns and a flat cap, suffering from advanced lung disease.[12] He associates the activity of coal mining with the proliferation of socialism in Britain in the twentieth century, as well as the intertwined fates of socialism and industrialization. Over the course of the movie he extends the association to include Eastern European socialist industrialization, tying these issues to Prometheus' ambiguous gift of fire. He thus draws clear parallels to the social benefits derived from industrialization and the concurrent destruction caused by it.

The film blends the grim realism of the mine closures with myth, voiced in rhyming couplets. Harrison draws on the myths of the ancient Greeks not only to provide a non-incendiary, or less-incendiary, political framework for the discussion surrounding the mine closures, but also to provide a means of expressing the profound suffering and destruction that has been inflicted upon the mining communities. As Harrison has stated:

> Most Greek tragedy shifts its timescale from immediate suffering to some long-term redemption through memorial ritual or social amelioration, or simply through the very play being performed. The performed suffering was old, the redemption contemporary. The appeal to futurity is not simply that 'time heals' because it brings forgetfulness and oblivion, but because creative memory is at work, giving suffering a new form, a form to allow the suffering to be shared and made bearable across great gaps of time.[13]

Harrison's use of Promethean mythology draws both upon ancient Greek sources, as well as later artistic and political interpretations.[14] He takes the narrative framework of *Prometheus Bound* as the overarching structure for his film/poem, including the story of the theft of fire and the resultant vindictive animosity of Zeus towards both Prometheus and the human race. Through the use of the myth, Harrison's story becomes not just about the plight of British miners in the late-twentieth century, but

[12] Harrison's choice of hero was remarkable in the context of the media coverage that the strikes had received in Britain in which the miners had been almost universally vilified. As Edith Hall put it, '... in defending the mining communities, Harrison has accepted into art heroes even less acceptable than destitute vagrants. It is one thing for a poet to support oppressed causes which have been legitimized by mainstream western liberal ideology, such as women and ethnic minorities in whose name countless productions and adaptations of Greek tragedy have emerged over the last three decades. It is quite another thing to make heroes out of the white male working class, especially the National Union of Mineworkers.' Hall (2002: 133).

[13] Harrison (1998: vii–viii).

[14] For a summary of the mythology surrounding Prometheus, see Gantz (1993: 152–66).

about mankind's eternal struggle for a better lot in life. The nineteenth-century poet Percy Bysshe Shelley had similarly turned to the story of Prometheus in his lyrical drama *Prometheus Unbound*. He used the Aeschylean play as a model for his own verse, expressing his unease with the French Revolution, and his perception that it had not led to freedom, but rather the exchange of one tyrant for another. As Lloyd-Jones observed, 'To the Romantic poets of the revolutionary era, the Titan tortured by Zeus for his services to mankind appeared as a symbol of the human spirit in its struggle to throw off the chains which priests and kings had forged for it.'[15] Prometheus captures the imagination because he is defiant in the face of tyrannical power despite his chains, and because he represents hope in the face of immeasurable suffering. His gift of fire, smuggled down from Olympus in a fennel reed, equally illuminates the imagination, with both its potential benefits to the human race, and its innate potential for destruction. The challenge for Harrison was how to represent Prometheus and what he symbolizes in relationship to the British miners and the larger socialist dream to the audience. Harrison's solution was to create a central character through whose eyes we see much of the story, who over the course of the film will come to embody the defiant spirit of Prometheus in the face of tyrannical power and immeasurable suffering, while at the same time depicting the communal suffering of the mining communities by illustrating the terrifying fates of the miners and their wives, as well as their children.

At the heart of the film is an old man; a miner who had lived through all the strikes only to watch almost every British coal mine close in the 1990s. The movie is set during the closure of the last working coal mine in Yorkshire in the early 1990s. Studies on the consequences of the mine closures, or 'industrial contraction', have found that the closures have not only resulted in profound social and psychological problems for the ex-miners and their immediate families, but have also severely impacted the physical fabric of the communities. A recent study concluded:

> The consequences of industrial contraction are negatively experienced at all levels of community life. Among those miners affected by pit-closure, psychological well-being is impaired by the consequent loss of identity, both as worker and principal breadwinner, by uncertainty and isolation, and by the intrusion of threatening experiences such as the requirements to fill out application forms and attend interviews in the face of stiff competition for jobs. The brunt of male frustration and anxiety is often borne by their spouses and families. Female partners find themselves buckling under

[15] Lloyd-Jones (1990: 238).

> the burden of having a depressed male around the home, while their children may become emotionally alienated from their parents with possible repercussions for their schooling. Across the community as a whole, relationships break down as rituals are abandoned, former friendships degenerate into rivalries and youth disaffection is expressed in criminality, drug-taking and disrespect toward traditional pillars of authority.[16]

It was this pervasive societal decay, and its epic proportions, stretching not only across the north of England, through Scotland and Wales, but also across the formerly socialist regions of Eastern Europe, that Harrison sought to convey.

IO AND THE NEREIDS

The suffering represented spans all generations—from the children being raised amidst the conflict, social decay, and hopelessness, the parents suddenly struggling to support their families, especially the males who had previously been the primary providers of income within the household,[17] to the senior citizens who are watching almost all of their hard-earned advances accumulated over the course of the twentieth century being lost within a single decade with no hope for future recovery. This narrative, like life in these communities, centres on the male characters, son, father, grandfather, but Harrison also tells an equally compelling narrative of the suffering of women in these communities by mapping their narratives onto the female roles in Aeschylus' *Prometheus Bound*: the chorus of Nereids and Io. The chorus of Nereids is formed by the local women who work at the Oceanus fish factory, one of the few remaining sources of employment in the community.[18] Having entered

[16] Waddington and Parry (2001).

[17] The psychological burden on the miners is succinctly put in the film/poem when the old miner, in trying to explain to his grandson why his father had not really meant to hurt him, either physically or emotionally, when he had hit him upside the head earlier in the morning, says, 'He'd not usually clout thee, would thi dad. He's laid off after today and he feels bad... He's lost his job, love! He feels small.' Harrison (1998: 17).

[18] Levels of employment for women in mining communities has traditionally been lower than in non-mining communities for both social and economic reasons. 'Jobs for women are scarce in mining communities and in 1984 more than 50 per cent of our female sample were earning no money. Most of these described themselves as housewives rather than unemployed suggesting that, for the majority, paid work was not even seen as a viable proposition. In our communities in 1984, 39 per cent of the women we surveyed said they were doing some paid work. By 1988 work opportunities for women had worsened considerably. An even smaller minority of 29 per cent were earning and most of these

the factory, they exit having lost their individual and communal identities as they had once existed within their community, and now appear as mannequins draped in gauze, with blue ribbons of hair, floating down the Humber River like products for export, through Europe, to the ancient site of Eleusis, where they are immolated along with Prometheus.[19] The role of Io is taken on by the wife and mother of the household whose frenzied wandering is a central strand of the film's narrative. At the beginning of the film, her son is slapped upside the head for using the newspapers to start the morning fire that his father had been collecting, which contained stories about the miners strike in 1984 and then the subsequent mine closures in the decade that followed. Having quarrelled with his father, the boy runs out of the house, despite his mother calling after him from her bedroom window, 'Jack, come back. He didn't mean it. He's upset, your Dad.'[20] She pulls on her clothes and goes out in search of him and over the course of the movie runs through Yorkshire and then is chased through Europe by Zeus' henchmen Kratos and Bia, until in Bulgaria she is killed like a cow in an abattoir and her remains incinerated.

Unlike its Greek model, the female narrative of *Prometheus* is a virtually silent narrative, yet an integral one for the story Harrison is telling about the social decay of the Yorkshire mining communities.[21] Charity Scribner observes, 'In *Prometheus*, Harrison renders his women nearly mute, yet magnifies their screen presence. The single line spoken by the mother of the Yorkshire family consists of eleven words and does not take on the meter that defines most of the *Prometheus* ('Jack, come back. He didn't mean it. He's upset, your Dad' [Harrison 11]).[22] The violence inflicted upon the women in the film/poem is a metaphor for the destruction which the mine closures wrought upon the women in mining families. While mining communities are usually discussed in terms of the men who work in the mines,

> without women mining communities would not exist; they would be labour camps... pit work in the form we know it in the nineteenth and twentieth

worked for less than half-time.' Waddington, Wykes, and Critcher (1991: 78). These numbers suggest that for most mining families the possibility of women supplementing the diminished income of their husbands both during and subsequent to the strike was extremely limited.

19 For still images of the chorus of Nereids, see Harrison (1998: 34, 57, and 58).

20 Harrison (1998: 11).

21 For a discussion of the presence of female voices in the Aeschylean *Prometheus Bound* and the lack thereof in Harrison's film/poem, see Woodward (1999).

22 Scribner (2003: 81–3).

> century was only possible because of the way in which women worked in the home. Housework was as central to the winning of coal as the graft of the miner underground. Just as the industry defines the class position of the miner, the organization of pit production defines the family position of the miner's wife.[23]

And, as subsequent studies have found, 'pit closure is an outcome which impacts more greatly on women than on men'.[24] Though while the consequences and stresses of the mine closures were felt most acutely by the women,

> the demoralizing effects of pit closure on the wider mining communities are evident in the deterioration of the physical environment, control over young people and participation in community life. The closure of a mine and redundancy or transfer of its employees fragment social cohesion. Pit closure brings the loss of such community facilities as recreation grounds and the withdrawal of a range of informal services, such as housing maintenance and snow clearance, which the pit and its men provided.[25]

In short, the physical and emotional fabric of the entire community began to unravel, causing enormous suffering for the women in those communities who traditionally bore the 'greater responsibility for the emotional maintenance of the family'.[26] It is in this context of societal disintegration that Harrison situates his female characters. The chorus of Nereids provides an anonymous perspective on the communal destruction, while the mother figure provides a very intimate picture of the effects of the mine closures.

Scribner and Woodward have commented on the lack of voice that Harrison provides to women in the film/poem, in distinct contrast to the strong voices that he has provided to women in much of his other poetry, dramatic or otherwise. However, neither situates this lack of voice in the social context of working-class communities. The world depicted by Harrison reflects his perception and the reality of the gender structures and roles of women in these communities. The only female voices uttering articulate words in the film/poem are the mother and grandmother in early scenes. In both instances the women speak within their households to members of their household.[27] Harrison's depiction of women within these communities having a voice only in their home is

[23] Williamson (1982: 118–19).

[24] Waddington, Critcher, Dicks, and Parry (2001: 90).

[25] Waddington, Critcher, Dicks, and Parry (2001: 80).

[26] Waddington, Critcher, Dicks, and Parry (2001: 55).

[27] In addition to the mother calling after her son, the grandma chastises her husband, 'Are you lighting up again, you barmy bastard? You'll be underground again sooner than

supported both by the description of working-class culture presented in Richard Hoggart's seminal book, *The Uses of Literacy*, and in more recent sociological work on working class culture and social dynamics.[28] A recent study by Waddington, Critcher, Dicks, and Parry concluded that 'in these communities, women's experiences were framed by the response of their partners so that the male agenda predominated'.[29] The researchers acknowledge in their conclusion to their chapter on women and families that, despite trying to talk about women in the four mining communities covered in their surveys, they 'have ended up talking largely about men'.[30] The reason for this male dominated narrative in both sociological studies of these communities and Harrison's film/poem about one family in one such community is that 'in traditional working-class communities the actual or imminent collapse of the main industry also threatens male identity, from which the community has historically drawn its concepts of the female role, of family life and of culture more generally'.[31] It is this reality that Harrison is attempting to convey. Unlike the Nereids in *Prometheus Bound*, Harrison's Nereids cannot simply offer advice and sympathy and then return home to the watery depths far away from Prometheus' suffering. Similarly there is no hopeful prophecy that his Io will, in some far away land, regain her human dignity.

The mother figure is introduced awaking in bed, apparently alarmed. Whether her alarm stems from a bad dream or apprehension about her husband's final day in the pit and the consequences of the mine closure on her family is unclear. The audience next sees her leaning out of an upstairs window calling to her young son who had fled the house after a quarrel with his father, which stemmed directly from the frustration and anxiety caused by the mine closures.[32] Despite the fact that she is clad only in a silk slip, at this point she is not sexualized, nor is there a sense that her well-being is threatened. She is simply a mother distressed by a quarrel between her husband and her son. As the men follow the colliery brass band to the mine for their last day of work in the pits, we see the

you think. And if you're going to be carving damned coal all day put some papers down.' Harrison (1998: 12–13).

[28] Hoggart (1957). For a study focusing specifically on working class dynamics in communities affected by the coal mine closures, see Waddington, Critcher, Dicks, and Parry (2001).

[29] Waddington, Critcher, Dicks, and Parry (2001: 55).

[30] Waddington, Critcher, Dicks, and Parry (2001: 69).

[31] Waddington, Critcher, Dicks, and Parry (2001: 70).

[32] For a still image of this scene, see Harrison (1998: 11). For further still images of the Io figure, see Harrison (1998: 51, 53, 68, 74, and 78).

woman, now clad in shoes, a skirt, shirt and sweater, running out of the house and along the streets looking for her young son. We see her again, a short time later running along the canal path past a barge laden with coal. She is clearly panicked by the discord in her family, but there is no sense yet of a threat to her own physical being. This depiction of the mother within a family affected by the mine closures experiencing psychological distress and fear for her family's well-being reflects the conclusions drawn in a 1991 study. That study 'found that the more the husband was experiencing problems at work, the greater was the propensity for his spouse to exhibit such symptoms of psychological distress as nervousness, restlessness and having "frightening thoughts"'.[33] Before we see the mother again, however, we see Kratos and Bia forcefully take the coal miners from the colliery and truck them to Germany, where they are tipped into a pit of molten metal—humans smelted for industrial purposes, with a clear insinuation that England is being cleansed of its troublesome coal miners.

With this act of profound violence in the background evoking the darkest moments in twentieth-century European history, when we see the boy's mother again (who has herself run across Europe and is now in Germany) gathering kindling wood to start a fire, there is a clear sense that more than the unity of her family is in jeopardy. This sense of physical danger is immediately confirmed by the voice of Hermes, who says of Kratos and Bia:

> ...
> *I've let them have her as their toy*
> *to drive demented then destroy.*
> *To death, through Dresden from Doncaster*
> *dogged and hounded, faster, faster,*
> *she'll suffer, this fire-kindling Frau,*
> (in the likeness of a Friesian cow),
> the sort of fate that's been assigned
> to those considered not one's kind,
> those hate's gadflies force to flee,
> schizophrenic, gypsy, refugee.
> They'll turn the screw of paranoia
> then, fun done, finish her in ... *Feuer.*[34]

And indeed, over the remaining course of the movie we see her incessantly hounded by Kratos and Bia, becoming ever more frantic, with an

[33] Waddington, Critcher, Dicks, and Parry (2001: 61).
[34] Harrison (1998: 45).

escalating sense of physical threat. The threat becomes increasingly one of not only physical violence but also of sexual violence as the layers of clothing that she left the house with are slowly stripped away over the course of a number of scenes. Eventually she is fleeing her pursuers wearing nothing but the silk slip which she had been wearing in the first scene in which she appeared. In the end, however, we discover that violence that has stalked her for much of the movie is not sexual in nature, in part because her pursuers see her not as human but as beast. She is forced into an abattoir where she is slaughtered in the same fashion as the cow that preceded her through the chutes. As her body is hoisted up with a chain around her leg, causing her last piece of clothing to slide up, revealing her naked body, she is presented as having been stripped of everything: her sexuality, her family, her life, her identity as human.

The fate of Harrison's chorus of Nereids is similarly bleak. They begin the movie as local women employed at the Oceanus fish factory, but are converted by Hermes into a Greek chorus of his fashioning.[35] The chorus that is formed is exactly the sort of tragic chorus that Harrison detests. Hermes describes the chorus:

> This choir's just Zeus's little quirk.
> They handled scales so well at work.
> What sport to squeeze these lumpen proles
> into the choral corset of posh roles,
> to warble a mournful little number. . . .[36]

Harrison, from his first play onward, has insisted that the idea of the Greek chorus as Victorian ladies in white nighties chanting in unison is anathema to Greek drama.[37] Hermes, on the other hand, believes that verse drama is posh drama, requiring both a physical appearance and speaking voice that these Yorkshire women lack.[38] The Nereids of this

[35] It is worth noting that where the women find employment is with a large multinational company that makes its profits from exploiting natural resources to the point of depletion and collapse.

[36] Harrison (1998: 34).

[37] In the introduction to their adaptation of *Lysistrata*, *Aikin Mata*, Harrison and James Simmons wrote that the European tradition of Greek choruses consisted of 'effete angelic choral speaking and emasculated dancing'. Harrison and Simmons (1966: 10).

[38] Richard Hoggart comments on the difference in appearance between the classes in *The Uses of Literacy*: 'This may be a fancy, but I am often struck by an apparent difference in the fatness of the different classes, say between that of a middle-aged working-class woman and that of a prosperous middle-aged business-man. One has a white and matt quality, the other is tightly rounded, shiny and polished; one makes me think of gallons of tea, hundredweights of bread, and plates of fish-and-chips; the other of steaks in station hotels.' Hoggart

chorus are witnesses to the action, but not participants in the action, despite the fact that they will share Prometheus' fiery fate. The chorus of the *Prometheus Bound* have agency and are able to offer both advice and sympathy to the chained Titan, attempting to mediate between him and Zeus. For Harrison's Zeus, like Thatcher, there is no possible mediation. In 1981 Thatcher stated, in response to the hunger strikes by IRA prisoners in the prison known as the Maze, 'Crime is crime is crime: it is not political'. Few would doubt that she felt this was equally applicable to the miners who were striking illegally in 1984. There is little advice that this chorus could provide, even if they had the appropriate voice and the inclination to speak about their suffering in public.[39] A tyrant cannot be negotiated with; they can be obeyed, or they can be disobeyed, and the penalty for disobedience paid, as the exemplar of Prometheus and Zeus illustrates.

Hermes not only creates a chorus that insists on changing the appearance of the women to one that he feels is more appropriate to tragedy, but he also strips them of their local dialect, allowing them only to sing a song that has no words. Hermes is insistent that poetry is the domain of the gods, and forbidden to those who speak the local dialect:

> In local lingo, note, gods rhyme
> effortlessly all the time.
> Poetry of this posh sort'll
> never come from a mere mortal.
> It's quite beyond mere mortal reach,
> this pure Olympian form of speech.
> It's a pure Olympian privilege
> forbidden folk from Ferrybridge.[40]

Harrison co-opts both the language of the gods and the chorus to make poetry and tragedy political, and to make it speak for those who have been rendered voiceless, pointing out the dark history of the lands through which they float, and associating that history with Zeus' animosity towards mankind. As the Nereids sail down the Danube through

(1957: 39). Hermes cannot stand for ordinary women of this sort to represent the community of the chorus in Greek tragedy.

[39] For an extensive account of female activism during the strike, see Seddon (1986). For some sense of the numbers of women who participated in such actions, see Waddington, Wykes, and Critcher (1991: 74–93).

[40] Harrison (1998: 20–1). Soon after this as the boy and his grandfather begin to speak in rhyming couplets, Hermes associates this use of poetic diction by the Yorkshire working-class with the theft of fire. See Harrison (1998: 23).

the locks of Portile de Fier, Hermes comments on the twentieth-century history of the region:

> KRATOS (Force) and (Violence) BIA,
> who miss their old SS career,
> had recent sport in two regimes
> on either side of these Danube's streams.
> Where our sugary chorus glide
> through killing fields in either side,
> BIA (Violence) and KRATOS (Force)
> found two dictators to endorse,
> the best they'd had since World War II,
> Milosevic and Ceausescu,
> who made the Danube red not blue.
> And poor mortals think that song redeems
> the ravages of such regimes.[41]

Harrison associates the dark history of violence and suffering throughout twentieth-century Europe with the British mine closures through the act of the chorus bearing silent witness. Like his Io, Harrison's Nereids may be lacking an articulate voice in the public realm, but he insists that their stories are inseparable from the public narrative of the male coal miners which was so prominent in the British press from the mid-1980s through to the early 1990s, as well as the larger narrative of the loss of the socialist dream throughout Europe at the close of the century. For Harrison the narrative is not one of mine closures and economics, but of a cultural genocide unleashed on entire communities under the guise of the economic good of the larger state.

CONCLUSION

The female narrative that Harrison is telling is a narrative of violence against women—not the physical and sexual violence so frequently presented in film and other media, but a violence that has systematically worked to break down all of the traditional female bonds of security, both familial and communal. It is not that Harrison is unaware that there are other female narratives that could be told in the context of his film/poem that are narratives of physical and sexual violence against women. Nor does he ignore these narratives completely. As the statue of

[41] Harrison (1998: 72–4).

Prometheus, which is being trucked from Yorkshire through Europe to Greece, crosses the German/Czech border, the camera pans over the roadside stop selling garden gnomes and the prostitutes selling their bodies. Hermes, in passing, comments:

> A man drives from Dresden in his new
> 'free market' BMW,
> finds a quiet place and parks
> and gets sucked off for 50 Marks.
> Old East-bloc men can now afford a
> quick blow-job across the border,
> when Deutschmarks fell into their laps
> at the Berlin Wall's collapse.
> After blow-jobs they buy these
> new deities from Vietnamese,
> who buy these dwarves from Poles and sell
> to New Europe's clientele.[42]

The women standing beside the road, Harrison seems to be suggesting, are another commodity to be bought, sold, and traded in the new free-market economy that followed the collapse of the old Eastern Soviet Bloc countries.[43] It is this commoditization that links these women on the German/Czech border with the chorus of Nereids and Io, and indeed the miners themselves. All have become commodities whose value is determined by market demands and who, like the coal pits themselves, can be declared economically unviable, and be gutted of anything of value that remains, then abandoned.

The British working classes have traditionally lived subsistence lifestyles in which the core of working-class attitudes were attached to 'a sense of the personal, the concrete, the local: it is embodied in the idea of, first, the family and, second, the neighbourhood.'[44] For many in these communities, this way of life came under attack by Thatcher's government and its economic policies. As one miner recently commented, while reflecting on the strike of 1984, 'We had a community culture in a mining village, self-policing, looking out for one another, and then all

[42] Harrison (1998: 49–50).

[43] According to a European Union Commissioner, former Eastern bloc countries are believed to be the place of origin of approximately two-thirds of the women being trafficked internationally for the purposes of prostitution. See Vandenberg (1997). The association between the death of the working-class and the increased commoditization and trade of human beings is also explored in Season 2 of David Simon and Ed Burns' television series *The Wire*, produced by HBO. There, too, the women being trafficked are of Eastern European origin.

[44] Hoggart (1957: 33).

of a sudden we were thrown into Thatcher's class war... It was her war, not ours. She determined it and we lost...'[45] For the government, the miners' strike and the subsequent mine closures were necessary steps to improving the British economy and ensuring that control of the economy rested firmly with the government. Its concerns were national and global, as opposed to the familial and local concerns of the miners and their families. It is the local story that Harrison is telling, trying to present the scope of suffering experienced through the use of myth and Greek tragedy. To use Edith Hall's words, *Prometheus* is a 'howling lament' that presents a narrative of the aftermath of the miner's strike that the mainstream media never told.[46] Far from being 'the enemy within', the mining communities represented the twentieth-century aspirations of the working class, which the government systematically undermined to the point of collapse, not only removing their livelihoods, but also destroying the community and familial structures that had anchored their lives for generations. For daring to seek security for their communities, their families, and the ongoing financial security that would allow them to make do, these mining communities faced all the resources that the state could muster against them, from massive police forces which often employed violence, to denial of state benefits in their times of need, because their actions had been decreed by the state to be criminal. A lack of articulate speech, often a defining feature of the working class, does not negate suffering, though often it allows those with an eloquent grasp of language to inflict suffering and to insist that such suffering is necessary. *Prometheus* is about facing both public and personal holocausts, and while the fate of the male workers has been a very public narrative in Britain, Harrison also insists on the private familial and feminine narratives of suffering.

[45] Wainwright (2009). [46] Hall (2002: 140).

Part V

Historical Women

11

Between Family and the Nation: Gorgo in the Cinema[1]

Konstantinos P. Nikoloutsos

This chapter examines the portrayal of Gorgo, wife of Sparta's legendary King Leonidas, in two Hollywood productions: *The 300 Spartans*, a 1962[2] CinemaScope epic produced by Twentieth-Century Fox under the direction of Rudolph Maté, and the 2007 action film *300* coproduced by Warner Bros. Pictures, Legendary Pictures, and Virtual Studios under the direction of Zack Snyder. My goal here is twofold: first, to investigate the extent to which Gorgo's representation is faithful to or departs from ancient historical sources; second, to identify the cinematic mechanisms and discursive practices that account for the differences between the depiction of Gorgo in Greek literature and that on the big screen.

Building on the theoretical premise that motion pictures set in the classical world mirror modern concerns and anxieties, this chapter will argue that, although in both films under examination Gorgo wears an ancient Greek garment, underneath this garment we find a contemporary woman. As I aim to demonstrate, both cinematic portraits of Gorgo are constructed in accordance with western stereotypes of gender and sexuality, thereby offering visual testimony to the changes in attitudes to

[1] I am grateful to the OUP anonymus readers, as well as to Paul Cartledge, Anthony Corbeill, David Levene, Maria Marsilio, and Gonda Van Steen for their comments and suggestions that helped me improve my chapter significantly. Many thanks are also due to Alison Futrell for her response at *Feminism and Classics V*, organized at the University of Michigan in May 2008, where this paper was first presented. All mistakes remain with me alone.

[2] Prior to its official domestic release on 29 August 1962, *The 300 Spartans* premiered in Philadelphia, PA on ca. 31 December 1961. See the entry F6.5024 in *The American Film Institute Catalog of Motion Pictures Produced in the United States, Volume F6, Features Films, 1961–1970*. In the late 1950s onwards, it became customary for major US studios to seek to test the reception of prestige pictures through a limited number (sometimes just one) of big-city, reserved-seat roadshows organized well before the general mass release. See, e.g., Solomon (1988: 132–7); Hall and Neale (2010: 161).

these issues in recent decades. This, however, is not the only finding that is important for historical and artistic reasons. Both films, I shall show, seek to master ancient Greek history and project a monolithic picture of Spartan society through a highly stylized and grossly anachronistic image of her 'first lady' as an iconic wife, mother, and queen, a woman who matches her husband in loyalty, patriotism, and intelligence. In further exploring this elevation of Gorgo to a symbol of the family and the nation, I shall argue that, while her domestication in Maté's film is in full agreement with the policy of Containment adopted by the US government during the Cold War period, her alignment with the rhetoric of politicized womanhood in *300* reproduces a binarism central to post-September 11 American ideology, that between the liberal white West and the oppressive Muslim Orient.

GORGO AND THE POLITICS OF SPECTATORSHIP

300 opens at a campfire, where Dilios (David Wenham), the only Spartan survivor from the battle of Thermopylae, narrates the events of Leonidas' life until he became king of Sparta: his birth, the harsh testing rites he passed since his early childhood according to the citizen training system of ἀγωγή that Sparta implemented to produce brave warriors,[3] and finally his coronation. This filmic technique of character construction does not apply to Gorgo. Although Spartan girls, unlike girls elsewhere in Greece, followed an arduous programme of physical training, similar to that for boys, to become fit partners for men and fit mothers for future warriors,[4] neither film associates Gorgo with this long-established tradition. Furthermore, neither of them provides any other background information about Gorgo before she is established as a queen on the

[3] The heir-apparent to the two Spartan thrones was exempted from the obligation of going through the ἀγωγή. See, e.g., Cartledge (2001: 44, 63, 85). Leonidas, however, did have to pass this ordeal since he was not a crown prince, as he is erroneously portrayed in *300*.

[4] On the physical education of girls in ancient Sparta, see, e.g., Hodkinson (2000: 227–8); Cartledge (2001: 83–4, 114); Pomeroy (2002: 12–29). The novelized version of the script of *The 300 Spartans*, which was written by British author John Burke in 1961, and published in the US in August 1962 to coincide with the film's official domestic release, makes a rather provocative reference to the physical training that girls received in Sparta. Recalling the image of boys exercising in a field at the foot of Mt. Taygetus, the narrator of the book, seer Megistias, adds: 'There were girls, too, running and wrestling. Like the boys, they were naked; and they had the roughness and strength of boys, too. The sons they bore must be true Spartans' (Burke 1962: 6). This is an elaboration of the opening scene included in the script dated 5 September 1960, which was filmed but cut before *The 300 Spartans* was released. See Levene (2007: 385 n. 10); Nikoloutsos (2013: 266–7 n. 15).

big screen. Since the focal point of both films is the heroic last stand of Leonidas and his small band of soldiers against the hordes of Persian king Xerxes at the narrow pass of Thermopylae in the late summer of 480 BC, such details about Gorgo are redundant. Another reason for this biased representation lies in the androcentric nature of ancient historical accounts, themselves produced by men, in which women appear only occasionally. This concentration on male deeds undermines the depiction of rounded female characters. As Alastair Blanshard and Kim Shahabudin note about this problem in reconstructing ancient history on the big screen: 'Filmmakers are faced with the choice of either perpetuating the gender bias of ancient accounts and limiting their accounts to the deeds of men or violating their commitment to historical accuracy and inventing female characters.'[5]

Gorgo appears three times in Herodotus (5.48; 5.51; 7.239).[6] Similarly, in the two films under examination, her presence is limited to a few, scattered scenes. Embedded in a male-centred narrative in which she plays a peripheral role, she lacks individuation and historical specificity. As Susan Linville explains about the portrayal of women in history-based films:

> [I]t is the process of *not* telling women's histories that makes possible women's deployment in these narratives as symbolic answers.... [W]omen's lack of distinct histories and their resulting fragmentary status are preconditions for their iconic functions.[7]

To better understand how Gorgo is fashioned to suit the ideological and artistic goals of each film, first we must look at some information about the historical Gorgo and the way this is altered, compressed, or even erased on the big screen.

Born presumably in the early 510s BC,[8] Gorgo was the only child of Cleomenes I, king of Sparta from the Agiad line. Since Cleomenes left no son when he died in 490 BC, the throne had to pass, according to the Spartan custom of royal succession, to his nearest male kinsman. His

[5] Blanshard and Shahabudin (2011: 118).

[6] Six aphorisms, one of which is based on an anecdote narrated in Herodotus (5.51), are attributed to Gorgo by Plutarch (*Mor.* 240 d–e). None of the ancient sources on Gorgo are to be taken at face value. Her portrait is meant to be in line with fundamental principles of Lycurgus' constitution; it also reflects popular perceptions about the Spartans in the non-Spartan world. See Paradiso (1993); Pomeroy (2002: 76); Cartledge (2003: 123).

[7] Linville (2004: 15).

[8] As Herodotus (5.51) narrates, Gorgo was eight or nine years old when Aristagoras, the tyrant of Miletus, visited Sparta in 500 BC to ask her father Cleomenes for his support in the Ionian revolt against the Persians.

father and previous Agiad king, Anaxandridas II, had three sons from his first wife. Dorieus, the oldest of them, was killed during an unsuccessful attempt to found a colony in Sicily. As a result, Cleomenes was succeeded by his second half-brother, Leonidas, who had meanwhile taken Gorgo as his wife.[9] To match Leonidas in status and capitalize on the American fascination with royalty, Gorgo is elevated to queen in both films under examination.[10] Her representation as such, however, is far from being accurate. Administrative power in ancient Sparta was shared by two hereditary kings, one from the Agiad family and one from the Eurypontid family. The historical Leonidas, therefore, was not a monarch, a single absolute ruler like a modern king. Portraying Leonidas as the sole head of the Spartan city-state and a born king, as is the case in *300*,[11] highlights his hegemonic masculinity. Furthermore, the use of the title 'queen' by Spartan royal women is not attested before the early third century BC, shortly after its occurrence on inscriptions from Macedonia. This, of course, does not mean that the woman so titled was equal to the king in terms of power.[12]

Women in ancient Sparta were normally married in their late teens.[13] The wedding of Leonidas with Gorgo, therefore, must have taken place in the late 490s BC. Born in the early 540s, Leonidas was in his late forties when he married Gorgo. This means that he was her senior by approximately three decades. In order for Sparta's royal couple to look appealing to the viewer and inspire identification, this huge age disparity is obliterated and the two characters are portrayed as generational peers in both

[9] See Hdt. 5.42–5, 7.205.

[10] The depiction of Gorgo as a queen in *The 300 Spartans* was an idea of Spyros Skouras (Synodinou 1998: 183), the Greek-born president of Twentieth-Century Fox, who was close to everyone in the Greek royal family, especially Queen Frederica (Curti 1967: 241). On the ways in which Gorgo's representation is informed by the public image of Frederica, see Nikoloutsos (2013: 281–2).

[11] By contrast, *The 300 Spartans* acknowledges, verbally and visually, Sparta's dual kingship on several occasions in the scenes before Leonidas' departure for Thermopylae. Despite the film's efforts to be historically accurate in this matter, Leotychides, Leonidas' fellow king, remains on the margins of the narrative, allowing Leonidas to emerge as the actual ruler of Sparta. The part is played by an uncredited actor with one line of dialogue. Moreover, Demaratus, the former Spartan king from the Eurypontid line who was forced to go to exile and sought refuge in Persia, describes Leotychides to Xerxes as a usurper of the throne and Leonidas as 'a true Spartan king. His name means lion, and he lives up to it. There is no man who can match him in courage and skill in battle, nor in devotion to his country.'

[12] See Carney (1991), (2000: 225–8); Pomeroy (2002: 75–6).

[13] See Pomeroy (1995: 38), (2002: 44, 56 n. 22).

films.[14] Ancient history, thus, changes to suit modern aesthetic criteria and beliefs about the ideal age difference between husband and wife in order for the marriage to be happy. If the age gap that separates Leonidas and Gorgo in ancient Greek literature was reproduced on the big screen and the two looked physically incongruous, the model of conjugal harmony they are crafted to epitomize would be undermined. This mismatch would, in turn, fail to satisfy the voyeuristic instincts of the spectators, denying them the pleasure of looking at a young, loving couple.

The shaping of Gorgo in accordance with the politics of spectatorship is extended over other aspects of her marriage to Leonidas. Gorgo was not only Leonidas' wife; she was also his step-niece. Just as in other cities in Greece, so too in Sparta endogamy was a common practice, especially among the members of the ruling elite. As Sarah Pomeroy explains:

> Since the Spartan population was small and xenophobic, it could be characterized as endogamous in general. There were never more than 10,000 *homoioi* (men of equal status or similars) or, consequently, more than 500 elite. . . . The problem of finding a suitable spouse was intensified in the case of the kings: the small pool of eligible brides included members of the royal families and daughters or widows of wealthy or influential men.[15]

Sparta's small citizen body was not the only reason for adopting this tradition. Endogamy was also an excellent strategy for gaining economic and sociopolitical advantage. The marriage of Leonidas to his step-niece is, like other attested marriages between members of the two royal houses of Sparta, a union 'whose clear purpose was to consolidate the lineage's property holdings'.[16] As the only child of a reigning king, Gorgo was a *patrouchos* (holder of the patrimony), the sole heiress of her father's entire wealth, the management of which passed, along with the throne, to Leonidas. Within the context of this arranged marriage, then, Gorgo becomes a 'vehicle for the devolution of property and with it property-power among elite males'.[17]

This ancient custom would be too dangerous to be portrayed on the big screen. Marriage between two individuals with a close blood relationship is nowadays classified as incest, and is socially and legally taboo. To enable audience identification, both films feign ignorance of the

[14] Anna Synodinou and Richard Egan were respectively thirty-four and thirty-nine years old when they played Gorgo and Leonidas in *The 300 Spartans*. Lena Headey and Gerald Butler who played the parts in *300* were thirty-four and thirty-six years old respectively.

[15] Pomeroy (2002: 73).

[16] Hodkinson (2004: 114).

[17] Cartledge (2003: 126–7).

endogamous nature of Leonidas' marriage to Gorgo and cast it as the union of two people bound to each other by means of mutual love and devotion. As I have argued in a recent essay about the strategies that Hollywood employs to reconstruct classical antiquity for popular consumption, Greek history 'is revived and reinterpreted according to the moral standards of the present'.[18]

The alignment of Sparta's royal couple with the rhetoric of compulsory love in *The 300 Spartans* does not stem only from the need to please the viewer and facilitate the mental process whereby s/he seeks to establish a sense of intimacy with the screen image. The erasure of the blood relationship between Leonidas and Gorgo is also in agreement with the proscriptions of the Motion Picture Production Code (commonly known as the Hays Code) and its intended protection of family values.[19] Devised by William H. Hays, president of the Motion Picture Producers and Distributors of America (MPPDA), and fully enforced from 1934 until 1968, when it was abandoned in favour of the rating system that is still used in the US, the Code was a set of guidelines determining what the films produced or distributed by major studios should avoid showing in order to obtain the seal of approval from MPPDA (renamed the Motion Picture Association of America in 1945) and be released at cinemas. Acknowledging the influence that motion pictures could have on the viewers, especially young ones, the Code placed upon the industry the obligation of safeguarding and promoting the moral values of American society. One of the Code's 'particular applications' (i.e., the precise listing of forbidden material that followed the introductory section entitled 'general principles') in the addenda to its original 1930 draft was concerned with sex and declared with religious zeal: 'the sanctity of the institution of marriage and the home shall be upheld'.[20] To this end, among other provisions, the Code banned representations of erotic perversion and restricted physical expressions of desire, stipulating that scenes of passion should be included only if they were essential to the plot. In that case, the amount of passion projected on the big screen was curtailed. For, as the Code specified, prolonged kissing and lustful embraces were prohibited.[21]

The 300 Spartans adheres to these principles and limits the physical interaction between Leonidas and Gorgo. The couple is cast together in only two scenes in the entire film. The first time is when Leonidas

[18] Nikoloutsos (2008: 224).

[19] On the Hays Code and films set in the classical world, see Nikoloutsos (2008: 225) and Day in this volume.

[20] Doherty (1999: 362).

[21] See Doherty (1999: 354, 363).

(Richard Egan) returns home from an emergency summit at Corinth, where delegates from various Greek city-states gathered to decide on a common course of action against the invasion of Xerxes' vast army.[22] The second time is when he announces to Gorgo (Anna Synodinou) his decision to march to Thermopylae with his personal bodyguard, ignoring the orders of the Council, which asked him to depart after the celebration of the sacred festival of Carneia. Both scenes are structured so as to anticipate some physical intimacy between the couple. The first scene opens with Gorgo anxiously awaiting her husband's arrival at the palace. She has been informed that Leonidas has come back from his mission at Corinth, but went straight to the Council without stopping at home first—something he has never done before, as she confesses to her (fictitious) niece, Ellas (Diane Baker). Gorgo is in despair and hugs her husband after Ellas withdraws, just as she does in the second scene when she fails to convince Leonidas to change his mind and realizes that she might not see him alive again. Their embracing, however, is too brief—it lasts only a few seconds—and is very reserved. Synodinou places her arms around Egan's back in a mechanical, robot-like manner (Fig. 11.1), thereby perpetuating the stereotypical association of the Spartans with moderation and self-control in ancient moralizing discourses.[23] Despite the romantic atmosphere produced in both scenes by the music of Greek composer Manos Hadjidakis, the film denies Leonidas and Gorgo a kiss, although their faces are close enough and in the first scene they even

Figure 11.1 Gorgo (Anna Synodinou) embracing Leonidas (Richard Egan) in *The 300 Spartans*, dir. Rudolph Maté.

[22] This detail is anachronistic. The congress actually took place at Isthmus in 481 BC. See Hdt. 7.172.

[23] On ancient views on Spartan moderation and austerity, see Hodkinson (2000: 19–64).

touch each other.[24] The film thus draws a distinction between onscreen and offscreen space, between the permissible and the forbidden, between what can be shown to the spectators and what must be left to their imagination.

Hollywood under the Code, however, does not set the imagination of the spectator free. To the contrary, it seeks to monitor and tame it. As Thomas Doherty explains:

> Adhering to the catechism's injunction that sin resided in three places ('thought, word, and deed'), the genius of Hollywood's system of censorship lay in the sophisticated critical scrutiny accorded not only what was seen, said, and meant onscreen but what was apprehended from offscreen as well. True dream police, the Code censors extended their surveillance beyond the visible world and into the space of the spectator's mind.[25]

Correspondingly, in *The 300 Spartans* the diegetic elements operate so as to shape, and constrain, the mental construction of the nondiegetic space. Leonidas and Gorgo address each other as 'my love' in the film, thereby demonstrating that their marriage is based on deep and enduring respect and affection. In the first scene in which they are cast together, Gorgo, before embracing Leonidas, tells him that, when he left for Corinth, she consulted the old priest Megistias who read the entrails of a lamb he sacrificed and made a double prophecy: 'He said you will be the Spartan King best remembered among men. And he said that, for centuries to come, women will sing songs about my love for you.' In the second scene, she urges Leonidas to reconsider his decision to march to Thermopylae with such a small force, but then realizes that war is a male domain and adds passively: 'All I know is that I cannot live without you.' To put her mind at rest, Leonidas replies: 'You must trust me, Gorgo. I love you more than life itself.' What is said on screen is clear, unambiguous, and in line with the Code's definition of 'pure love' as a suitable subject.[26] Thus, when the diegesis is over and the camera retires, the image of Leonidas and Gorgo planted in the spectator's mind is that of a royal couple who conform to their iconic role and resist carnal

[24] By contrast, this kiss is granted to Ellas and Phylon, the younger couple in the film. Although they kiss three times in the same scene, in keeping with the Code's regulations, their kisses are brief and their mouths are closed. Another of the Code's prohibitions was horizontal kissing. Thus, when Xerxes kisses queen Artemisia in his tent, she is lying on the bed, while he is sitting and leaning over her.

[25] Doherty (1999: 11).

[26] As the Code specified, '*Pure love*, the love of a man for a woman permitted by the law of God and man, is the rightful subject of plots. The passion arising from this love is not the subject for plots.' Quoted from Doherty (1999: 354–5).

pleasure, as opposed to their 2007 counterparts who embrace sex and adultery, as I discuss below.

The desexualization of the intimate moments between Leonidas and Gorgo is also in line with the instructions given to the production team by Spyros Skouras, the Greek-born president of Twentieth Century-Fox (1942–62). *The 300 Spartans* was originally an Italian production based on a mediocre script. Fearing that it would be full of historical inaccuracies if it was filmed according to the conventions of the *peplum*, a trend (*filone*)[27] that was at its peak in Italy at the time, Skouras acquired the rights from producer Giorgio Venturini and moved the project to Greece.[28] Filming began at Lake Vouliagmeni, about twelve miles north of Loutraki, on 7 November 1960 and lasted for nearly three months.[29] Given the absence of big names in the lead roles, the film's publicity campaign during the production period concentrated on its effort to recreate, at an enormous budget[30] and with thousands of extras, one of the most iconic battles of classical antiquity in a way that was faithful to the historical record. According to an article published in the newspaper *Τὸ Βῆμα* on 6 December 1960, Fox submitted the script for inspection to the Greek Ministry of Education.[31] As the article notes, all departures from the historical sources concerned minor characters and were approved by the Greek authorities since they were deemed to be harmless to the credible reconstruction of Spartan society on screen.[32]

[27] The *peplum* was not a separate genre, but rather a trend in Italian filmmaking that had a currency at a certain time (1958–65) and produced hundreds of titles. The bibliography on the *filone* is vast. See, e.g., Lucanio (1994); Dyer (1997: 165–83); Günsberg (2005: 97–132); Pomeroy (2008: 29–59) and his essay in this volume; Brunetta (2009: 161–4); Shahabudin (2009); Blanshard and Shahabudin (2011: 58–76); Burke (2011); Nikoloutsos (2013: 264–5).

[28] '*Η ταινία που γέννησε τους 300*' [The Film that Gave Birth to *300*], *Ελευθεροτυπία*, 10 March 2007, p. 36. See also Synodinou (1998: 184).

[29] Lake Vouliagmeni was proposed to Fox as an ideal location by the Greek Cartographic Service on account of its morphology that is similar to that of ancient Thermopylae which has been radically altered by natural forces. Nowadays, there is no narrow pass, and the sea is several miles away from the location where the battle took place. See '*Οἱ ἕλληνες φαντάροι εἶναι ἀπαράμιλλοι καὶ ὡς πέρσαι*' [The Greek Soldiers are Incomparable Even as Persians], *Τὸ Βῆμα*, 6 December 1960, p. 2.

[30] On the original and final budget of the film, as well as its publicity in the press of the time, see Nikoloutsos (2013: 266 n. 13).

[31] The original Italian script was revised by co-producer George St. George who allegedly drew on Herodotus, Thucydides, and Plutarch. He also consulted English historian Roger Beck, English classicist and writer of historical novels Rex Warner, and Prince Peter of Greece. See *Τὸ Βῆμα* [n. 29 above], p. 2.

[32] The Greek Ministry of Education requested that Spartan king Demaratus who was living as an exile at the Persian court be portrayed not as traitor, but as a patriot serving Greece with the deceiving advice he was supplying Xerxes. See *Τὸ Βῆμα* [n. 29 above], p. 2.

To illustrate the studio's commitment to historical accuracy further, the article reports that when Richard Egan asked for the inclusion of more passion in the film as a counterbalance to its dry historicity, Skouras, who patrolled the production, rejected the request stating:

> «Ὄχι ἔρωτες. *Πιστή ἀναπαράστασι τῆς ἱστορίας ὥστε νά μποροῦν νά τήν δοῦν ἐποικοδομητικά καί τά παιδιά». Μ' αὐτή τή βασική ἐντολή γυρίζεται «Ὁ Λέων τῆς Σπάρτης» γιά νά δείξη μέσω τῆς ἔγχρωμης ὀθόνης τοῦ σινεμασκόπ σέ ἑκατομμύρια ἀνθρώπους πάνω στή γῆ μία ἀπό τίς σπουδαιότερες μάχες τῆς ἱστορίας τῆς Ἑλλάδος καί τοῦ κόσμου.*[33]
>
> 'No romance. Faithful representation of history so that children will also be able to watch it constructively'.[34] *The Lion of Sparta*[35] is being filmed in line with this basic guideline in order to show, through the color screen of CinemaScope, to millions of people on earth one of the most important battles in the history of Greece and the world.[36]

This act of self-censorship is in line with the Code's concern for the proper nurturing of the young.[37] Nonetheless, Skouras' claim to historical accuracy is misleading. Whereas it recognizes the need for the erotics of the film to conform to the goals of a self-imposed pedagogical agenda—itself a masquerade for the need of the film to cash in by attracting a large and diverse audience of all ages—it conceals the very fact that the scenes between Gorgo and Leonidas are (along with several other scenes depicting moments of private life) unattested in the ancient sources. These scenes, too, succumb to the mechanisms of cinematic narration and partake largely of fiction.

By contrast, *300* follows a more honest representational strategy. The film lacks the ambition of *The 300 Spartans* to become a form of visual historiography and educate the masses.[38] *300* does not engage in the

[33] The text is reproduced in its original form without any correction of the accent marks. Publications in katharevousa stopped making systematic use of the grave accent in the 1950s and replaced it with the acute.

[34] Interestingly enough, Frank Miller was one of those children who were inspired by the film. See Grossman (2007: 60); Turner (2009: 129); Cyrino (2011: 20).

[35] This was the working title of the film. See the entry F6.5024 in *The American Film Institute Catalog of Motion Picture Produced in the United States, Volume F6, Features Films, 1961–1970*. The original title of the film as an Italian *peplum* was *Termopili*. See Synodinou (1998: 184); Nikoloutsos (2013: 264).

[36] Translations from modern Greek are my own.

[37] The Hays Code recognized two levels of comprehension: 'Maturer minds may easily understand and accept without harm subject matter in plots which does younger people positive harm.' Quoted from Doherty (1999: 11).

[38] On *The 300 Spartans* as a means for the construction of collective memory, see Nikoloutsos (2013: 369–72).

historical discourse precisely because it does not draw, at least directly, on ancient sources. The film is based on the 1998 graphic novel of the same title by American writer and illustrator Frank Miller (produced in co-operation with his former wife, colourist Lynn Varley) and reproduces its plot and aesthetics. Gorgo is a rather unimportant figure and appears on only one page in Miller's book. Leonidas is about to march to Thermopylae with his personal bodyguard when she comments: 'North. The *Hot Gates*. This explains your *enthusiasm* last night' (emphasis in the original). The ancient toponym is translated in English not for the sake of historical clarity, but to tease the reader through the allusion to steamy sexual intercourse between the couple on the eve of Leonidas' departure for the fatal battle with the Persians.

In the tradition of Wolfgang Petersen's *Troy* (2004) and Oliver Stone's *Alexander* (2004), both of which sought to sexualize the ancient Greek world on the big screen, *300* recreates this sexual encounter between Leonidas and Gorgo that is missing from Miller's book. The scene exudes passion and sensuality, offering the viewer (male and female alike) the pleasure of looking at, and identifying with, a couple that is compatible, both physically and mentally. As Stacey Scriver notes, 'it is a soft-focus scene complete with gentle music and punctuated by gasps of pleasure. It is a representation of the pure love between a man and a woman, a husband and a wife.'[39] As opposed to *Troy* and *Alexander* where the sex between Achilles and Briseis, and Alexander and Roxane, respectively, is violent and forced, the sex between Leonidas (Gerard Butler) and Gorgo (Lena Headey) in *300* is mutually desired and enjoyable. The two characters alternate positions—with Gorgo first on top, then at the bottom—thereby offering a demonstration of the freedom and gender parity that the film, incorrectly, casts as a characteristic of Spartan society.[40]

The scene, however, does more than use sex to illustrate the supposed democratic structures of Spartan society. Earlier in the film, when a Persian emissary arrives asking for 'earth and water', a token of Sparta's submission to the power of Xerxes, Leonidas refers to Athenians, quite pejoratively, as 'boy lovers'.[41] Although historically inaccurate,

[39] Scriver (2009: 190).

[40] As opposed to their Athenian counterparts, Spartan elite women, including Gorgo, are attributed a considerable amount of autonomy and power over the male members of their family and society at large in ancient literature. Modern scholars are divided among those who allow for greater credibility to surviving sources [Zweig (1993a); Pomeroy (2002: 93–9)] and those who read them with scepticism [Dewald (1981: 105); Paradiso (1993: 111–14); Millender (1999); Powell (1999); Hodkinson (2000: 94–103), (2004); Cartledge (2001: 106–26); Hazewindus (2004: 15–41, 237–43)].

[41] The perception of Sparta as anti-Athens has dominated the western imagination since the early nineteenth century. See e.g., Macgregor Morris and Hodkinson (2011: xi).

this dissociation of Sparta from the institution of pederasty,[42] practised with variations in several Greek city-states, is a disclaimer that aims to enhance the machismo of Spartan men and cast them, in the eyes of the spectators, as the only Greeks who can fearlessly stand against the vast army of Xerxes (Rodrigo Santoro) who is portrayed as a feminized oppressor. Gorgo is fully aligned with the efforts of the film to dehomoeroticize ancient Sparta and becomes a tool whereby Leonidas is straightened up for popular consumption. To titillate the male viewer and counterbalance the film's concentration on the pumped-up pectorals of Spartan soldiers, the camera focuses on Gorgo's breast while Leonidas is making slow, passionate love to her, as opposed to the quick and emotionless sex that she is forced to have with traitor Theron (Dominic West), an invented character, in exchange for his support in persuading the Spartan Council to send reinforcements to her husband. The fusion of the statue-like bodies of Leonidas and Gorgo stands in sharp contrast to the orgiastic sex in which the deformed female slaves of Xerxes' harem engage so lustfully when the hunchback traitor Ephialtes visits his tent. In this scene, therefore, Gorgo serves as a vehicle whereby a Hollywood cliché is reproduced and perpetuated: good and good-looking people have good and 'healthy' sex.

GORGO AND COLD WAR CONTAINMENT

In a recent article, I focused on Leonidas' armour in *The 300 Spartans* and showed that it is reminiscent of that of Roman emperors.[43] This fusion of Greek and Roman antiquity is of course anachronistic and finds an explanation in the history of the making of the film. When Skouras acquired the rights from Venturini, the film was at the pre-production stage. He thus negotiated the purchase of the entire preparatory work of

[42] On Spartan pederasty, see Cartledge (2001: 91–105). Surprisingly, Burke's novel, based on the script of *The 300 Spartans*, makes an explicit reference to Spartan pederasty. The seer Megistias, watching the young Teucer exercising, notes: 'When he was a boy there had been many men who loved him with the love which we held higher than the love of a man for a woman. I had been one of those who had admired from a distance—an aging man myself, stricken by his youthful perfection, yet knowing even then that he was destined for the love of a woman' (1962: 6).

[43] See Nikoloutsos (2013: 272–5). On the tendency to Romanize the Greeks in terms of sets and costumes in films produced in Italy in order to make them more 'familiar' and acceptable to American audiences, see Nisbet (2006: 34) and Vivante in this volume.

the Italians,[44] including the costumes.[45] The Greek film industry was at an embryonic stage, producing only a few titles per year, and lacked the means of manufacturing the large quantity of period costumes needed for an historical epic with thousands of extras.[46] By contrast, Italy had both the experience and the technology. Since the early 1950s, Cinecittà and other studios had served as filming locations for several Hollywood epic productions, including *Quo Vadis* (1951), *Ulysses* (1954), *Helen of Troy* (1956), and *Ben Hur* (1959). This foreign artistic activity provided the stimulus for the genesis of the *peplum*. These were basically low-budget films. As Shahabudin notes: 'There was often only enough money available to finance a day or two of shooting.'[47] As a result, the *pepla* were made without historical advisors and often recycled sets and props in order to reduce the production cost.[48] Originally a *peplum*, *The 300 Spartans* displays this very characteristic of the *filone*, according to which it did not really matter if the costumes and settings did not look Greek or Roman, as long as they somehow looked 'ancient'.[49]

This blending of historical periods and dressing styles is prevalent in the costumes that Gorgo wears in the film. A basic narrative trait of the *pepla* is the dichotomization of characters, male and female alike, into good/moral and bad/immoral.[50] Thus, as Fernando Lillo Redonet notes, 'Gorgo and Ellas personify purity and innocence, whereas Artemisia [Queen of Halicarnassus and mistress of Xerxes] is shown as a *femme fatale*.'[51] To suit the image of a modest wife-queen, Gorgo wears two gowns that resemble the austere Doric *peplos*, which envelops the female body like a tube.[52] As opposed to the light Ionic *chitôn* that accentuates

[44] See *Ελευθεροτυπία* [n. 15 above], p. 36; Synodinou (1998: 184).

[45] Designed by Ginette Devaud, the costumes were made at Peruzzi's *Casa d'arte di Firenze*, which made costumes for numerous *pepla*, including *Ercole e la regina di Lidia* (US release title *Hercules Unchained*), *La battaglia di Maratona* (US release title *The Giant of Marathon*), *Saffo, venere di Lesbo* (US release title *The Warrior Empress*), *Il colosso di Rodi* (*The Colossus of Rhodes*), and *Il tiranno di Siracusa* (US release title *Damon and Pythias*). See the list at http://www.imdb.com/company/co0055382 (accessed 1 March 2011).

[46] On the history of the Greek film industry during this period, see Bakogianni in this volume.

[47] Shahabudin (2009: 201).

[48] See Dyer (1997: 166); Pomeroy (2008: 58).

[49] As Paul (2010b: 142) astutely notes, this collectivization of antiquity is best illustrated by the alternative title of the genre, 'sword-and-sandals'.

[50] On this polarity, see Lagny (1992: 168); Günsberg (2005: 103); Lillo Redonet (2008: 118, n. 6); Pomeroy in this volume.

[51] Lillo Redonet (2008: 119).

[52] On tube-like *peploi* in sculptural representations from ancient Sparta, see Kokkorou-Alevras (2006: 90) and Fig. 29, 31, 62, 71, and 72 Kaltsas (2006).

the breasts, hips, and buttocks, the Doric *peplos* (made of heavier material) conceals physical details, thereby negating a woman's sexuality. Its simplicity emphasizes her chastity and moral sternness.[53] Gorgo's royal gowns reproduce the basic stylistic features of the *peplos*. They are both straight, floor-length garments girdled at the waist. Certain elements they bear, however, are incompatible with depictions of *peploi* in the Greek visual arts from the archaic and early classical periods. One of her dresses, for example, is decorated with wide borders in crimson. This detail is anachronistic. Such stripes, in various hues of purple, were used to adorn the tunics of Roman aristocrats and served as an indicator of social status.[54] The other dress that she wears is held in place with double fibulae and braided cross-bands that pass over her shoulders and around her breast, and end in a cord belt whose ends are hanging along the garment. Cross-bands form part of the iconography of the Ionic *chitôn* in Greek antiquity. Similarly, the type of belt that is placed tightly around Gorgo's waist is a basic accessory of a married woman's tunic in imperial Rome.[55] This blending of dressing styles is not without symbolic value. Just as the knot on Gorgo's belt signifies that her chastity is locked up and she is bound to one man, her husband, so too the cross-bands that secure her breast denote that she is constrained and fully aligned with the dress and behavioural codes of patriarchal society.

By contrast, the representation of Artemisia (Anne Wakefield) as a *femme fatale* includes self-conscious, exaggerated femininity and extreme artificiality. As Stella Bruzzi notes about screen sirens:

> The symbolic iconography of the classic *femme fatale* is a limited, clearly demarcated register of clothes, based on the contrast of light and dark (... [which is] indicative of [her] duplicity), frequent wardrobe changes (not necessarily motivated by action) and the insertion of distinctive, often anachronistic garments or accessories.[56]

Gorgo's wardrobe is limited to two *peploi*. Artemisia, on the other hand, wears a different garment every time she appears on screen. This continuous change of looks is a metonym for her mutable, treacherous character. Artemisia is an ally of Xerxes until the end of the film, where her identity as a Greek spy is disclosed. Gorgo's *peploi* consist of one piece, are minimally decorated, and of one colour: white. Artemisia's

[53] See Lee (2005: 61–3); Cleland et al. (2007: 143).

[54] See Stone (2001: 15); Goldman (2001: 221–2); Cleland et al. (2007: 138, 201).

[55] See Cleland et al. (2007: 19). Ellas also wears cross-bands and the same type of belt. On this type of belt, see Sebesta (2001: 48).

[56] Bruzzi (1997: 126).

gowns are voluminous, red or in various hues of blue, and adorned with golden details and accessories. These colours carry symbolic connotations in the *peplum*. White is used to indicate a good character; dark (black/blue) and sharp (red) colours signal an evil character.[57] For example, when Xerxes has been unable to defeat Leonidas for days, Artemisia visits him in his tent and tricks him by advising him to announce to his soldiers that the gods ordered him to withdraw the troops back to Persia to avoid winning a Pyrrhic victory at Thermopylae.[58] In this scene, Artemisia wears a blue dress matched with a *himation* in a darker shade of blue. Acknowledging her scheming mind, Xerxes makes a comment that reproduces patriarchal stereotypes about women and equates Artemisia to Pandora and her biblical counterpart, Eve: 'It was a dark day when the first woman came into this world.'[59]

The construction of Artemisia's image as a seductress and devourer of men[60] is complemented by her flawless make-up and elaborate coiffure. To gain the glamorous look of the *femme fatale*, her eyes are artfully painted in green and paired with long faux eyelashes and red lips.[61] Her dark black hair is perfectly arranged in a ponytail with curls falling symmetrically on the sides and the forehead, giving her the lethal, serpentine look of Medusa (Fig. 11.2).[62] Shaped like the coils of the snake and paired with a slender neck and curvy shoulders that she leaves exposed when she arrives at Xerxes' tent, Artemisia's locks become a metonym for her transgressiveness and self-empowerment. Her ability to ensnare and victimize men is also emphasized by the golden snake armlets that she wears when Xerxes kisses her in his lavish tent. By contrast, Gorgo wears minimal make-up, no jewellery,[63] and has her hair tied in a plain high bun. This knot has a symbolic meaning. It underscores Gorgo's

[57] This stereotypical choice of colours in the *pepla* is a device for generating an immediate response from the viewers. 'The audience must recognize immediately which characters to side with' (Ghigi 1977: 738). Quoted from Günsberg (2005: 103). On these colours in the *peplum*, see also Wood (2005: 72).

[58] This is a piece of advice that Artemisia provides to Xerxes after his defeat at Salamis. See Hdt. 8.102.

[59] Herodotean narrative equates Artemisia to another aberrant figure in the ancient gender system, Athena. See Vignolo Munson (1988: 94).

[60] An orientalized and sexualized queen is often depicted as a man-eater in *peplum* films. See, e.g., Lagny (1992: 175–6); Günsberg (2005: 119–25); Shahabudin (2009: 206–11).

[61] For make-up styles in historical epics, see Annas (1987: esp. 59, 61–3) and Llewellyn-Jones in this volume.

[62] On the assimilation of the heroine in epic films to Medusa, see Vivante in this volume.

[63] On the use of jewellery by Spartan women, see Pomeroy (1995: 38); Hodkinson (2000: 229).

Figure 11.2 Artemisia (Anne Wakefield) in the tent of Xerxes (David Farrar) in *The 300 Spartans*, dir. Rudolph Maté.

modesty and denotes that, as opposed to a dissolute Eastern queen, she, a wife/queen in the Greek West, is restrained, held together.

Gorgo and Artemisia are crafted to represent two different models of femininity: procreative/domestic *vs.* recreative/extra-domestic.[64] Artemisia has five battleships under her command when she sails from Halicarnassus to Greece. In terms of gender, the ship is in direct opposition to the feminine. It is the 'locus for all-male-labor, comradeship and merriment, a male community on the move'.[65] Throughout the film, she wanders in the barracks, a strictly male domain. Artemisia has autonomy and affords to defy gender stereotypes because her land is female-led. As Herodotus relates, when her husband died, *she* held the royal power, although she had a young son, and joined Xerxes' expedition against Greece not out of coercion, but because of her 'manly courage' (ἀνδρηίη). Her aberrant behaviour impresses Herodotus[66] to such an extent that he calls her θῶμα (marvel) (7.99). By contrast, Gorgo, coming from a man-led city, is confined in the house. She and her niece Ellas engage in the typical duties of women in classical antiquity, spinning and weaving (Fig. 11.3). This picture, however, is in sharp contrast with ancient accounts, according to which Spartan women, elite and non-elite, were freed from domestic labour that was performed by enslaved Helots from the neighbouring region of Messenia.[67] In Maté's film, just as in Snyder's

[64] This is a standard polarity in the *peplum*. See Günsberg (2005: 119–32).

[65] Günsberg (2005: 125).

[66] It is worth noting that Herodotus was also from Halicarnassus. His account, therefore, might not be objective.

[67] See Hodkinson (2000: 227); Pomeroy (2002: 30–2); Kennell (2010: 86).

Figure 11.3 Gorgo (Anna Synodinou) and Ellas (Diane Baker) spinning and weaving in *The 300 Spartans*, dir. Rudolph Maté.

300, Sparta is depicted as a slave-free society in order to suit modern utopian perceptions of it as an embodiment of egalitarianism.

Gorgo is cast as a loyal wife. Like Penelope, she stays at home and patiently waits for her husband to return from the emergency meeting of the leaders of Greek city-states at Corinth. When Leonidas enters the palace, he is so concerned that his plan to march north to Thermopylae was met with resistance by the Spartan Council that he forgets to greet his wife. Leonidas returns to Sparta only to depart again. The film thus aligns masculinity with mobility, and femininity with fixity. This is a common narrative trope in the *peplum* films. As Maggie Günsberg points out: 'While domestic femininity depends on the return and presence of its patriarch, heroic masculinity defines itself in diametric opposition to and absence from the private sphere.'[68] Leonidas apologizes to Gorgo for forgetting to greet her. Like a good, submissive wife, she takes no offence and tells him: 'And you haven't asked about your son.... Today he fought with his toy sword against a boy a whole head taller than him and defeated him.' Raising a boy to become a soldier who will fight for Sparta emphasizes Gorgo's character as a caring, responsible mother and a patriotic woman.[69] At the same time, begetting a son, and heir, highlights Leonidas' hegemonic masculinity. Gorgo refers to the boy not as 'our son' but '*your* son', thereby casting herself as a procreation vessel, a vehicle whereby primogenitary succession—the bedrock of

[68] Günsberg (2005: 115).

[69] On the equation of womanhood with motherhood in ancient Sparta, see Pomeroy (2002: 57–62).

patriarchy in Greek antiquity and western societies—continues uninterrupted.

The construction of Gorgo as a domesticated woman should be understood within the broader sociopolitical context in which the film was produced. *The 300 Spartans* has been read as a metaphor for Cold War global politics and the rivalry between, on the one hand, the US and its NATO allies, represented by the united Greek city-states, and, on the other hand, the USSR and the Communist Bloc, represented by the wicked Persians.[70] One of the main doctrines promoted in the US after the end of World War II was that of Containment. Coined by American diplomat and political adviser George Kennan in 1947, the term referred to the efforts of the US administration to prevent the spread of communism in non-communist countries—to 'contain', that is, communism within its borders. The adoption of this foreign policy paralleled the rise of a domestic politics of containment that saw the home as the very site in and by which to contain and regulate the desires of American men and women. The construction of such a space necessitated a recasting of traditional gender roles that had been disrupted after the Great Depression and World War II. As Elaine May explains:

> The Great Depression of the 1930s brought about widespread challenges to traditional gender roles that could have led to a restructured home. The war intensified these challenges and pointed the way toward radical alterations in the institutions of work and family life. Wartime brought thousands of women into paid labor force when men left to enter the armed forces. After the war, expanding job and educational opportunities, as well as the increasing availability of birth control might well have led young people to delay marriage or not marry at all, and to have fewer children if they did marry.[71]

Cold War victory, at the level of production and consumption, required the reinforcement of traditional American manhood achieved through the re-assumption by men of the role of the breadwinner and the return of women to the house.[72] By the early 1950s, American popular imagination associated communism with seductive and voracious femininity.

[70] See Clough (2004: 374–8); Levene (2007: 386, 392; 399–400); Lillo Redonet (2008: 120–1); Blanshard and Shahabudin (2011: 105–7).

[71] May (2008: 5–6).

[72] On 24 July 1959, at the height of the Cold War, American Vice President Richard Nixon and Russian Premier Nikita Khrushchev met at the US Trade and Cultural Fair in Moscow and had an impromptu 'Kitchen Debate'. Leaning on the railing in front of a model General Electric oven, they debated capitalism and communism by referencing both nuclear weapons and washing machines. At one point, Khrushchev said: 'Your capitalistic attitude toward women does not occur under Communism.' Nixon replied: 'I think that this

For example, in Mickey Spillane's novel *Kiss Me Deadly* (1952)—adapted into a classic *film noir* in 1955—women who serve as secret agents for the Russians are portrayed as taking advantage of men who are unable to resist their sensual powers. *The 300 Spartans* uses a similar scenario with Artemisia deploying her dynamism and appeal to victimize Xerxes. This scenario suggests that the Persian Empire, and by extension the Communist Bloc, is a world where the women are men and the men are women and slaves. This world threatens to overcome Greece/the US, the place of tradition and normality.

> Such popular-culture images suggested that any effective containment of communism would require the containment of femininity and an assertion of the traditional gender hierarchy. The Cold War thus provided powerful impetus for a pronounced cultural emphasis on conventional domesticity as a pillar of American life.[73]

Gorgo is fashioned to suit this ideology of the Cold War era. Her containment, however, does not mean that she is completely passive. To the contrary, the house becomes the site of her agency and social action. During the palatial ceremony in which the young Phylon (Ellas' fictitious boyfriend) is recognized as a Spartan warrior, Gorgo entrusts him with the shield and recounts the following Spartan laws:

> You must treasure freedom above life. Shun pleasure for the sake of virtue. Endure pain and hardship in silence. Obey orders implicitly. Seek the enemies of Greece wherever they may be, and fight them fearlessly, until victory or death. Now taking the place of your dead mother, I'm giving you this shield. There are but these five words to remember: *Ἢ τὰν ἢ ἐπὶ τᾶς*.

Drawn from Plutarch (*Mor.* 241.16) who puts it into the mouth of an anonymous Spartan mother, the famous aphorism *Ἢ τὰν ἢ ἐπὶ τᾶς* (either this or upon this, either come back victorious with your shield or dead upon it) aims to add credibility to this fictitious scene and highlight Gorgo's role as an agent through whom moral values are transmitted across generations. Gorgo displays an awareness of the onus that her position as a queen places upon her and acts as an initiator of young men into the symbolic order and the obligations of manhood.

By contrast, the Gorgo of *300* lacks a strong sense of morality. The film recreates the scene from Miller's comic book in which she hands the shield to her husband upon departure for Thermopylae and utters

attitude towards women is universal. What we want to do, is make life more easy for our housewives.' On this famous debate, see the essays in Oldenziel and Zachmann (2009).

[73] Winter (2003: 100).

the exhortation a Spartan mother would supposedly give her son when he was about to go to war. On the one hand, the scene reduces gender to biology, casting Gorgo as both mother and wife, and highlights her fertility by placing this encounter in a wheat field, thereby evoking the stereotypical equation of women with the earth. Like a woman, the earth gives birth, but at the same time opens up to receive the dead soldier. In this scene, therefore, Gorgo becomes a symbol of both life and death, both womb and tomb. On the other hand, she emblematizes the nation and addresses her husband not by his name but as 'Spartan', thereby imposing upon him the obligation of loyalty to and defence of his motherland. This initial casting of Gorgo as a symbol of the family and the state is undermined in the rest of the film. By offering herself to Theron in exchange for political support, Gorgo breaks away from the symbolic order to which she basically owes her position as a queen and ceases to operate as a paradigm of virtue and integrity, attributes for which she stands out in Herodotus (5.49–51)[74] and Plutarch (*Mor.* 240.1–4). Simply put, the Gorgo of *300* is cast as Sparta's first lady, but in the end fails to act like a lady.

GORGO IN THE POST-9/11 ERA

Although Gorgo is cast as an iconic woman in *The 300 Spartans*, a symbol of the private and the public, she plays a minor role in the diegesis. As Maureen Molloy notes about the ambiguous representational status of first ladies in film, their inclusion in the script is, paradoxically, fundamental yet peripheral.[75] Once Leonidas leaves Sparta for Thermopylae, Gorgo is nothing but a memory. She disappears from the screen to re-enter the narrative as a name at a crucial juncture, after the first battle between the Greeks and the Persians. A servant sent by her arrives at Thermopylae to deliver a secret message to Leonidas: the Council decided not to send troops to back him up, but instead to fortify Isthmus, the passageway to the Peloponnese. Melting the wax that covers the surface of the wooden tablet in one of the area's many hot springs in order to reveal the message, Leonidas comments: 'My wife is a very clever woman. Even if the messenger had been captured, no one would have guessed that there was a message hidden under the wax.' Based on an

[74] For an interpretation of this Herodotean anecdote, see Dewald (1981: 105); Hazewindus (2004: 15–41, 237–43).

[75] Molloy (1999: 160). See also Linville (2004: 69–70).

anecdote narrated by Herodotus (7.239),[76] this brief episode reproduces the stereotypical association of women with cunningness and deception. At the same time, in keeping with post-war gender ideology, it illustrates the traditional exclusion of women from the sphere of formal politics, thereby echoing the patriarchal belief that history is made only by men.

By contrast, to inspire female identification,[77] Gorgo is granted a much more prominent role in Snyder's film. *300* extricates the Spartan queen from her marginal position in Frank Miller's androcentric narrative and undertakes to restore her as a distinct historical entity, albeit in a manner that results in a reductive symbolization similar to that in Maté's film. While Miller devotes only a page to Gorgo in his graphic novel, 'Snyder's *300* introduces [her] as the political... equal to Leonidas.'[78] Not only does she leave the house to join Leonidas in meeting Xerxes' messenger at the Spartan *agora*. Acting like a peer[79] rather than a subordinate wife, as is the case with her precursor in *The 300 Spartans*, she stands beside (and not behind) her husband, as she scornfully addresses councilman Theron who accompanies the stranger. When the Persian emissary demands earth and water as tokens of Sparta's submission to the will of Xerxes, Gorgo replies quite boldly: 'Do not be coy or stupid, Persian. You can afford neither in Sparta.' In Miller's book, it is Leonidas, the epitome of the alpha male, who warns Xerxes' envoy of the city's indomitable spirit. Putting these words in Gorgo's mouth instantiates the parity of gender that the film, inaccurately, casts as a characteristic of early 5th-century Spartan society.[80] Unaccustomed to women expressing themselves in public fora, the Persian ambassador asks insultingly: 'What makes this woman think

[76] The exiled Spartan king Demaratus informed his people of Xerxes' plan to march against Greece by inscribing the message on a wooden tablet and melting wax over it. When the tablet arrived in Sparta, the Lacedaemonians could not guess its meaning until Gorgo advised them to scrape the wax away and find the message hidden underneath.

[77] See Cyrino (2007a: 4); Scriver (2009: 187).

[78] Cyrino (2011: 23).

[79] As Frank Miller comments in the *Special Features* DVD, 'she and Leonidas had what I suspect was more a partnership than a marriage'.

[80] While elite Spartan women retained the freedom of speech within the household, the right to enter the *agora* or the Council was an integral part of male citizenship. Plutarch (*Pyrrhos* 27.2) narrates that during the siege of Sparta in 273 BC, Archidamia, mother of King Agis IV, appeared before the Council with a sword in her hands to reproach the Elders for proposing to rescue the women by sending them to Crete. Gorgo, too, draws a sword and kills Theron in the Council. The Archidamia anecdote, however, is an example of female intervention in political affairs from the third century BC and cannot be used as evidence for the status of Spartan women during the early fifth century. Furthermore, Archidamia acts as a representative of all Spartan women, as opposed to Gorgo who represents a single case. See Hodkinson (2004: 119, 125).

she can speak among men?' Gorgo's response is an ancient aphorism that is detached from its original context and is inserted in the script to underscore her otherness: 'Because only Spartan women give birth to real men.'[81]

The modern issue of women's empowerment and involvement in decision-making processes informs this scene all the way till the end. To punish the blasphemous intruder, Leonidas kicks him into a bottomless pit. For a minute, however, he has second thoughts and looks to his wife for approval.[82] Gorgo remains still, but then nods her head, thereby endorsing an act that will have serious repercussions for Sparta and Greece as a whole.

Snyder's Gorgo is as dynamic and outspoken as she is beautiful[83] and seductive. She exudes both regal authority and sex appeal. Her look is carefully crafted, reproducing contemporary aesthetics of femininity: long, sleek hair—a defining part of a woman's appearance in commercials and magazines—full lips, perfectly shaped eyebrows, and an enhanced mole on the cheek—a beauty mark popularized by Marilyn Monroe and more recently by Cindy Crawford. While Maté's Gorgo is dressed in *peploi* that highlight her modesty and respectability, the Spartan queen of *300* shows off her skin freely. In the scene in which she appears before the Council in order to persuade its members to send reinforcements to her husband at Thermopylae, she wears a dark brown gown with long sleeves that cover her arms. This conservative, classy outfit accentuates her position as Sparta's 'first lady' and the respect she commands, and at the same time reproduces modern stereotypes about power dressing and the external appearance of women in male-dominated environments. With this sole exception, in the rest of the film Gorgo wears sensual,

[81] This aphorism is attributed to Gorgo when an anonymous woman from Attica asked her why Spartan women are the only women who are able to exercise power over their men. See Plut. *Mor.* 240.5.

[82] The second time Leonidas seeks guidance from Gorgo is when he must decide whether or not to obey the oracle that forbids him from marching to Thermopylae. Gorgo advises him: 'It is not a question of what a Spartan citizen should do, nor a husband, nor a king. Instead ask yourself, my dearest love, what should a free man do?' Commenting on both scenes in the *Special Features* DVD, Butler notes: 'What I love about Leonidas is he is probably the most decisive character I've ever played. But in his moment of indecision, he needs backup. He needs a second opinion. He needs assurance. He looks both times to his wife.'

[83] The myth of Helen helped shape a certain perception about Spartan women in the Greek world. In Homer (*Od.* 13.412) Sparta is called *καλλιγύναικα* (a land of beautiful women) although the epithet applies to other regions as well (e.g., Achilles' Phthia). See Hughes (2005: 55–67). In the seventh century, the Delphic oracle declared: 'Of all the earth, Pelasgic Argos is best, and Thessalian horses, and Lacedaemonian women' [quoted from Pomeroy (2006: 362)]. The ascription of beauty to a woman named Gorgo is, of course, paradoxical. In Greek mythology, Gorgo was an alternate name for Medusa, the epitome of ugliness in the classical world. The serpentine look of Medusa is reproduced through Gorgo's braids that are shaped like the coils of the snake at the back of her head.

white gowns that leave her shoulders, back, cleavage, hips, and (one of her) legs exposed. Her dresses combine soft fabrics (that skim over and accentuate her curves) with hard materials, such as leather straps and metal details—a combination evocative of her feminine and masculine side, her double identity as lover and warrior, both doll and Amazon.

This image of Gorgo projected in *300* is not without contemporary sociopolitical overtones. Just as her 1962 counterpart is domesticated to suit the Cold War ideology of Containment, so too Snyder's Gorgo is cast as an emancipated woman, in terms of looks and personality, to serve as a vehicle whereby the film reproduces, and at the same time seeks to capitalize upon, the post-9/11 coding of the West in mass media as a place where all people, regardless of gender, enjoy freedom of movement and speech, as opposed to the oppressive Islamic Orient where basic human rights are violated.[84] Gorgo is fashioned to act as a counter-icon to women in Muslim societies who must comply with a very strict dress code and conceal their entire body, sometimes even their eyes and hands, under a dark-coloured shroud called hijab (also known as abaya, burqa, or chador—depending on the style and region) that negates individuality and personal freedom. Gorgo's autonomy and intrusion into the male domain serve as a reminder that in certain countries in the Islamic world women are not even allowed to drive or appear in public without their male guardian. The only chance they have to break away from the muteness and invisibility to which religious laws have condemned them is, as media in the West often portray them, when they are deployed by militant organizations to act as suicide bombers. Gorgo, on the other hand, emerges as a utopian symbol for women in western societies, illustrating that they can successfully negotiate their relationship to established power structures and gain political representation equal to that of their male peers.

Gorgo's construction as a 'phallic woman' is, nonetheless, undermined in the rest of the film. To influence the Council, she needs help from Theron. Although she gains an opportunity to address its members, she fails to convince them to send reinforcements to her husband at Thermopylae. The film, therefore, reconstructs an idealized version of the past to call attention to issues of a problematic present and show that, although women in western societies have advanced their position in the political and professional domains in recent decades, they still have to operate within a sociocultural system with strong patriarchal roots,

[84] The polarity between the liberal West and the despotic East dates back to the fifth century. See Hall (1989). For interpretations of Snyder's *300* along this ideological axis, see, e.g., Basu et al. (2007); D'Arcens (2009) (with further bibliography); Scriver (2009); Žižek (2009: 68–71).

which considers the production of history and power as the province of males. As in *The 300 Spartans*, the Gorgo of *300* is resurrected from the pages of ancient history and is inserted in a film narrative, which is concerned more with the problems of the present than offering an accurate picture of the classical past. Although both films have nothing reliable to say about the position of women in ancient Sparta, investigating the various ways in which the past and the present interact with each other on the screen illustrates the central position that classical antiquity occupies in contemporary thinking, its catalytic role in shaping modern identities and the production of ideologies in western societies.

12

Representing Olympias: The Politics of Gender in Cinematic Treatments of Alexander the Great[1]

Kirsten Day

INTRODUCTION

For a movie director interested in historical epic subjects, Alexander the Great seems an obvious choice: he was a charismatic conqueror whose short life was full of action and adventures that covered nearly the entire then-known world. Yet ironically, films focused on the life of a man universally known by the epithet 'the Great' have been both few in number[2] and disappointing in execution. The two most prominent of these, Robert Rossen's 1956 *Alexander the Great* and Oliver Stone's 2004 *Alexander*, were critical[3] and commercial failures despite their big

[1] I am grateful to Augustana College for generously providing the funding which helped to advance the research on this paper. Thanks as well to Elizabeth Carney, Konstantinos Nikoloutsos, and Marilyn Skinner for providing me with copies of their then-forthcoming work.

[2] The first appearance of Alexander in cinema was the 1941 Bollywood film *Sikander* directed by Sohrab Modi (Nikoloutsos 2008: 244 n. 4). There have since been a handful of less prominent Alexander productions, such as a 1964 TV pilot starring William Shatner, and a number of Alexander projects that never got off the ground—most notably, Baz Luhrmann and Martin Scorsese were each contemplating major motion pictures based on Alexander at the same time Stone was formulating his film. Robert Rossen's *Alexander the Great* and Oliver Stone's *Alexander*, however, are the only two major motion pictures based on Alexander's life that have reached the big screen. For an overview of various Alexander projects, both finished and never completed, see Reames-Zimmerman (2004: 12) and Nisbet (2006: 87–135).

[3] Not only was *Alexander the Great* a 'box office bomb', *The Harvard Lampoon* proclaimed it the worst film of 1956, and Richard Burton himself apologized for it: 'I know all "epics" are awful, but I thought *Alexander the Great* might be the first good

budgets[4] and clear attempts at epic grandeur. In addition, classicists and historians have criticized both directors for omitting or conflating important historical events.[5] But regardless of their popular and critical reception, films focused on subjects from antiquity can, when viewed with scholarly detachment, offer valuable information about the events and cultures they nominally depict, while analysis of points of deviation from the facts as they are presented in the historical record can provide important insights into our own society's values and perspectives. Because both Rossen and Stone purportedly aim for a high degree of historical accuracy in general,[6] each director succeeds in bringing some

one. I was wrong' (*Tatara* n.d.). Stone's film, likewise, was poorly received for the most part: the assessments of *LA Times* movie critic Kenneth Turan—'*Alexander*, Not-So-Great' (2004)—and Baylor University's Carol King—'*Alexander* the Great Disappointment' (2004)—are typical. There were some critics, however, who received each film more positively: for instance, the Directors Guild of America nominated Rossen's *Alexander* for 'Outstanding Directorial Achievement in Motion Pictures' (Tatara n.d.), and Reames defends Stone's film in her article 'Fire-bringer' (n.d.).

[4] Rossen's film was budgeted at 2 million dollars but far exceeded that cost (Casty 1969: 33; Tatara n.d.). Stone's *Alexander* cost $155 million to make and grossed just over $34 million in the US and $133 million abroad (www.boxofficemojo.com, accessed 11/30/08, noted in Nikoloutsos 2008: 244 n. 2; see also Scott 2004b). Stone (2010: 337–8) argues that despite its domestic failure, the film could be considered a success in foreign markets.

[5] Borza (2004: 1) assesses Rossen's *Alexander the Great* as 'not a good film', citing, among other problems, ahistorical sets along with other historical inaccuracies; Carney (2010: 141), too, criticizes Rossen's sets, contrasting their authenticity unfavourably when compared to Stone's surprisingly accurate recreations of material culture in general (Angelina Jolie's wardrobe, as Carney 2010: 154 and Llewellyn-Jones 2010: 250 note, excepted). Both Reames-Zimmerman (2004: 13, 15) and Llewellyn-Jones (2010: 248–51) also overview historically accurate details in Stone's *Alexander*; places where Stone took what can be considered reasonable liberties for pragmatic or artistic reasons; and other areas where his choices are less well-justified.

[6] Solomon (2001a: 42) calls *Alexander the Great* 'one of the most historically faithful of all movies about the ancient world and perhaps one of the most intelligent, too', noting that it includes a number of memorable episodes recounted in Plutarch's *Life of Alexander*. Others disagree: for instance, while acknowledging that Rossen's film was intended as 'a bid for the "real" Alexander', towards which end Prince Peter of Greece was enlisted as historical advisor (Nisbet 2006: 91), Nisbet suggests that 'Greece's Prince Peter has done little to earn his cheque' (2006: 97); on *Alexander the Great*, see also Nikoloutsos (2008: 224–8). For Prince Peter's involvement with *The 300 Spartans*, another movie anchored in Greek history, see Nikoloutsos (2013: 265 n. 10) and in this volume. Stone enlisted eminent Alexander scholar Robin Lane Fox as his historical advisor, and together, according to Borza (2004: 2), they sought out the 'scholarly expertise of Lane Fox's Oxford colleagues and other British experts'. While critics have often taken Stone to task for having the 'temerity' to frame himself as a historian (Rosenstone 2000: 27), Stone has vigorously defended himself against this charge (Stone 2000: esp. 40), insisting that film is not the same as written history and that those who contend that he equates the two have prompted misunderstandings and unfair criticisms of his work (Toplin 2000: 6); perhaps in response, Stone's film includes a disclaimer 'tagged onto the end of the interminable credits' noting that the film is merely

aspects of Alexander's life and times to light. For classicists interested in the lives of women in antiquity, the portrayal of Olympias in these films is of particular interest. Each director to some extent succeeds in illustrating how women like Olympias exerted both direct and indirect influence in a patriarchal culture where women typically served as pawns in men's power struggles. At the same time, both filmmakers mould historical realities—through subtle choices of emphasis and omission, as well as through conscious alterations of the historical record—to reflect a contemporary vision of gender dynamics in accordance with current social agendas or personal concerns.[7] By analysing the depiction of Olympias and related male-female relationships in these two films, I aim to show both where they succeed in suggesting how women navigated positions of power and to identify where modern notions of gender dynamics take over, resulting in an anachronistic vision of how women functioned in this era.

THE HISTORICAL OLYMPIAS

While women in classical period Athens were almost totally disenfranchised, in the transitional society of fourth-century BCE Macedonia, fewer restraints were placed on women's lives.[8] In the royal family in particular, we begin to see evidence of women achieving power by promoting male alliances—both overtly and through stereotypical 'women's methods' such as intrigue, deception,[9] and when necessary, through their sexuality. Our ancient sources indicate that Alexander's mother Olympias is one of the earliest and most prominent participants in this sort of power

'inspired by certain historical events' (Borza 2004: 2; see also Chaniotis 2008 for a defence of Stone's choices as a filmmaker depicting historical subject matter). Among others (see esp. Petrovic 2008), Carney (2010: 140) has noted that both filmmakers draw not only on Plutarch and Justin—reputable ancient historical sources, but those most interested in character and 'lurid storytelling'—rather than on Arrian's somewhat drier account, but also on *The Alexander Romance*, a rather fanciful ancient novel based on the life of Alexander.

[7] While films are by nature collaborative efforts, both directors exert an unusual amount of control over their productions: shortly after World War II, Rossen established his own production company for this very reason (Tatara n.d.). Stone, similarly, develops his own projects, focusing on subjects in which he has personal interest. In addition, each man served as both director and scriptwriter for his Alexander project, and Rossen additionally produced his film and did his own research (Shahabudin 2010: 103). Few 'Hollywood artists', as Toplin (2000: 9) puts it, have 'such an extensive beginning-to-end personal and emotional investment in their projects'.

[8] Pomeroy (1990: 8–11); Carney (2000: 3–4).

[9] Carney (2006: 23).

politicking.[10] Although our sources disagree on the issue, for example, she may have prompted her son's belief that he was fathered by the god Zeus-Ammon[11] in a bid both to promote his reputation and to whet his ambitions. She also managed to pass on her Aeacid identity to her son in spite of the strong patrilineal nature of Macedonian society, so that her own reputation was elevated when Alexander identified himself as an Aeacid.[12]

Nor were Olympias' machinations limited to relatively harmless information manipulation and identity politics. Determined to ensure Alexander's succession, she likely arranged the murder of Philip's last wife Cleopatra and her newborn child. Although uncertain, it is possible that she also was involved in the assassination of Alexander's father Philip, whose timely death made way for her own son's immediate succession to the throne. During Alexander's reign, Olympias also played a more public, if less dramatic, role in the politics of the Macedonian state. For instance, having received plunder from her son, she made offerings at Delphi, and along with her daughter, she distributed grain when there was a shortage.[13] Some sources, in fact, treat Olympias and her daughter, as Elizabeth Carney puts it, 'like heads of state',[14] while others suggest that she had a hand in public policy.[15] After her son's death, Olympias worked as a succession advocate for her infant grandson Alexander IV. To this end, she was certainly responsible for the deaths of Alexander's mentally-deficient half-brother Philip Arrhidaeus, who was recognized as king together with Alexander IV, and his wife Adea Eurydice, along

[10] Because of her connections with Alexander, our information on Olympias is more extensive than that found on most ancient women; at the same time, as Nikoloutsos points out in his article in this volume, it is difficult to construct a credible portrait of women from antiquity from ancient sources which are often biased or work from some sort of agenda.

[11] According to Arrian *Anab.* 4.10.2, Alexander's official historian Callisthenes alluded to Olympias' lies about Alexander's birth. Plut. *Alex.* 3.2, citing Eratosthenes, says that as Alexander prepared to embark on his campaign against the Persian Empire, Olympias took him aside and told him something secret about his birth and urged him to act in accordance with his lineage; on the other hand, Plutarch adds that others say Olympias denied playing a part in this story and in fact asked Alexander to stop slandering her to Hera; noted in Carney (2010: 137–8). While Carney herself questions the issue, many scholars have concluded that Olympias was the source of the idea of her son's divine origins.

[12] In Arrian *Anab.* 1.11.8, for example, Alexander says that he was descended from the *genos* of Neoptolemus; noted in Carney (2010: 137). See also Arr. *Anab.* 4.1.26; Just. *Epit.* 11.2.1, 12.15.1, 16.3; Paus. 1.9.8; Curt. 8.4.26; Diod. 17.1.5; Strab. 13.1.27.

[13] Carney (2010: 138).

[14] Carney (2010: 138) citing *SEG* IX 2.

[15] Hyp. *Eux.* 19–20, 25 noted in Carney (2010: 138).

with numerous members of a rival political faction.[16] Her efforts on her grandson's behalf, in fact, extended to leading an army to Macedonia in the hopes of eliminating rival threats to his position. When this effort failed and she was captured, she faced execution 'like a queen in a tragic drama'.[17]

As such, Olympias used every means traditionally available to her as a woman—and some that were not—in order to promote the succession of her heirs, playing power politics even to the death. These efforts, however, should not be attributed to selfless maternal instincts alone. Olympias' advocacy of her offsprings' interests served her own, since it enhanced her own power, wealth, and prestige as well.[18]

OLYMPIAS IN ROSSEN'S *ALEXANDER THE GREAT*

Despite a number of problems, the first part of Rossen's film, as Eugene Borza has argued, is 'a serious study of Macedonian court intrigue... based squarely on Plutarch's *Life of Alexander*, and it is a faithful rendering of that ancient biographer not only in spirit but also in many details'.[19] Accordingly, Rossen's Olympias is a strong, charismatic character who effectively negotiates for power using the three primary avenues available to women: information management, male kinship connections, and her own sexuality.

Rossen depicts Olympias as grooming Alexander's reputation and his disposition towards greatness from the moment he is born. First, she cultivates the notion that Alexander is the son of a god by sending notice of his birth to Philip with the message: 'To Philip: Hail and rejoice. On this day to Olympias, your queen and wife, a god was born.' It is made clear, moreover, that it is Olympias herself who is promoting this notion. When Philip asks, 'A god?', he is told, 'Those were the queen's words.' When Philip returns from the battlefield and meets his son for the first time, she reinforces this idea: when Philip proudly calls Alexander 'Little lion', she corrects him: 'Little god'. And when Philip asks the meaning of the omen of a falling star that Olympias' Egyptian soothsayer has said accompanied Alexander's birth, Olympias replies, 'That a god was born to me... of a god.' Like Alexander's historical mother, Rossen's

16 Carney (2010: 137). 17 Carney (2010: 139).

18 Carney (2010: 139). For a fuller account of Olympias' life, see Carney (2006).

19 Borza (2004: 1). See again Petrovic (2008) and Carney (2010: 140) for more on Plutarch as biographer rather than historian.

Olympias attempts to bolster her own position and power by providing her son with mythic kinship connections. Rossen's implication that the Egyptian soothsayer is her lover,[20] in addition, suggests the possibility that Olympias is using her sexual charms to obtain his 'professional' backing for her scheme to propagate the mythology surrounding her son. Olympias also uses her sexuality to exert power over her husband. By suggesting that she has taken an Egyptian lover and perhaps conceived a child by him, Olympias places Philip in an awkward position: admitting he has been cuckolded would damage his reputation. Indeed, Parmenio suggests that she revels in having asserted herself in this way: 'What she herself thinks I don't know, but this I do know: she's a woman and she taunts you.'

Olympias also draws her son into her web of identity politics. Even in his crib, Olympias works to shape Alexander's view of himself, comparing him to Achilles and telling him that like the Homeric hero, he shall be greater than his father. It is later made clear that Olympias is cultivating her son's belief in his divine paternity when Alexander asks his mother point blank if the throne is his by right of birth, and she offers a corrective: 'By *divine* right.' Rossen implies that Alexander has absorbed these lessons when the young man tells Aristotle that like Achilles, his life will be short and glorious, and again when he reads to his friends excerpts from the *Iliad* concerning Achilles' glory. Aristotle confirms that Alexander has ingrained Olympias' suggestions of his divinity when he later says to Philip: 'Alexander is many things . . . he's your son, but he's also hers. And he believes himself to be a god.' In working thus to shape the self-image and public perception of her son, Olympias lays the groundwork for obtaining a measure of real power for herself, and she does so in two of the traditional ways available to women of this time: through the manipulation of information and by capitalizing on her male kinship connections.

As Alexander comes of age and prepares to assume his place as Philip's regent, Olympias' attempts to obtain power through her son become more overt. When Alexander enters Pella, she tells him, 'Philip has gone mad! . . . He accuses everyone of conspiring against him. Even me . . . ,' explaining that Philip wants to get rid of her so that he can marry again. She advises Alexander, 'Whatever he asks of you, do. Whatever he says, agree with. For when you're regent—when you're regent, then we'll rule.' Philip, too, recognizes that as a woman, Olympias' primary means

[20] This Egyptian lover is a non-historical figure Rossen has borrowed from *The Alexander Romance*, on which see Carney (2010: 147); Shahabudin (2010: 109).

of exerting power is through her male kinship connections. He warns Alexander, 'She can only rule through you. You are her power. And her pawn.' According to Philip, her efforts on Alexander's behalf once again take the form of information manipulation—he reports that she has been fostering rumours that the Macedonian army is defeated and that Philip himself is dying or dead[21]—and by capitalizing on male kinship connections—she has enlisted the support of her brother, king of Epirus, whose army now threatens Macedonia.

Olympias' intrigues in Rossen's film, however, are not restricted to fomenting rumours. After Alexander's friend Pausanias is publicly humiliated by Attalus, Olympias uses her feminine wiles to manipulate the young man, redirecting his anger toward Philip and implanting the idea that assassinating Philip will bring him glory. When Alexander overhears and questions her about her intentions, she sows in him seeds of doubt about Philip, telling him that Philip has named his new son by Eurydice[22] 'Karanos' after the king who first founded the Macedonian royal family[23]; 'What's in Philip's mind?' she asks. After Pausanias acts on her suggestion and kills Philip, Rossen makes clear that it is Olympias who is to be viewed as responsible when Alexander in disgust throws the bloody dagger at her feet. Nor is this the only death in which Olympias has a hand: when Eurydice dies soon after Philip's assassination, Attalus tells Alexander that although the record will read that it was a suicide, in truth Olympias was behind both Eurydice's death and that of her newborn son.

Not only do the broad strokes of Rossen's portrayal of Olympias' actions find their origins in our ancient sources; Rossen's Olympias is also ruthless, ambitious, and politically savvy, characteristics that accord reasonably well with the historical record. At the same time, whereas the textual record suggests that Olympias herself was not an exceptionally sexual person,[24] the presence of an ahistorical Egyptian lover, Danielle

[21] Olympias later confirms that Philip's accusations are true: 'Who else should I have fought for except you? What other love do I have? There *were* rumours of his death. He *was* being defeated. There were others who put forth their claim to the crown.'

[22] Most sources call Philip's last wife 'Cleopatra', but Arrian *Anab.* 3.6.5 refers to her as 'Eurydice' (noted in Carney 2010: 146, et al.). Both Rossen and Stone employ the name 'Eurydice', perhaps because Cleopatra was also the name of Alexander's sister, but also to avoid confusing an audience for whom the name 'Cleopatra' would immediately call to mind Cleopatra VII of Egypt.

[23] Both films make Eurydice's child male; although ancient sources are contradictory (see Athen. 13.557d; Paus. 8.7.7; Just. *Epit.* 9.7.12, 11.2.3; Diod. 17.2.3), most scholars agree that there was time for only one baby, most likely the girl mentioned in Athenaeus. See, e.g., Carney (2010: 161 n. 48).

[24] Carney (2010: 141).

Figure 12.1 Olympias (Danielle Darrieux) with her son Alexander (Richard Burton) in *Alexander the Great*, dir. Robert Rossen.

Darrieux's suggestive performance, and an iconographical presentation of Olympias as a 'femme fatale'[25] imply a connection between Olympias' lust for power and her sexuality. For example, her appearance in the scene where Alexander is appointed regent—following which she voices her own ambition to rule alongside him—emphasizes her demonic, man-devouring character. The spiral locks of her ponytail paired with her green dress with its multiple-button closures on the shoulders that expose her skin beneath imply Olympias' serpent-nature, while her diadem with its horn-like projections give her a lethal, demon-like quality (Fig. 12.1). Later, in the scene where she plants the idea of Philip's assassination in Pausanias' head, Olympias wears a similar outfit, but this time, the dress is bright red, associating her with the blood Pausanias will soon spill, while her relaxed, reclining pose and her calculated pouring of wine enhances the image of her as sexually dangerous. Even her listing in the credits as 'the French Star Danielle Darrieux' seems designed to capitalize on Western notions of French women as sexually appealing and voracious when compared to their more modest and chaste English-speaking counterparts.

In addition, although Alexander's life was undoubtedly shaped to a large extent by his relationship with his two very colourful parents, Rossen's depiction of this hero is influenced by anachronistic notions of

[25] For further discussion of the iconography of the *femme fatale*, see Nikoloutsos' discussion of the visual presentation of Gorgo and Artemisia in this volume.

Freud's Oedipus Complex.[26] Our historical sources indicate that the young Alexander was indeed eager to get out from under his father's wing and seek a measure of glory for himself. For example, when Pixodarus, satrap of Caria, sent to Philip seeking to make a military alliance through a marriage connection between his own daughter and Philip's feeble-minded son Arrhidaeus, Alexander intervened, sending an envoy in the hopes of redirecting Pixodarus' offer to himself. When Philip found out, he upbraided Alexander severely and brought back his envoy in chains (Plut. *Alex.* 10.1–3). Alexander and his mother also undoubtedly enjoyed a close relationship. In addition to engaging in political jockeying on her son's behalf, Olympias is also cast as a doting mother in the ancient sources; Plutarch, for instance, tells us that, much to his tutor's consternation, Olympias used to hide delicacies for Alexander in his chests of bedding and clothes (*Alex.* 22.5). While there is, therefore, reason for seeing Alexander's relationship with his father as somewhat strained and that with his mother as particularly close, Rossen's depiction strays too far into the anachronistic territory of Freudian psychology.

Throughout the film, Rossen's Alexander, like the historical one, is eager to distinguish himself as a military and political leader distinct from his father. However, in Rossen's depiction, this ambition is cast as a resentment that is both overly dramatic and too heavily emphasized. Although, to his credit, Rossen is restrained enough to leave Alexander's role in Philip's assassination ambiguous,[27] that he conceived of this hostility as Oedipal is suggested by his comment that the longer version of his film, which originally ran for three hours, was better, since it 'unveils the various guilts Alexander felt towards his father much more deeply—for instance his chase of Darius. It is not just a simple chase to kill the Emperor of the Persian Empire. The chase for Darius is tied up with his tremendous feeling that as long as a father figure is alive in royalty, he has to kill him.'[28] Likewise, there are subtle suggestions in the film that the close relationship Alexander shares with his mother crosses the boundary into Oedipal territory as well, such as Barsine's comment to Alexander that 'No other woman is my rival—except your mother . . . '.

Thus, his attention to historical authenticity notwithstanding, Rossen's conception of Alexander's character seems to be shaped by the intervening influence of Freudian psychology. Although the use of Freudian themes

[26] Freudian overtones in Rossen's film have also been recognized by Shahabudin (2010: 98–100).

[27] See Solomon (2001a: 43).

[28] Quoted in Casty (1969: 34) and Tatara (n.d.).

in films set in classical antiquity is not uncommon, such artistic licence is problematic, for, as Jeanne Reames notes, 'despite its Greco-mythic title, the "Oedipus Complex" is modern Freudian—not ancient Greek—and it certainly didn't apply to a Macedonian court that practiced royal polygamy'.[29] In addition, Marilyn Skinner has pointed out that 'despite his varied proclivities, biographers depict Alexander as essentially moderate and disciplined in his appetites (at least up until his final years), and particularly self-controlled regarding sex'.[30] Victor Hanson, on the other hand, argues that 'it's less likely that sex was at the root of Alexander's relationships with his mother Olympias and his companion Hephaistion, and his various liaisons with Eastern princesses, than that Alexander was—unlike his lusty Macedonian compatriots—rather asexual'.[31] Because of its anachronistic nature and its unsuitability to Alexander's character, Rossen's depiction goes too far in subtly characterizing these parent-child dynamics as manifestations of Oedipal tensions.

ADDITIONAL CONSIDERATIONS OF GENDER IN ROSSEN'S *ALEXANDER THE GREAT*

Despite contamination by modern psychological notions, Rossen's portrait of Olympias, as noted above, adheres more or less to ancient traditions regarding both her character and the roles she played in Macedonian court intrigues. In addition to the depiction of Olympias, several other aspects of Rossen's film suggest an attempt to provide a relatively accurate portrayal of gendered relations in the ancient world. For instance, references to Philip's multiple marriages are in line with the Macedonian practice of polygamy. This issue, far from being skirted, is indeed emphasized when Alexander first tells Philip's future wife Eurydice, 'my father, as you know, has had many wives and mistresses and many children by them', and then later repeats, 'My father, as I said, had many wives and mistresses.' Because Olympias is 'divorced' before Philip weds Eurydice, his marriages might be understood as serial rather than concurrent[32]; nonetheless, in 1956, at a time when the Production Code

[29] Reames (n.d.). [30] Skinner (2010: 130). [31] Hanson (2004).

[32] As Carney (2010: 161 n. 46) notes, 'No ancient author apart from the frequently mistaken Justin (who does not understand polygamy) suggests that Philip divorced Olympias . . .'. See Athen. 13.557d; Plut. *Alex.* 9.4–5; Just. 9.7.5–7.

was in full force,[33] the presence of Philip's multiple partners is a daring point to foreground and effectively illustrates for contemporary viewers ancient practices which are at odds with modern notions of gender relations and morality.

Rossen's film also effectively suggests the political nature of marriage in the ancient world. For instance, as he is dying, the Persian king Darius writes to Alexander and offers him the hand of his daughter, suggesting that the union will help unite Macedonians and Persians through their mutual offspring. Darius' suggestion thus reinforces Rossen's framing of Alexander's conquests as a somewhat noble attempt to bring diverse peoples together and bring superior Hellenic culture to less enlightened societies. This idea is further strengthened by Rossen's identification of Darius' daughter as Roxane, who was historically the daughter of Oxyartes of Bactria, and by the transference of Alexander's marriage to Roxane to the mass ceremony at Susa where Alexander compelled more than eighty Macedonian officers to take brides from Persian and Median noble families (Arrian *Anab*. 7.4.4–5). The political nature of the union is further emphasized by the juxtaposition between the silent and passive Roxane and the outspoken, forthright Barsine, who is clearly Alexander's primary romantic interest.[34] While Alexander's affair with Barsine is supported by the historical record,[35] she is there but a minor character. By bringing her to the forefront, Rossen underscores the pragmatic nature of his marriage to Roxane through a contrast. While Alexander's union with Roxane helps, in some way, to illustrate the difference between marital practices then and now, at the same time it points to Rossen's concern with keeping his hero in line with modern sensibilities. By conflating Roxane with Stateira, the eldest daughter of Darius III, and Parysatis, youngest daughter of Artaxerxes III Ochus, both of whom

[33] Noted in Nikoloutsos (2008: 225); for more on the Hays Code, see also Nikoloutsos in this volume.

[34] Because the Hays Code was in effect during the filming of *Alexander the Great*, the sexual aspect of Alexander and Barsine's relationship is not shown explicitly (Nikoloutsos 2008: 225). The scene in Miletus where Alexander wakes up in bed while Barsine finishes dressing, however, has strong post-coital implications. Nisbet (2006: 97–8) notes that the current tendency towards prudishness also led Rossen to purge references to nudity, particularly male nudity, from his film; for instance, sculptures are fig-leafed, put in shorts, or deprived of their genitals altogether 'to appease contemporary sensibilities' (Nisbet 2006: 98).

[35] Noted in Plut. *Alex*. 21.4. Barsine was involved with Alexander in 332 or 331 BCE after Parmenion captured her at Damascus following the battle of Issus. Ancient sources indicate that it was a sexual relationship, but not a marriage. She reportedly bore Alexander a son named Heracles (Nikoloutsos 2008: 244 n. 9); see also Carney (2000: 101–5 and 149–50).

Alexander in actuality took to wife at Susa (Arrian 7.4.4–5), Rossen reinscribes Alexander as a monogamous hero who meets with contemporary notions of morality.[36]

Similarly, Rossen disambiguates Alexander's sexuality in order to accommodate 1950s mores. Ancient sources report a close and intimate relationship between Alexander and his companion and age-mate Hephaestion (Curt. 3.12.16). While this relationship seems to have had a sexual component during adolescence, modern scholars disagree as to whether or not this persisted into adulthood.[37] Whatever the nature of their adult relationship, Alexander's sexuality does not seem to have fallen outside of norms for Macedonian society.[38] Their intimacy and the well-known suggestion of its sexual nature, however, made the person of Hephaestion problematic for contemporary homophobic audiences. Rossen, therefore, plays down Hephaestion's importance in Alexander's life as far as is possible without omitting him entirely. In *Alexander the Great*, he is mentioned but once, and then in conjunction with a handful of Alexander's other generals and companions. As Nisbet puts it, 'Rossen's enthusiasm for historical name-checking mandates his inclusion... [but] his Hephaestion is a nonentity, a gaping absence in the narration.'[39] By acknowledging Hephaestion's existence, Rossen maintains an appearance of historicity, yet his elision from the larger narrative dodges the thorny question of the precise nature of their relationship and saves Alexander from the stain of association with what was seen as deviant sexuality. In order to accommodate the minimization of Hephaestion's role in Alexander's life, he transfers Alexander's excessive grief for Hephaestion's death to Cleitus, and takes the added precaution of emphasizing the platonic nature of their friendship by having Alexander repeatedly address Cleitus as 'brother'.[40]

For the same reason, Rossen omits from his narrative entirely the eunuch Bagoas, with whom our sources tell us Alexander also had a sexual relationship. As Marilyn Skinner notes, by Greek standards, this

[36] Nikoloutsos (2008: 224).

[37] For example, Reames-Zimmerman (1999: 93) argues that sexual activity between Alexander and Hephaestion was likely confined to adolescence. For more on this controversy, see Skinner (2010: 128–9).

[38] Nonetheless, both Reames-Zimmerman (1999: 81) and Skinner (2010: 120) point out that, while normal within its Macedonian context, Alexander and Hephaestion's relationship does not fit the expected criteria for ancient sexual practices. For an overview of ancient sexual expectations and practices in classical antiquity, see Skinner (2010: 120–6). Both Reames-Zimmerman (1999: 84ff.) and Skinner (2010: 126–30) discuss exceptions to the accepted model and examine probable practices in Macedonia, as well as the relationship between Alexander and Hephaestion in particular.

[39] Nisbet (2006: 98).

[40] Nikoloutsos (2008: 227–8).

relationship is fairly unproblematic. As a foreigner from a subject population, an adolescent, and a eunuch, he 'fits impeccably' as the passive partner in the scheme of dominance/submission widely practised in the Greek world.[41] Yet since the very presence in Alexander's cohort of a eunuch, which does not fit neatly into rigid gender categories, runs contrary to 1950s expectations of manhood, he is simply written out of the script.

Rossen not only plays down or ignores any of Alexander's connections that might impune his manhood; as Konstantinos Nikoloutsos notes, he also takes pains to emphasize his masculinity by depicting him as attracted to and attracting every woman he interacts with, including his father's new wife Eurydice.[42] In addition, although Barsine, as noted above, receives little attention in the historical record, her role in Rossen's film is expanded and emphasized, becoming in fact the primary intimate connection of his adult life. Not only do they have a prolonged affair, but Barsine is also the only person who speaks her mind to him publicly with impunity. Indeed, she appears at his side on his deathbed as his most prominent mourner, even pushing to the side his legitimate wife, Roxane. As such, Rossen strives both to 'straighten' out Alexander's sexuality and to intensify it in order to present his hero in accordance with the hetero-normative expectations of his own day.

Thus, while in many ways Rossen's treatment of Alexander's life shows great concern for historical accuracy and complex characterization, contemporary standards of morality and the Hollywood Production Code then in force led to a reorganization of the details of Alexander's sexual life. The result was an unambiguously masculine heterosexual hero whose morals remain uncompromised by the same-sex interests and polygamous unions recorded by ancient biographers. The authenticity of the gendered framework of Rossen's film is thus itself compromised by current notions of morality that equate anything but unambiguous masculinity and heterosexuality with deviance. Moreover, Rossen may be subtly influenced, too, by his own personal identification with his hero. Alan Casty has recognized Rossen's affinity for characters that serve as models for his own life, noting that Rossen himself rose from poor beginnings to reach the height of his profession '[l]ike so many of his own heroes, entangled in the paradoxes of power and identity . . . '.[43] Kim Shahabudin, in addition, argues that Rossen's blacklisting in the early 1950s, as a result of his initial refusal to cooperate with the House Un-American Activities Committee, influenced his portrayal

[41] Skinner (2010: 128). [42] Nikoloutsos (2008: 224). [43] Casty (1969: 3–4).

of Alexander as an 'idealist misunderstood by his contemporaries'.[44] As such, his tendency to focus on young men like Alexander seems to stem from his own experiences and ideals.[45] Rossen's identification with Alexander would likely have led him to the sorts of alterations which would make him an acceptable hero to contemporary audiences.

This 'cleaning up' of Alexander's image, moreover, is not limited to his sexuality. Rossen also takes pains to emphasize Alexander's nobility of purpose as well. Alexander himself, in speaking to the Athenians, tells them that Greece is 'a nation with a destiny: a divine mission to bring Greek culture and civilization to all the world...'. As Eugene Borza notes, though this may have been a by-product of Alexander's conquests, it was 'not a component of his policy'.[46] In addition, Rossen promotes the idea that Alexander is a democratizing figure after the 'Brotherhood of Mankind' theory advocated by W.W. Tarn in the mid-20th century, an idea modern scholars have criticized as 'not being rooted in the evidence from antiquity'.[47] While this idea, as noted above, is suggested in his marriage to Roxane, it is most evident in the character of Barsine, who twice proudly announces that she is both Greek and Persian,[48] and who urges her husband Memnon not to join forces with the Persians, arguing that Alexander's victory will keep the glories of Athens alive. That Rossen purposefully attributed this 'noble purpose' to Alexander he makes clear in describing Alexander as 'A man born before his time, a catalytic agent, he emerged from an era of warring nationalisms to try for the first time in history to get the peoples of Asia and Europe to live together.'[49] In this way, despite an admirable willingness to show Alexander as a complex and often flawed character, Rossen takes pains to clean up his sexuality and imbue his ambition and his conquests with a noble justification, seemingly in response to current social considerations and his own personal need to elevate a character with whom he identifies on a more personal level.

[44] Shahabudin (2010: 112; see also 102–5).

[45] Casty (1966–7 and 1969: 3–4).

[46] Borza (2004: 4).

[47] Borza (2004: 4); see also Harrison (2010: 224ff.) for a discussion of the historical status of Tarn's ideas in light of the extant evidence. Cartledge and Greenland (2010: 6) note that while Alexander's personal agenda remains unclear, a more likely motivation from a propagandistic standpoint was 'revenge for Persian sacrileges committed on Greek soil a century and a half earlier'. See also Harrison (2010: 230–1).

[48] See Nikoloutsos (2008: 225) and Shahabudin (2010: 101). According to Plutarch *Alex.* 21.4, Barsine is the daughter of the satrap of Phrygia Artabazus, but received a Greek education (noted in Nikoloutsos 2008: 225).

[49] Quoted in Casty (1969: 33) and Tatara (n.d.).

OLYMPIAS IN STONE'S *ALEXANDER*

Like Rossen, Stone depicts Olympias as a strong, ambitious woman who actively pursues power by manipulating information, exploiting her sexuality,[50] and capitalizing on her relationship with her son. Like both the Olympias of the historical record and the heroine of Rossen's film, Stone's character attempts to connect her son, and thus herself, to mythological royalty by instilling in him the idea that Zeus, not Philip, is his father. She also promotes in Alexander a particular pride in his Aeacid lineage by alluding frequently to her descent from Achilles and referring to Alexander himself as 'my little Achilles'.[51] Furthermore, Stone's Olympias attempts to influence the goings-on in the royal court directly. She tries, for example, to convince Alexander that Philip's marriage to Eurydice will threaten his claim to the throne, and thus urges him to take action,[52] advising him not only to strike back against Philip, but also to repress his love for Hephaestion and marry a noble Macedonian girl so that he can beget an heir and secure his claim to the throne before he leaves for Asia. To her dismay, Alexander defends both Philip and his love for Hephaestion. Accordingly, Stone makes Olympias alone responsible for Philip's death, insisting that Alexander himself had no knowledge of the plot beforehand.[53] After Alexander leaves for Asia, Olympias' continued participation in politics is demonstrated through their correspondence, wherein she offers him political advice and informs him of court intrigues.

In this way, Stone attempts to depict Olympias as a 'hardened political player', as he puts it in his Director's Commentary. At the same time, however, like Rossen, he has clearly been influenced by Freud's Oedipal theories and sees Oedipal tensions as shaping the dynamic between

[50] Stone's emphasis on Olympias' sexuality, evident through both casting and costuming, can hardly be missed by even the most casual viewer.

[51] Carney (2010: 150–1) observes that ironically, because Stone more or less ignores the prominent place of Homeric heroes as cultural role models, 'Homeric values'—along with her attempts to promote her son's connection with Achilles—'become simply and idiosyncratically those of Olympias.'

[52] Most explicitly in Chapter 21. In discussing Stone's film, I am following the widescreen special edition Director's Cut.

[53] According to Carney (2010: 147), while it is a real possibility that Olympias may have engineered Philip's assassination, it is unlikely that Alexander knew nothing of it. Carney also points out that Stone's film downplays the possible involvement of other figures associated with the Macedonian royal court and provides only a watered-down hint ('a spanking scene with sexual undertones') of the gang rape of Pausanias, Philip's actual assassin, who was motivated to act by Philip's failure to punish the offenders. Plut. *Alex.* 10.4; Diod. 16.93.7–8; Arist. *Pol.* 1311b; Just. *Epit.* 9.6.5–6; noted in Carney (2010: 161 n. 44).

mother and son.[54] By contrast, in Stone's film, as opposed to Rossen's, the Oedipal overtones do not remain subtle and largely in the background. Instead, Stone purposefully overemphasizes the sexual nature of the relationship between Olympias and Alexander and associates a ridiculous number of snakes with Olympias to visually drive home his Oedipal agenda.[55] As a result, his film becomes less the story of Alexander and his historic conquests and more a character study in Freudian psychology.[56] Indeed, as Stone makes clear in the Director's Commentary, his primary objective in this film is to explore Alexander's psychological motivations by setting forth the nature of his relationships with his parents as Oedipal. Interestingly, he later seemed baffled to learn that many scholars see his application of Freudian psychology to the ancient world as problematic, reasoning that 'Freud clearly acknowledged that many of his theories were based on Greek myth'.[57]

In order to further his Oedipal agenda, Stone's film includes a series of barely restrained physical interactions between mother and son that come to a climax when Alexander confronts his mother about whether or not she had a hand in Philip's death. As tensions build, Alexander protests that he did not want Philip to die, and expresses violent impulses towards his mother. When she reminds him that Zeus is his father and advises him to act like it, he responds, 'My first act would be to kill you. You murdered me in my cradle; you birthed me in a sack of hate.' Stone implies, however, that these violent feelings are largely an attempt to repress his sexual attraction to his mother: when Olympias asks Alexander if he has learned nothing from Philip's death, he responds, 'No, from you mother,' and gives her an aggressive, sexual kiss on the lips.

Equally as telling is Stone's use of Roxane.[58] While Alexander's marriage to Roxane is outwardly framed as a politically motivated attempt to

[54] In an interview, Stone notes that in his film, Alexander 'does "marry" his mother as Oedipus did, without knowing it, and when he kills Cleitus, he unconsciously is murdering his own father' (Crowdus 2005: 19; see also 20).

[55] Plutarch *Alex.* 2.6 says that Olympias used snakes in cult practices; since this is not adequately demonstrated in the movie (noted in Carney 2010: 151), however, Olympias' attachment to snakes becomes primarily a means of characterizing her as a dangerous other and of driving home Stone's Oedipal theme. I would note, however, that Stone himself asserts that he is merely using them to characterize her as a 'lonely woman', much as some people today—like his own mother—keep cats or dogs. See Crowdus (2005: 19; see also Director's Commentary, Chapter 20).

[56] The Oedipal elements in *Alexander* have been widely recognized: see, for example, Reames (n.d.); King (2004); Borza (2004: 5); Crowdus (2005: 13); Pierce (2008: 58); Petrovic (2008: 175–83); Carney (2010: 156); Platt (2010: 291).

[57] Crowdus (2005: 16).

[58] Borza (2004: 3) notes that Stone's depiction of Roxane deviates considerably from the portrait drawn in the ancient sources: 'Alexander's Bactrian wife Roxane was hardly the

democratically unite diverse peoples[59]—demonstrating that like Rossen, Stone has been influenced by Tarn's notion that Alexander was driven by a 'noble purpose'[60]—the obvious implication is that the union is equally motivated by subconscious Oedipal desires. Stone drives this message home to viewers through the casting of Rosario Dawson as a counterbalance to Angelina Jolie's Olympias. In his Director's Commentary, Stone makes plain that he intended the audience to see Roxane as an avatar of Olympias when he comments that '[Angelina is] a strong woman, as is Rosario' and notes that Roxane's 'accent . . . somewhat reflects Angelina's outsiderness, her ethnicity',[61] thereby effectively making Dawson's Roxane into 'the equivalent of his [Alexander's] mother, Olympias'. Stone reinforces this connection visually by giving Olympias and Roxane similar snake bracelets, each of which is removed and placed on a bedside table in parallel scenes where Alexander is in bed with the woman in question—with Olympias when he is a child, and with Roxane on their wedding night.[62] Lest the viewer miss these hints, Stone highlights his intention through dialogue: after their wedding, Alexander describes Roxane as 'a pale reflection of my mother's heart',[63] while Olympias herself asks her

tempestuous vixen of the Oliver Stone film. Historically she seems to have been a devoted wife and mother, content to play her traditional female role of producing children for the king, one of whom may have died in India as an infant, the other born after Alexander's death in 323 BC.'

[59] Ptolemy's statement in Stone's film that Alexander's marriage to Roxane had 'no political significance' both contradicts this implication, and is an overstatement: while not of royal blood, Roxane was the daughter of a Bactrian chief, and this marriage connection was intended to mollify the inhabitants of an area he was having a difficult time controlling.

[60] Borza (2004: 4) has noted that Stone's and Lane Fox's 'shared a need to give meaning to Alexander's conquests, even when there wasn't any' which led them to fall back on 'that tired old saw, a version of [Tarn's] Brotherhood of Mankind theory . . . '. See also Crowdus (2005: 14), Nisbet (2006: 128), and Harrison (2010: 220–4). In an interview with Crowdus, Stone himself confirms this by speculating that Alexander was 'the first globalist' who 'probably came to believe in the concept of "one world, one king"—with himself as the king, of course, as an enlightened monarch, the ideal Greek philosopher-king' (2005: 15; see also 23). For Stone's response to criticism of his inclusion of Tarn's notions, see Stone (2010: 339–41 and 345–8). For an alternate perspective, see Reames (n.d.), who argues that Stone 'deliberately undercut[s] Tarn's optimistic fiction'.

[61] Chapters 20 and 32. Carney (2010: 154) suggests that because both Jolie's and Dawson's accents are fictional whereas those of all the male characters in the film are real, the implication is that 'Stone and the two actresses saw their characters as less real, less historic than the male roles'.

[62] In Chapter 3, Olympias removes her snake-bracelet and places it on a bedside table before she lies down with the young Alexander; in Chapter 20, Alexander notices his new bride Roxane's snake bracelet and removes it, placing it on a bedside table before he joins her in bed. Stone makes explicit note of the similarity in these bracelets in his Director's Commentary (Chapter 20).

[63] Chapter 20.

son in a letter, 'Who is this woman you call your queen, Alexander? Do not confuse us.' If even these suggestions are too subtle, Stone includes a scene which makes his meaning unmistakable: when Alexander attacks Roxane after Hephaestion's death, he splices the scene with footage from Philip's near-rape of Olympias at the beginning of the film.[64] Alexander's implication that Roxane plotted to kill Hephaestion, moreover, not only further aligns the two women, but also deprives the historical Roxane—who may instead have plotted to kill Alexander's Persian wife in order to ensure her own son's right of succession—of political acumen, attributing her motivations, as he did with Olympias, to mere sexual jealousy instead.[65]

Thus, while Stone's Olympias exhibits ambition, intelligence, and political savvy, her value as a model for how women might have negotiated positions of power for themselves in fourth-century BCE Macedonia is overwhelmed by the prominence of his Oedipal agenda.[66] In addition, while both Angelina Jolie's Olympias and Rosario Dawson's Roxane are framed as strong women, their strength is situated to a large extent in their sexuality. Elizabeth Carney takes Stone to task for this, complaining that he 'compound[s] the sexual stereotyping of women in general and Olympias in particular that is already present in virtually all the ancient sources (and often uncritically accepted in modern scholarship) by introducing new sexist elements into the saga'.[67] This characterization is particularly inappropriate, moreover, in the case of Olympias, who, as noted above, our ancient sources suggest was not a particularly sexual person.[68] Interestingly, Stone undercuts even this source of power with scenes where first Olympias and later Roxane come near to being raped.[69] In

[64] Chapter 35. Stone again demonstrates that his Oedipal overtones were consciously inserted in his Director's Commentary: 'He never attacks his mother, but he attacks Roxane. In so doing, he resembles his father' (Chapter 35).

[65] See Carney (2010: 155–6).

[66] Carney (2010: 139), in fact, argues that the 'development of the character of Olympias and what proved to be the limitations of the portrayal of that character lay at the heart of Stone's film, and (I believe) at the heart of its commercial and artistic failure'.

[67] Carney (2010: 141). Later in the same volume, Stone responds to Carney's criticisms and defends his characterization (2010: 338–9).

[68] Carney (2010: 141–2). Carney (2010: 142–4) locates the origins of this characterization in the Greek *Alexander Romance*.

[69] In Chapter 4, Philip attacks Olympias, who is saved when the young Alexander's shouts alert the servants. In Chapter 20, Alexander forcibly takes Roxane on their wedding night, but her initial resistance later shifts to consent. In Chapter 35, Alexander attacks Roxane after Hephaestion's death in a scene where Philip's earlier attack on Olympias is explicitly referenced; Roxane is saved when she informs Alexander that she is carrying his son. Thus, interestingly, both women are only 'saved' from violent male attack by their function as vessels for male offspring.

doing so, he emphasizes Olympias' victimhood and suggests that the motivation for her actions is sexual vengeance rather than political expediency.[70] In fairness, the Persian queen Stateira is represented as a noble female figure whose strength is not located in her sexuality; but at the same time, her character is left undeveloped, and the minimal screen time devoted to her is framed by images of Darius' concubines posing seductively for Alexander and his men[71] and by the overbearing presence of Olympias herself.[72] Thus, the prevailing image of women's power in Stone's *Alexander* is a predominantly reductive one: that of the sexualized, domineering, anxiety-provoking Oedipal mother.

Stone likewise suggests in Alexander a corresponding Oedipal resentment towards his father. Although he avoids the implication that Alexander played a role in Philip's death, Stone suggests Alexander's Oedipal hostility by framing the character of Cleitus as a proxy for his father. According to ancient sources,[73] Alexander was incited to anger when his longtime companion Cleitus questioned his policies, and the resulting argument ended with Alexander taking Cleitus' life. In recreating this episode, Stone takes the opportunity to suggest that Cleitus functions as a psychological surrogate for Philip by having Alexander imagine his father momentarily in Cleitus' place. Not insignificantly, Alexander's rage turns murderous in Stone's film when Cleitus says, 'You and your barbarian mother live in shame.' Thus for Stone, Alexander running Cleitus through with a spear becomes a clear manifestation of Oedipal resentment,[74] an agenda he acknowledges, once again, on his Director's Commentary: 'Cleitus becomes the proxy of the father, kills his father, marries his mother, Oedipus—knowledge that came too late.'

In light of Stone's self-proclaimed interest in historical accuracy, his conscious choice to insert an anachronistic Oedipal theme seems somewhat puzzling. However, comments on the director's cut suggest that his concern with Oedipal tensions may have more to do with Stone himself than with his historical subject,[75] in that he hammers away incessantly at

[70] See Carney (2010: 145).

[71] Despite Stateira's noble and virtuous depiction, Llewellyn-Jones (2010: 273–4) demonstrates that 'the women of the Persian court'—Stateira included—'are used only as visual stimuli, and the true nature of the harem in the Achaemenid period—the role royal women played within the power structure of the inner court and, by extension, the empire—is entirely overlooked in favour of hackneyed "Oriental" images'.

[72] Chapter 14.

[73] Curt. 8.1.22–52; Plut. *Alex.* 50–1; Arrian *Anab.* 4.8.

[74] See Reames (n.d.).

[75] Nisbet (2006: 132) suggests that for Stone's historical advisor Robin Lane Fox, too, this project tapped into personal wishes and desires to the extent that his identification with the character compromised his objectivity: 'Lane Fox himself... entered a magically

the dominant role the mother plays in a young man's life. He comments, for instance, that Olympias 'defines [Alexander's] limits', that 'the mother is undermining the relationship with Roxane', and that 'His mother won't let him go... the mother is always there, like a consciousness, pulling him away from his wife, making it almost impossible for him to have a satisfying relationship with Roxane.' In the end, Stone rationalizes his perspective by saying, 'I think mothers have a lot to do with these stories, as do fathers too. The mother, the father, they shape our destiny....'[76]

Additionally, Stone's preoccupation with the image of a strong, domineering mother is not limited to the film under consideration here. As Susan Linville notes, 'The cinema of Oliver Stone is replete with images of bad mothering....'[77] In her examination of Stone's 1995 film *Nixon*, Linville demonstrates that Stone presents Pat Nixon as 'a double for the dreaded phallic mother to whom she is opposed, yet with whom the film at times also aligns her'. This conceptualization is most evident in a scene showing Pat admonishing Nixon about the infamous tapes: 'a shot from his point of view reveals [his mother] Hannah's uncanny image effacing Pat. Nixon, it is implied, cannot hear his wife's criticisms without hallucinating that Hannah's cold, penetrating eyes are judging him, an experience represented as fraught with the castration anxiety that Freud's analysis of the uncanny details.'[78] Interestingly, the editing here is reminiscent of that in the scene in *Alexander*, discussed above, where Alexander imagines Philip in Cleitus' place in the course of their deadly argument. Additionally, in *Nixon*, as in *Alexander*, the early influence of the mother is positioned as so character-forming that it shapes not only the psyche of the son, but the very direction of global events.[79] And in both films, Stone connects the mother's influence to the

rejuvenating second adolescence. Leading the charge and looking over the daily rushes, he was finally confirmed in what he had said all those years back in his 1973 biography of Alexander. Only a chap of his own all-round calibre (gentleman and scholar, polymath, rider to hounds) could hope to understand what had made the real Alexander tick....' He goes on to note that 'Lane Fox's old-school insistence on an objective and fact-bounded "real" Alexander ends up delivering a passionately *personal* Alexander, a larger-than-life and richly imagined persona...' (2006: 133).

[76] Director's Commentary, Chapter 39 (end credits). Stone, in fact, dedicated the film to his own mother (noted in Carney 2010: 149).

[77] Linville (2004: 67).

[78] Linville (2004: 70, 73).

[79] Although Nixon's own account suggests that Stone's portrait of Nixon's relationship with his mother might have a basis in reality (Linville 2004: 162 n. 1), Stone's characteristic choice of subject matter and emphasis is telling. Linville cites 'the indictment of the soldiers' mothers in *Born on the Fourth of July* (1989) and *Heaven and Earth* (1993)—not to mention

development in the son of sexual proclivities that are positioned as outside the norm.[80] Elizabeth Carney attributes the recurrence of such mother issues in Stone's films to 'the writer-director's own unhappy early experiences'.[81] In this way, Stone's Oedipal agenda seems to tell us more about his own personal anxieties than about those of Alexander the Great.[82] Overall, the value of Stone's portrait of Olympias and its usefulness in informing audiences about how women in the Macedonian court negotiated power is greatly compromised by this anachronistic Oedipal agenda.

ADDITIONAL CONSIDERATIONS ABOUT GENDERED DEPICTIONS IN STONE'S *ALEXANDER*

Stone's film is problematic in its depiction of sexuality and gendered power structures in other ways as well. To begin with, Stone has been heavily criticized by the gay community for his ambiguous presentation of the precise nature of the relationship between Alexander and Hephaestion. Despite his insistence, according to Warner Brothers' president Alan F. Horn, that 'Alexander was a bisexual character',[83] gay viewers were disappointed that the intimacy between Alexander and Hephaestion was not presented as explicitly sexual.[84] For instance, in Chapter 16, Alexander expresses his great love for Hephaestion, but the awkward hug that follows where we would expect a passionate kiss implies that the two may be no more than 'Platonic soulmates', as, indeed, Stone refers to them in this scene's Director's Commentary. While

the auto-da-fe of Mallory's sitcom mom in *Natural Born Killers* (1994)' as supporting evidence (2004: 162 n. 2) for her characterization of Stone's career as 'matrophobic filmmaking with a vengeance' (2004: 68).

[80] Stone conceives Nixon-as-a-young-boy's submission to his mother's authoritarianism as shaping his own adult personality, and then links Nixon's authoritarianism to 'his lukewarm heterosexuality', dramatized through Nixon's retreat from Pat's advances (Linville 2004: 82). For more on Stone's conception of Alexander's sexuality, see below.

[81] Carney (2010: 149). Carney notes that Stone rejects the idea that the prevalence in his work of an estranged father and problematic mother stems from his relationship with his own parents. For more on these issues, see Carney (2010: 162 n. 54 and 55).

[82] Turan (2004), too, has observed that Stone's film suggests his close personal identification with Alexander, saying it 'plays like a fantasy self-portrait' of writer-director Oliver Stone.

[83] Waxman (2004).

[84] For more on the gay press's disappointment in Stone's depiction of Alexander's sexuality, see Nikoloutsos (2008: 229–30).

Stone's depiction is technically in line with the views of contemporary scholars who believe that based on information in extant sources, the precise nature of the relationship between Alexander and Hephaestion is unknowable,[85] classicists have criticized Stone's understanding of ancient sexual categories, the problems with which are suggested by his application of the term 'bisexual' itself to a figure from antiquity.[86]

The insistence on a 'historically accurate' depiction of Alexander's (bi-)sexuality[87] paired with a reluctance to make this explicit onscreen suggests that to some extent Stone wanted to have it both ways. He hoped to depict the 'real' Alexander without alienating contemporary audiences uncomfortable with heroes who do not live up to a hyper-masculine, heterosexual ideal. In addition, Stone's inclusion of a dysfunctional Oedipal relationship between Alexander and his mother and the extension of that dysfunction to his relationship with his wife seems subtly designed to allow him to 'get away' with his open portrayal of Alexander's sexuality, which Stone describes as 'trisexual' or 'pansexual'.[88] And despite his openness to presenting his subject with an alternative sexual orientation, Stone's comment that 'I wanted Colin to experiment with the bisexual nature of Alexander so he has to play the weaknesses that were in his character'[89] betrays a troubling attitude that positions deviation from clear-cut heterosexuality as a fault.[90] At the same time, Stone's film locates the origins of this 'weakness' in Alexander's relationship with his mother, replicating the modern stereotype of an 'inherent connection between an overbearing-doting mother and the identity of a conflicted homosexual man'.[91] By implying that the women in Alexander's life—especially Olympias—are the cause for his sexual orientation, Stone pursues an all-too familiar and hackneyed line of reasoning which gender studies scholars have been challenging for

[85] Skinner (2010: 129); see also Reames-Zimmerman (1999) and Cartledge (2004: 228).

[86] For more on how male sexual roles in Stone's film accord with ancient sexual practice, see Nikoloutsos (2008: 230–2) and Skinner (2010: 127–30).

[87] Horn relates Stone's interest in portraying Alexander as bisexual to his strong desire to be 'historically accurate' (Waxman 2004), an ironic association in light of the problems with describing a figure from the ancient world using a term derived from modern notions of sexuality.

[88] Director's Commentary: Chapter 14.

[89] Director's Commentary: Chapter 21.

[90] In addition, Stone's description of the eunuch Bagoas (Director's Commentary, Chapter 14) as 'a third species' suggests discomfort with minority gender categories as well.

[91] Vieron (2010: 6). Crowdus (2005: 13) and Reames (2010: 185) also note that Stone reduces Hephaestion to a one-dimensional soul mate for Alexander, erasing the important political and military roles he played, thereby further problematizing the depiction of this male-male relationship (see also Reames 2010: 185–7).

decades,[92] while at the same time ignoring the well-established scholarly recognition that these sorts of sexual categorizations did not apply in antiquity in the first place.[93]

Nonetheless, Stone deserves some credit for breaking with the expectations of sex and gender traditionally associated with heroic epic storytelling. As Nikoloutsos has observed, '[u]nlike Rossen ... Stone takes the ancient protocols of sexuality into serious consideration'.[94] For instance, Stone is bold enough to privilege Alexander's relationship with Hephaestion, whether or not it has an apparent sexual element, as more important to him than his connection to Roxane. In contrast to the great love that Hephaestion and Alexander profess for one another, Ptolemy's voice-over places love as the third and last reason for Alexander's marriage.[95] Moreover, on Alexander's wedding night, Hephaestion comes into the room and places a ring on the fourth finger of Alexander's left hand in a symbolic marriage; Nikoloutsos thus concludes that '*Alexander* does take a pioneering stand in regard to same-sex coupling by presenting the relationship between Alexander and Hephaestion as a romantic bond analogous to that of companionate marriage.'[96]

Stone's inclusion of the eunuch Bagoas—whom, as I mentioned above, Rossen omitted entirely—also merits acknowledgement. As noted earlier, Alexander's relationship with Bagoas, who clearly functioned as the passive partner in the dominance/submission scheme, accords readily with Greek sexual expectations.[97] Contemporary American audiences, however, are less comfortable with the presentation of a character

[92] As Richard Goldstein put it in a review from *The Advocate*, Stone's Alexander 'is a neurotic mess. He wasn't queer because same-sex love was honorable in his time but because he suffered from mother horror and father fixation—a good candidate for reparative therapy'. Quoted in Nikoloutsos (2008: 230).

[93] While Stone himself purports to recognize that there is a real difference in sexual categories in the ancient world (see Crowdus 2005: 22–3), he also betrays a misunderstanding of ancient perspectives when he applies the term 'bisexual' to ancient practices, as noted above, and again when he describes Alexander as having a 'fascinating blend of masculine and feminine qualities', citing the value he and other heroes placed on physical beauty, as well as the fact that 'they wrestled and ran around naked' (Crowdus 2005: 22)—attitudes and activities the ancients would surely not have viewed as effeminate.

[94] Nikoloutsos (2008: 231).

[95] Nikoloutsos (2008: 240–1).

[96] Nikoloutsos (2008: 243).

[97] Skinner (2010: 128). Nikoloutsos' understanding of Bagoas contradicts Skinner's: '... Bagoas's status as a eunuch marks him as a departure from the protocols of classical Greek homoerotics. Greek authors of the classical period had contempt for eunuchs as one of the many trappings of Asiatic despotism' (Nikoloutsos 2008: 232).

of ambiguous gender,[98] and Stone deserves credit not only for making him a presence, but for the clear implication of a sexual element to his relationship with Alexander. Although Stone cut from the theatrical release a scene where Alexander goes to bed with Bagoas, he retained one where the two engage in a sexually passionate kiss.[99] As Nikoloutsos observes, others, too, are 'implicated in this logic of sexual plurality and non-fixity of male desire'. Homoerotic kisses are also exchanged between Alexander and Cleitus and between Cassander and Perdiccas, while Philip himself rapes his future assassin Pausanias.[100] Although the details of Pausanias' rape are historically inaccurate, 'the act itself'—with Philip in the active role—'is compatible with the ancient protocols of sexuality', as are the aforementioned kisses.[101] Stone's film therefore has a 'much more diverse erotic agenda than the cinematic Alexander of the 1950s'.[102] Despite problems with historical accuracy and the anachronistic construction of gender and sexuality in this film, Stone's Alexander, unlike Rossen's, suggests to viewers unfamiliar with classical antiquity that the rigid gender categories and inflexible notions of sexual norms prevalent in America today did not necessarily apply in Macedonian society.[103] While Stone is to be credited for this, it is likely that his willingness to focus on a hero whose masculinity is less than clear-cut contributed to the failure of his film at the domestic box-office in particular. As Jon Solomon notes, *Alexander* 'was released during a period of homophobic frenzy in the United States', as evidenced by the

[98] Nikoloutsos (2008: 236) notes that Stone's Alexander, too, is marked by gender ambiguity. After he enters inner Persia, Alexander adopts Eastern ways, and for the rest of the film, he is 'constantly in drag', outfitted in blonde wigs and feminine clothing and wearing heavy jewellery and eye make-up.

[99] Waxman (2004). Nikoloutsos (2008: 233) points out, however, that Stone's Bagoas is silent and passive in direct contrast to the historical Bagoas, who was 'politically active despite his sexual passivity': he intervened with Alexander to save the life of Nabarzanes and convinced Alexander to sentence the satrap Orsines to death (Curt. 10.1.25–38 noted in Nikoloutsos 2008: 233).

[100] Nikoloutsos (2008: 229).

[101] Nikoloutsos (2008: 232). '[P]ederasty', Nikoloutsos goes on to observe, 'was a well-established practice in ancient Macedonia and aristocratic youths engaged in it, sometimes beyond adolescence.'

[102] Nikoloutsos (2008: 228).

[103] Carney (2010: 156) argues that 'Stone, despite his good intentions, fails to convey the normality of the relationship [between Alexander and Hephaestion] in the context of the ancient world.' While Carney's point may be valid when considering this relationship in isolation, I would argue that the overarching presentation of gender and sexuality in Stone's film does begin to hint at real difference in expectations between our culture and Alexander's.

vote to ban same-sex marriage in eleven states.[104] In addition to this climate of resistance to alternate sexualities in American society in general, Jerry Pierce demonstrates that Stone's characterization bumps up against generic expectations as well. Because his lead character 'shirks his heteroperformative duties and abandons himself to his decadent desires', Stone's presentation of Alexander not only runs counter to the audience's expectations of an epic hero, but is even aligned more closely with the typically 'feminized and tyrannical antagonists' of this genre.[105] While American audiences in general are increasingly tolerant of depictions of alternative gender and sexual identities in film and television at least on the margins, we still seem unwilling to accept such ambiguity in a central heroic male character.[106]

CONCLUSION

Modern productions on classical subjects inevitably come up short when scholars scrutinize them for historical accuracy. These works are more productively viewed as dialogues with the past which not only inform us about antiquity and why it continues to engage us, but also offer us an opportunity to learn about the present by examining where past and present intersect and deviate.[107] While both Rossen's and Stone's films through the character of Olympias offer insight into the dynamics of power and gender at play in Alexander's time, it is important to recognize the veneer of modern social and artistic agendas superimposed on historical realities so that we may better understand both the world of the historical Alexander and the impulses that continue to lead us to connect with classical subjects.

In both Robert Rossen's *Alexander the Great* and Oliver Stone's *Alexander*, the authenticity of the gendered framework is compromised by social considerations and the directors' personal agendas. Yet each film provides us with something of value in promoting an understanding of the ancient world. While Rossen's film suffers from the imposition of

[104] Solomon (2010b: 43).

[105] Pierce (2008: 62 and 54 respectively). See Pierce (2008) for a detailed examination of how Stone's presentation of Alexander is antithetical to the heroes of more commercially and critically successful films.

[106] Witness the omission of reference to participation in male-male relationships by figures like Achilles, Julius Caesar, and Mark Antony in recent works such as Wolfgang Petersen's 2004 *Troy* and HBO's 2005–7 series *Rome*.

[107] Joshel et al. (2001: 2); see also Day (2008: 3–4).

mid-20th century intolerance for alternative sexualities or questionable masculinities, at the same time, it not only offers us a reasonable facsimile of what the historical records tell us was Olympias' role in Alexander's early life, but also provides modern viewers with an inkling of how women in the ancient world in general, and in the Macedonian court in particular, might have negotiated positions of power by manipulating information, capitalizing on kinship connections, and utilizing their sexuality. Stone's film, in contrast, tells us far less about how Olympias in particular is portrayed in the historical record, and is less successful as well in showing how women exerted power in the ancient world. At the same time, Stone's film begins to get across the idea that our conceptions of sexuality and gender are not 'natural' and, indeed, they functioned far differently in the ancient world than they do today. Therefore, while both films undoubtedly have their flaws, each provides a small and useful glimpse into the particulars of women's lives in classical antiquity.

13

'An Almost All Greek Thing': Cleopatra VII and Hollywood Imagination

Lloyd Llewellyn-Jones

> Poor lady, resting in her queenly tomb. All these ages and ages she had little idea her system of vamping men of her time would pass down the centuries and be preserved in moving pictures.
>
> Louella Parsons, *Chicago Herald*, September 1917.

The focus of this chapter is the Hollywood portrayal of the life of the Ptolemaic Egyptian queen Cleopatra VII. I begin the investigation by drawing the reader's attention to a scene that opens the second half of Joseph Mankiewicz' 1963 epic movie *Cleopatra*. The setting is the royal precinct of Alexandria, where an Isis-crowned Cleopatra (Elizabeth Taylor), accompanied by her chief minister, the learned Sosigenes (Hume Cronyn), offers incense to a veiled golden statue of the dead and deified Julius Caesar. As she offers up her prayers, she contemplates her future relationship with Rome. In the scene Cleopatra wears a necklace composed of gold coins stamped with Caesar's image. The scene, as recorded in Mankiewicz' shooting-script,[1] runs as follows:

CLEOPATRA: (looking at the statue) Would [Caesar] have approved, do you think?

SOSIGENES: Definitely. Perhaps the veil of Isis would have bothered him just a bit –

[1] The final shooting script for *Cleopatra* is dated 18 September 1961, although in reality a definitive shooting script did not exist even after filming had ceased and the picture was being edited. Joseph Mankiewicz was occupied with major re-writes on a daily basis throughout the filming of *Cleopatra*. The process is chronicled in Wanger and Hyams (1963) and Brodsky and Weiss (1963).

CLEOPATRA: Three years. And Rome remembers him only by the image on a gold coin...

SOSIGENES: (looking at her necklace) Are they those I brought back with me? (Cleopatra nods) After all, when Octavian had them struck off, it was to commemorate Caesar's deification.

CLEOPATRA: So that he could inherit Caesar's divinity together with all the rest.
Even a dead god cannot rewrite his will.

SOSIGENES: Antony did present Caesarion's claims to the senate. He kept that much of his promise.

CLEOPATRA: He will keep the rest of it...

SOSIGENES: (doubtfully) After almost three years since Caesar's death—more than a year since Phillipi?

CLEOPATRA: Antony will come. He will need Egypt.

SOSIGENES: Egypt is you.

CLEOPATRA: That's what I meant, of course. Antony will need me.

In this scene, both Sosigenes and Cleopatra propound the idea that the queen is intimately identified with her kingdom; indeed, the notion that Cleopatra *is* Egypt lies at the very heart of the movie. In this respect, the film follows the popular preconception that Egypt and Cleopatra are perpetually unified. In fact, it is a vision which seems to have been endorsed by the historical Cleopatra VII *Philopator kai Philopatris*. Dorothy Thompson has argued that Cleopatra's choice of the royal epithet *Philopatris*—'The Queen Who Loves Her Country'—indicated that her loyalty lay not in her Macedonian heritage, but in her Egyptian identity; her *patris* was Egypt.[2] Her use of Pharaonic religious imagery and the Egyptian artistic legacy, as well as her ability to speak the Egyptian language, were clearly intended to promote her as the natural heiress to an ancient and glorious civilization, in the eyes of both her native Egyptian subjects and her foreign enemies. Most famously, on the exterior walls of the temple of Hathor at Dendera in Upper Egypt, Cleopatra VII commissioned twenty-foot high carved images of herself in traditional Pharaonic pose as the mother goddess Isis and of her offspring and heir, Caesarion, as the divine son Horus.[3]

[2] Thompson (2003).

[3] For Cleopatra VII's building constructions at Dendera, see Arnold (1999: 211–24). See also Ray (2003). For a good image of the Dendera relief, showing scale, see Hughes-Hallett (1990: plate 1). More generally for Cleopatra VII's use of Pharaonic imagery and her identification with Egypt, see Chauveau (2000: 102 ff.); Hölbl (2001: 271–93); Ashton (2008: 31–146); Fletcher (2008). Recently, seven Egyptian-style statues of Ptolemaic royal women have been re-identified as Cleopatra VII. See Ashton (2001a) and (2001b). However, some of the arguments for these identifications appear highly suspect. For comments on Ashton's identifications, see Bianchi (2003).

But when Elizabeth Taylor's Cleopatra is told, 'you are Egypt', no one thinks to correct the line to 'you are Greek-Egypt' or, better, 'you are a Macedonian who through historical right of conquest now reigns in Egypt'. Cleopatra is Egypt; but Cleopatra is not necessarily *Hellenistic* Egypt. The 'Greekness' of Cleopatra is subsumed beneath her Egyptian identity, while the Hellenistic world she inhabited is ignored altogether. 'Hellenistic' means very little to the average cinemagoer, simply because the Hellenistic period per se has never captured the imagination of filmmakers. In fact the Hellenistic world has been disregarded by Hollywood movie directors who have tended to cut off Greek history with the death of Alexander the Great (as portrayed by Richard Burton in 1956 or Colin Farrell in 2004) and pick it up again (but this time in a decidedly Roman context) with the accession of Cleopatra VII.

Hollywood clearly has difficulty in defining what 'Hellenistic' means. Since the period is characterized by a succession of interrelated Macedonian dynasties battling it out for space in a decidedly un-Greek world—Syria, Egypt, Asia Minor—Hollywood finds it difficult to classify the period both in terms of visualization and narrative. Hollywood does not know what to make of a hybrid culture. That is why when it does turn its attention to the Greek period of Egyptian history, its thirtieth Dynasty, and attempts to retell the story of Cleopatra VII, the queen is rooted, visually at least, not in the Hellenistic world at all, but in the Pharaonic past, and in the Egyptian New Kingdom (*c.*1550–1154 BC) to be more precise.

In this chapter I will explore popular twentieth-century images of the Egyptian queen as portrayed in the *Cleopatra* movies produced by Hollywood over six decades to see how this conception of Cleopatra as Egypt came about. Of course, Cleopatra has been a very popular icon with moviemakers since the rise of Hollywood. In fact, some of the earliest forays into epic filmmaking—Georges Méliès' *Cléopâtre* (1899) and the Italian *Marc Antonio e Cleopatra* (dir. Guazzoni, 1913)—took the Cleopatra story as their theme and created out of it a nationalistic spectacle of Roman moral probity versus Oriental decadence.[4] In this chapter, however, I want to touch on several renditions of the Cleopatra story produced by Hollywood studios,[5] namely the Fox Film Corporation's 1917 Theda Bara silent feature (directed by J. Gordon

[4] See Wyke (1997: 84–6).

[5] Therefore, I reluctantly eliminate the sublime British-made *Caesar and Cleopatra* (dir. Pascal, 1946) starring Vivien Leigh from this study. However, for a discussion see Hamer (1997).

Edwards, but which unfortunately only survives today in movie stills),[6] the 1934 Cecil B. DeMille motion picture staring Claudette Colbert (produced by Paramount Pictures), and the 1963 Twentieth Century-Fox epic staring Elizabeth Taylor and directed by Joseph Mankiewicz.

There are two aspects of the representations of Cleopatra that need to be addressed: first the question of the portrayal of the queen in film narrative and secondly her visualization in film design. These elements are interrelated and interdependent; both are fundamentally important aspects of the epic genre.

HOLLYWOOD'S 'INAUTHENTIC AUTHENTICITY'[7]: CLEOPATRA IN FILM NARRATIVE

How did the celluloid treatments of Cleopatra's history reflect her race, origin, and identity? While her *patris* might have been Egypt, nonetheless, Cleopatra VII's Macedonian ancestry and the importance of that lineage in the wide world of Hellenistic politics were crucial to the queen's public persona; the Greekness of Cleopatra VII, of the Ptolemies generally, and of their capital city, Alexandria, was of primary importance to the Ptolemaic system of government, to their culture, and to their ethics. The Pharaonic elements of kingship were important tools for the Ptolemies, but their Greekness was never completely subsumed beneath native Egyptian culture.[8] Their Greekness allowed the Ptolemies to function in a world of Greek rulers, a series of dynasties spread throughout the Mediterranean and the Near East, which were united by a common Greek language, ideology, and culture.

FILM NARRATIVE: *CLEOPATRA*, 1917

The loss of the negative of the 1917 *Cleopatra* film makes it difficult to reconstruct the plot outline or the treatment of Cleopatra's identity

[6] The American Film Institute lists Bara's *Cleopatra* among its top ten most important missing films. For a discussion see Thompson (1996: 68–78). Very recently a few seconds of footage have been rediscovered: http://www.imdb.com/news/ni0101658/ (accessed 25 September 2012). See further http://www.youtube.com/watch?v=OWn7L2pL5dI (accessed 25 September 2012).

[7] 'Inauthentic Authenticity' was coined by Solomon (2001a: 31).

[8] On this crucial interaction of Greek and Egyptian cultures, see especially the important work of Stevens (2003).

within the narrative structure.[9] However, newspaper reviews of the period generally assert that the film attempted to depict a faithful retelling of Cleopatra's life, noting, for example, 'The story, true to the main facts of history, shows the ambitious and beautiful Queen Cleopatra using her sex to juggle with the political history of Rome and Egypt.'[10] Maude Miller of the Ohio Board of Censors wrote enthusiastically that, 'The producers have followed history in a remarkable way.'[11]

Nevertheless, it would seem that the two love-affairs of the historical Cleopatra were not enough to satiate the lustful appetite of Theda Bara's vampish queen:[12] another (fictional) lover was introduced into the plot, a young man named Pharon (Alan Roscoe), the son of the Priest of Osiris, and the rightful (i.e. non-Macedonian) heir to the Egyptian throne. In the plot he leaves the city of Abouthis (probably Abydos) and heads towards Alexandria in order to rid Egypt of the licentious siren and to take over the reins of government. But gradually Pharon falls in love with Cleopatra, who at first treats him cruelly and spurns his love until he offers her one final service as a display of his passionate devotion—for it is Pharon who hands Cleopatra the fatal asp.

The 1917 *Cleopatra* is the only film to suggest political unrest and an ever-present nationalistic movement, which were consistent features of Ptolemaic history, although (admittedly) the plot seems to have utilized this political feature merely to play up Pharon's (unrequited) love story.[13] The loss of the negatives makes any further discussion difficult.

FILM NARRATIVE: *CLEOPATRA*, 1934

Despite the fact that the Alexandrian court is inhabited by persons with Greek names (Sosigenes, Pothinus, Apollodorus), the script for Cecil B. DeMille's 1934 portrayal of the life of the queen entirely underplays Cleopatra's ethnic origins.[14] In fact, it is difficult to place DeMille's Cleopatra in any kind of context, since we are told nothing of her background, and we are not even aware that she is from a long line of

[9] An attempt at reconstructing the plot is made by Thompson (1996: 68–70).

[10] *Motion Picture News* (5 January 1918: 102).

[11] *Motion Picture News* (5 January 1918: 102).

[12] For Bara's *femme fatale* Cleopatra, see Hughes-Hallett (1990: 267–72); Golden (1996); and Genini (1996: 39–41).

[13] For anti-Ptolemaic uprisings, see, for example, Hölbl (2001: 307–9).

[14] For a background to the making of the 1934 *Cleopatra*, see Birchard (2004: 275–82) and Louvish (2007: 321–31).

kings (of any race). Cleopatra is just Cleopatra. She does not need a history or a pedigree; for DeMille, the name speaks for itself and provides all the information necessary for this particular history lesson. As DeMille wrote in his autobiography, '[Cleopatra] was the imperious Queen. She was the vivacious, alluring woman. She was Egypt.'[15]

The screenplay by Waldemar Young and Vincent Lawrence consciously underplays Cleopatra's history prior to her meeting with Caesar (Warren William).[16] The script informs the viewer that she has a brother named Ptolemy (an amalgamation of the historical Ptolemies XIII and XIV), but the audience does not see him and there is certainly no hint in the movie that she follows Ptolemaic precedent and is married to him. The screenplay makes it clear that the young Cleopatra is caught up in some kind of court faction, but it does not provide any details, although the figure of Ptolemy's corrupt chief minister, the eunuch Pothinus (Leonard Mudie), looms large in the first quarter of the movie before he is killed off—not on the orders of Caesar though, but rather by the machinations of Cleopatra. The script is silent about the fate of the shadowy Ptolemy.

The first half of the film, the affair with Caesar, curiously condenses time and is plotted at breakneck speed. The proceedings suggest that upon landing at Alexandria, Caesar is ushered into the palace where he has a meeting with Ptolemy and Pothinus (although this is not portrayed on screen). Then, following Plutarch and later legend,[17] Cleopatra is delivered to him in a carpet and she begins to work her charms. That night she kills Pothinus and continues to seduce Caesar. It is made clear that the two rulers consummate their relationship there and then, and so the next morning Cleopatra finds herself unopposed queen of Egypt.

The movie then cuts to Rome for the first time, approximately a fortnight after the dramatic events in Alexandria. Caesar and Cleopatra enter Rome in triumph as the Roman plebs marvel at the queen's beauty. The next morning, the Ides of March, Caesar and Cleopatra meet to discuss their plans for empire and marriage before Caesar leaves to declare his intentions to the Senate. However, 'history' intervenes and within hours Caesar lies dead in the Forum and Cleopatra, still in her wedding gown, is heading back to the Nile. Within days though, she is sailing up the Cydnus to meet Antony (Henry Wilcoxon) and her destiny.

[15] DeMille (1960: 309).

[16] A video clip makes clear that DeMille's goal was to capture the affair with Mark Antony: http://www.youtube.com/watch?v=Dhz00dsSrMk (accessed 25 September 2012).

[17] Plut. *Caesar* 49.

The swift plotting of the screenplay means that DeMille's treatment of the story has no room for the appearance of the child Caesarion, who, the historical Cleopatra claimed, was sired by Caesar; there is precious little time in the movie for his conception, let alone his birth. Needless to say, there is no mention of Cleopatra's three children by Antony either (perhaps motherhood was contrary to DeMille's idea of Cleopatra's sophisticated sensuality). Accordingly, in DeMille's vision, Egyptian history begins and ends with Cleopatra; she has no past, since she has no ancestry, and, because of her lack of children, she is denied a posterity. But Cleopatra *is* Egypt, and, in a Shakespearean-type motif, she is addressed as such throughout the film.

The screenplay's silence about Cleopatra's lineage is actually reflected in the lines themselves (the script draws heavily on the Hollywood screwball comedies of the 1930s for its witty socialite dialogue, wisecracks and self-parody).[18] A scene set at Calpurnia's elegant Fifth-Avenue-style *soirée* in Rome, for example, has a group of nobles gossiping about the scandalous goings-on in Egypt (as they probably did in real life); the subject of Cleopatra soon arises and one young woman innocently asks, 'Is she black?' Her question is answered by peals of laughter.

There is an innate confusion about the queen's appearance: coming as she does from Africa, the natural Roman (i.e. American) assumption is that she is a black queen ruling over a black people (the thought is still prevalent among feminist Afro-American scholars today).[19] But in fact Cleopatra's arrival within the city quells all rumours—for this Cleopatra's white skin shines like alabaster and even surpasses the dazzling blonde curls worn by her Egyptian handmaidens. DeMille, of course, does not think it necessary to provide his audience with an explanation of why, historically, Cleopatra cannot be black. Instead he follows the principle that if legend tells us that Cleopatra was the most beautiful woman in the ancient world, then it was obvious that she should be

[18] A clear example of self-parody of epic film dialogue occurs during a passionate moment between Antony and Cleopatra:

ANTONY: Together we could take over the world!
CLEOPATRA: Nice of you to include me.

See Louvish (2007: 327): 'The whole film...is played tongue-in-cheek, with the script played at soap-opera level and containing frisky jests on the classical texts it derived from: "You and your Friends! Romans! Countrymen!" Octavian rebukes Antony for playing up to the crowd.'

[19] See Foss (1997: 82). He notes, '[Cleopatra's] mother is not known for certain. Given all the uncertainties of her ancestry...her blood is estimated as 32 parts Greek, 27 parts Macedonian and 5 parts Persian...If she was black, no one mentioned it.'

played by the most beautiful woman in the modern world; in 1934, that was popularly held to be Claudette Colbert.[20]

FILM NARRATIVE: *CLEOPATRA*, 1963

By 1963, however, tastes had changed, and it was the violet-eyed Elizabeth Taylor who embodied Egypt's most famous monarch, and (it could be argued) the public image of Cleopatra has never been excelled or even equalled since Taylor first applied the famous black eyeliner.

The film itself has received much critical comment, most of it hostile. Taylor herself reputedly referred to the picture as 'a disease', while Mankiewicz admitted that 'the picture was conceived in a state of emergency, shot in confusion and wound up in blind panic'.[21] *Cleopatra* is often regarded as a lumbering giant of a movie, which lacks momentum and drive.[22] But that is to ignore the integrity of the piece; the producers, the director, and the lead players genuinely attempted to create an authentic retelling of the Cleopatra story, at least as far as narrative was concerned. In a letter to the head of Twentieth Century-Fox, the film's producer, Walter Wanger, articulated the film's ethic:

> The goal to achieve is not a compromise production or a film of expedience, but an original, exciting, romantic historical film that will enthral the audience.... We are telling the amazing story of the most remarkable woman of all times, showing her entire life from the age of nineteen to her dramatic death at thirty-nine years of age. Covering for the first time in the theatre the contrasting lives of Caesar and Antony and the enmity of Octavian. All this against the greatest panorama of world conquest. The spectacular sequences, such as Cleopatra's entrance into Rome... the battle of Actium, and the orgies in Alexandria, will not be the stereotyped spectacles of the usual 'big' pictures, but overall dramatic concepts never before [seen] on the screen.[23]

[20] On Colbert and her screen style, see Tapert (1998: 166–85).

[21] Cited in Tanitch (2000: 80).

[22] *Time* (exact date not stated) noted, for example, 'as drama and as cinema, *Cleopatra* is riddled with flaws. It lacks style both in image and action. Never for an instant does it whirl along on wings of epic élan; generally it just jumps from scene to ponderous scene on the square wheels of exposition.' Cited in Vermilye and Ricci (1993: 156). For an overview of the filming process and its aftermath see Medved and Medved (1984: 97–105). See also Brodsky and Weiss (1963) and Richards (2008: 152–6).

[23] Wanger and Hyams (1963: 77).

As for Cleopatra herself, Wagner regarded her not as some *femme fatale* of Shakespeare or Theda Bara imagining, not the sex kitten of Shaw or DeMille, but as 'a fascinating, brilliant young woman, admirably reared in rulership. She is a great administrator. She understands military tactics. Her sense of responsibility as a governing chief is enormous... She speaks seven languages and many dialects.'[24]

The screenplay draws faithfully (if indiscriminately) on the histories of Suetonius, Appian, and Plutarch, as well as on the popular Italian novel *The Life and Times of Cleopatra* by C.M. Franzero. As Wanger noted, 'it is [Mankiewicz's] plan to stay very close to history. The lives of the chief protagonists, as chronicled in Plutarch, Suetonius, Appian and other ancient sources, are crammed with dramatic event and structure.'[25] In fact, Mankiewicz drolly made reference to some key classical texts within the script itself, and some of Cleopatra's best lines were calculated to make audiences laugh: 'I have been reading your commentaries on Gaul', she announces to Rex Harrison's Julius Caesar, with the same bored inflection shared by thousands of schoolchildren worldwide.

The influence of ancient writers on the film's representation of the queen permeates the film; to such an extent, in fact, that the Greco-Roman sources are almost quoted verbatim. In one early scene set in the palace at Alexandria Caesar is briefed about the current state of affairs in the Ptolemaic family. His Admiral, Agrippa (Andrew Keir), and chief aide, Rufio (Martin Landau), read the details of Cleopatra's early history from an intelligence document, a scroll purportedly written by Cicero:

AGRIPPA: (reading) '...actually of Macedonian descent, no Egyptian blood—officially admitted—that is'. (He looks up) I wish Cicero would spare us his personal comments on these reports...

CAESAR: (his eyes almost shut with weariness) That's all Cicero is. One endless personal comment...

AGRIPPA: (continues to read) '...reputed to be extremely intelligent, and sharp of wit. Queen Cleopatra is widely read, well-versed in the natural sciences and mathematics. She speaks seven languages proficiently. Were she not a woman, one would consider her an intellectual.' Nothing bores me so much as an intellectual—

CAESAR: Makes a better admiral of you, Agrippa....

RUFIO: (grins) Here's something perhaps of more interest to the navy... (he reads now) '...often arrogant in manner, and of a violent temper. Relentless, and utterly without scruple. In attaining her objectives, Cleopatra has been known to employ torture, poison, and even her own sexual talents—which are said to be considerable.'

[24] Cited in Bernstein (2000: 349–50).

[25] Wanger and Hyams (1963: 63).

(The men laugh)

> *RUFIO*: (continuing) '. . . Her lovers, I am told, are listed more easily by number than by name. It is said that she *chooses*, in the manner of a man, rather than wait to be chosen after womanly fashion.'

In this early scene, emphasis is laid on Cleopatra's Macedonian ancestry as well as her considerable talents—sexual and intellectual. These, of course, are familiar themes in the ancient portrayals of the queen.[26] The script also offers an explanation of the custom of Egyptian brother–sister marriage and the audience is left in no doubt that the young Cleopatra is *brother-loving* in the fullest sense of the term. In fact, during an early meeting, Caesar confronts Cleopatra with a tirade of abuse concerning her unorthodox family history and the dynasty's relationship to Egypt as a whole:

> *CAESAR*: (He strides towards Cleopatra) You, the descendant of generations of in-bred, incestuous mental defectives—how dare you call me barbarian?
> *CLEOPATRA*: Barbarian!
> *CAESAR*: Daughter of an idiotic flute-playing drunkard who bribed his way to the throne of Egypt—
> *CLEOPATRA*: Your price was too high, remember?
> *CAESAR*: You call me barbarian? . . . I'm fed up to the teeth with the smug condescension of you worn-out pretenders! Parading on the ruins of your past glories. Keep out of my affairs and do as I say!
> *CLEOPATRA*: Do as you say? Literally? As if I were something you had conquered?
> *CAESAR*: If I choose to regard you as such.

In this scene, Mankiewicz manages to put Cleopatra firmly into her historic and dynastic locale; he alludes to the Ptolemaic practice of brother–sister marriage and its possible long-term genetic effects, to the fact that the dynasty rules Egypt without historical authority (Caesar calls the Ptolemies 'pretenders'), and to the dubious financial dealings of Cleopatra's father, Ptolemy XII 'Auletes', undertaken with the Romans in order to secure his unstable throne.[27]

Interestingly, without going into such lurid detail herself, Mankiewicz's Cleopatra also confirms her non-Egyptian ancestry in a remarkably witty and self-depreciating remark thrown to Antony during their

[26] A collection of ancient sources on Cleopatra is provided by Wyke (1992), (2002: 195–243); Flamarion (1997); Lovric (2001); and Jones (2006).

[27] On Ptolemaic inbreeding, see Ogden (1999: 97). On the financial dealings of Ptolemy XII with the Romans, see Hölbl (2001: 222–4) and Sullivan (1990: 229–34).

meeting on her lavish barge at Cydnus. The subject centres around philhellenism, as Cleopatra compliments Antony (Richard Burton) on his elaborate leopard-skin-trimmed Greek armour:

CLEOPATRA: I find what you are wearing most becoming. Greek—isn't it?
ANTONY: I have a fondness for almost all Greek things...
CLEOPATRA: As an almost all Greek thing—I'm flattered.

Cleopatra's statement of national identity is short and swift, and rather derisory; blink and you might miss it, but it is there, captured on celluloid, and a tribute to the production's striving for historical precision, at least in the story-line.[28]

In addition, unlike the 1934 DeMille treatment, Mankiewicz's version of Cleopatra's history (which is far more factual and weighty) lays considerable emphasis on the Caesarion story, for, contrasting with DeMille, Mankiewicz is keenly aware of Cleopatra's Greek pedigree and Hellenic persona and is concerned that Cleopatra should not stand divorced from her past or future, or from her family-line, or from the international politics of the Hellenistic world at large.[29] In this movie Egypt is assimilated into the bigger picture. Mankiewicz is also keen to make Cleopatra a mother figure, fertile and bounteous; envisioning herself as Egypt, in one scene Cleopatra declares herself to be the life-giving Nile. She tells Caesar of her rounded thighs, that her hips are set well apart and declares, 'such women, they say, bear sons'. The son that the 1963 Cleopatra does indeed bear knows his lineage and knows that he is set to continue the royal line of the Ptolemies, a fact endorsed by his prominent entrance into Rome seated at the side of his goddess-mother. There is, even so, still no mention of the queen's children by Antony; instead all of Cleopatra's maternal feelings and aspirations for empire are focused on the son of Julius Caesar.

Nevertheless, it would seem that as far as public awareness of Cleopatra's ancestry goes, the Ptolemies are pretty well served by the 1963 epic treatment. The Greekness of Cleopatra is not hidden away like some shameful family secret, despite the dynasty's interpersonal shortcomings.

[28] One of the best accounts of the web of incest and murder spun by the Ptolemies is provided by the American poet Barbara Chase-Riboud (b. 1949) in her 1987 poem *Portrait of a Nude Woman as Cleopatra*. See Lovric (2001: 20–1).

[29] For the historical Caesarion, see especially Andreae and Rhein (2006: 61–76, 164–75). One wonders if the president of Fox at the time, the Greek-born Spyros P. Skouras, intentionally played up Cleopatra's Greek ancestry. On Skouras' involvement in productions set in Greek antiquity, see Nikoloutsos (2013: 265–72; 275, 278, 281 n. 58) and in this volume.

DESIGNS ON THE PAST

Turning now to the subject of film set and costume design, it should be noted at the outset that, in general, Hollywood presents a very conservative view of the ancient world. The epics' art direction does not take risks. Their sense of the past is largely based on visual conventions inherited from Victorian historical paintings and stage designs, so that the presentation of ancient life varies little in Hollywood filmmaking. Hollywood's coordinated conception of epic backgrounds was clearly a function of finance, because the studio heads believed that big budget films could not risk challenging popular notions of ancient life with revisionist (or even accurate) visual depictions of the ancient world as foreign, or perilous, or savage, or even dirty. Experienced moviegoers knew what Rome, or Greece, or Egypt was *supposed* to look like, and any film that seriously challenged these traditional preconceptions was not likely to gain popular acceptance or do well at the box office.[30]

Hollywood's penchant for the grandiose was anticipated by the late nineteenth century Academic Painters like Long, Alma-Tadema, Gérôme, Leighton, and Poynter who cleaned up history and overlaid it with a Victorian love of fussy elaborate detail.[31] The ancient world as conceived by these nineteenth-century artists is incredibly lavish—far grander, probably, than the original ever was. D.W. Griffith and Cecil B. DeMille were certainly familiar with the work of these painters, and it is clear that the Academic paintings of ancient life heralded the way for the filmic recreations of the twentieth century. Effectively, Victorian artists created the stereotypes of what the Greek, Roman, or Egyptian past should look like.[32]

Even though the Hollywood studio art departments had at their disposal the lavish resources of the research departments, the photographs provided by the travelling research teams, and the illustrated texts available in the vast libraries of MGM, Warner Brothers, Paramount, and Fox, the pursuit of archaeological accuracy was not

[30] The 1954 film *The Silver Chalice* (dir. Saville) set in late first century AD Syria and Judaea radically altered the standard epic design formula. The film's set and costume designs are a blend of the semi-abstract and the impressionistic. Because of its experimental design (coupled with a poor script) the movie was a box office flop. See Hirsch (1978: 34–6); Elley (1984: 117–18); Richards (2008: 72–3).

[31] For the Academic Painters and their recreations of antiquity, see Liversidge and Edwards (1996); Ash (1989, 1995, 1999); Wood (1983). The Hollywood debt to the nineteenth-century artists is still felt today. See Landau (2000: 64–5). For the influence of Victorian theatre design on cinema art direction, see Finkel (1996) and Mayer (1994).

[32] See Robinson (1955); Christie (1991); Dunant (1994).

necessarily guaranteed; Hollywood's view of the antique past is *based* on historical reality but tends, nevertheless, to be heavily glamorized. The immaculate palaces, temples, forecourts, arenas, barges, and market-places of the epic milieu, the burnished gold, the marble, the silks and the draperies, look inescapably like opulent movie fantasies rather than faithful depictions of ancient reality. Amazed at the visual magnificence of *The Ten Commandments* (dir. DeMille, 1956), the movie mogul James Thurbur allegedly exclaimed, 'Jeez, it makes you realize what God could have done if He'd had the money.'[33]

The dazzling beauty of the epic sets, with their rigorous denial of dirt, suggests a conspiratorial revision of historical truth: the typical *mise en scène* of the Hollywood epic was too elaborate and systematic to pass off as an artistic vision of the past, and so the directors' claims of authenticity were often beside the point. John Cary goes some way towards explaining the dichotomy: 'If authenticity is brought into our conscious too laboriously,' he notes, 'the drama suffers. DeMille, perhaps unconsciously, understood this and, unlike Marie Antoinette, if bread was what people wanted, bread—and lots of it—was what he gave them.'[34]

CLEOPATRA'S PALACE: PROBLEMS IN SET DESIGN

When it comes to representing Ptolemaic Alexandria, Hollywood clearly finds itself in something of a dilemma. The production designers of the three Hollywood films about Cleopatra found it difficult to visualize a major Hellenistic city that merges traditional and well known Egyptian architectural motifs with elements of, equally familiar, Classical Greek architecture. What can Hollywood do with a hybrid culture? Archaeological finds at Alexandria and investigations into the literary sources suggest that the vast palace of the Ptolemaic monarchy was principally Greek in design and construction although it included notably impressive and often monumental Pharaonic structures. These were either built by the Ptolemies themselves in imitation of ancient building styles or else they were genuine ancient buildings pilfered from their original locations by the Greek-speaking rulers.[35]

[33] MacDonald Fraser (1988: 5).

[34] Cary (1974: 91). On DeMille, his approach to history, and the film design process, see Llewellyn-Jones (2005).

[35] See discussions in Grimal (1998: 86–104); Green (1996: 127–41, 191–203).

The sets in DeMille's 1934 *Cleopatra* ignore the Hellenistic aspect entirely, as much, indeed, as the script overlooks Cleopatra's Macedonian lineage. Much of the film's action takes place on a studio set representing a high and airy hall that overlooks one of the palace courtyards. The set is decorated with a lotus-pillar colonnade, with pylon gateways, rooftop terraces, and pediments, all of which are borrowed from New Kingdom Egyptian temple designs. The hall itself is hung with curtain swags with tasselled borders and large marble pediments, on top of which sit proud granite statues of Pharaonic lions, actually copied from a pair of lions erected in Nubia by Tutankhamun and now housed in the British Museum.[36] It is interesting to note that just as DeMille's Cleopatra is eternal Egypt, so her palace is eternal Egyptian, Pharaonic Egyptian at that, and New Kingdom Egyptian to be specific. There is no call for a genuine Hellenistic Alexandria here, with its unique and fascinating mixture of Greek and Egyptian styles. A vision of eternal Egypt will suffice.

However, on a preliminary viewing, the opening ten minutes of Mankiewitz's 1963 *Cleopatra* seem to contradict the notion of a timeless Egypt and confirm Fox's publicity announcement that,

> Untold effort has gone into the over-all design of the physical production for 'Cleopatra'.... [The] detailed, authentic craftsmanship of the film's production designers, costume designers, and set decorators... establish the style and taste of the settings, and help provide the proper mood and atmosphere for the story that is told.[37]

The film opens on the bloody spectacle of the aftermath of the Battle of Phrasalus as the bodies of the dead are burned on funeral pyres, and then cuts to the first of the movie's many 'spectacle' scenes, the wharf-market and royal palace at Alexandria. The establishing panorama-shot along the coastline provides the audience with an unrivalled recreation of the ancient city and includes such landmarks as the Pharos (lighthouse). The film's art director, John De Cuir, had only three months to rebuild the ancient city on the production's Cinecittà lot, although two previously thwarted attempts to build the set on locations in England and California had given him plenty of time to perfect his designs and consult his research notes. The architectural elements designed by De Cuir alert the viewer to the fact that the story is set in a Hellenistic city. The palace façade itself looks authentically Hellenistic enough too; there is certainly no hiding the fact that its inspiration is Greek for it is embellished with Doric columns, sculpted pediments, and painted *metopes*. But the set

[36] See Russmann (2001: 130–1).

[37] Quoted from the un-authored 1963 Press Book p. 16.

design neatly incorporates some Egyptian elements too: human-headed sphinxes, a great scarab beetle, a seated statue of Isis, an Egyptian-style kiosk and, of course, a giant sphinx guarding the entrance to the harbour itself all help the viewer to locate the Egyptian spin on the essentially Hellenic design. Interestingly, recent (underwater) archaeological investigation at Alexandria supports De Cuir's vision; the later Ptolemies utilized large-scale Egyptian architecture on a more routine basis than was once supposed. Alexandria, and especially the royal quarter, would have been an eclectic mixture of Greek and Egyptian building styles.[38]

However, upon stepping inside the palace, the cinema audience enters another world; here the Hellenistic elements of the façade give way to a riot of Egyptianizing motifs (although the occasional piece of classical sculpture is allowed to creep in). Cleopatra's palace is vast: its throne rooms, reception rooms, dining rooms, and private chambers glisten and gleam with mosaics and alabaster columns. Caesar's massive guest-bedchamber, for example, has a polished marble floor and a papyrus-effect wall-mural that depicts a variety of Pharaonic religious scenes more fitting for a New Kingdom tomb or temple than a palace. The tomb-like decoration of the palace is made even more obvious in other sets, such as a corridor leading into the queen's apartments which is decorated with raised golden bas-reliefs, winged pediments, and gilded guardian statues. It is interesting to note how frequently well-known images of earlier Egyptian artworks are utilized within the set design to create this image of timeless Egypt. One of Cleopatra's private chambers, for example, is furnished with chairs and tables modelled on those found in the tomb of queen Hetepheres of the Egyptian Old Kingdom,[39] while her barge is hung with expensive 'Grecian' drapes but also includes copies of the famous black-skinned guardian (or *Ka*) statues discovered in the tomb of Tutankhamun.[40] The queen's palace bedchamber, however, is more reminiscent of a Napoleonic boudoir than anything that a Greek, Roman, or Egyptian noblewoman would have recognized. The king-size bed itself is pure Dorchester Hotel, 1963.[41]

[38] For the architecture of the royal quarter, see Foreman (1999).

[39] IV Dynasty, reign of Khufu, *c.* 2585 BCE. For details, see Reisner and Smith (1955: 33–4, plates 27–29); Lehner (1985).

[40] XVIII Dynasty, reign of Tutankhamun, *c.*1347–1337 BCE. See Saleh and Sourouzain (1987: no. 180).

[41] A section of the 1963 Press Book entitled 'The Designer's Contribution' includes fifteen full colour illustrations of various sets used throughout the film. A section of *Life International* magazine, 20 May 1963, is devoted to the filming of *Cleopatra*. One particular segment (pp. 72–3) is entitled 'Heroic Settings Designed for Larger-Than-Life Heroes' and includes good images of the Alexandrian set.

The idea that the ancient past also contains traces of the fashionable present is a very important element of the Cleopatra films: Theda Bara's 1917 Cleopatra lives in a world of plush oriental rugs and potted palms, a reflection of the late Edwardian taste for busy and fussy interior design. The wall paintings of her palace are cod-Egyptian and the hieroglyphs are gobbledygook, but they do reflect the popular taste in Orientalism prevalent at the time. Claudette Colbert's Cleopatra, on the other hand, lives in a splendid clean-line *art-deco* palace, an *hommage* in itself to the Egyptomania that was sweeping through Europe and America in the 1920s and 1930s.[42] In actuality, as cinema audiences first wondered at Cleopatra's gleaming palace and its fixtures and furnishings, they would have realized that it was not at all dissimilar to the *art-deco* movie theatres in which the film was originally played.[43]

CLEOPATRA'S WARDROBE: EPIC COSTUME DESIGN

Without fail, Hollywood visually represents the queen as pure Egyptian; in all three films, the design of Cleopatra's wardrobe rejects authentic Hellenistic or Greco-Roman fashions in favour of a fantasy Pharaonic look. As far as the filmmakers are concerned, the justification for these creations is always the giant Egyptian-style relief of Cleopatra carved into the wall at the rear of the temple of Dendera. It is never the sculpted portrait busts of the queen in Greek mode, nor is it ever her Roman-type coin imagery that becomes the basis of her filmic designs. The Dendera relief satisfies the image of Cleopatra as eternal Egypt and is used to qualify the art directors' claims that Cleopatra's look is based on her authentic ancient representations. Filmmakers do not acknowledge that the Egyptian costume worn by the queen at Dendera is only part of the story.

It is doubtful that the real Cleopatra wore anything like the costume depicted on the Dendera relief outside public ceremonial events. One has the feeling that the Ptolemaic rulers saw the advantage of, and even enjoyed, being portrayed in traditional Pharaonic dress, and they were no doubt accustomed to wearing a wide array of Egyptian crowns, regalia, and costume at ceremonial events; certainly, temple reliefs show an enormous range of headgear that seems to have been 'invented' by or

[42] See in particular Ziegler (1994: 506–51).
[43] See Curl (1994: 212–20) and Montserrat (2000: 89).

for the Ptolemies.[44] But for the Ptolemaic kings and queens, Egyptian dress was *fancy dress*, albeit a masquerade costume that could have a political resonance. Ptolemaic sculpture, coinage, and other artefacts, together with literary texts, strongly suggest that on a daily basis the Greek rulers wore Greek-style clothes, or, by the late Ptolemaic age, even Roman-style clothing.[45] Greek dress helped the Ptolemies to function in the Hellenistic world. On her later coinage (minted with Antony), Cleopatra VII's Roman *stola* and Roman coiffure demands that she be taken seriously by Rome.[46] Egyptian clothing was probably reserved for priestly, civic, or even national ceremonials.

In her excellent study of the use and abuse of Cleopatra's imagery in past centuries, Lucy Hughes-Hallett has demonstrated how Cleopatra has been made into a contemporary model, with each successive generation anxious to claim her as their own.[47] The growing taste for the neoclassical in art inspired a gradual increase in the representation of the queen as a Greek-Roman noblewoman,[48] but in the early years of the nineteenth century the popular perception of Cleopatra as a Hellenistic queen began to change.

Following the invasion of Egypt by Napoleon and the subsequent publication of Baron Denon's mammoth *Description d'Égypte*, public perceptions of Cleopatra quickly began to alter as the detailed drawings of the *Description* allowed for the first time an understanding of how ancient Egyptian queens looked and dressed.[49] This information proved too tempting to be ignored and it was not long before new images of Cleopatra in Pharaonic costume began to appear. Since it was popularly assumed that Cleopatra *was* Egypt, it was natural to re-dress her as a native ancient Egyptian; consequently her Greek imagery was quickly set aside and ultimately forgotten.

It was also at this time that theatrical portrayals of Cleopatra picked up on the new knowledge of her Egyptian surroundings and similarly began to portray her as an Egyptian queen.[50] By the latter half of the nineteenth century, and with the discipline of Egyptology firmly established, stage designers commissioned to illustrate the Cleopatra story, concentrated

[44] See Forbes (1996).

[45] For the famous description of the Greek-style clothing of Ptolemy VIII, see Athenaeus XII 549e. See further, Gambato (2001).

[46] See illustrations in Walker and Higgs (2001: 144, Fig. 4.3 and arguably Fig. 4.2).

[47] Hughes-Hallett (1990). The process began early, in the reign of the Roman emperor Augustus; see Wyke (1992).

[48] See Ziegler (1994: 568–72) and Walker and Higgs (2001: 346–7, Fig. 368).

[49] Ziegler (1994: 562). For the *Description* see Curl (1994: 114–16).

[50] Ziegler (1994: 398–9).

more of their efforts into producing authentic reproductions of Pharaonic Egypt and a Cleopatra who was firmly located in the 'look' of the New Kingdom.[51]

DESIGNER HISTORY: CLEOPATRA IN HIGH-HEELS

By the mid-nineteenth century the familiar representation of Cleopatra as a sexy, bejewelled, breast-exposing Egyptian queen was firmly established in the Western imagination. It was this type of imagery that inspired the early filmmakers. But films themselves are products of their time and, even in the earliest silent pictures, in order to make the remote ancient world a little more palatable and familiar to the movie audiences, elements of contemporary living were frequently incorporated into the 'look' of the film. In fact, one of the most interesting dilemmas in designing ancient spectacles was how to reconcile a modern perspective with the historical horizon of the period described, and how to conciliate the 'look' of the past with the 'look' of the present day without committing serious anachronisms.

The art director of an epic film is particularly aware of the process of creating historical authenticity which at one and the same time appeals to contemporary taste. As the film-theorist C.S. Tashiro suggests, more than anything else, make-up, hairstyles, and costumes in the typical epic are often adjusted to the period when the film was made to become the primary focus of what he terms 'Designer History'.[52] This is never more noticeable than in the *Cleopatra* movies; it is no surprise to see Cleopatra in high-heels. These particular movies were, after all, major vehicles for important and influential female stars, and the Hollywood star-system allowed major actresses like Bara, Taylor, and Colbert a say in how their film wardrobes would look.[53] Consequently, there is an undeniable *contemporary* emphasis for the Egyptian-style costumes of Hollywood's Queen of the Nile.

There is no known designer for the 1917 Cleopatra, and it is possible that much of the costume design, hairstyling, and make-up may have

[51] The French School in particular (especially the likes of Gérôme, Rixens, Cananel, and Moreau) played up the eroticism of the ancient Egyptian Cleopatra in oil paintings dated from 1860–1900. See Ziegler (1994: 574–80); see also Foreman (1999: 94, 100–1, 152).

[52] Tashiro (1998: 95–118). See further Llewellyn-Jones (forthcoming).

[53] On the role of fashion and the star system, see Davis (1993: 205–32) and Gaines and Herzog (1990).

been done by the performers themselves. Theda Bara's Cleopatra looks rather ample by modern standards, but in 1917 her Cleopatra look was a wow with the fans. In the late teens, Europe and America were in the grip of a wave of exotic and erotic Orientalist fantasies such as the Ballet Russe's *Scheherazade,* Richard Strauss' opera *Salome,* and the erotic dance-performances of Mata Hari and Little Egypt. Thus, with her hair set in contemporary ringlets and her eyelids shaded in heavy make-up, Bara's Cleopatra was crafted in the classic vamp-mode, and perfectly in accord with the times. Today one might think her costumes (and there were over fifty-five of them) rather amusing, but Hollywood publicity claimed that they were immaculately researched copies of Cleopatra's originals. In fact, it was claimed that Bara herself 'worked for months with a curator of Egyptology at the Metropolitan Museum in New York'[54] where she studied ancient items of clothing and jewellery and, more generally, the lifestyle of the ancient Egyptians.[55] Her months of 'research' were later endorsed by the actress's poses and tableaux. In fact, so imbued was Theda Bara (whose name, incidentally was deliberately coined to be an anagram of 'Arab Death') with a feeling for the period, that she was quoted as having declared that she 'felt the blood of the Ptolemies coursing through [her] veins'.[56] As she stated, 'It is not a mere theory in my mind. I have a positive knowledge that I am a reincarnation of Cleopatra. I live Cleopatra, I breathe Cleopatra, I *am* Cleopatra.'[57]

The publicity material mixed elements of historical authenticity together with notions of eroticism, and in a *Motion Picture News* review of November 1917, the reader was encouraged to reflect on the reactions of a man leaving a cinema where he has just witnessed Bara's Cleopatra in full vamp:

[54] Genini (1996: 39).

[55] The idea that Bara, like other stars of early cinema, designed her own costumes is endorsed by her own memoirs of the filming of her 1918 movie, *Salome*: 'I wanted to be a different Salome, so I ordered the wig-maker to send me a wig of tawny, blond hair. It was almost to be like a lion's mane, wild, unruly and weird. But the man had no imagination. He sent me one with Pickford curls. So I'm a brunette Salome after all'. Quoted in Golden (1996: 167).

[56] Wagenknecht (1962: 179). See Golden (1996: 130).

[57] Cited in Golden (1996: 130). The 1917 Press Book accompanying *Cleopatra* contained an article asking, 'Is Theda Bara a Reincarnation of Cleopatra?' Several arguments in favour of the proposition were advanced: '1) The character of Cleopatra and the character of Theda Bara are similar in many respects. 2) In appearance, so far as can be definitely ascertained, Miss Bara and the Siren of the Nile were similar. 3) Miss Bara's last name is similar to an Egyptian word meaning "Soul of the Sun". 4) The prophecy of Rhadmes fits Cleopatra as easily as Miss Bara.'

> His mind will drift back to the first half of the picture where Miss Bara wore a different costume in every episode. Different pieces of costume rather; or better still different varieties of beads. His temperature will ascend with a jump when he recalls the easy way in which the siren captivated Caesar and Pharon and Antony... He might suddenly realize that his mother back in Hohokus would shut her eyes once or twice for fear that the beads might break or slip, but then—mother never did understand Egyptian history after all.[58]

In fact, the suggestive peek-a-boo nature of Bara's costumes became a major feature of film reviews. The film critic of the *New York Dramatic Mirror*, for example, noted in a review published on 27 October 1917, 'Those who like to see Theda Bara should not fail to take advantage of the opportunity afforded in *Cleopatra*, for certainly you will never see *more* of her.'

So while Bara's pearl-encrusted costumes were thrilling to see on the screen, and while they certainly did not entirely look like everyday wear of the period, they could not be labelled as serious attempts to recreate Cleopatra's wardrobe.

DeMille's 1934 film is filled with the lush exoticism that was his trademark: feathers, gold, glittering jewels, and scantily clad young women fill the screen of his *Cleopatra*.[59] Colbert's Cleopatra make-up was the pure 1930s glamour formula, with thin, plucked brows, heavy lashes, dark shadow on the eyelids, and full, rounded lips. Couture dresses in the 1930s were often cut on the bias, and this smooth, clinging style seemed particularly well suited for this particular re-telling of the story. The bias-cut gowns created for Colbert by the designer Travis Banton were immaculately tailored constructions that skilfully emphasized every curve of her slim body; in effect, the ravishingly simple costumes were carefully designed and made to act as a 'second skin' for Colbert, who insisted that Banton bare as much of her bosom as possible, believing that drawing attention to her breasts would divert attention from her short neck.[60] The result was a series of daring but elegant designs, perfectly in accord with *art-deco* fashion, which were both up-to-the-minute *and* pleasing as recreations of a fantastic Egyptian past. Colbert's Cleopatra-look both exploited the contemporary mode of

[58] *Motion Picture News*, 3 November 1917. See further Wyke (1997: 89–90).

[59] For DeMille's attitude towards historical costuming, see Llewellyn-Jones (2005) and (forthcoming).

[60] One of Banton's original costume designs, together with a surviving lamé gown worn by Colbert, is illustrated in McConathy and Vreeland (1976: 146–7). See further Bailey (1983: 280–1); Tapert (1998: 166–85); Annas, La Valley and Maeder (1987: 48–9); LaVine (1981: 141).

Egyptianization in dress, and accelerated its popularity overnight.[61] The silhouette of Colbert's costumes is not the straight, vertical line of ancient Egypt, but a 1930s figure-hugging cut that skims the hips and flares out elegantly below the knees to form a 'fish tail' trailing onto the floor. This contemporary treatment of the skirt, together with the halter necklines (one of Banton's hallmarks), was at the cutting edge of fashion in 1934.

When Mankiewicz's *Cleopatra* first went into production at Pinewood studios in England in 1959, the theatre designer Oliver Massel was hired to design Elizabeth Taylor's costumes. He came up with a series of designs that reflected both ancient Egypt and late 1950s couture, and, interestingly, also spoke of the queen's Greek heritage.[62] In one rare wardrobe test-photograph, Taylor wears a Greek style *chitoniskos* (short belted tunic) and has her hair dressed in a Greek-style topknot. From the few stills and costume-shots that survive, it would appear that Messel was keen to assimilate Cleopatra with the original Greek palace that had been designed and built for her by John De Cuir on the wet and windy Pinewood lot. But after the relocation of the shoot to the Cinecittà Studios in Rome, Messel was dismissed (or refused to sign a new contract; the evidence is sketchy)[63] and the task of creating Taylor's costumes was given over to leading Hollywood designer Irene Sharaff. As Walter Wanger recalls:

> 29 April 1961: Irene Sharaff agreed to design Elizabeth's costumes... I first approached Miss Sharaff, who is one of the top Broadway designers, to do the costumes for *Cleopatra* in 1958. Irene, who is tall, sharp eyed and candid [although Tom Mankiewicz, the director's son, later labelled her as 'not very pleasant'], brushed it off with, 'It wouldn't be possible to do *Cleopatra* without making it look like *Aida*.'[64]

[61] On Egyptomania in the dress of the 1920s and 1930s, see Ziegler (1994: 526–8) and Montserrat (2000: 85–7).

[62] In this respect, Messel's designs were in keeping with those he created for Vivien Leigh's Cleopatra in the 1945 *Caesar and Cleopatra*. Interestingly, British publicity rhetoric shared much in common with that of Hollywood. In a *Picture Post* report dated 15 December 1945, it was noted that, 'envoys [were] sent to all the museums to check up the right way of putting a band of silk on one of Caesar's togas... Miss Leigh's black wigs had to be plaited into 80 strands each night so that they were properly crinkled the next day;... 2,000 costumes were made... they used a hundredweight of dyes;... more than 500 pieces of jewellery were used.'

[63] The relationship between Messel and the American producers was obviously strained from the beginning of the project. See Wanger and Hyams (1963: 48). Wanger writes, 'Oliver Messel, the costume designer, is complaining about his position and authority.'

[64] Wanger and Hyams (1963: 73). The relationship between star-designer and Hollywood star appears to have been good. Wanger (1963: 83) writes: '12 June 1961: Brought Liz together with Irene Sharaff for the first time. An important meeting because I want them to like each other. Thank heavens, it came off well.' A report in *Life International*, 23 October

With Sharaff contracted to design Taylor's gowns, the rest of the costumes were divvied up between the Italian designer Vittorio Nino Novarese and Hollywood's Reinie Conley;[65] Rex Harrison's outfits, however, also became the responsibility of Sharaff.[66] Her published memoirs for this period make an important contribution to understanding the decisions about the production of the 1963 film. In a typical piece of confident Hollywood rhetoric, Sharaff assures the reader that her designs were based upon months of research in Egyptian museums, and draws attention to her use of the ancient literary and visual sources. When, for example, she designed Taylor's famous gold Isis gown—worn by Cleopatra for her lavish entry into Rome and, ultimately for her suicide, she sensibly noted that,

> The bas-relief at Dendera . . . shows the elaborate crown and collar of an Egyptian goddess . . . [but] it did not mean that during her life [Cleopatra] dressed like that, except for sacred ceremonial occasions. The few photographs I found of sculpture and coins . . . suggest only that she was plump, had a large nose, and that her hair was dressed much like any other Roman matron of her times. The trade relations between the two countries must have carried continual mutual influences. Cleopatra, as a Macedonian, as a ruler, and as a woman, was undoubtedly astute and surely delighted in anything novel from Rome or ports on the trade routes to add to her personal adornment. The script called for 60 changes of costume for Cleopatra, from a girl of seventeen to a woman of thirty-seven. One tends to think of Cleopatra looking the same through her relatively short life, but of course the maturing had to be indicated. I found this was easiest to handle by dividing the costumes into three groups. . . . All the ceremonial costumes were based on Egyptian tomb paintings; the second group were clothes such as a Roman woman of the upper classes might have worn; and the last group made use of one of the oldest garments, the *djellabah*.[67]

Nevertheless on viewing the film, Sharaff's three categories of dress-styles are hard to identify: there is nothing in the design of Cleopatra's wardrobe that suggests the clothing of a Greek noblewoman; the look is purely Egyptian, but with a reflection of early 1960s aesthetic, in particular the tightly clinched corseted waists and Christian Dior-style tailoring techniques, so perfectly suited to Elizabeth Taylor's voluptuous figure.

1961, has Sharaff calling Taylor a 'dreamboat'. Sharaff later went on to design Taylor's wedding outfit for her (first) marriage to Richard Burton.

65 An original design for a priestess by Reinie Conley is illustrated in Annas, La Valley, Maeder, and Jenssen (1987: 18).

66 Wanger and Hyams (1963: 93); Sharaff (1976: 112–13).

67 Sharaff (1976: 106).

Walter Wanger's reminiscences for 26 July 1961 record that, 'Liz is on a diet again. . . . She likes her clothes to fit skin tight. One or two pounds can make all the difference, and Liz is always concerned about looking her best, naturally.'[68]

Sharaff found justification for squeezing Taylor into her corseted bodices and tight skirts from her naïve analysis of ancient Egyptian sculptures which completely failed to take into account the ancient artistic requisites and preoccupations concerning the ideal female body.[69] Her memoirs note,

> I was lucky enough to find a photograph of a small headless statue in the Cairo Museum, whose dress gave me a clue to designing Cleopatra's costumes. The tight-fitting bodice showed fine lines of tarunto or, as it is more commonly called, quilting, one of the oldest forms of decoration.[70]

Under the banner of historical authenticity, Sharaff was able to create a series of breathtaking costumes which somehow managed to be 1960s chic, displaying full and uplifted breasts to set off minute clinched waistlines. Moreover, capitalizing on a contemporary 1960s trend towards more conspicuous eyes, Taylor's *Cleopatra* make-up incorporated the historical Pharaonic fashion of brows and eyes thickly outlined with black *kohl* and heavily shadowed lids and sockets. Wanger's journal claims that the elaborate make-up creations were invented by Taylor herself:

> Elizabeth's make-up, conceived and designed by her, consists of one of the most glamorous eye-dos I have ever seen. To achieve the effect she wanted she stuck a lot of spangles on her lids, which created a wonderful appearance, but it took two hours just for her to put on her make-up.[71]

So much for historical authenticity, or the boast of the film's academic research pedigree! What is interesting in these reports, though, is the apparent dichotomy between the official Hollywood rhetoric, which stresses historical precision via painstaking research, and a rather slapdash attitude whereby the female star is allowed to design her own make-up without the aid of any 'specialist'.[72] The attitude pervades the entire production design; at one point in her notes even Sharaff admits that, 'Although silk-jersey is a modern fabric, when it is softly pleated it

[68] Wanger and Hyams (1963: 85).
[69] On the depiction of the clothed female body in Egyptian art, see Robins (1993: 180–5).
[70] Sharaff (1976: 106, 108).
[71] Wanger and Hyams (1963: 139–40).
[72] On the use of make-up in period films, see Annas (1987: 63). She notes, for example, that '*Spartacus* (1960) was quite simply a film about brown eyeshadow.'

hangs like the material we see on Roman statues. As silk-jersey drapes wonderfully well, many of Cleopatra's costumes were made from it.'[73]

The efforts of the Hollywood publicity machine to stress the historical authenticity of the film were often undercut by the stars themselves. Elizabeth Taylor, in a *Photoplay* article of 1962, for example, noted that,

> The day the picture is over, I'll come over in a truck and carry my entire wardrobe of sixty dresses off. You may call it a slight case of pilfering, but these gowns are too gorgeous to be left behind... They'll make the most wonderful ball gowns and party dresses. This one I'm wearing now is pure 22 carat gold. All of them are precious. But what is more important, they're as modern as tomorrow. I think I'll set a new trend. Not only with the dresses but the hairdos and such—the Cleopatra look.[74]

No sooner said than done. The catwalks of all the major fashion houses for 1963 were crammed with black-wigged models wearing variations on the Cleopatra theme as a new wave of Egyptomania swept over another generation of fashion lovers. In the summer of 1963, Cleopatra was chic.

CONCLUSION

What then is the purpose of using Pharaonic costumes and predominantly Pharaonic sets to tell the motion picture story of a Greek ruler living in a Greek city? It would appear that the design teams of all the *Cleopatra* movies were concerned to separate the two main players in the story: the Egyptians and the Romans, and so each of the two peoples are given design characteristics which stereotype their ancient nationalities. In the *Cleopatra* films, the Ptolemies inhabit a vast gold palace resembling Karnak temple and wear clothing dating back to the New Kingdom. The Romans live in splendid white marble villas and they habitually wear togas or full armour. The Greek Ptolemies *cannot* be dressed like Greeks because in popular imagination Greek and Roman clothing are one and the same, a variety of white drapes disported around the body in various ways or, alternatively, anatomical military cuirasses. Egyptian dress, however, is very different: the use of wigs, headdresses, and make-up distances the Egyptians from the Romans, sets them apart, and highlights their national identity, however misguided that notion is in historical reality. The design elements used for the *Cleopatra* films are

[73] Sharaff (1976: 106). [74] *Photoplay* April 1962, p. 30.

used as visual clues that help the audience locate a scene and recognize the nationality of a character.

Sometimes filmmakers were aware of Cleopatra's Macedonian lineage and played on this in the film narrative, but the desire to make her into an Egyptian monarch was too potent a force, and so she was always *visualized* (in costume terms) as a Pharaonic ruler. But the designed image of Cleopatra is in itself a product of history in which the nineteenth-century rediscovery of Ancient Egypt played a key role. Moreover, the parameters laid down by epic film design (based as it is on Victorian Academic painting and theatre design), demands that Cleopatra inhabits a fantastic, larger-than-life world that is at one and the same time distant and contemporary, alien and desirable. As Cleopatra, Theda Bara, Claudette Colbert, and Elizabeth Taylor each in their own way evoked the ancient past while incorporating the stylistic influences of the day. Despite the digressions from history, movie audiences found their portrayals convincing; not many seem to have questioned how or why a Greek woman got to be the queen of Egypt. What really mattered for the average moviegoer was the chance to experience the intermingling of the glamour of Hollywood with the legend of Cleopatra.

Bibliography

Achtner, Wolfgang (1994). 'Obituaries: Sylva Koscina', *The Independent*, 31 December [website], http://www.independent.co.uk/news/people/obituaries–sylva-koscina-1388934.html (accessed 15 April 2013).

Ackerman, Robert (2002). *The Myth and Ritual School: J. G. Frazer and the Cambridge Ritualists*. New York: Routledge.

Adamson, Walter L. (1980). *Hegemony and Revolution: A Study of Antonio Gramsci's Political and Cultural Theory*. Berkeley: University of California Press.

Aitken, Ian (2001). *European Film Theory and Cinema: A Critical Introduction*. Edinburgh: Edinburgh University Press.

Akbar, Arifa (2008). 'Pitt's Voyage through Classics Continues with "The Odyssey"', *The Independent, Film* section, 18 October [website], http://www.independent.co.uk/arts-entertainment/films/news/pitts-voyage-through-classics-continues-with-the-odyssey-965448.html (accessed 15 April 2013).

Allan, William (2002). *Euripides: Medea*. London: Duckworth.

Allen, Alena (2007). 'Briseis in Homer, Ovid, and *Troy*', in Martin M. Winkler (ed.), *Troy: From Homer's Iliad to Hollywood Epic*. Oxford: Blackwell, 148–62.

Allen, Paula Gunn (1986). *The Sacred Hoop: Recovering the Feminine in American Indian Traditions*. Boston: Beacon Press.

Andersen, Lars K. ([1994] 2003). 'A Stone-Turner from Lyngby', in Jan Lumholdt (ed.), *Lars von Trier: Interviews*. Jackson, Miss.: University Press of Mississippi, 88–99.

Andreae, Bernard and Karin Rhein (2006) (eds). *Kleopatra und die Caesaren*. Munich: Himer Verlag.

Annas, Alicia (1987). 'The Photogenic Formula: Hairstyles and Makeup in Historical Films', in Edward Maeder, Alicia Annas, Satch LaValley, and Elois Jenssen (eds), *Hollywood and History: Costume Design in Film*. London: Thames and Hudson Ltd., 52–77.

———, Satch La Valley, and Edward Maeder (1987). 'The Three Faces of Cleopatra', in Edward Maeder, Alicia Annas, Satch LaValley, and Elois Jenssen (eds), *Hollywood and History: Costume Design in Film*. London: Thames and Hudson Ltd., 43–51.

Anonymous (2005). 'Trojan Looks', *Channel Guide Magazine*, February: 3.

Anonymous (n.d.). 'The Top 15 Wicked Film Critics' Descriptions of Diane Kruger, AKA "Helen of Troy"', *No Apologies! Press* [website], http://www.noapologiespress.com/presents/kruger.html (accessed 6 September 2012).

Arnold, Dieter (1999). *Temples of the Last Pharaohs*. Oxford: Oxford University Press.

Arrowsmith, William (1978). 'Editor's Foreword', in William Arrowsmith (ed.), *Euripides Iphigeneia at Aulis*. Translated by William S. Merwin and George E. Dimock, Jr. Oxford: Oxford University Press, v–xiii.

Ash, Rosemary (1989). *Sir Lawrence Alma-Tadema*. London: Thames and Hudson.

——(1995). *Lord Leighton*. London: Thames and Hudson.

——(1999). *Victorian Masters and Their Art*. London: Thames and Hudson.

Ashton, Sally-Ann (2001a). 'Identifying the Egyptian-Style Ptolemaic Queens', in Susan Walker and Peter Higgs (eds), *Cleopatra of Egypt from History to Myth*. London: British Museum Press, 148–55.

——(2001b). *Ptolemaic Royal Sculpture from Egypt: The Interaction Between Greek and Egyptian Traditions*. Oxford: BAR International Series 923.

——(2008). *Cleopatra and Egypt*. Oxford: Wiley-Blackwell.

Atwood, Margaret (1987). *Selected Poems, 1965–1975*. London: Houghton Mifflin Harcourt.

——(2005). *The Pelopiad*. Ediburgh: Canongate.

Aubert, Natacha (2008). 'Roger Moore en Romulus. Tite-Live lu par Cinecittà (*L'Enlèvement des Sabines*, Richard Pottier, 1961)', in Tomas Lochman, Thomas Späth, and Adrian Stähli (eds), *Antike im Kino*. Basel: Verlag der Skulpturhalle Basel, 194–201.

B, Lynn [no surname] (2004). 'Diane Kruger: Gorgeous Girl Next Door', *A Girl's World* [website], http://www.agirlsworld.com/rachel/hangin-with/dianekruger.html (accessed 6 September 2012).

Babington, Bruce and Peter W. Evans (1993). *Biblical Epics: Sacred Narrative in the Hollywood Cinema*. Manchester: Manchester University Press.

Badley, Linda (2006). 'Danish Dogma: "Truth" and Cultural Politics', in Linda Badley, R. Barton Palmer, and Steven Jay Schneider (eds), *Traditions in World Cinema*. Edinburgh: Edinburgh University Press, 80–94.

——(2010). *Lars von Trier*. Urbana/Champaign, Ill.: University of Illinois Press.

Bailey, Margaret J. (1983). *Those Glorious Glamour Years: Classic Hollywood Costume Design of the 1930s*. London: Columbus Books.

Bainbridge, Caroline (2007). *The Cinema of Lars von Trier: Authenticity and Artifice*. London: Wallflower Press.

Baine, Wallace (2004). 'The Passion of the Brad', *Santa Cruz Sentinel*, 14 May.

Bakogianni, Anastasia (2008). 'All is Well that Ends Tragically: Filming Greek Tragedy in Modern Greece', *Bulletin of the Institute of Classical Studies*, 51: 119–67.

——(2009). 'Voices of Resistance: Michael Cacoyannis' *The Trojan Women* (1971)', *Bulletin of the Institute of Classical Studies*, 52: 45–68.

——(2011). *Electra Ancient and Modern: Aspects of the Tragic Heroine's Reception*. London: Institute of Classical Studies.

——(2013). 'Who Rules this Nation? (*Ποιός Κυβερνά αυτόν τον Τόπο;*): Political Intrigue and the Struggle for Power in Michael Cacoyannis' *Iphigenia* (1977)', in Anastasia Bakogianni (ed.), *Dialogues with the Past: Classical Reception Theory and Practice* Vol. 1. London: Institute of Classical Studies (forthcoming).

Bartel, Heike and Anne Simon (2010) (eds). *Unbinding Medea: Interdisciplinary Approaches to a Classical Myth from Antiquity to the 21st Century*. London: Legenda.

Basu, Subho, Craige Champion, and Elisabeth Lasch-Quinn (2007). '*300*: The Use and Abuse of Greek History', [website], http://www.spiked-online.com/index.php/site/article/3918/ (accessed 9 July 2011).

BBC News, Friday 5 March 2004. [website], http://news.bbc.co.uk/1/hi/uk/3514549.stm (last accessed 5 September 2012).

Bean, Jennifer M. and Diane Negra (2002) (eds). *A Feminist Reader in Early Cinema*. Durham, North Carolina: Duke University Press.

Benioff, David (2003). '*Troy*', *Internet Movie Script Database* [website], http://www.imsdb.com/Movie%20Scripts/Troy%20Script.html (accessed 6 September 2012).

——(n.d.). 'Web Access... David Benioff', *BBC* [website], http://www.bbc.co.uk/films/webaccess/david_benioff_1.shtml (accessed 6 September 2012).

Bennetts, Leslie (2004). 'Aspects of Brad', *Vanity Fair*, June [website], http://bradfans.net/articles/2004/vanityfair.php (accessed 15 April 2013).

Berger, John (1972). *Ways of Seeing*. London: BBC/Penguin.

Bergren, Ann (1979). 'Helen's Web: Time and Tableau in the *Iliad*', *Helios*, 7: 19–34.

——(1981). 'Helen's "Good Drug": *Odyssey* IV 1–305', in Stephanus (Stephen) Kresic (ed.), *Contemporary Literary Hermeneutics and Interpretations of Classical Texts*. Ottawa: Ottawa University Press, 201–14.

——(1983). 'Language and the Female in Early Greek Thought', *Arethusa*, 16: 69–95.

Bernstein, Matthew (2000). *Walter Wagner, Hollywood Independent*. Berkeley: University of California Press.

Berry, Oliver (2003). '*Cold Mountain*' [website], http://www.kamera.co.uk/reviews_extra/cold_mountain.php (last accessed 10 October 2012).

Berthelius, Marie and Roger Narbonne ([1987] 2003). 'A Conversation with Lars von Trier', in Jan Lumholdt (ed.), *Lars von Trier: Interviews*. Jackson, Miss.: University Press of Mississippi, 47–58.

Berti, Irene and Marta García Morcillo (2008) (eds). *Hellas on Screen: Cinematic Receptions of Ancient History, Literature and Myth. Heidelberger Althistorische Beiträge und Epigraphische Studien, Bd. 45*. Stuttgart: Franz Steiner Verlag.

Beye, Charles Rowan (1982). *Epic and Romance in the Argonautica of Apollonius*. Carbondale, Ill.: Southern Illinois University Press.

Bianchi, Robert S. (2003). 'Images of Cleopatra VII Reconsidered', in Sally-Ann Ashton and Susan Walker (eds.), *Cleopatra Reassessed*. London: British Museum Press, 13–23.

Biancofiore, Angela (2007). '*Médée* de Pier Paolo Pasolini: "mauvaise conduite" de l'Étrangère au sein de la polis', *Italies*, 11: 87–102.

Birchard, Robert S. (2004). *Cecil B. DeMille's Hollywood*. Lexington: University Press of Kentucky.

Björkman, Stig (1996). *Breaking the Waves*. Paris: Petite Bibliothèque des Cahiers du Cinema.

——(2003) (ed.). *Trier on von Trier*. Translated by Neil Smith. London: Faber and Faber.

Björkman, Stig and Lena Nyman ([1995] 2003). 'I am Curious, Film: Lars von Trier', in Jan Lumholdt (ed.), *Lars von Trier: Interviews*. Jackson, Miss.: University Press of Mississippi, 100–102.

Blanshard, Alastair and Kim Shahabudin (2011). *Classics on Screen: Ancient Greece and Rome on Film*. London: Bristol Classical Press.

Blondell, Ruby (2002). *The Play of Character in Plato's Dialogues*. Cambridge: Cambridge University Press.

——(2005). 'How to Kill an Amazon', *Helios*, 32: 73–103.

——(2009). '"Third cheerleader from the left": From Homer's Helen to Helen of *Troy*', *Classical Receptions Journal*, 1.1: 1–26.

——(2010). '"Bitch that I Am": Self-Blame and Self-Assertion in the *Iliad*', *Transactions of the American Philological Association*, 140.1: 1–32.

Boedeker, Deborah (1997). 'Becoming Medea: Assimilation in Euripides', in James J. Clauss and Sarah Iles Johnston (eds), *Medea: Essays on Medea in Myth, Literature, Philosophy, and Art*. Princeton: Princeton University Press, 127–48.

Bondanella, Peter (1983). *Italian Cinema: From Neorealism to the Present*. New York: The Ungar Publishing Company.

——(2001). *Italian Cinema: From Neorealism to the Present*. 3rd edition. New York: Continuum.

Bordwell, David, Janet Staiger, and Kristin Thompson (1985). *The Classical Hollywood Cinema: Film Style and Mode of Production to 1960*. New York: Columbia University Press.

Borza, Eugene N. (December 2004). 'Movie Commentary: Alexander', *AIA Online Publication*. http://www.archaeological.org/pdfs/papers/AIA_Alexander_Review.pdf (accessed 10 October 2012).

Bridges, Emma, Edith Hall, and Peter John Rhodes (2007) (eds). *Cultural Responses to the Persian Wars: Antiquity to the Third Millennium*. Oxford: Oxford University Press.

Briggs, Ward (2010). 'Review of Arthur J. Pomeroy, "*Then it was Destroyed by the Volcano*"', *International Journal of the Classical Tradition*, 17: 156–61.

Brilliant, Richard (1995). 'Kirke's Men: Swine and Sweethearts', in Beth Cohen (ed.), *The Distaff Side: Representing the Female in Homer's Odyssey*. Oxford: Oxford University Press.

Brockliss, William, Pramit Chaudhuri, Ayelet Haimson Lushkov, and Katherine Wasdin (2012). 'Introduction', in William Brockliss, Pramit Chaudhuri, Ayelet Haimson Lushkov, and Katherine Wasdin (eds), *Reception and the Classics: An Interdisciplinary Approach to the Classical Tradition*. Cambridge: Cambridge University Press, 1–16.

Brodsky, Jack and Nathan Weiss (1963). *The Cleopatra Papers. A Private Correspondence*. New York: Kessinger Publishing.

Brown, Blain (2002). *Cinematography: Theory and Practice*. Amsterdam: Butterworth Heineman.

Brunetta, Gian Piero (2009). *The History of Italian Cinema: A Guide to Italian Film from Its Origins to the Twenty-First Century*. Translated from Italian by Jeremy Parzen. Princeton: Princeton University Press.

Bruzzi, Stella (1997). *Undressing Cinema: Clothing and Identity in the Movies*. New York: Routledge.

Buckley, Réka (2008). 'Glamour and the Italian Female Film Stars of the 1950s', *Historical Journal of Film, Radio and Television*, 28:3: 267–89.

Buitron, Diana, Beth Cohen, Norman Austin, and George Dimock (1992). *The Odyssey and Ancient Art: An Epic in Word and Image*. New York: Edith C. Blum Art Institute, Bard College.

Burke, Frank (2011). 'The Italian Sword-And-Sandal Film from *Fabiola* to *Hercules and the Captive Women*: Texts and Contexts', in Flavia Brizio-Skov (ed.), *Popular Italian Cinema: Culture and Politics in a Postwar Society*. New York: I. B. Tauris & Co. Ltd., 17–51.

Burke, John (1962). *The 300 Spartans*. New York: Signet Books.

Burnett, Anne P. (1998). *Revenge in Attic and Later Tragedy*. Berkeley: University of California Press.

Burr, Ty (2004). 'Pitt Looks Pretty, but the Star Makes a Strained Achilles in Lumbering "Troy"', *Boston Globe*, 14 May.

Cacoyannis, Michael. (1984). 'Discussion: Ancient Drama and the Film', in Ariadne-Koumari Sanford (ed.), *Le Théâtre Antique de nos Jours: Symposium International á Delphes 18–22 Août 1981*. Athens: Centre Culturel Européen de Delphes Athènes, 211–28.

——(1995). '*Μιχάλης Κακογιάννης: Αυτοπαρουσίαση*', in *Μπάμπης Κολώνιας* (επιμ.), *36° Φεστιβάλ Κινηματογράφου Θεσσαλονίκης:*

Μιχάλης Κακογιάννης. Cultural Organization of the European Capital: Thessaloniki. Athens: Kastaniotis Publications, 12–15.

Cammarota, M. Domenico (1987). *Il cinema peplum*. Rome: Fanucci Editore.

Carney, Elizabeth D. (1991). 'What's in a Name? The Emergence of a Title for Royal Women in the Hellenistic Period', in Sarah B. Pomeroy (ed.), *Women's History and Ancient History*. Chapel Hill: University of North Carolina Press, 154–72.

——(2000). *Women and Monarchy in Macedonia*. Norman: University of Oklahoma Press.

——(2006). *Olympias, Mother of Alexander the Great*. New York: Routledge.

——(2010). 'Olympias and Oliver: Sex, Sexual Stereotyping, and Women in Oliver Stone's *Alexander*', in Paul Cartledge and Fiona Rose Greenland (eds), *Responses to Oliver Stone's* Alexander: *Film, History, and Cultural Studies*. Madison: University of Wisconsin Press, 135–67.

Carter, David M. (2007). *The Politics of Greek Tragedy*. Exeter: Bristol Phoenix Press.

Cartledge, Paul (2001). *Spartan Reflections*. Berkeley: University of California Press.

——(2003). *The Spartans: The World of the Warrior-Heroes of Ancient Greece, from Utopia to Crisis and Collapse*. Woodstock: The Overlook Press.

——(2004). *Alexander the Great: The Hunt for a New Past*. New York: Overlook.

——and Fiona Rose Greenland (2010) (eds). 'Introduction', in Paul Cartledge and Fiona Rose Greenland (eds), *Responses to Oliver Stone's* Alexander: *Film, History, and Cultural Studies*. Madison: University of Wisconsin Press, 3–12.

Cary, John (1974). *Spectacular! The Story of Epic Films*. London: Castle Books.

Casty, Alan (1966–67). 'The Films of Robert Rossen', *Film Quarterly*, 20.2: 3–12.

——(1969). *The Films of Robert Rossen*. New York: Museum of Modern Art.

Cavallini, Eleonora (2005). 'A Proposito di *Troy*', in Alberto Boschi and Alessandro Bozzato (eds), *I Greci al Cinema: Dal Peplum 'D'Autore' alla Grafica Computeriazzata*. Bologna: Digital University Press, 53–79.

——(2008). 'Phryne: From Knidian Venus to Movie Star', in Irene Berti and Marta García Morcillo (eds), *Hellas on Screen: Cinematic Receptions of Ancient History, Literature and Myth. Heidelberger Althistorische Beiträge und Epigraphische Studien, Bd. 45*. Stuttgart: Franz Steiner Verlag, 203–18.

Celli, Carlo and Cottino-Jones, Marga (2007). *A New Guide to Italian Cinema*. New York: Palgrave Macmillan.

Chaniotis, Angelos (2008). 'Making Alexander Fit for the Twenty-First Century: Oliver Stone's *Alexander*', in Irene Berti and Marta García

Morcillo (eds), *Hellas on Screen: Cinematic Receptions of Ancient History, Literature and Myth. Heidelberger Althistorische Beiträge und Epigraphische Studien, Bd. 45*. Stuttgart: Franz Steiner Verlag, 185–201.

Chauveau, Michel (2000). *Egypt in the Age of Cleopatra*. Ithaca: Cornell University Press.

Chiasson, Charles (2013). 'Re-politicising Euripides: The Power of the Peasantry in Michael Cacoyannis' *Electra* (1962)', in Anastasia Bakogianni (ed.), *Dialogues with the Past: Classical Reception Theory and Practice*. Vol. 1. London: Institute of Classical Studies (forthcoming).

Christie, Ian (2000). 'Between Magic and Realism: Medea on Film', in Edith Hall, Fiona Macintosh, and Oliver Taplin (eds), *Medea in Performance 1500–2000*. Oxford: Legenda, 144–65.

Christie, Irad (1991). 'Cecil B. DeMille: Grand Illusions', *Sight and Sound*, 1.8: 18–21.

Christopoulos, Georgios and Ioannis Bastias (2000) (dir. of publication). *The History of the Hellenic Nation. Vol. 16: Modern Hellenism from 1941 to the End of the Century*. Athens: Athens Publishing Inc.

Clack, Jerry (1973). 'The Medea Similes of Apollonius Rhodius', *Classical Journal*, 68: 310–15.

Clader, Linda Lee (1976). *Helen: The Evolution from Divine to Heroic in Greek Epic Tradition* (Mnemosyne, Bibliotheca Classica Batava: Supplementum 42). Leiden: Brill.

Clare, R. J. (2002). *The Path of the Argo*. Cambridge: Cambridge University Press.

Clauss, James J. (1993). *The Best of the Argonauts: The Redefinition of the Epic Hero in Book 1 of Apollonius's Argonautica*. Berkeley: University of California Press.

——(1997). 'Conquest of the Mephistophelian Nausicaa: Medea's Role in Apollonius' Redefinition of the Epic Hero', in Sarah Iles Jonston and James J. Clauss (eds), *Medea: Essays on Medea in Myth, Literature, Philosophy, and Art*. Princeton: Princeton University Press, 149–77.

——(2008). '*Hercules Unchained: Contaminatio, Nostos, Katabasis* and the Surreal', *Arethusa*, 41: 51–66.

——and Sarah Iles Johnston (1997) (eds). *Medea: Essays on Medea in Myth, Literature, Philosophy, and Art*. Princeton: Princeton University Press.

Clayton, Barbara (2004). *A Penelopean Poetics: Reweaving the Feminine in Homer's Odyssey*. Lanham: Lexington Books.

Cleland, Liza, Glenys Davies, and Lloyd Llewellyn-Jones (2007). *Greek and Roman Dress from A to Z*. London: Routledge.

Clogg, Richard (2002). *A Concise History of Greece*. 2nd edition. Cambridge: Cambridge University Press.

Clough, Emma (2004). 'Loyalty and Liberty: Thermopylae in the Western Imagination', in Thomas J. Figueira (ed.), *Spartan Society*. Swansea: The Classical Press of Wales, 363–84.

Cohen, Beth (1985) (ed.). *The Distaff Side: Representing the Female in Homer's* Odyssey. Oxford: Oxford University Press.

Cohen, David S. (2004). '*Troy*: From Script to Screen: An Interview with David Benioff', *Scr(i)pt*, May/June, 36–40.

Collins, Leslie (1988). *Studies in Characterization in the Iliad.* Frankfurt am Main: Athenäum.

Conacher, D. J. (1967). *Euripidean Drama: Myth, Theme and Structure.* Toronto: University of Toronto Press.

Constantinidou, Soteroula (1994). 'The Vision of Homer: The Eyes of Heroes and Gods', *Antichthon*, 28: 1–15.

Cowie, Peter (2004). *Revolution! The Explosion of World Cinema in the 60s.* London: Faber and Faber.

Crofts, Stephen. (2006). 'Reconceptualising National Cinema/s', in Valentina Vitali and Paul Willemen (eds), *Theorising National Cinema.* London: British Film Institute, 44–58.

Crowdus, Gary (2005). 'Dramatizing Issues that Historians Don't Address: An Interview with Oliver Stone', *Cineaste*, 30.2: 12–23.

Csapo, Eric and William J. Slater (1994). *The Context of Ancient Drama.* Ann Arbor: University of Michigan Press.

Curl, James Stevens (1994). *Egyptomania: The Egyptian Revival: A Recurring Theme in the History of Taste.* Manchester: Manchester University Press.

Curti, Carlo (1967). *Skouras: King of Fox Studios.* Los Angeles: Holloway House Publishing Company.

Cyrino, Monica S. (2005). 'She'll Always Have Paris: Helen in Wolfgang Petersen's *Troy*', *Amphora*, 4: 10–11, 18.

——(2007a). 'Film Review: *300*', *Amphora*, 6.1: 1, 4–5.

——(2007b). 'Helen of Troy', in Martin M. Winkler (ed.), *Troy: From Homer's* Iliad *to Hollywood Epic.* Oxford: Blackwell, 131–47.

——(2011). 'This is Sparta!: The Reinvention of Epic in Zack Snyder's *300*', in Robert Burgoyne (ed.), *The Epic Film in World Culture.* New York: Routledge, 19–38.

——(2013) (ed). *Screening Love and Sex in the Ancient World.* New York: Palgrave Macmillan.

D'Arcens, Louise (2009). 'Iraq, the Prequel(s): Historicizing Military Occupation and Withdrawal in *Kingdom of Heaven* and *300*'. *Screening the Past* 29 [online journal], http://www.latrobe.edu.au/screeningthepast/26/early-europe/kingdom-of-heaven-300.html (accessed 8 July 2011).

Danek, Georg (2007). 'The Story of Troy through the Centuries', in Martin M. Winkler (ed.), *Troy: From Homer's* Iliad *to Hollywood Epic.* Oxford: Blackwell, 68–84.

Davis, Ronald L. (1993). *The Glamour Factory. Inside Hollywood's Big Studio System.* Dallas: Southern Methodist University Press.

Day, Kirsten (2008). 'Introduction', *Celluloid Classics: New Perspectives on Classical Antiquity in Modern Cinema*. Special issue of *Arethusa*, 41.1: 1–9.

De Giusti, Luciano (1990). *I film di Pier Paolo Pasolini*. 3rd edition. Rome: Gremese Editore.

de Lauretis, Teresa (1987). *Technologies of Gender. Essays on Theory, Film, and Fiction*. Bloomington: Indiana University Press.

Decker, Kerstin (1997). 'Echter als das Original. "Medea" und "Epidemic", zwei bisher unbekannte Filme Lars von Triers bei den "Televisionen unter freiem Himmel" in Berlin', *Der Tagesspiegel*, 10 July 1997, 22.

DeMille, Cecil B. (1960). *The Autobiography of Cecil B. DeMille*. New York: W. H. Allen.

DeNicola, Deborah (1999) (ed.). *Orpheus and Company: Contemporary Poems on Greek Mythology*. Hanover: University Press of New England.

Dewald, Carolyn (1981). 'Women and Culture in Herodotus' *Histories*', in Helen P. Foley (ed.), *Reflections of Women in Antiquity*. Philadelphia: Gordon and Breach Science Publishers, 91–125.

Diggle, James (1994). 'Review of Mellert-Hoffmann's Untersuchungen zur "Iphigenie in Aulis" des Euripides', in *Euripidea. Collected Essays*. Oxford: Clarendon Press, 48–50.

Dimock, Jr. George E. (1978). *Euripides: Iphigenia at Aulis*. Oxford: Oxford University Press.

Doane, Mary Ann (1987). *The Desire to Desire. The Woman's Film of the 1940s*. Bloomington: Indiana University Press.

Dodds, E. R. (1951). *The Greeks and the Irrational*. Berkeley: University of California Press.

Doherty, Thomas (1999). *Pre-Code Hollywood: Sex, Immorality, and Insurrection in American Cinema, 1930–1934*. New York: Columbia University Press.

Drake, Stillman (1978). *Galileo at Work: His Scientific Biography*. Chicago: University of Chicago Press.

Drouzy, Maurice (1982). *Carl Th. Dreyer né Nilsson*. Paris: Editions du Cerf.

——— (1986) (ed.). *Carl Th. Dreyer: Jésus de Nazareth; Médée*. Paris: Editions du Cerf.

Duffy, Carol Ann (1999). *The World's Wife: Poems*. London: Picador.

Duflot, Jean (1970). *Entretiens avec Pier Paolo Pasolini*. Paris: Éditions Pierre Belfond.

Dunant, Caroline (1994). 'Olympian Dreamscapes: The Photographic Canvas. The Wide-Screen Paintings of Leighton, Poynter and Alma-Tadema', in Jacky Bratton, Jim Cook, and Christine Gledhill (eds), *Melodrama: Stage, Picture, Screen*. London: BFI Publishing, 82–93.

Dyer, Richard (1992). 'Don't Look Now: The Male Pinup', in Mandy Merck (ed.), *The Sexual Subject: A Screen Reader in Sexuality*. London: Routledge, 265–76.

Dyer, Richard (1997). *White*. London: Routledge.

——(1998). *Stars*. 2nd edition. London: BFI Publishing.

——(2004). *Heavenly Bodies: Film Stars and Society*. 2nd edition. New York: St. Martin's Press.

Easthope, Anthony (1986). *What A Man's Gotta Do. The Masculine Myth in Popular Culture.* London: Paladin Grafton Books.

Ebbott, Mary (1999). 'The Wrath of Helen: Self-Blame and Nemesis in the *Iliad*', in Miriam Carlisle and Olga Levaniouk (eds), *Nine Essays on Homer*. Lanham, Md.: Rowman and Littlefield, 3–20.

Edelstein, David (May 2004). 'War is Hellenic: The Blood and Eroticism of *Troy*', *Slate* [online journal], http://www.slate.com/articles/arts/movies/2004/05/war_is_hellenic.html (accessed 6 September 2012).

Edwards, Mark W. (1987). *Homer: Poet of the Iliad.* Baltimore: John Hopkins University Press.

Eisenstein, Sergei ([1949] 1977). *Film Form: Essays in Film Theory*. Edited and translated by Jay Leyda. New York: Harcourt.

Eliade, Mircea ([1954] 1991). *The Myth of the Eternal Return*. Translated by Willard Trask. Princeton: Princeton University Press.

——(1959). *The Sacred and the Profane*. Translated by Willard Trask. New York: Harcourt, Brace and World.

——([1960] 1967). *Myths, Dreams, and Mysteries: The Encounter Between Contemporary Faiths and Archaic Realities*. Translated by Philip Mairet. New York: Harper and Row.

Elley, Derek (1984). *The Epic Film: Myth and History*. London: Routledge & Kegan Paul.

Ellis, John (1992). *Visible Fictions: Cinema, Television, Video*. New York and London: Routledge.

Faraci, Devin (May 2004a). 'Interview: Diane Kruger', *Cinematic Happenings Under Development* [website], http://www.chud.com/news/may04/may8troy1.php3 (accessed 31 October 2005; no longer accessible 6 September 2012).

——(May 2004b). 'Interview: David Benioff', *Cinematic Happenings Under Development* [website], http://www.chud.com/news/may04/may11troy3.php3 (accessed 31 October 2005; no longer accessible 6 September 2012).

Felson-Rubin, Nancy (1994). *Regarding Penelope: From Character to Poetics.* Princeton: Princeton University Press.

Felson, Nancy and Slatkin, Laura M. (2004). 'Gender and Homeric Epic', in Robert Fowler(ed.), *The Cambridge Companion to Homer*. Cambridge: Cambridge University Press, 91–114.

Figueira, Thomas J. (2004) (ed.). *Spartan Society*. Swansea: The Classical Press of Wales.

Finkel, Alicia (1996). *Romantic Stages. Set and Costume Design in Victorian England.* London: McFarland.

Finley, John H. (1978). *Homer's Odyssey*. Cambridge, Mass.: Harvard University Press.

Fischer, Paul (May 2004). 'Diane Kruger Launches International Career with "Troy"', *Film Monthly* [online journal], http://www.filmmonthly.com/Profiles/Articles/DianeKruger/DianeKruger.html (accessed 6 September 2012).

Flamarion, Edith (1997). *Cleopatra: From History to Legend*. London: Thames and Hudson.

Fletcher, Joann (2008). *Cleopatra the Great: The Woman Behind the Legend*. London: Hodder.

Flynn, Gillian (2004). 'Men and Myth', *Entertainment Weekly*, 14 May: 24–31.

Foley, Helene P. (1978). 'Reverse similes and sex role in the *Odyssey*', *Arethusa*, 11: 7–26.

——(1985). *Ritual Irony: Poetry and Sacrifice in Euripides*. Ithaca: Cornell University Press.

Forbes, David C. (1996). 'Follies: Crowns of the Ptolemies', *KMT. A Modern Journal of Ancient Egypt*, 7.3: 42–3.

Foreman, Laura (1999). *Cleopatra's Palace: In Search of a Legend*. London: RandomHouse.

Forst, Achim (1998). *Breaking the Dreams: Das Kino des Lars von Trier*. Marburg: Schüren Verlag.

——(2002). 'Leidende Rächerin: Lars von Triers *Medea*', in Ulrich Eigler (ed.), *Bewegte Antike: Antike Themen im modernen Film*. Stuttgart/Weimar: Metzler Verlag, 67–79.

Foss, Michael (1997). *The Search for Cleopatra*. London: Arcade Publishing.

Fox, Robin Lane (2004). *The Making of Alexander*. London: R&L.

Fraser, George MacDonald (1988). *The Hollywood History of the World*. London: Penguin Books.

Fraser, P. M. (1972). *Ptolemaic Alexandria*. 3 volumes. Oxford: Oxford University Press.

Frazer, Sir James George (1922). *The Golden Bough: A Study in Magic and Religion* (one volume edition). New York: Macmillan.

French, Philip (May 2004). 'Troy', *Guardian Unlimited* [online journal], http://film.guardian.co.uk/News_Story/Critic_Review/Observer_Film_of_the_week/0,1217624,00.html (accessed 6 September 2012).

Freud, Sigmund ([1908] 1958). 'The Relation of a Poet to Daydreaming' in *On Creativity and the Unconscious: The Psychology of Art, Literature, Love and Religion*. Translated I.F. Grant. New York: Harper, 44–54.

Fusillo, Massimo (1996). *La Grecia secondo Pasolini: mito e cinema*. Florence: La Nuova Italia Editrice Scandicci.

Futrell, Alison (2005). '*Troy* the Film', paper presented at panel on '*Troy*, the Movie', American Philological Association annual meeting, 8 January.

Gadamer, Hans-Georg (1991). *Truth and Method*. 2nd revised edition. Translated by Joel Weinsheimer and Donald G. Marshall. New York: Crossroad.

Gaines, Jane and Charlotte Herzog (1990). *Fabrications: Costume and the Female Body*. London: Routledge.

Gambato, Maria (2001). 'The Female Kings: Some Aspects of the Representation of the Eastern Kings in the *Deipnosophistae*', in David Braund and John Wilkins (eds), *Athenaeus and his World: Reading Greek Culture in the Roman Empire*. Exeter: Exeter University Press, 227–30.

Gamel, Mary-Kay (1999). 'Introduction to *Iphigenia at Aulis*', in Ruby Blondell, Mary-Kay Gamel, Nancy Sorkin Rabinowitz, and Bella Zweig (eds and trans.), *Women on the Edge: Four Plays by Euripides*. London: Routledge, 305–27.

Gantz, Timothy (1993). *Early Greek Myth: A Guide to Literary and Artistic Sources*. Baltimore: Johns Hopkins University Press.

García, Nacho (2008). 'Classic Sceneries: Setting Ancient Greece in Film Architecture', in Irene Berti and Marta García Morcillo (eds), *Hellas on Screen: Cinematic Receptions of Ancient History, Literature and Myth. Heidelberger Althistorische Beiträge und epigraphische Studien, Bd. 45*. Stuttgart: Franz Steiner Verlag, 21–38.

Genini, Ronald (1996). *Theda Bara: A Biography of the Silent Screen Vamp, with a Filmography*. London: McFarland.

Gentili, Bruno and Franca Perusino (2000) (eds). *Medea nella letteratura e nell'arte*. Venice: Marsilio Editori.

Ghigi, G. (1977). 'Come si spiegano le fortune dei *pepla* su cui sembra si ritorni a puntare', *Cineforum*, 17: 733–46.

Giannini, Pietro (2000). 'Medea nell'epica e nella poesia lirica arcaica e tardo-arcaica', in Bruno Gentili and Franca Perusino (eds), *Medea nella letteratura e nell'arte*. Venice: Marsilio Editori, 13–27.

Gilbert, John (1995). *Change of Mind in Greek Tragedy*. Göttingen: Vandenhoeck and Ruprecht.

Giordano, Michele (1998). *Giganti Buoni. Da Ercole a Piedone*. Rome: Gremese Editore.

Girard, René (1965). *Deceit, Desire, and the Novel: Self and Other in Literary Structure*. Translated by Yvonne Freccero. Baltimore: John Hopkins University Press.

Golden, Eve (1996). *Vamp. The Rise and Fall of Theda Bara*. New York: Vestal Press.

Goldman, Norman (2001). 'Reconstructing Roman Clothing', in Judith L. Sebesta and Larissa Bonfante (eds), *The World of Roman Costume*. Madison: University of Wisconsin Press, 213–37.

Goldsmith, David F. (2004). '*Troy*: David Benioff's Trojan Horse Screenplay Conquers Hollywood', *Creative Screenwriting*, 11.3: 54–7.

Graf, Fritz (1997). 'Medea, the Enchantress from Afar: Remarks on a Well-Known Myth', in James J. Clauss and Sarah Iles Johnston (eds), *Medea: Essays on Medea in Myth, Literature, Philosophy, and Art*. Princeton: Princeton University Press, 21–43.

Graver, Margaret. (1995). 'Dog-Helen and Homeric Insult', *Classical Antiquity*, 14: 41–61.

Green, Peter (1996). *Alexandria and Alexandrianism*. Malibu: Getty Trust.

——(1997). *The Argonautika by Apollonios Rhodios: Translated, with Introduction, Commentary and Glossary*. Berkeley: University of California Press.

——(2004). 'Heroic Hype, New Style: Hollywood Pitted against Homer', *Arion*, 12: 171–87.

Greene, Naomi (1990). *Pier Paolo Pasolini: Cinema as Heresy*. Princeton: Princeton University Press.

Gregory, Justina (2008). 'Euripidean Tragedy', in Justina Gregory (ed.), *A Companion to Greek Tragedy*. Oxford: Blackwell, 251–70.

Gress, Elsa (1988) (tr.). '*Medea*: Screenplay Manuscript by Carl Th. Dreyer in Cooperation with Preben Thomsen', in Jytte Jensen (ed.), *Carl Th. Dreyer*, New York: Museum of Modern Art, 79–92.

Grimal, Nicolas (1998). *La gloire d'Alexandrie*. Paris: Pettit Palais.

Grimm, Günther (1998). *Alexandria. Die erste Königsstadt der hellenistischen Welt*. Mainz Am Rhein: von Zabern.

Grossman, Lev (2007). 'The Art of War', *Time*, 169.11: 58–61.

Gundle, Stephen (2007). *Bellissima: Feminine Beauty and the Idea of Italy*. New Haven: Yale University Press.

Günsberg, Maggie (2005). *Italian Cinema: Gender and Genre*. New York: Palgrave Macmillan.

Gurd, Sean A. (2005). *Iphigenias at Aulis: Textual Multiplicity, Radical Philology*. Ithaca: Cornell University Press.

Hall, Edith (1989). *Inventing the Barbarian: Greek Self-Definition Through Tragedy*. Oxford: Oxford University Press.

——(2002). 'Tony Harrison's *Prometheus*: A View from the Left', *Arion*, 10: 129–40.

——(2004). 'Introduction: Why Greek Tragedy in the Late Twentieth Century?', in Edith Hall, Fiona Macintosh, and Amanda Wrigley (eds), *Dionysus Since 69: Greek Tragedy at the Dawn of the Third Millennium*. Oxford: Oxford University Press, 1–46.

——(2008). *The Return of Ulysses: A Cultural History of Homer's Odyssey*. Baltimore: The Johns Hopkins University Press.

Hall, Sheldon and Steve Neale (2010). *A Hollywood History: Epics, Spectacles, and Blockbusters*. Detroit: Wayne State University Press.

Hamer, Mary (1997). 'Timeless Histories: A British Dream of Cleopatra', in Matthew Bernstein and Gaylyn Studlar (eds), *Visions of the East. Orientalism in Film*. London: I.B. Tauris, 269–91.

Hanson, Victor Davis (2004). 'Gay Old Times? Oliver Stone Perpetuates a Classical Myth', *National Review Online* [online journal], http://www.victorhanson.com/articles/hanson121804.html (accessed 10 October 2012).

Hardin, Richard F. (2011). 'Review of Heike Bartel, Anne Simon (ed.), *Unbinding Medea: Interdisciplinary Approaches to a Classical Myth from Antiquity to the 21st Century*. London: Legenda, 2010.' *Bryn Mawr Classical Review* [online journal] http://bmcr.brynmawr.edu/2011/2011-02-22.html (accessed 10 October 2012).

Hardwick, Lorna (2003). *Reception Studies* in *Greece and Rome*: *New Surveys in the Classics* 33. Oxford: Oxford University Press.

——(2007). 'Contests and Continuities in Classical Traditions: African Migrations in Greek Drama', in John Hilton and Anne Gosling (eds), *Alma Parens Originalis? The Receptions of Classical Literature and Thought in Africa, Europe, the United States, and Cuba.* Oxford: Peter Lang, 43–72.

Harrison, T. W. and James Simmons (1966). *Aikin Mata*. Ibadan: Oxford University Press.

Harrison, Thomas (2010). 'Stone, *Alexander*, and the Unity of Mankind', in Paul Cartledge and Fiona Rose Greenland (eds), *Responses to Oliver Stone's* Alexander*: Film, History, and Cultural Studies.* Madison: University of Wisconsin Press, 219–42.

Harrison, Tony (1998). *Prometheus*. London: Faber and Faber.

——(2007). *Collected Film Poetry*. London: Faber and Faber.

Hatzichronoglou, Lena (1993). 'Euripides' *Medea*: Woman or Fiend', in Mary DeForest (ed.), *Woman's Power, Man's Game: Essays on Classical Antiquity in Honor of Joy K. King*. Wauconda, Ill.: Bolchazy-Carducci Publishers, 179–93.

Hayes, John. (n.d.) 'The Making of *Helen of Troy*', *Wide Screen Movies Magazine* [online journal], http://widescreenmovies.org/WSM01/helen.htm (accessed 6 September 2012).

Hazewindus, Minke W. (2004). *When Women Interfere: Studies in the Role of Women in Herodotus' Histories*. Amsterdam: J. C. Gieben.

Hedreen, Guy (1996). 'Image, Text, and Story in the Recovery of Helen', *Classical Antiquity*, 15: 152–92.

Heilbrun, Carolyn ([1985] 1990). 'What Was Penelope Unweaving?', in *Hamlet's Mother and Other Women*. New York: Columbia University Press, 103–11.

Heitman, Richard (2005). *Taking Her Seriously: Penelope and the Plot of Homer's* Odyssey. Ann Arbor: University of Michigan Press.

Henderson, Robert M. (1972). *D.W. Griffith. His Life and Work*. Oxford: Oxford University Press.

Heyer, Virginia (1948). 'In Reply to Elgin Williams', *American Anthropologist*, 50: 163–6.

Hirsch, Forster (1978). *The Hollywood Epic*. London: Gazelle Books.

Hirschberger, Martina (2000). 'Das Bild der Gorgo Medusa in der griechischen Literatur und Ikonographie', *Lexis*, 18: 55–76.

Hjort, Mette and Scott MacKenzie (2003) (eds). *Purity and Provocation: Dogma 95*. London: British Film Institute Publishing.

Hodkinson, Stephen (1986). 'Land Tenure and Inheritance in Classical Sparta', *Classical Quarterly*, 36.2: 378–406.

——(2000). *Property and Wealth in Classical Sparta*. London: Duckworth and the Classical Press of Wales.

——(2004). 'Female Property Ownership and Empowerment in Classical and Hellenistic Sparta', in Thomas J. Figueira (ed.), *Spartan Society*. Swansea: The Classical Press of Wales, 103–36.

——and Anton Powell (1999) (eds). *Sparta: New Perspectives*. London and Swansea: Duckworth and the Classical Press of Wales.

Hoggart, Richard (1957). *The Uses of Literacy*. Harmondsworth: Penguin.

Hölbl, Günther (2001). *A History of the Ptolemaic Empire*. London: Routledge.

Holmberg-Lübeck, Maria (1993). *Iphigenia, Agamemnon's Daughter: A Study of Ancient Conceptions in Greek Myth and Literature Associated with the Atrides*. Stockholm: Almavisit & Wiksell Int.

Homeyer, Helene (1977). *Die spartanische Helene und der trojanische Krieg: Wandlungen und Wanderungen eines Sagen-Kreises vom Altertum bis zur Gegenwart*, Palingenesia 12. Wiesbaden: Steiner.

Hose, Martin (2008). *Euripides. Der Dichter der Leidenschaften*. München: C. H. Beck.

Hughes, Bettany (2005). *Helen of Troy: The Story Behind the Most Beautiful Woman in the World*. New York: Vintage Books.

Hughes-Hallett, Lucy (1990). *Cleopatra: Histories, Dreams and Distortions*. London: Harpercollins.

Hunter, Richard (1987). 'Medea's Flight: The Fourth Book of the Argonautica', *Classical Quarterly*, 37: 129–39.

——(1993a). *The Argonautica of Apollonius: Literary Studies*. Cambridge: Cambridge University Press.

——(1993b) (trans.). *Apollonius of Rhodes: Jason and the Golden Fleece*. Oxford: Oxford University Press.

Ieranò, Giorgio (2000). 'Tre Medee del Novecento: Alvaro, Pasolini, Wolf', in Bruno Gentili and Franca Perusino (eds), *Medea nella letteratura e nell'arte*, Venice: Marsilio Editori, 177–97.

Ignatieff, Andrew (2004). 'A Journey Worthy of Ulysses', *Anglican Journal* [online journal] http://www.anglicanjournal.com/issues/2004/130/ (accessed 10 October 2012).

Isler-Kerényi, Cornelia (2000). 'Immagini di Medea', in Bruno Gentili and Franca Perusino (eds), *Medea nella letteratura e nell'arte*. Venice: Marsilio Editori, 117–38.

Jacobson, Howard (1974). *Ovid's Heroides*. Princeton: Princeton University Press.

James, Paula (2009). 'Crossing Classical Thresholds: Gods, Monsters and Hell Dimensions in the Whedon Universe', in Dunstan Lowe and Kim Shahabudin (eds), *Classics for All: Reworking Antiquity in Mass Culture*. Newcastle upon Tyne: Cambridge Scholars Publishing, 237–60.

Jameson, Fredric (2002). *A Singular Modernity: Essay on the Ontology of the Present*. New York: Verso.

Jauss, Hans (1982). *Toward an Aesthetic of Reception*. Translated by Timothy Bahti. Introduction by Paul de Man. Minneapolis: University of Minnessota Press.

Jensen, Jytte (1988) (ed.). *Carl Th. Dreyer*. New York: Museum of Modern Art.

Johnston, Claire ([1973] 1991). 'Women's Cinema as Counter-Cinema', in Claire Johnston (ed.), *Notes on Women's Cinema*. Glasgow: Screen, 24–31.

Jones, Patricia J. (2006). *Cleopatra: A Sourcebook*. Norman: University of Oklahoma Press.

Joseph, Susan and Marguerite Johnson (2008). 'An Orchid in the Land of Technology: Narrative and Representation in Lars von Trier's *Medea*', *Arethusa*, 41: 113–32.

Joshel, Sandra R., Margaret Malamud, and Maria Wyke (2001). 'Introduction', in Sandra R. Joshel, Margaret Malamud, and Donald T. McGuire, Jr. (eds), *Imperial Projections: Ancient Rome in Modern Popular Culture*. Baltimore: The Johns Hopkins University Press, 1–22.

Jung, Carl G. (1933a). 'Archaic Man', in Carl G. Jung, *Modern Man in Search of a Soul*. San Diego: Harcourt Brace Jovanovich, 125–51.

——(1933b). 'The Spiritual Problem of Modern Man', in Carl G. Jung, *Modern Man in Search of a Soul*. San Diego: Harcourt Brace Jovanovich, 196–220.

——(1933c). 'The Stages of Life', in Jung, *Modern Man in Search of a Soul*. San Diego: Harcourt Brace Jovanovich, 95–114.

——(1933d). *Modern Man in Search of a Soul*. San Diego: Harcourt Brace Jovanovich.

——(1971). 'The Relations Between the Ego and the Unconscious', in Joseph Campbell (ed.), *The Portable Jung*. Translated by R. F. C. Hull. New York: The Viking Press, 79–128.

Kahil, Lilly B.G. (1988). 'Hélène', in *Lexicon Iconographicum Mythologiae Classicae*, v. 4. Zürich, München: Artemis Verlag, 498–563.

Kallendorf, Craig W. (2007). 'Introduction', in Craig W. Kallendorf (ed.), *A Companion to the Classical Tradition*. Oxford: Blackwell, 1–4.

Kaltsas, Nikolaos (2006) (ed.). *Athens-Sparta*. New York: Alexander S. Onassis Public Benefit Foundation (USA).

Kaplan, E. Ann (1997). *Looking for the Other: Feminism, Film, and the Imperial Gaze*. London: Routledge.

——(1998). 'Classical Hollywood Film and Melodrama', in John Hill and Pamela Church Gibson (eds), *The Oxford Guide to Film Studies*. Oxford: Oxford University Press, 272–88.

——(2000). 'Is the Gaze Male?', in Ann E. Kaplan (ed.), *Feminism and Film*. Oxford: Oxford University Press, 119–38.

Katz, Marylin A. (1991). *Penelope's Renown: Meaning and Indeterminacy in the Odyssey*. Princeton: Princeton University Press.

Kaufmann, Walter (1974) (trans. and ed.). *Friedrich Nietzsche: The Gay Science*. New York: Random House.

Kennell, Nigel M. (2010). *Spartans: A New History*. Malden: Willey-Blackwell.

King, Carol J. (2004). '*Alexander* the Great Disappointment', *CAMWS Newsletter*, 14.2: 5.

King, Katherine Callen (1987). *Achilles: Paradigms of the War Hero from Homer to the Middle Ages*. Berkeley: University of California Press.

Kitto, H. D. F. (1961). *Greek Tragedy: A Literary Study*. London: Methuen & Co. Ltd.

Kluckhohn, Clyde (1949). *Mirror for Man: The Relation of Anthropology to Modern Life*. New York: McGraw-Hill Book Company.

Kokkorou-Alevras, Georgia (2006). 'Laconian Stone Sculpture from the Eighth Century B.C. until the Outbreak of the Peloponnesian War', in Nikolaos Kaltsas (ed.), *Athens-Sparta*. New York: Alexander S. Onassis Public Benefit Foundation (USA), 89–94.

Koliopoulos, John S. and Thanos M. Veremis (2002). *Greece: The Modern Sequel. From 1821 to the Present*. London: Hurst & Company.

Kolker, Robert P. (1998). 'The Film Text and Film Form', in John Hill and Pamela Church Gibson (eds), *The Oxford Guide to Film Studies*. Oxford: Oxford University Press, 11–29.

——and Peter Beicken (1993). *The Films of Wim Wenders: Cinema as Vision and Desire*. Cambridge: Cambridge University Press.

Kolonias, Babis (1995) (ed.). *Michael Cacoyannis*, in Babis Kolonias (ed.), *36th Film Festival of Thessaloniki: Michael Cacoyannis*. Cultural Organization of the European Capital: Thessaloniki. Athens: Kastaniotis Publications.

Komar, Kathleen K. (2003). *Reclaiming Klytemnestra: Revenge or Reconciliation*. Champaign, Ill.: University of Illinois Press.

Kostof, Spiro (1989). *Caves of God: Cappadocia and its Churches*. Oxford: Oxford University Press.

Kovacs, David (2002) (ed.). *Euripides: Bacchae, Iphigenia at Aulis, Rhesus*. Cambridge, Mass.: Harvard University Press.

——(2003). 'Towards a Reconstruction of *Iphigenia Aulidensis*', *Journal of Hellenic Studies*, 123: 77–103.

Kruger, Kathryn Sullivan (2001). *Weaving the Word: The Metaphorics of Weaving and Female Textual Production*. London: Susquehanna University Press.

Kvistad, Ivar (2010). 'Cultural Imperialism and Infanticide in Pasolini's *Medea*', in Heike Bartel and Anne Simon (eds), *Unbinding Medea: Interdisciplinary Approaches to a Classical Myth from Antiquity to the 21st Century*. London: Legenda, 224–37.

Lagny, Michèle (1992). 'Popular Taste: The *Peplum*', in Richard Dyer and Ginette Vincendeau (eds), *Popular European Cinema*. London: Routledge, 163–80.

Lancia, Enrico and Roberto, Poppi (2003) (eds). *Dizionario del cinema italiano: Le atrici*. Rome: Gremese Editore.

Landau, Diana (2000). *Gladiator: The Making of the Ridley Scott Epic*. New York: Boxtree.

Landy, Marcia (1994). *Film, Politics, and Gramsci*. Minneapolis: University of Minnesota Press.

——(1996a). *Cinematic Uses of the Past*. Minneapolis: University of Minnesota Press.

——(1996b). '"Which Way is America?" Americanism and the Italian Western', *Boundary 2*, 23.1: 35–59.

LaVine, W. Robert (1981). *In a Glamorous Fashion. The Fabulous Years of Hollywood Costume Design*. London: Allen.

Lawall, Gilbert (1966). 'Apollonius' *Argonautica*: Jason as Antihero', *Yale Classical Studies*, 19: 119–69.

Lee, Mireille M. (2005). 'Constru(ct)ing Gender in the Feminine Greek *Peplos*', in Liza Cleland, Mary Harlow, and Lloyd Llewellyn-Jones (eds), *The Clothed Body in the Ancient World*. Oxford: Oxbow, 55–64.

Lehner, Mark (1985). *The Pyramid Tomb of Hetep-heres and the Satellite Pyramid of Khufu*. Mainz: Peter von Zabern.

Levene, David S. (2007). 'Xerxes Goes to Hollywood', in Emma Bridges, Edith Hall, and Peter John Rhodes (eds), *Cultural Responses to the Persian Wars: Antiquity to the Third Millennium*. Oxford: Oxford University Press, 383–403.

Levine, Stuart (2008). 'Powerful TV women must face backlash', *msnbc.com*. 13 July [website], http://www.msnbc.msn.com/id/25613199/ (accessed 10 October 2012).

Lillo Redonet, Fernando (2008). 'Sparta and Ancient Greece in *The 300 Spartans*', in Irene Berti and Marta García Morcillo (eds), *Hellas on Screen: Cinematic Receptions of Ancient History, Literature and Myth. Heidelberger Althistorische Beiträge und epigraphische Studien, Bd. 45*. Stuttgart: Franz Steiner Verlag, 117–30.

Linville, Susan E. (2004). *History Films, Women, and Freud's Uncanny*. Austin: University of Texas Press.

Liversidge, Michael J. H. and Catherine Edwards (1996) (eds). *Imagining Rome: British Artists and Rome in the Nineteenth Century*. London: Merrell Holberton.

Llewellyn-Jones, Lloyd (2005). 'The Fashioning of Delilah: Costume Design, Historicism and Fantasy in Cecil B. DeMille's *Samson and Delilah* (1949)', in Liza Cleland, Mary Harlow and Lloyd Llewellyn-Jones (eds), *The Clothed Body in the Ancient World*. Oxford: Oxbow, 14–29.

——(2009). 'Hollywood's Ancient World', in Andrew Erskine (ed.), *The Blackwell Companion to the Ancient World*. Oxford: Blackwell, 564–79.

——(2010). '"Help Me, Aphrodite!": Depicting the Royal Women of Persia in *Alexander*', in Paul Cartledge and Fiona Rose Greenland (eds), *Responses to Oliver Stone's* Alexander: *Film, History, and Cultural Studies*. Madison: University of Wisconsin Press, 243–81.

——(forthcoming). *Designs on the Past: How Hollywood Created the Ancient World*. Edinburgh: Edinburgh University Press.

Lloyd-Jones, Hugh (1990). 'Zeus in Aeschylus', in Hugh Lloyd-Jones, *The Academic Papers of Hugh Lloyd-Jones: Greek Epic, Lyric, and Tragedy*. Oxford: Clarendon Press, 238–61.

Lochman, Tomas, Thomas Späth, and Adrian Stähli (2008) (eds). *Antike im Kino*. Basel: Verlag der Skulpturhalle Basel.

Loffreda, Pierpaolo (2001) (ed.). *L'età dell'oro*. Pesaro: Edizioni di Cineforum.

Loraux, Nicole (1993). *The Children of Athena: Athenian Ideas about Citizenship and the Division between the Sexes*. Translated by Caroline Levine. Foreword by Froma I. Zeitlin. Princeton: Princeton University Press.

——(2002). 'Greek Tragedy: Political Drama or Oratorio', in Nicole Loraux (ed.), *The Mourning Voice: An Essay on Greek Tragedy*. Translated by Elizabeth Trapnell Rawlings. Foreword by Pietro Pucci. Ithaca: Cornell University Press, 1–13.

Louvish, Simon (2007). *Cecil B. DeMille and the Golden Calf*. London: Faber and Faber.

Lovric, Michelle (2001). *Cleopatra's Face: Fatal Beauty*. London: British Museum Press.

Lowe, Dunstan and Kim Shahabudin (2009) (eds). *Classics For All: Reworking Antiquity in Mass Culture*. Newcastle upon Tyne: Cambridge Scholars Publishing.

Lowe, Nick (2005). 'Writing *Troy*', paper presented at panel on '*Troy*, the Movie', American Philological Association annual meeting, 8 January.

——(2007). 'The Screen of Orpheus', *Arion*, 15: 149–56.

Lowenthal, David (1985). *The Past is a Foreign Country*. Cambridge: Cambridge University Press.

Lucanio, Patrick (1994). *With Fire and Sword: Italian Spectacles on American Screens, 1958–1968*. Metuchen: The Scarecrow Press, Inc.

Lucantonio, Gabrielle (1998). *Lars von Trier*. Rome: Dino Audino Editore.

——(2005). 'Presentazione/Introduction', in Booklet to DVD *Lars von Trier, Medea*. Rome: Raro Video.

Lucas, Tim (2007). *All the Colors of the Dark*. Cincinnati: Video Watchdog.

Lumholdt, Jan (2003) (ed.). *Lars von Trier: Interviews*. Jackson, Miss.: University Press of Mississippi.

Luschnig, C. A. E. (1988). *Tragic Aporia: A Study of Euripides' Iphigenia at Aulis*. Ramus Monographs 3. Berwick, Vic.: Aureal Publications.

Lyons, Sir John (1999). 'The Vocabulary of Color with Particular Reference to Ancient Greek and Classical Latin', in Alexander Borg (ed.), *The Language of Color in the Mediterranean: An Anthology on Linguistic and Ethnographic Aspects of Color Terms*. Stockholm: Almquist & Wiksell International, 38–75.

MacDonald Fraser, George (1988). *The Hollywood History of the World*. Marlborough: Michael Joseph Ltd.

MacGregor, Ian, with Rodney Tyler (1986). *The Enemies Within: The Story of the Miner's Strike, 1984–5*. London: Collins.

Macgregor Morris, Ian and Stephen Hodkinson (2012). 'Introduction', in Stephen Hodkinson and Ian Macgregor Morris (eds), *Sparta in Modern Thought: Politics, History and Culture*. Swansea: The Classical Press of Wales, vii–xxvi.

Machamer, Peter (1998) (ed.). *The Cambridge Companion to Galileo*. Cambridge: Cambridge University Press.

MacKinnon, Kenneth (1986). *Greek Tragedy into Film*. Rutherford, N.J.: Fairleigh Dickinson University Press.

——(2002). *Love, Tears, and the Male Spectator*. London: Associated University Presses.

Maeder, Edward, Alicia Annas, Satch La Valley, and Elois Jenssen (1987) (eds). *Hollywood and History. Costume Design in Film*. Los Angeles: Thames and Hudson Ltd.

Malamud, Bernard ([1952] 2003). *The Natural*. London: Faber & Faber.

Marcus, Millicent (1986). *Italian Film in the Light of Neorealism*. Princeton: Princeton University Press.

Martindale, Charles (2006). 'Introduction: Thinking through Reception', in Charles Martindale and Richard F. Thomas (eds), *Classics and the Uses of Reception*. Oxford: Blackwell Publishing, 1–13.

——(2007). 'Reception', in Craig W. Kallendorf (ed.), *A Companion to the Classical Tradition*. Oxford: Blackwell, 297–311.

May, Elaine T. (2008). *Homeward Bound: American Families in the Cold War Era*. New York: Basic Books.

Mayer, David (1994). *Playing Out the Empire. Ben-Hur and Other Toga Plays and Films. A Critical Anthology*. Oxford: Clarendon Press.

Mayer, Kenneth. (1996). 'Helen and the Διὸς βουλή', *American Journal of Philology*, 117: 1–15.

McCart, Gregory (2007). 'Masks in Greek and Roman Theatre', in Marianne McDonald and J. Michael Walton (eds), *The Cambridge Companion to Greek and Roman Theatre*. Cambridge: Cambridge University Press, 247–67.

McCarthy, Todd (2004). 'Troy', *Variety*, 5 May.

McConathy, Dale and Diana Vreeland (1976). *Hollywood Costume: Glamour, Glitter, Romance*. New York: Harry N. Abrams.

McDonald, Marianne (1983). *Euripides in Cinema: The Heart Made Visible*. Philadelphia: Centrum Philadelphia.

——(1991). 'Cacoyannis's and Euripides' *Iphigenia*: The Dialectic of Power', in Martin M. Winkler (ed.), *Classics and the Cinema*. Bucknell Review. Lewisburg: Bucknell University Press, 127–41.

——(2001). 'Eye of the Camera, Eye of the Victim: Iphigenia by Euripides and Cacoyannis', in Martin M. Winkler (ed.), *Classical Myth and Culture in the Cinema*. Oxford: Oxford University Press, 90–101.

——(2008). 'A New Hope: Film as a Teaching Tool for Classics', in Lorna Hardwick and Christopher Stray (eds), *A Companion to Classical Receptions*. Oxford: Blackwell, 327–41.

——and Kenneth MacKinnon (1983). 'Cacoyannis vs. Euripides: From Tragedy to Melodrama', in Niall Slater and Bernhard Zimmermann (eds), *Intertextualität in der griechisch-römischen Komödie*. Stuttgart: M&P Verlag für Wissenschaft und Forschung, 222–34.

——and Martin M. Winkler (1991). 'Interviews with Michael Cacoyannis and Irene Papas (conducted over the telephone in November and December 1988)', in Martin M. Winkler (ed.), *Classics and the Cinema*. Bucknell Review. Lewisburg: Bucknell University Press, 159–84.

————(2001). 'Michael Cacoyannis and Irene Papas on Greek Tragedy', in Martin M. Winkler (ed.), *Classical Myth and Culture in the Cinema*. Oxford: Oxford University Press, 72–89.

McGrath, Charles (2004). 'Brad Pitt's Big Fat Greek Toga Party', *New York Times*, 9 May: 38.

McGuire, William (1982). *Bollingen: An Adventure in Collecting the Past*. Princeton: Princeton University Press.

Meagher, Robert E. (1995). *Helen: Myth, Legend, and the Culture of Misogyny*. New York: Continuum Publishing Co.

Medved, Harry and Michael Medved (1984). *The Hollywood Hall of Shame. The Most Expensive Flops in Movie History*. New York: HarperCollins.

Mendelsohn, Daniel (2004). 'A Little *Iliad*', *New York Review of Books*, 24 June: 46–9.

Menu, Michel (1996) (ed.). *Médée et la Violence*. Colloque international organisé à l'université de Toulouse-Le Mirail (CRATA). Toulouse: Presses Universitaires du Mirail.

Merkel, Inge ([1987] 2000). *Odysseus and Penelope: An Ordinary Marriage*. Translated by Renate Latimer. Riverside: Ariadne Press.

Michelakis, Pantelis (2001). 'The Past as a Foreign Country? Greek Tragedy, Cinema and the Politics of Space', in Felix Budelmann and Pantelis Michelakis (eds), *Homer, Tragedy and Beyond: Essays in Honour of P. E. Easterling*. London: Society for the Promotion of Hellenic Studies, 241–57.

——(2004). 'Greek Tragedy in Cinema: Theatre, Politics, History', in Edith Hall, Fiona Macintosh and Amanda Wrigley (eds), *Dionysus since 69: Greek Tragedy at the Dawn of the Third Millennium*. Oxford: Oxford University Press, 199–217.

Michelakis, Pantelis (2006a). *Euripides. Iphigenia at Aulis*. London: Duckworth.

——(2006b). 'Reception, Performance, and the Sacrifice of Iphigenia', in Charles Martindale and Richard F. Thomas (eds), *Classics and the Uses of Reception*. Oxford: Blackwell, 216–26.

——(2013). *Greek Tragedy on Screen*. Oxford: Oxford University Press.

Michelini, Ann N. (1999–2000). 'The Expansion of Myth in Late Euripides: *Iphigeneia at Aulis*', in *Euripides and Tragic Theatre in the Late Fifth Century*. Special issues of *Illinois Classical Studies* 24–5: 41–57.

Millender, Ellen G. (1999). 'Athenian Ideology and the Empowered Spartan Woman', in Stephen Hodkinson and Anton Powell (eds), *Sparta: New Perspectives*. London and Swansea: Duckworth and the Classical Press of Wales, 355–91.

Miller, Frank and Lynn Varley (2006). *300*. Milwaukie: Dark Horse Books.

Miller, Nancy K. (1981). 'Emphasis Added: Plots and Plausibilities in Women's Fiction', *Proceedings of the Modern Language Association*, 96: 36–48.

Mimoso-Ruiz, Duarte (1981). 'La *Medea* de Dreyer (Sur un Manuscrit pour un film non realisé de 1965)', *Orbis Litterarum*, 36: 332–42.

Mimoso-Ruiz, Duarte-Nuno (1996). 'Le Myth de Médée au Cinéma', in Michel Menu (ed.), *Médée et la Violence*. Toulouse: Presses Universitaires du Mirail, 251–68.

Molloy, Maureen (1999). 'Death and the Maiden: The Feminine and the Nation in Recent New Zealand Films', *Signs*, 25.1: 153–70.

Montserrat, Dominic (2000). *Akhenaten. History, Fantasy and Ancient Egypt*. London: Routledge.

Most, Glenn W. (2006) (trans. and ed.). *Hesiod: Theogony, Works and Days, Testimonia*. Cambridge, Mass.: Harvard University Press.

Müller, Marion ([2000] 2002). *Vexierbilder: Die Filmwelten des Lars von Trier*. St. Augustin: Gardez! Verlag.

Mulvey, Laura (1975). 'Visual Pleasure and Narrative Cinema', *Screen*, 16.3: 6–18.

——(1989a). 'Visual Pleasure and Narrative Cinema', in Laura Mulvey, *Visual and Other Pleasures*. London: Macmillan, 14–26.

——([1981] 1989b). 'Afterthoughts on "Visual Pleasure and Narrative Cinema", inspired by King Vidor's *Duel in the Sun*', in Laura Mulvey, *Visual and Other Pleasures*. London: Macmillan, 29–37.

Munn, Mike (1982). *The Stories Behind the Scenes of the Great Film Epics*. Watford: Model Books.

Murnaghan, Sheila (1987). *Disguise and Recognition in the Odyssey*. Princeton: Princeton University Press.

——and Deborah H. Roberts (2002). 'Penelope's Song: The Lyric Odysseys of Linda Pastan and Louise Glück', *Classical and Modern Literature*, 22: 1–33.

Neale, Steve (2000). *Genre and Hollywood*. London: Routledge.

Negra, Diane (2002). 'Immigrant Stardom in Imperial America: Pola Negri and the Problem of Typology', in Jennifer Bean and Diane Negra (eds), *A Feminist Reader in Early Cinema*, 374–403.

Nikoloutsos, Konstantinos P. (2008). 'The *Alexander* Bromance: Male Desire and Gender Fluidity in Oliver Stone's Historical Epic', *Helios*, 35.2: 223–51.

——(2010). 'Appropriating Greek Myth: Iphigenia and Argentine Patriarchal Society in Inés de Oliveira Cézar's *Extranjera*,' *Classical Receptions Journal*, 2.1: 92–113.

——(2012). 'Introduction', *Reception of Greek and Roman Drama in Latin America*. Special issue of *Romance Quarterly*, 59:1: 1–5.

——(2013). 'Reviving the Past: Cinematic History and Popular Memory in *The 300 Spartans* (1962)', *Classical World*, 106.2: 261–83.

Nisbet, Gideon (2006). *Ancient Greece in Film and Popular Culture*. Exeter: Bristol Phoenix Press.

Ogden, Daniel (1999). *Polygamy, Prostitutes and Death. The Hellenistic Dynasties.* Swansea: Classical Press of Wales.

Oldenziel, Ruth and Karin Zachmann (2009) (eds). *Cold War Kitchen: Americanization, Technology, and European Users*. Cambridge: Massachusetts Institute of Technology.

Orrison, Katherine (1999). *Written in Stone: Making Cecil B. DeMille's Epic 'The Ten Commandments'*. New York: Vestal Press.

Osborne, Robin (1987). *Classical Landscape with Figures: The Ancient Greek City and its Countryside*. London: George Philip.

Paglia, Camille (1997). 'Homer on Film: A Voyage through *The Odyssey*, *Ulysses*, *Helen of Troy*, and *Contempt*', *Arion*, 5:2, 166–97.

Paige, Nicholas (2004). 'Bardot and Godard in 1963 (Historicizing the Postmodern Image)', *Representations*, 88: 1–25.

Papadopoulou, Thalia (1997). 'The Presentation of the Inner Self: Euripides' *Medea* 1021–55 and Apollonius Rhodius' *Argonautica* 3, 772–801', *Mnemosyne*, 50: 641—64.

Paradiso, Annalisa (1993). 'Gorgo, la Spartana', in Nicole Loraux (ed.), *Grecia al femminile*. Bari: Laterza, 107–22.

Pasolini, Pier Paolo (1960). *Orestiade*. Turin: Giulio Einaudi.

——(1969). *Medea* (film). DVD: 2002, Los Angeles, CA: Vanguard Cinema.

——(1970). *Medea*. Milan: Aldo Garzanti Editore.

——(1975). 'Pasolini sur *Médée* et *Les Mille et une nuits*', *Pour le Cinema*, 23 November 1975. http://www.inf.fr/art-et-culture/cinema/video/I04163215/pasolini-sur-medee-et-les-mille-et-une-nuits.fr.html (accessed 10 October 2012).

——(1979). *Descrizioni di descrizioni*. Graziella Chiarcossi (ed.). Turin: Giulio Einaudi Editore.

——(1982). 'The Ashes of Gramsci', in Pier Paolo Pasolini, *Poems: Selected and Translated by Norman MacAfee*. New York: Vintage Books, 3–23. [First published in 1957 as *Le ceneri di Gramsci*.]

Pastan, Linda (1988). *The Imperfect Paradise*. New York: W. W. Norton and Company.

Paul, Joanna (2007). 'Working with Film: Theories and Methodologies', in Lorna Hardwick and Christopher Stray (eds), *A Companion to Classical Receptions*. Oxford: Blackwell Publishing, 303–14.

——(2010a). 'Oliver Stone's *Alexander* and the Cinematic Epic Tradition', in Paul Carteldge and Fiona Rose Greenland (eds), *Oliver Stone's* Alexander: *Film, History, and Cultural Studies*. Madison: University of Wisconsin Press, 15–35.

——(2010b). 'Cinematic Receptions of Antiquity: The Current State of Play', *Classical Receptions Journal*, 2.1: 136–55.

——(2013). *Film and the Classical Epic Tradition*. Oxford: Oxford University Press.

Pavlock, Barbara (1990). *Eros, Imitation, and the Epic Tradition*. Ithaca: Cornell University Press.

Pendergast Tom and Sara (2000) (eds). 'Cacoyannis, Michael', in the *International Dictionary of Films and Filmmakers. Vol. 2: Directors*. 4th edition. Detroit and London: St. James Press, 147–8.

Petersen, Wolfgang (n.d.). 'The Historical Troy and the *Iliad*', *Troy Movie Production Notes* [website], http://troymovie.warnerbros.com/ (accessed 17 October 2006; no longer accessible 6 September 2012).

Petrovic, Ivana (2008). 'Plutarch's and Stone's *Alexander*', in Irene Berti and Marta García Morcillo (eds), *Hellas on Screen: Cinematic Receptions of Ancient History, Literature and Myth. Heidelberger Althistorische Beiträge und Epigraphische Studien, Bd. 45*. Stuttgart: Franz Steiner Verlag, 163–83.

Pfrommer, Michael (1999). *Alexandria. Im Schatten der Pyramiden*. Mainz Am Rhein: Von Zabern.

Phinney, Edward (1967). 'Narrative Unity in the *Argonautica*, the Medea-Jason Romance', *Transactions of the American Philological Association*, 98: 327–41.

Pierce, Jerry Benjamin (2008). 'Great Ambiguity: How Oliver Stone's Alexander was Defeated by its More Masculine Cinematic Rivals', *Journal of the Indiana Academy of the Social Sciences*, XII: 46–65.

Platt, Verity (2010). 'Viewing the Past: Cinematic Exegesis in the Caverns of Macedon', in Paul Cartledge and Fiona Rose Greenland (eds), *Responses to Oliver Stone's* Alexander: *Film, History, and Cultural Studies*. Madison: University of Wisconsin Press, 285–304.

Pollitt, J. J. (1974). *The Ancient View of Greek Art: Criticism, History, and Terminology*. New Haven: Yale University Press.

Pomeroy, Arthur J. (2008). *'Then It Was Destroyed by the Volcano': The Ancient World in Film and on Television*. London: Duckworth.

Pomeroy, Sarah B. ([1984] 1990). *Women in Hellenistic Egypt: From Alexander to Cleopatra*. Detroit: Wayne State University Press.

——(1995). *Goddesses, Whores, Wives, and Slaves: Women in Classical Antiquity*. New York: Schocken Books.

——(2002). *Spartan Women*. Oxford: Oxford University Press.

——(2006). 'Women and Ethnicity in Classical Greece: Changing the Paradigms', in Konrad H. Kinzl (ed.), *A Companion to the Classical Greek World*. Oxford: Blackwell Publishing, 350–66.

Porter, Katherine Anne (1970). *The Collected Essays and Occasional Writings of Katherine Anne Porter*. New York: Delacorte Press.

Potter, Amanda (2009). 'Hell has no Fury like a Dissatisfied Viewer: Audience Responses to the Presentation of the Furies in *Xena: Warrior Princess* and *Charmed*', in Dunstan Lowe and Kim Shahabudin (eds), *Classics for All: Reworking Antiquity in Mass Culture*. Newcastle upon Tyne: Cambridge Scholars Publishing, 217–36.

Powell, Anton (1999). 'Spartan Women Assertive in Politics? Plutarch's Lives of Agis and Kleomenes', in Stephen Hodkinson and Anton Powell (1999) (eds), *Sparta: New Perspectives*. London and Swansea: Duckworth and the Classical Press of Wales, 393–419.

Prettejohn, Elizabeth, Peter Trippi, Robert Upstone, and Patty Wageman (2008) (eds). *J.W. Waterhouse: The Modern Pre-Raphaelite*. London: Royal Academy of Arts.

'Production notes' (2006) studies on Wim Wenders' *Don't Come Knocking* at http://thecia.com.au/reviews/d/don-t-come-knocking.shtml (accessed 10 October 2012).

Prümm, Karl, Silke Bierhoff, and Matthias Körnich (1999) (eds). *Kamerastile im aktuellen Film: Berichte und Analysen*. Marburg: Schüren Verlag.

Quart, Leonard and Albert Auster (2002). 'American Film and Society since 1945', in Steven J. Ross (ed.), *Movies and American Society*. Oxford: Blackwell, 221–40.

Rabel, Robert J. (2007). 'The Realist Politics of *Troy*', in Martin M. Winkler (ed.), *Troy: From Homer's* Iliad *to Hollywood Epic*. Oxford: Blackwell, 186–201.

Rabinowitz, Nancy Sorkin (1993). *Anxiety Veiled: Euripides and the Traffic in Women*. Ithaca: Cornell University Press.

Ray, James (2001). 'Alexandria', in Susan Walker and Peter Higgs (eds), *Cleopatra of Egypt from History to Myth*. London: British Museum Press, 32–7.

——(2003). 'Cleopatra in the Temples of Upper Egypt: The Evidence of Dendera and Armant', in Susan Walker and Sally-Ann Ashton (eds), *Cleopatra Reassessed*. London: British Museum Press, 9–11.

Reames, Jeanne (2010). 'The Cult of Hephaestion', in Paul Cartledge and Fiona Rose Greenland (eds), *Responses to Oliver Stone's* Alexander*: Film, History, and Cultural Studies*. Madison: University of Wisconsin Press, 183–216.

——— (n.d.). 'Fire Bringer: Oliver Stone's *Alexander*' [website], http://myweb.unomaha.edu/~mreames/Beyond_Renault/review2.html (accessed 10 October 2012).

Reames-Zimmerman, Jeanne (1999). 'An Atypical Affair? Alexander the Great, Hephaestion Amyntoros and the Nature of their Relationship', *Ancient History Bulletin*, 13.3: 81–96.

——— (2004). 'A History of Alexander on the Big Screen', *Amphora*, 3.2: 12–15.

Rehm, Rush (2003). *Radical Theatre: Greek Tragedy and the Modern World*. London: Duckworth.

Reisner, George A. and W. Stevenson Smith (1955). *A History of the Giza Necropolis II*. Cambridge, Mass.: Harvard University Press.

Renger, Almut-Barbara and Jon Solomon (2012) (eds). *Ancient Worlds in Film and Television: Gender and Politics*. Leiden: Brill Academic Publishers.

Richards, Jeffrey (2008). *Hollywood's Ancient Worlds*. New York: Hambledon Continuum.

Richter, Virginia (2008). 'Opfer und Rache in Lars von Triers *Medea* und *Dogville*', in Ulrich Meurer, Marie-Elisabeth Mitsou, and Maria Oikonomou (eds), *Perseus' Schild: Griechische Frauenbilder im Film*. Neuried: ars una Verlag, 67–99.

Robins, Gay (1993). *Women in Ancient Egypt*. London: British Museum Press.

Robinson, David (1955). 'Spectacle', *Sight and Sound*, 25: 22–7, 55–6.

Rodley, Lyn (1985). *Cave Monasteries of Byzantine Cappadocia*. Cambridge: Cambridge University Press.

Roisman, Hanna (2008). 'Helen and the Power of Erotic Love: From Homeric Contemplation to Hollywood Fantasy', *College Literature*, 35.4: 127–50.

Romney, Jonathan (2003). 'Cold Mountain: Gone with the wind? No ma'am, it went that way', *The Independent on Sunday*, *Films* section, 28 December.

Rose, Peter W. (2001). 'Teaching Classical Myth and Confronting Contemporary Myths', in Martin M. Winkler (ed.), *Classical Myth and Culture in the Cinema*. Oxford: Oxford University Press, 291–318.

Rose, Toby ([1992] 2003). 'Lars von Trier, Director', in Jan Lumholdt (ed.), *Lars von Trier: Interviews*. Jackson, Miss.: University Press of Mississippi, 86–7.

Rosenberg, Jan (1983). *Women's Reflections: The Feminist Film Movement*. Ann Arbor: University of Michigan Research Press.

Rosenstone, Robert A. (2000). 'Oliver Stone as Historian', in Robert Brent Toplin (ed.), *Oliver Stone's USA: Film, History, and Controversy*. Lawrence: University Press of Kansas, 26–39.

Ross, Steven J. (2002) (ed.). *Movies and American Society*. Oxford: Blackwell.

Rubino, Margherita (2000). *Medea Contemporanea: Lars von Trier, Christa Wolf, scrittori balcanici*. Genova: D.AR.FI.CL.ET.

Ruby, Jay (2000). *Picturing Culture: Explorations of Film and Anthropology*. Chicago: University of Chicago Press.

Russell, James (2007). *The Historical Epic and Contemporary Hollywood: From Dances with Wolves to Gladiator*. London: Continuum.

Russell, M. E. (May 2004). 'Helmer of Troy', *In Focus* [online journal], http://www.infocusmag.com/04may/petersenuncut.htm (accessed 18 October 2006; no longer accessible 6 September 2012).

Russmann, Edna R. (2001). *Eternal Egypt. Masterworks of Ancient Art from the British Museum*. London: British Museum Press.

Ryan, George C. (1965). 'Helen in Homer', *Classical Journal*, 61: 115–17.

Ryan-Scheutz, Colleen (2007). *Sex, the Self and the Sacred: Women in the Cinema of Pier Paolo Pasolini*. Toronto: University of Toronto Press.

Saleh, Mohamed and Hourig Sourouzain (1987). *The Official Catalogue of the Cairo Museum*. Cairo: American University in Cairo Press.

Salles, Walter (2008). 'Walter Salles on Wim Wenders', in Jason Wood and Ian Haydn Smith (eds), *Wim Wenders*. London: Axiom Books, 19–28.

Sandrini, Luca, and Alberto Scandola (1997) (eds). *La paura mangia l'anima: Il cinema di Lars von Trier*. Verona: Cierre Edizioni.

Scheid, John and Jesper Svenbro (1996). *The Craft of Zeus*. Cambridge, Mass.: Harvard University Press.

Schepelern, Peter (2010). 'The Element of Crime and Punishment: Aki Kaurismäki, Lars von Trier and the Traditions of Nordic Cinema', *Journal of Scandinavian Cinema*, 1: 87–103.

Scherer, Margaret R. (1967). 'Helen of Troy', *Metropolitan Museum of Art Bulletin*, 25: 367–83.

Schmidt, Ernst Günter (1996). 'Achilleus und Helena—ein verhindertes antikes Traumpaar. Ps.-Hesiod, Frauenkatalog Frgm. 204, 87–92 M.-W.', in R. Faber and B. Seidensticker (eds), *Worte, Bilder, Töne: Studien zur Antike und Antikerezeption*. Würzburg: Königshausen & Neumann, 23–38.

Scholes, Robert and Robert Kellog (1966). *The Nature of Narrative*. New York: Oxford University Press.

Schwartz, Barth David ([1992] 1995). *Pasolini Requiem*. New York: Vintage Books.

Scott, A. O. (2004a). 'Greeks Bearing Immortality', *New York Times*, 14 May: 16.

——(2004b). 'A Territory Alexander Couldn't Conquer', *The New York Times*, 26 December [online edition] http://www.nytimes.com/2004/12/26/movies/26ston.html (accessed 10 October 2012).

Scribner, Charity (2003). *Requiem for Communism*. Cambridge, Mass.: Massachussetts Institute of Technology Press.

Scriver, Stacey (2009). 'Subjectivity, Identity and 300 Spartans', *Psychoanalysis, Culture and Society*, 14.2: 183–99.

Scully, Stephen (2007). 'The Fate of Troy', in Martin M. Winkler (ed.), *Troy: From Homer's* Iliad *to Hollywood Epic*. Oxford: Blackwell, 119–30.

Seabrook, Jeremy and Trevor Blackwell (1993). 'Coal seams stitched up', *New Statesman and Society*, 9 July 1993.

Sebesta, Judith L. (2001). 'Symbolism in the Costume of the Roman Woman', in Judith L. Sebesta and Larissa Bonfante (eds), *The World of Roman Costume*. Madison: University of Wisconsin Press, 46–53.

Sebesta, Judith L. and Larissa Bonfante (2001) (eds). *The World of Roman Costume*. Madison: University of Wisconsin Press.

Seddon, Vicky (1986) (ed.). *The Cutting Edge: Women and the Pit Strike*. London: Lawrence & Wishart.

Segre, Michael (1998). 'The Never-Ending Galileo Story', in Peter Machamer (ed.), *The Cambridge Companion to Galileo*. Cambridge: Cambridge University Press, 388–416.

Shahabudin, Kim (2007). 'From Greek Myth to Hollywood Story: Explanatory Narrative in *Troy*', in Martin M. Winkler (ed.), *Troy: From Homer's* Iliad *to Hollywood Epic*. Oxford: Blackwell, 107–18.

——(2009). 'Ancient Mythology and Modern Myths: *Hercules Conquers Atlantis* (1961)', in Dunstan Lowe and Kim Shahabudin (eds), *Classics for All: Reworking Antiquity in Mass Culture*. Newcastle upon Tyne: Cambridge Scholars Publishing, 196–216.

——(2010). 'The Appearance of History: Robert Rossen's *Alexander the Great*', in Paul Cartledge and Fiona Rose Greenland (eds), *Responses to Oliver Stone's* Alexander: *Film, History, and Cultural Studies*. Madison: University of Wisconsin Press, 92–116.

Sharaff, Irene (1976). *Broadway and Hollywood: Costumes Designed By Irene Sharaff*. New York: Van Nostrand Reinhold Company.

Siafkos, Christos (2009). *Μιχάλης Κακογιάννης: Σε Πρώτο Πλάνο*. Athens: Psichogios Publications S. A.

Siciliano, Enzo (1982). *Pasolini: A Biography*. Translated by John Shepley. New York: Random House.

Siclier, Jacques (1962). 'L'âge du péplum', *Les cahiers du cinéma*, 131: 26–38.

Siegel, Janice (2007). 'The Coens' *O Brother, Where Art Thou?* and Homer's *Odyssey*', *Mouseion* 7, 213–45.

Sieglohr, Ulrike (2000) (ed.). *Heroines without Heroes: Reconstructing Female and National Identities in European Cinema 1945–51*. London: Cassell.

Sillanpoa, Wallace (1981). 'Pasolini's Gramsci', *Modern Language Notes*, 96: 120–37.

Skinner, Marilyn B. (2010). '*Alexander* and Ancient Greek Sexuality: Some Theoretical Considerations', in Paul Cartledge and Fiona Rose Greenland (eds), *Responses to Oliver Stone's* Alexander: *Film, History, and Cultural Studies*. Madison: University of Wisconsin Press, 119–34.

Sloane, Leonard (1969). 'Yellow Submarine Art Is the Thing Today', *New York Times*, 24 August 1969: F 15.

Smith, Paul (1993). *Clint Eastwood: A Cultural Production*. Minneapolis: University of Minnesota Press.

Sobchak, Vivian (2003). 'Surge and Splendor: A Phenomenology of the Hollywood Historical Epic', in Barry Keith Grant (ed.), *Film Genre Reader III*. Austin: University of Texas Press, 296–323.

Soldatos, Giannis (2002a). *Ιστορία του Ελληνικού Κινηματογράφου*. 1ος *Τόμος*: *1900- 1967*. Athens: Egokeros.

——(2002b). *Ιστορία του Ελληνικού Κινηματογράφου*. 2ος *Τόμος*: *1967–90*. Athens: Egokeros.

——(2004). *Ιστορία του Ελληνικού Κινηματογράφου*. 4ος *Τόμος*: *Ντοκουμέντα 1900–1970*. Athens: Egokeros.

Solomon, Aubrey (1988). *Twentieth Century Fox: A Corporate and Financial History*. Metuchen: The Scarecrow Press, Inc.

Solomon, Jon (1995–1996). 'In the Wake of "Cleopatra": The Ancient World in the Cinema since 1963', *The Classical Journal*, 91: 113–14.

——(2001a). *The Ancient World in the Cinema*. Revised and expanded edition. New Haven: Yale University Press.

——(2001b). 'The Sounds of Cinematic Antiquity', in Martin M. Winkler (ed.), *Classical Myth and Culture in the Cinema*. Oxford: Oxford University Press, 319–37.

——(2007). 'Viewing *Troy*: Authenticity, Criticism, Interpretation', in Martin M. Winkler (ed.), *Troy: From Homer's* Iliad *to Hollywood Epic*. Oxford: Blackwell, 85–98.

——(2010a). 'Review Article: Film Philology: Towards Effective Theories and Methodologies', *International Journal of the Classical Tradition*, 17: 435–49.

——(2010b). 'The Popular Reception of *Alexander*', in Paul Cartledge and Fiona Rose Greenland (eds), *Responses to Oliver Stone's* Alexander: *Film, History, and Cultural Studies*. Madison: University of Wisconsin Press, 36–51.

Sorlin, Pierre (1991). *European Cinemas, European Societies: 1939–1990*. London: Routledge.

——(2008). 'Les deux périodes antiquisantes du cinéma italien', in Tomas Lochman, Thomas Späth, and Adrian Stähli (2008) (eds), *Antike im Kino*. Basel: Verlag der Skulpturhalle Basel, 88–98.

Spelling, Ian (2004). 'War! What is it Good for?', *Film Review*, 645: 72–4.

Spina, Luigi (2008). 'By Heracles! From Satyr-Play to *Peplum*', in Irene Berti and Marta García Morcillo (eds), *Hellas on Screen: Cinematic Receptions of Ancient History, Literature and Myth. Heidelberger Althistorische Beiträge und epigraphische Studien, Bd. 45*. Stuttgart: Franz Steiner Verlag, 57–64.

Stacey, Jackie (1994). *Star Gazing*. London: Routledge.

Stack, Oswald (1969). *Pasolini on Pasolini: Interviews with Oswald Stack*. Bloomington: Indiana University Press.

Stanley, Alessandra (2004). 'Trojan Fever Breaking Out, both Seriously and Less So', *New York Times*, 12 May.

Stead, Jean (1987). *Never the Same Again: Women and the Miner's Strike*. London: The Women's Press.

Stefanutto Rosa, Stefano (2002). 'Rossana Podestà: an Illustrious Career' [website], http://www.torchieflash.com/rpodesta/rossanainterview.htm (accessed 28 February 2009).

Steimatsky, Noa (2009). 'The Cinecittà Refugee Camp (1944–50)', *October*, 138: 22–50.

Steiner, Deborah Tarn (2001). *Images in Mind: Statues in Archaic and Classical Greek Literature and Thought*. Princeton: Princeton University Press.

Stephan, Inge (2006). 'Zwischen Archaisierung und Aktualisierung: Medea-Filme von Pasolini, Trier, Dassin und Stöckl', in Inge Stephan, *Medea: Multimediale Karriere einer mythologischen Figur*. Köln/Weimar/Wien: Böhlau Verlag, 212–39.

Stevens, Susan A. (2003). *Seeing Double: Intercultural Poetics in Ptolemaic Alexandria*. Berkeley: University of California Press.

Stevenson, Jack (2002). *Lars von Trier*. London: British Film Institute Publishing.

——(2003). *Dogme Uncut: Lars von Trier, Thomas Vinterberg, and the Gang that Took on Hollywood*. Santa Monica, CA: Santa Monica Press.

Stocking, Jr. George (1974) (ed.). *The Shaping of American Anthropology 1883–1911: A Franz Boas Reader*. New York: Basic Books.

Stoddart, Helen (1995). 'Auteurism and Film Authorship Theory', in Joanne Hollows and Mark Jancovich (eds), *Approaches to Popular Film*. Manchester: Manchester University Press, 37–58.

Stone, Oliver (2000). 'Stone on Stone's Image (As Presented by Some Historians)', in Robert Brent Toplin (ed.) *Oliver Stone's USA: Film, History, and Controversy*. Lawrence: University Press of Kansas, 40–65.

——(2010). 'Afterword', in Paul Cartledge and Fiona Rose Greenland (eds), *Responses to Oliver Stone's* Alexander*: Film, History, and Cultural Studies*. Madison: University of Wisconsin Press, 337–51.

Stone, Shelley (2001). 'The Toga: From National to Ceremonial Costume', in Judith L. Sebesta and Larissa Bonfante (eds), *The World of Roman Costume*. Madison: University of Wisconsin Press, 13–45.

Stuttaford, Andrew (June 2004). 'The Fall of Troy', *National Review Online* [online journal], http://www.nationalreview.com/stuttaford/stuttaford200406020832.asp (accessed 6 September 2012).

Sullivan, Richard D. (1990). *Near Eastern Royalty and Rome*. Toronto: University of Toronto Press.

Suzuki, Mihoko (1989). *Metamorphoses of Helen: Authority, Difference, and the Epic*. Ithaca: Cornell University Press.

Synodinou, Anna (1998). *Πρόσωπα και Προσωπεία: Αυτοβιογραφικό Χρονικό*. Athens: Adelphoi Vlassis.

Tanitch, Robert (2000). *Blockbusters! 70 Years of Best-Selling Movies*. London: Batsford Ltd.

Tapert, Anette (1998). *The Power of Glamour: The Women who Defined the Magic of Stardom.* London: Aurum Press.

Tapper, Michael ([1990] 2003). 'A Romance in Decomposition', in Jan Lumholdt (ed.), *Lars von Trier: Interviews.* Jackson, Miss.: University Press of Mississippi, 71–80.

Tashiro, Charles S. (1998). *Pretty Pictures: Production Design and the History Film.* Austin: University of Texas Press.

Tatara, Paul (n.d.). 'Review of *Alexander the Great* for Turner Classic Movies' [website], http://www.tcm.com/thismonth/article/?cid=178898&rss=mrqe (accessed 10 October 2012).

Thompson, Dorothy J. (2003). 'Cleopatra VII: The Queen in Egypt' in Susan Walker and Sally-Anne Ashton (eds), *Cleopatra Reassessed.* London: British Museum Press, 31–4.

Thompson, Frank (1996). *Lost Films: Important Movies That Disappeared.* New York: Citadel Press.

Thompson, Kristin (1999). *Storytelling in the New Hollywood: Understanding Narrative Technique.* Cambridge, Mass.: Harvard University Press.

Tirard, Laurent (2002). *Moviemakers' Master Class: Private Lessons from the World's Foremost Directors.* London: Faber and Faber.

Toplin, Robert Brent (2000). 'Introduction', in Robert Brent Toplin (ed.), *Oliver Stone's USA: Film, History, and Controversy.* Lawrence: University Press of Kansas, 3–25.

Topper, Kathryn (2007). 'Perseus, the Maiden Medusa, and the Imagery of Abduction', *Hesperia*, 76.1: 73–105.

Travers, Peter (May 2004). 'Troy', *Rolling Stone* [online journal], http://www.rollingstone.com/movies/reviews/troy-20040514 (accessed 6 September 2012).

Turan, Kenneth (2004). '*Alexander*, Not-So-Great', *NPR* [website], http://www.npr.org/templates/story/story.php?storyId=4185352 (accessed 10 October 2012).

Turner, Julia (May 2004). 'The Many Faces of Helen', *Slate* [online journal], http://www.slate.com/id/2100449/ (accessed 6 September 2012).

Turner, Susanne (2009). 'Only Spartan Women Give Birth to Real Men: Zack Snyder's *300* and the Male Nude', in Dunstan Lowe and Kim Shahabudin (eds), *Classics For All: Reworking Antiquity in Mass Culture.* Newcastle upon Tyne: Cambridge Scholars Publishing, 128–49.

van Beekus, Antonius (2004). 'Under Siege', *totalDVD*, 67: 18–25.

Vandenberg, Martina (1997). 'The Invisible Woman', *The Moscow Times*, 8 October.

Vandiver, Elizabeth (2004). 'From Noman to Inman: the *Odyssey* in Charles Frazier's *Cold Mountain*', *Classical and Modern Literature*, 24: 125–48.

Vermilye, Jerry and Mark Ricci (1993). *The Films of Elizabeth Taylor.* New York: Virgin Books.

Viano, Maurizio (1993). *A Certain Realism: Making Use of Pasolini's Theory and Practice*. Berkeley: University of California Press.

Vidal, Gore (1992). *Screening History*. London: Andre Deutsch Ltd.

Vieron, Matt (2010). 'Stone's Olympias: Stereotyping the Son through the Mother', paper presented at *Film & History* conference. Hyatt Regency: Milwaukee, WI.

Vignolo Munson, Rosario (1988). 'Artemisia in Herodotus', *Classical Antiquity*, 7.1: 91–106.

Vincendeau, Ginette (1998). 'Issues in European Cinema', in John Hill and Pamela Church Gibson (eds), *The Oxford Guide to Film Studies*. Oxford: Oxford University Press, 440–8.

Vivante, Bella (2014). 'Enacting Divinity: Helen as Model for Spartan Women's Identity', in Ellen Millender (ed.), *Unveiling Spartan Women*. Swansea: Classical Press of Wales (forthcoming).

Voskaridou, Stella (2013). 'Cacoyannis' Trilogy: Out of the Spirit of Music', in Anastasia Bakogianni (ed.), *Dialogues with the Past: Classical R eception Theory and Practice*, Vol. 1. London: Institute of Classical Studies.

Waddington, David, Chas Critcher, Bella Dicks, and David Parry (2001). *Out of the Ashes? The Social Impact of Industrial Contraction and Regeneration on Britain's Mining Communities*. Norwich: The Stationery Office.

——— and David Parry (2001). 'Managing Industrial Decline: The Lessons of a Decade of Research on Industrial Contraction and Regeneration in Britain and other EU Coal-producing Countries', paper presented at conference in 2001—Confronting Change: North East England and Eastern European Coalfields, Newcastle, 10–15 November 2001.

———, Maggie Wykes, and Chas Critcher (1991). *Split at the Seams? Community, continuity and change after the 1984–5 coal dispute*. Milton Keynes: Open University Press.

Wagenknecht, Edward C. (1962). *Movies in the Age of Innocence*. Norman: University of Oklahoma Press.

Wainwright, Martin (2009). 'The Miner and the Copper', *The Guardian*, 24 February 2009 [online edition], http://www.guardian.co.uk/politics/2009/feb/24/miners-strike-photo-don-mcphee (accessed 5 September 2012).

Walcott, Derek (1993). *The Odyssey: A Stage Version*. London: Faber & Faber.

Walker, Alexander (1966). *The Celluloid Sacrifice: Aspects of Sex in the Movies*. New York: Hawthorn Books.

Walker, Susan and Peter Higgs (2001) (eds). *Cleopatra of Egypt from History to Myth*. London: British Museum Press.

Walton, J. Michael ([2009] 2010). *Euripides our Contemporary*. Revised edition. London: Methuen Drama.

Wanger, Walter and Joe Hyams (1963). *My Life with Cleopatra*. London: Corgi.

Wasserstrom, Steven M. (1999). *Religion after Religion: Gershom Scholem, Mircea Eliade, and Henry Corbin at Eranos*. Princeton: Princeton University Press.

Waxman, Sharon (20 November 2004). 'Breaking Ground with a Gay Movie Hero', *The New York Times* [online edition], http://www.nytimes.com/2004/11/20/movies/MoviesFeatures/20alex.html (accessed 10 October 2012).

Weinberg, Joanna (2004). 'Homer Erotic', *Tatler*, 299.5: 144–9.

Wenders, Wim (2003). 'In defense of places', *Directors' Guild of America Magazine* 28.4, November [website], http://www.dga.org/Craft/DGAQ/All-Articles/0311-Nov-2003/In-Defense-of-Places.aspx (accessed 15 April 2013).

Wilk, Stephen R. (2000). *Medusa: Solving the Mystery of the Gorgon*. Oxford: Oxford University Press.

Wilkins, John (1990). 'The State and the Individual: Euripides' Plays of Voluntary Self-Sacrifice', in Anton Powell (ed.), *Euripides, Women and Sexuality*. London: Routledge.

Williamson, Bill (1982). *Class, Culture, and Community: A Biographical Study of Social Change in Mining*. London: Routledge.

Williamson, Margaret (1990). 'A Woman's Place in Euripides' *Medea*', in Anton Powell (ed.), *Euripides, Women, and Sexuality*. London: Routledge, 16–31.

Winkler, Martin M. (1995). 'Cinema and the Fall of Rome', *Transactions of the American Philological Association*, 125: 135–54.

——(2005). 'Neo-Mythologism: Apollo and the Muses on the Screen', *International Journal of the Classical Tradition*, 11.3: 383–423.

——(2007a). 'Editor's Introduction', in Martin M. Winkler *Troy: From Homer's* Iliad *to Hollywood Epic*. Oxford: Blackwell, 1–19.

——(2007b). 'Greek Myth on the Screen', in Robert D. Woodard (ed.) *The Cambridge Companion to Greek Mythology*. Cambridge: Cambridge University Press, 453–79.

——(2009). *Cinema and Classical Texts: Apollo's New Light*. Cambridge: Cambridge University Press.

Winter, Thomas (2003). 'Cold War', in Bret E. Carroll (ed.), *American Masculinities: A Historical Encyclopedia*. New York: SAGE Publications, 99–101.

Wood, Christopher (1983). *Olympian Dreamers. Victorian Classical Painters 1860–1914*. London: Constable.

Wood, Mary P. (2005). *Italian Cinema*. Oxford: Berg.

Woodhouse, C. M. (1984). *Modern Greece: A Short History*. London: Faber and Faber.

Woodward, Steve (1999). 'Voices in the Past and Present: Tony Harrison's Reworking of the Prometheus Myth', in Lorna Hardwick (ed.), *Tony Harrison's Poetry, Drama And Film: The Classical Dimension*. Milton Keynes: The Open University. http://www2.open.ac.uk/ClassicalStudies/GreekPlays/Colq99/woodward99.htm (accessed 5 September 2012).

Worman, Nancy (1997). 'The Body as Argument: Helen in Four Greek Texts', *Classical Antiquity*, 16: 151–203.

——(2001). 'This Voice which Is not One: Helen's Verbal Guises in Homeric Epic', in André Lardinois and Laura McClure (eds), *Making Silence Speak: Women's Voices In Greek Literature and Society*. Princeton: Princeton University Press, 19–37.

——(2002). *The Cast of Character: Style in Greek Literature*. Austin: University of Texas Press.

Wyke, Maria (1992). 'Augustan Cleopatras: Female Power and Poetic Authority' in Anton Powell (ed.), *Roman Poetry and Propaganda in the Age of Augustus*. London: Bristol Classical Press.

——(1997). *Projecting the Past: Ancient Rome, Cinema and History*. London: Routledge.

——(2002). *The Roman Mistress: Ancient and Modern Respresentations*. Oxford: Oxford University Press.

Yarnall, Judith (1994). *Transformations of Circe: The History of an Enchantress*. Urbana, Ill.: University of Illinois Press.

Zacharia, Katerina (2008). '"Reel" Hellenisms: Perceptions of Greece in Greek Cinema', in Katerina Zacharia (ed.), *Hellenisms: Culture, Identity, and Ethnicity from Antiquity to Modernity*. Aldershot, Hampshire: Ashgate, 321–53.

Zajko, Vanda and Miriam Leonard (2006) (eds). *Laughing with Medusa: Classical Myth and Feminist Thought*. Oxford: Oxford University Press.

Zeitlin, Froma I. (1995). 'Art, Memory and *Kleos* in Euripides' *Iphigenia in Aulis*', in Barbara Goff (ed.), *History, Tragedy, Theory: Dialogues on Athenian Drama*. Austin: University of Texas Press, 174–201.

——(1996). *Playing the Other: Gender and Society in Classical Greek Literature*. Chicago: University of Chicago Press.

Zemon Davis, Natalie (1997). 'Remaking Impostors: From Martin Guerre to Sommersby', *Hayes Robinson Lecture Series* no. 1, Egham, Surrey [website], http://www.rhul.ac.uk/history/documents/pdf/events/hrzemon-davis.pdf (accessed 10 October 2012).

Ziegler, Christine (1994). *Egyptomania. L'Égypte dans l'art occidental 1730–1930*. Montreal: National Gallery of Canada.

Žižek, Slavoj (2009). *In Defense of Lost Causes*. New York: Verso.

Zweig, Bella (1993a). 'The Only Women Who Give Birth to Men: A Gynocentric, Cross-Cultural View of Women in Ancient Sparta', in Mary DeForest (ed.), *Woman's Power, Man's Game: Essays on Classical Antiquity in Honor of Joy K. King*. Wauconda, Ill.: Bolchazy-Carducci Publishers, 32–53.

——(1993b). 'The Primal Mind: Using Native American Models to Study Women in Ancient Greece', in Nancy Sorkin Rabinowitz and Amy Richlin (eds), *Feminist Theory and the Classics*. New York: Routledge, 145–80.

Index

Note: Page references in *italics* denote references to illustrations and films; the suffix *n* indicates a footnote, the number following *n* indicates the footnote number where there is more than one footnote on the page.